62.47

Hitler's Generals on Trial

Hitler's Generals on Trial

THE LAST WAR CRIMES
TRIBUNAL AT NUREMBERG

Valerie Geneviève Hébert

University Press of Kansas

© 2010 by the University Press of Kansas
All rights reserved

Published by the University Press of Kansas (Lawrence, Kansas 66045),
which was organized by the Kansas Board of Regents and is operated and
funded by Emporia State University, Fort Hays State University, Kansas
State University, Pittsburg State University, the University of Kansas, and
Wichita State University

Library of Congress Cataloging-in-Publication Data

Hebert, Valerie, 1974–
  Hitler's generals on trial : the last war crimes tribunal at Nuremberg /
Valerie Geneviève Hebért.
      p. cm. — (Modern war studies)
  Includes bibliographical references and index.
  ISBN 978-0-7006-1698-5 (cloth : alk. paper)
  1. High Command Trial, Nuremberg, Germany, 1948–1949. 2. Leeb,
Wilhelm, Ritter von, 1876–1956—Trials, litigation, etc. 3. Germany.
Oberkommando der Wehrmacht—Trials, litigation, etc. 4. Nuremberg War
Crime Trials, Nuremberg, Germany, 1946–1949. 5. Command of troops—
Germany—History—20th century. I. Title.
  KZ1179.H54H43 2010
  341.6'90268—dc22   2009035149

British Library Cataloguing in Publication Data is available.

Printed in the United States of America

10 9 8 7 6 5 4 3 2 1

The paper used in this publication is recycled and contains 30 percent
postconsumer waste. It is acid free and meets the minimum requirements
of the American National Standard for Permanence of Paper for Printed
Library Materials Z39.48-1992.

For Glen and Livi,
and for my aunt Jean, who would have liked to see this book in print

Contents

Acknowledgments

Although writing a book is solitary work, it is not achieved without practical and intangible support from many sources. My thanks and appreciation are due especially to the various institutions and councils who provided generous awards and fellowship opportunities for travel, research, and writing. They are: the Fonds Québecois de la Recherche sur la Société et la Culture, the Social Sciences and Humanities Research Council of Canada, the Ontario Graduate Scholarship, the Joint Initiative in German and European Studies, the Harry S. Truman Library Institute, the German Historical Institute, and the Holocaust Educational Foundation. This work was also made possible in part by funds granted to the author through a Charles H. Revson Foundation Fellowship at the Center for Advanced Holocaust Studies, United States Holocaust Memorial Museum. The statements made and views expressed, however, are solely the responsibility of the author.

I am indebted as well to the helpful and patient staffs of the National Archives and Records Administration in College Park, Maryland, the Bundesarchiv in Koblenz, the Bundesmilitärarchiv in Freiburg, the Institut für Zeitgeschichte in Munich, the Stadtarchiv Nürnberg in Nuremberg, the Diamond Law Library at the Columbia Law School in New York, the Truman Library Institute in Independence, Missouri, the Library of Congress Manuscripts Division in Washington, D.C., and last, but certainly not least, the interlibrary loan office of Robarts Library, at the University of Toronto. I offer thanks also to the Nathanson Centre on Transnational Human Rights, Crime and Security at Osgoode Hall Law School at York University, and in particular to its director, Craig Scott, for providing me with a stimulating and constructive academic home in which to bring the manuscript to completion.

Whatever merits this book possesses I share with many friends and colleagues who generously gave of their time, thought, and expertise along the way. My doctoral supervisor, Michael Marrus, taught me the most about how to think and write as a historian. His enthusiastic support for and belief in this project never wavered, even when my own confidence did. Responsive and kind, I could not have asked for more in an academic mentor. Jim Retallack offered unending assistance in securing funding and office space.

Ed Morgan introduced me to the fascinating world of international law and provided insights into the compatibility of legal and historical analysis. Lawrence Douglas wrote the book that inspired this one, and contributed gentle yet incisive comments at critical points in its development. Jacques Kornberg modeled a rare combination of scholarly rigor and emotional sensitivity in his approach to the shattering history of the Holocaust and genocide. I hope that I have approximated that delicate balance here. Rebecca Wittmann, Hilary Earl, and Tomaz Jardim, my good friends and colleagues in war crimes trial research at the University of Toronto, freely gave their advice at all stages of my work. I would like to say a special thank-you to Hilary, who rescued me from my first book topic, suggesting that the High Command case might hold more interesting and rewarding potential for research. She was right.

For opportunities to present my work publicly, and for valuable critiques of parts of the manuscript, I wish to extend my thanks, among others named already, to Matt Berg, Doris Bergen, Suzanne Brown-Fleming, Marcus Funck, Simone Gigliotti, Geoff Hamm, Erin Hochman, Jennifer Jenkins, Geoff Megargee, Maria Mesner, Kim Christian Priemel, Mark Roseman, Dirk Schumann, Alan Steinweis, Alexa Stiller, Zev Weiss, Lisa Yavnai, and Peer Zumbansen. I am much obliged as well to Mike Briggs, Larisa Martin, and Karen Hellekson at the University Press of Kansas, for their faith and patience. My parents, Richard and Sheila Hébert, were wonderful and welcome company on one of my overseas research trips. They also showed an uncommon appreciation for how challenging this undertaking was, and their constant encouragement and reassurance that it was worthwhile saw me through some of its more daunting phases. Lisa Todd and Deb Neill read every chapter first and pushed me to achieve more than I thought possible. Our friendship, laughter, and commiseration motivated, emboldened, and sustained me. I am inexpressibly grateful for my daughter Olivia, who was born at the end of my doctoral studies. In a way no historical or legal source could, her birth and young life have shown me how precious and delicate life is. It has made the confrontation with this book's subject more difficult to bear. But the joy she brings me has made it all the more meaningful. Last, I reserve my deepest thanks for my husband, Glen Cordner, who never mentioned the many sacrifices my work required of him, except to say that in the end, they were all worth it.

Glossary of Acronyms

AWA	Allgemeines Wehrmactamt, or General Armed Forces Office
CCAP	Committee for Church Aid for Prisoners
CCL	Control Council Law
CCPAC	Chief of Counsel for the Prosecution of Axis Criminality
EDC	European Defense Community
EUCOM	Headquarters of the U.S. Army, European Command
HICOG	U.S. High Commission for Occupied Germany
IMT	International Military Tribunal, Nuremberg
IMTFE	International Military Tribunal for the Far East, Tokyo
JAG	Judge Advocate General
JCS	Joint Chiefs of Staff
MGO	Military Government Ordinance
NATO	North Atlantic Treaty Organization
OCCPAC	Office of the Chief of Counsel for the Prosecution of Axis Criminality
OCCWC	Office of the Chief of Counsel, War Crimes
OKH	Oberkommando des Heeres, or High Command of the Army
OKM	Oberkommando der Marine, or High Command of the Navy
OKW	Oberkommando der Wehrmacht, or High Command of the Armed Forces
OMGUS	Office of the Military Government, U.S.
RSHA	Reichssicherheitshauptamt, or Reich Security Main Office
RuSHA	Rasse- und Siedlungshauptamt, or Rase and Settlement Office
S.A.	Sturmabteilung, or Storm Detachment
S.D.	Sicherheitsdienst, or Security Service
SHAEF	Supreme Headquarters, Allied Expeditionary Force
SIPO	Sicherheitspolizei, or Security Police

SNP	Subsequent Nuremberg Proceedings
S.S.	Schutzstaffel, or Shock Troops
UNWCC	United Nations War Crimes Commission
USAEUR	United States Army, Europe
USFET	United States Forces, European Theater

The judicial process is a social process.
— Prosecution Closing Statement,
High Command Case

Introduction

The Nuremberg trials had several goals. Justice was only one. American political and judicial leaders who promoted and defended the war crimes trial plan regarded these proceedings as offering a rare and fleeting opportunity to educate the German people about their immediate past. They believed that by provoking an honest and thorough confrontation with the crimes of the Nazi regime and its organizations, the German people would be fully converted to democracy and more successfully integrate with the West. This, they hoped, would ensure a lasting peace. This book tells the story of the American-led High Command case, the last trial held at Nuremberg. In that telling, it also poses a central question: did the judicial exercise help the Germans in the understanding of and reconciliation with their traumatic and contested history?

Over nine months in 1948, the Americans brought fourteen field marshals and generals of the Wehrmacht (the German armed forces) to trial at Nuremberg for war crimes, crimes against peace, crimes against humanity, and the common plan or conspiracy to commit these crimes. The High Command case was the last in a series of twelve trials called the Subsequent Nuremberg Proceedings (SNP). This series of trials applied the same law and used the same courtroom as the International Military Tribunal, the first and still the best-known Allied trial at Nuremberg. The Subsequent Proceedings, however, were conducted under exclusively American auspices. With each trial focusing on one branch of the Nazi state, such as the judiciary, government ministries, the S.S. and police, medicine, industry, and the military, these proceedings aimed at proving and recording the criminality of the entire system. Given the Americans' view that the crime of aggressive war was the supreme crime, in that it comprised all "lesser" crimes, they regarded the High Command case as one of the most important postwar trials of German war criminals. What they did not anticipate was that the prosecution and conviction of soldiers became the fulcrum on which the debate over the legitimacy of the entire American war crimes trial program turned.

The proceedings generated a vast documentary record. The High Command case, the most comprehensive of the three trials of soldiers, produced

1

a transcript of over 10,000 pages. Prosecution and defense counsel wrote thousands more pages of briefs and memoranda and submitted 3,900 evidence exhibits, some of which were hundreds of pages long. They called eighty-nine witnesses to the stand. Each of the defendants testified at length. The charges raised in the High Command case included, among other offenses, the deliberate abuse and liquidation of millions of Soviet POWs, the murder of Western Allied soldiers and airmen, the extermination of East and West European civilians (particularly Jews, Communists, Romani, and the mentally and physically infirm), the killing of civilian hostages as collective punishment, draconian reprisals against so-called partisans, and participation in the slave labor program.

As a group, soldiers were more difficult to prosecute than, for example, members of the S.S. or Nazi doctors. On a general level, prosecutors had to overcome the widely held and frequently cited belief that atrocities occur in all wars, on all sides, and that there was nothing ideologically or qualitatively distinct about the German military's conduct. Many claimed that the Wehrmacht's behavior was commensurate with Soviet tactics and evolved only in response to conditions encountered in the field. They insisted that it was neither predetermined nor guided by any racial or political objectives. The trial also posed particular legal and rhetorical challenges. The prosecutors and judges had to deal with thorny, yet fundamental, jurisprudential issues such as command responsibility: the degree of responsibility an officer bears for the conduct of soldiers under his command, the limits of military necessity, and the defense of superior orders. Of course everyone at Nuremberg understood and accepted that it is the role and duty of any army in war to fight, kill, and occupy. Therefore, in order to secure convictions at trial, counsel had to disengage the dreadful necessities and awful realities of all wars from the specifically racially and ideologically motivated policies that characterized Nazi warfare. In practice, the prosecutors' and judges' task was not as difficult as one might have expected. The evidence of Wehrmacht criminality was, in the words of the chief prosecutor, "overwhelming."

The trial's German name, OKW-Prozess, is somewhat of a misnomer, as only three of the defendants held staff positions in the Oberkommando der Wehrmacht—that is, the Wehrmacht High Command. The others were field commanders and had fought the war from Norway to Greece and from the interior of France to the outskirts of Moscow. These officers had served from the prewar planning stages until the war's final days. At the most basic level, their successful invasion, defeat, and occupation of countries in Eastern and Western Europe gave other Nazi state agencies, such as the S.S. and police, access to the territories and victims against whom to perpetrate racially, politically, and ideologically motivated crimes. But the defendants' involvement in these atrocities went much deeper. From their staff positions at the OKW and their posts in the battlefield, they took a leading role in transforming Hitler's ideas and ambitions into concrete orders, and ensuring that these orders were carried out by the millions of men serving under their command.

Among the officers on trial was Lieutenant General Hermann Reinecke, chief of the General Armed Forces Office, who had overseen the creation and implementation of POW policy that resulted in the deaths (among others) of approximately 3.3 million Red Army soldiers from exposure, starvation, disease, neglect, exhaustion, and outright execution. Lieutenant General Walter Warlimont, chief of the Department of National Defense in the Wehrmacht Operations Staff, and Lieutenant General Rudolf Lehmann, chief of the Wehrmacht Legal Division, both experts in law, had drafted orders such as the horrific Barbarossa Jurisdiction Order, which allowed for the murder of countless men, women, and children on the pretext of partisan activity; and the notorious Commissar Order, which resulted in the execution of 600,000 Red Army commissars upon capture. Also present in the dock were Lieutenant General Karl von Roques, in whose area Soviet POW mortality rates had exceeded 80 percent, and General Hans Reinhardt, who had deported over 3,800 Soviet men, women, and children to Auschwitz-Birkenau to serve as slave laborers. They later perished in the gas chambers. Field Marshal Georg von Kuechler had distributed the Reichenau Order that called for "severe . . . revenge on subhuman Jewry," and General Hermann Hoth had instructed his troops that their survival depended on the merciless annihilation of "Bolshevik–Jewish agitators."

The tribunal convicted eleven of the fourteen defendants and sentenced them to prison terms spanning from time already served to life. The judges' stringent adjudication of guilt in combination with the prosecution's voluminous documentary evidence (material of the Wehrmacht's own creation) produced a legal and historical record that was sensitive to the realities of combat. But it also irrefutably established the Wehrmacht's conscious criminal complicity and participation in vicious Nazi policies and determined the defendants' individual shares of them. If the issue of the High Command case's didactic contribution were to conclude here, one might characterize it as a success. However, the trial's educative legacy is far more complex. This book shows that what came before and after the proceedings had a greater impact on the trial's didactic influence than what unfolded in the courtroom. The underlying argument is that in order to assess whether Nuremberg succeeded in its didactic goals, one must examine both the trial's representation of history and the public reception of that narrative. Accordingly, the book explains how the court proceedings shaped the interpretation of the Nazi past. It also reconstructs the sociopolitical circumstances before, during, and after the trial that determined the West Germans' response, and influenced how the American occupation authorities dealt with the trial records.

The High Command case began early in 1948 in an atmosphere of German antipathy and mistrust toward American war crimes trials. Shortly after the trial ended, the Nuremberg tribunals, having fulfilled their mandate, dissolved. The convicted, who were incarcerated at Landsberg prison in Bavaria, came under the jurisdiction of the Office of the U.S. High Commissioner for Germany. The High Commission thereby assumed the obligation to honor the sentences as well as authority over the disposition of the trial documents. However, occupation officials' responsibility for protecting the trial records and enforcing punishment soon came into conflict with new and pressing Cold War concerns and sensitivities. Despite the immediate postwar Allied injunction against Germany ever again possessing arms, the mounting fear of and hostility toward the Soviets convinced Western powers of the Federal Republic's strategic importance as a military force on the European continent. West Germany's newfound political capital provided opponents of the trials and their judgments with an opportunity to pry convicted war criminals loose from Allied custody. In early Allied–West German negotiations over rearmament, the West German government made the release of the soldiers held in Landsberg a clear condition for the reconstruction of their military.

The churches, the press, veterans' associations, and ordinary citizens alike joined the government in its efforts to free convicted soldiers. They accused the High Command case judges and prosecutors of not having understood the reality of combat in the East or the character of the enemy. They insisted that all military personnel, even senior officers, were inextricably bound by superior orders but had nonetheless behaved according to the laws of war. They denied outright the credibility and authenticity of the evidence implicating the army in Nazi policies. Because there were no war crimes, the argument continued, there was no basis for trials, and no justification for punishment. American authorities attempted to restore perspective to the outcry, reminding the public that there could be no military reason behind the slaughter of Jews, or a one-hundred-to-one policy of reprisals against innocent civilians accused of harming German troops. Opponents were undeterred.

The controversy unleashed by the High Command case was always about much more than the custody of a handful of officers at Landsberg. Calling the legitimacy of the trial into question—and indeed the struggle over the memory of the Wehrmacht's conduct in war—went to the heart of the German postwar national identity. By using the defendants' individual offenses to narrate the breadth and depth of Nazi criminality, trial organizers had sought to use the accused as symbols of a broader and more pervasive guilt and responsibility than the trial was capable of prosecuting. Given that 20 million "ordinary" Germans had served in the Wehrmacht, the evidence revealed in court implicated a greater proportion of the German population in ideological and racial crimes than any other state institution examined at Nuremberg. The trial and the enforcement of punishment represented a standing reproach of German complicity in Nazi crime. It also challenged the mainstream impression that Nazi criminals were sadistic monsters, and shortened the social and psychological distance that the Germans imagined separated them from war crime perpetrators. To be sure, they recognized this challenge, and in response, they created, perpetuated, and protected a counterimage of the Wehrmacht in war.

The myth of "die saubere Wehrmacht" (the upstanding Wehrmacht) held that the war was a righteous and desperate struggle against Communism, and that it had been fought honorably by ordinary Germans defending their home and heritage from eastern aggression. These soldiers, who had been no servants of Hitler, at best resisted participating in excesses, justifiable as they might have been. At worst, they reluctantly obeyed questionable orders from a few top-level commanders, under duress, and in response to a ruthless enemy. Atrocities against the Jews were the work of a small minority of fanatical S.S. men, who informed the army of their activities only after the fact, if at all. This distancing of the "people's army" from the undeniably criminal agencies of the Nazi state such as the Party, the S.S., and S.D. offered solace and refuge to a people emerging from catastrophic defeat and living under the opprobrium of world opinion. Exonerating the soldiers provided an alibi for almost the entire nation.

This alternative image of the Wehrmacht was integral to the postwar construction of West German national identity and resonated with the contemporary international political landscape. Because West Germany occupied a crucial place in the Western anti-Communist alliance, it could not be eliminated as a state. Nor could it function on the world stage as a nation of perpetrators. It therefore had to reinterpret its past. West Germany's new nationalism assumed the identity of victim: of Hitler's mad and destructive impulses and his absolute control over the country that left no room for dissent, of a disastrous bombing campaign that laid waste to its cities, of vengeful Red Army soldiers, of national division and expulsion, and of continued debasement by the former Allied powers through the imprisonment of so-called war criminals, who were being punished now for fighting an enemy that they had been justified in targeting all along. There was truth at the core of some of these claims, but in combination, and without context, they took the place of national self-reflection and obviated any sense of responsibility for having supported the Nazi regime and participating in its most ferocious crimes.

Free from the burden of guilt, and armed with a narrative that called the whole notion of "war crimes" into question, critics of the trial program sharpened and intensified their campaign. In time, the arguments employed to free convicted soldiers were extended to all criminals convicted in American courts, even though the majority had served in other state institutions. With ever-increasing determination, political, religious, public, and private institutions brought their opposition to bear on occupation authorities. Growing weary of the debate, and anxious as a result of growing international tensions, the Americans communicated with these groups in terms ever more remotely connected to the trials and the cruelties they had exposed. Officials refrained from referring to "war crimes" and "war criminals." Wishing to avoid provocation, the Americans even refused to publish the trial records in German. Eventually, the United States devised a series of processes to grant clemency and early parole to the convicted. By the spring of 1958, not a single war criminal convicted in any of the Subsequent Proceedings remained in prison. In the end, the Nuremberg project did not achieve justice, nor did it educate the German people about Nazi crime in any nuanced or lasting way. If nothing more, the Nuremberg experience offers compelling evidence for a closer union between political will and judicial efforts, if trials of atrocity are to fulfill their didactic ambitions.

The book concludes with observations about the long-term legacy of the High Command case and the American war crimes trial program at Nuremberg. Interpreting the German public's shocked and outraged response to a 1995 national exhibit on Wehrmacht crimes in the East as a symptom of the High Command case's didactic failure, and looking more broadly at West Germany's own halting and circumscribed confrontation with its past, we see all the more clearly what was lost when American authorities abandoned Nuremberg's goals of justice and education. In allowing the conclusions of the trials to recede ever further into the recesses of public memory, West Germany was able to perpetuate a view of history containing far fewer victims and almost no perpetrators. In time, thanks in no small part to the work of German historians, the truths first uncovered at Nuremberg took their place in public memory of the war. For the most part, however, memory's return came too late to hold the guilty to account. The attempt to educate the German people about the truth of the Nazi past was a core goal of the Nuremberg trials, and is the focus of this book. But Nuremberg was equally devoted to justice. What emerges from this study is that the two goals were and are inextricably linked. The pursuit of justice at Nuremberg sought to restore honor and value to the lives lost and injured. Punishment, the final expression of justice, forced this message onto the public imagination. Without punishment, this message was lost. Without truth, there was no reason to look for it.

1

From War Crimes to War Crimes Trials: The Evolution of American Judicial Policy, 1942 to 1948

The American case is being prepared on the assumption that an inescapable responsibility rests upon this country to conduct an inquiry, preferably in association with others, but alone if necessary, into the culpability of those whom there is probably cause to accuse of atrocities and other crimes. We have many such men in our possession. What shall we do with them? We could, of course, set them at large without a hearing. But it has cost unmeasured thousands of American lives to beat and bind these men. To free them without trial would mock the dead and make cynics of the living. On the other hand, we could execute or otherwise punish them without a hearing. But undiscriminating executions or punishments without definite findings of guilt, fairly arrived at, would violate pledges repeatedly given, and would not set easily on the American conscience or be remembered by our children with pride. The only other course is to determine the innocence or guilt of the accused after a fair hearing as dispassionate as the times and horrors we deal with will permit, and upon a record that will leave our reasons and motives clear.

—Justice Robert H. Jackson, American chief prosecutor at Nuremberg

WHEN PEACE CAME to Europe in spring 1945, there began the awful tallying of the war's devastation. In twelve years of Nazism and six years of combat, entire countries, such as Czechoslovakia and Poland, had ceased to exist, and cities from London to Berlin to Leningrad had been reduced to rubble. But by far the most devastating losses were human. The war claimed 60 million lives. Russia alone sacrificed 8 million of its soldiers to battle. The heaviest casualties were civilian: in Yugoslavia, 1.5 to 2 million; in Poland, 6 million; in Russia, 17 million.[1] Millions more so-called displaced persons crowded makeshift camps scattered around Europe. The formerly deported, enslaved, and imprisoned recounted experiences of savagery hitherto unknown to the record of human behavior. Film footage of liberated camps confirmed in horrifying detail what had for years already been known in principle: the Nazis had sought the systematic annihilation of an entire people. Through these images, the world learned of this human destruction anew. Reeling from the catastrophe, Allied nations groped and struggled to articulate a response. Indeed, calls for punishment had long echoed through the halls of government offices and civilian organizations. But growing now was the idea that here existed the opportunity not only for retribution, but for reassertion of the ideas and values whose recent near defeat was perhaps the most terrifying aspect of the war. Because the intentions and actions of German belligerents were undoubtedly criminal (in spirit, if not in letter), would a trial be the appropriate and adequate response? Could a judicial inquiry give meaning to the devastation suffered and the destruction inflicted? More and more voices, particularly within the United States, expressed the belief that it could. However, even though everyone "knew" what the Nazis had done, devising the mechanism to name, prove, and punish the crimes that had spanned the expanse of a continent, the duration of a regime, and implicated the population of a country was not nearly as obvious. This chapter will narrate the evolution of American judicial policy from the United States' first public utterance of retribution to the proceedings against the German High Command, its thirteenth and last war crimes trial at Nuremberg. It will establish how the Americans conceived of Nazi criminality and what they sought to accomplish by submitting it to judicial examination.

Toward the International Military Tribunal at Nuremberg

Within a few months of the start of the war, exiled governments of overrun and occupied nations called on the Allies to condemn Nazi atrocities. Although Nazi outrages were well-known to the Allied powers, such as the Wehrmacht's draconian hostage reprisal policy against civilians, and the massacre at Babi Yar, in which the S.S. shot more than 33,000 Jews in two days, wartime pronouncements on the intention to punish the perpetrators were vague and noncommittal. In the first years of hostilities, the United States' official neutrality released them from any public expectation to intervene (if only verbally or diplomatically) against these crimes. Further, once the December 1941 attack on Pearl Harbor brought the Americans into the war, the primary objects of their outrage were the Japanese. It was not until after the Normandy landing in mid-1944 that the American government and public confronted the evil of Nazism firsthand.[2] By contrast, Britain felt the pressure for action from governments-in-exile almost immediately. It responded with promises of punishment, such as Prime Minister Winston Churchill's 1941 announcement: "retribution for [Nazi] crimes must henceforth take its place among the major purposes of this war."[3] But neither the British nor the Americans intended to commit themselves to a particular policy, and both labored to remain aloof to contemporary international initiatives to lay the foundations for specific postwar actions.

It is significant that neither the United States, nor Britain, nor the USSR signed the January 1942 Declaration of St. James Palace, which proposed punishment through postwar trials. Issued by representatives of Belgium, Czechoslovakia, Greece, Luxembourg, the Netherlands, Norway, Poland, Yugoslavia, and the Free French National Committee, these nations promised that they "place[d] among their principal war aims the punishment, *through the channels of organized justice*, of those guilty of or responsible for these crimes, . . . and resolve[d] to see in a spirit of international solidarity that (a) those guilty or responsible, whatever their nationality, are sought out, handed over to justice and judged, (b) that the sentences are carried out."[4]

Allied reluctance to declare a position was not tenable for long. By the summer of 1942, reports of Nazi cruelties against civilians (Jewish and non-Jewish alike) poured in from all corners of the continent.[5] Allied statements now alluded more and more to the broad outlines of a punishment policy. As a result of mounting pressure from the Polish and Czech governments-in-exile, Churchill suggested the formation of a United Nations Commission on War Crimes, whose mandate would be to gather information on atrocities with a view to their eventual prosecution. Although promising in principle, unfortunately procrastination (particularly American) and discord (especially between the British and the Soviets) characterized the negotiations for the commission.[6] Throughout this period, the United States and Britain continued to issue statements regarding the punishment of war criminals and spoke vaguely about future tribunals in nations where atrocities had been committed.[7] However, these declarations were more about placating the governments-in-exile than they were indicative of sincere policy intentions.

When the United Nations War Crimes Commission (UNWCC) was finally inaugurated in October 1943 (over a year since it was first conceived, and without the participation of the Soviet Union), the major Allies still

reserved the prerogative of defining any future trial program. The personnel and activities of the commission reflected American and British reti-
cence. Herbert C. Pell, a man with no legal training or background in the
war crimes issue, was appointed chairman. Bereft of both investigative and
executive power, the commission ultimately became a repository of information and reports on alleged war crimes. In four and a half years of operation, it gathered the names of 36,529 suspected war criminals, but with no
prosecutorial authority, the commission remained entirely dependent on
Allied initiative to organize and hold proceedings.[8] Therefore, although
there had been many references to punishment, tribunals, and "justice," by
no means were the Allies committed to a particular course of action, much
less unified in basic guiding principles. The war crimes issue at that time
was simply not a high priority, and understandably so, as the war raged on.
However, this may also have been because in the cases of Britain and the
United States, neither country had experienced the horrifying reality of a
Nazi occupation. Moreover, both countries (particularly Britain) were skeptical of atrocity reports, remembering the exaggerations that emanated from
Belgium during World War I. Some officials feared the promise of retribution would spark reprisals against prisoners of war in German custody. Last,
their reluctance to give too much influence to the governments-in-exile and
a general uneasiness about working with the Soviets may account for the
delay in commitment to a trial policy.[9] As for the Soviets, feeling snubbed
by the UNWCC and embittered by the delayed opening of a second European front, they did not wait for Allied agreement before holding their own
trials. Proceedings were quick and death sentences were common, but the
cases involved only crimes committed against Soviet citizens.[10] The first
and only glimmer of Allied unity on the war crimes issue appeared on 1
November 1943. In discussions at Moscow, representatives from Britain, the
United States, and the USSR differentiated between localized crimes and
offenses that defied national boundaries. They bound the Allied governments to punish the latter, and broadest, category of crime:

> At the time of the granting of any armistice to any government which may
> be set up in Germany, those ... who have been responsible for, or have taken
> a consenting part in ... atrocities, massacres and executions will be sent back
> to the countries in which their abominable deeds were done in order that
> they may be judged and punished according to the laws of these liberated
> countries. ... Major criminals whose offenses have no particular geographical
> location ... will be punished by a joint decision of the governments of the
> Allies.[11]

Although the declaration did not specifically mandate trials, it did obligate the Allies to "punishment by joint decision." However, the Allied governments were not in agreement on the mechanism for punishment. In fact, the Big Three diverged strongly in their punishment plans. Although the Soviets maintained no ongoing discussion with the British and Americans, their proceedings against war criminals at Krasnodar and Kharkov clearly showed that the Moscow Declaration was no empty threat. Moreover, the Soviets were increasingly attracted to the potential propaganda benefits trials offered, in that they provided a stage to showcase the suffering of the Soviet people and the contribution they made to defeating the Nazis.[12]

The British were steadfastly opposed to trials of any kind. From early on in the war, their intention was to dispatch by summary execution a limited number of top Nazi leaders and to leave the punishment of so-called lesser criminals to the nations in whose territory or against whose nationals the offenses had been committed. There were two important reasons for their position. First, Secretary of the Foreign Office Anthony Eden feared that trials would drag on for years and forestall the return of a peaceful atmosphere in Europe. Second, and perhaps more significantly, the British were still smarting from the disastrous and humiliating attempt to conduct war crimes trials after World War I.[13]

Understandably, in 1944 and 1945, the British appeared little inspired by the prospect of trials. Rather, a quick and finite political disposition of the most notorious and indisputably criminal Nazi leaders seemed to hold out the most promise for a speedy transition to peace in Europe.[14] Although the French were later invited to take part in the organization and prosecution of the major war crimes trial, it played no significant part in the wartime discussions of the issue.[15]

The Americans ultimately led the campaign for the conduct of war crimes proceedings, but the government had not always been a dedicated advocate of trials. Indeed, even after the trial plan gained currency, it was not universally supported by all branches of the state. During hostilities, the policy for punishment of war criminals was not a prime concern for the American political leadership. Authorities were fearful of reprisals against their prisoners of war should they announce formal policy intentions and were wary of committing themselves to numerous, costly, and laborious proceedings. For as long as they could, the American government kept a low profile on war crimes issues and postponed making decisions.[16] It was only after D-day, as Allied forces closed in on Hitler's Germany, that high-level attention focused on the question of trials and general occupation policies, of which they would be an integral part.[17]

Because the British and American armies would bear primary responsibility for the occupation of West Germany, military authorities took the lead in developing this policy. In August 1944, the American War Department under Henry Stimson hastily produced a draft interim directive on occupation policy for Germany and a handbook to guide officers in its implementation. Although these documents ordered occupation authorities to intern officers of Nazi organizations such as the S.S. and Gestapo and to arrest all those who were suspected of having committed war crimes, they did not clearly explain what was to be done with them thereafter.[18] Meanwhile, pressure from the press and the American Jewish Conference was mounting, calling for punitive action.[19] In a statement on war criminals submitted to Secretary of State Cordell Hull on 25 August 1944, the American Jewish Conference declared: "[the] campaign of terror and annihilation [which] has been carried out with unexampled bestiality . . . cannot go unpunished without destroying the legal and moral foundations upon which our civilization rests."[20]

Secretary of the Treasury Henry Morgenthau Jr. was even more forceful in his observations, and his actions gave the war crimes issue the high-level attention that had for too long been lacking. Fearing that American policy makers were inclined to be "soft and coddling" toward Germany, Morgenthau called for a severe and vindictive peace agreement.[21] According to his plan, Germany as a nation would pay for the atrocities that he considered worse than their violations of the basic laws of war.[22] On 5 September 1944, he presented his views to President Theodore Roosevelt. He called for the deindustrialization and depopulation of the Ruhr and Saar, the ceding of East Prussia and Silesia to Poland and Russia, and the transformation of Germany into a nation "primarily agricultural and pastoral in character."[23] Trials were not to be wasted on the "arch-criminals of this war whose obvious guilt has generally been recognized by the United Nations. . . . They shall be apprehended . . . and identified . . . [and] shall be put to death forthwith by firing squads."[24] At least early on, Roosevelt was of like mind. He had already harshly critiqued the War Department's *Handbook of Military Government for Germany*. In a note to Stimson, he chided:

> This so-called handbook is pretty bad. . . . Too many people here and in England hold to the view that the German people as a whole are not responsible for what has taken place—that only a few Nazi leaders are responsible. That unfortunately is not based on fact. The German people as a whole must have it driven home to them that the whole nation has been engaged in a lawless conspiracy against the decencies of modern civilization.[25]

In principle, Stimson concurred with the need to confront the Germans with the crimes committed in their name, but he utterly rejected the notion of a vengeful peace, particularly the call for the economic debasement of Germany. Although seventy-seven years old and slowed by heart trouble, he proved a formidable opponent to Morgenthau, to whom he wrote: "My basic objection to the proposed methods of treating Germany which were discussed . . . was that in addition to a system of preventive and educative punishment they would add the dangerous weapon of complete economic oppression. Such methods, in my opinion, do not prevent war, they tend to breed war."[26]

This was one of the first indications of the growing commitment in the War Department, and soon also in the State Department, that occupation should have a constructive effect on postwar Germany. Punishment by judicial decision, they hoped, would reconcile the German people to their past, perform a kind of national catharsis, and lead the country back into the community of democratic nations. Further, recording and publicizing the crimes of the Third Reich and modeling the basic democratic principles of due process and human rights would, in their view, more likely restore and secure a lasting peace. Stimson presented these ideas to the president: "The very punishment of these men in a dignified manner consistent with the advance of civilization, will have all the greater effect upon posterity. Furthermore, it will afford the most effective way of making a record of the Nazi system of terrorism and of the effort of the Allies to terminate the system and prevent its recurrence."[27]

Across the ocean, British intransigence remained firm. On 4 September 1944, Lord Chancellor Sir John Simon prepared a memorandum at the War Cabinet's request that unequivocally declared Britain's opposition to trials:

> The method by trial, conviction and judicial sentence is quite inappropriate for notorious ringleaders. . . . Apart from the formidable difficulties of constituting the court, formulating the charge, and assembling the evidence, the question of their fate *is a political, not a judicial question*. It could not rest with judges, however eminent or learned, to decide finally a matter like this, which is of the widest and most vital public policy.[28]

For a short time, the Morgenthau–Simon view seemed to prevail. Roosevelt invited his treasury secretary to accompany him to the September 1944 Quebec Conference. Although the topic of punishment policy was not the priority of the talks, Roosevelt and Churchill quietly agreed that summary execution was the best solution, initialed a draft of the Morgenthau plan, and agreed to confer with Stalin to jointly compose a list of the top Nazis to be dispatched.[29] Later that month the Morgenthau Plan was leaked to the press, causing uproar in Germany and opening up questions of occupation and war crimes policy to public scrutiny. Roosevelt distanced himself from the plan, for fear of a negative backlash against him in the upcoming election, and Stimson moved quickly to take advantage of the policy vacuum. He handed the task of formulating a concrete war crimes trial plan to Assistant Secretary of War John J. McCloy, who in turn passed it to Lieutenant-Colonel Murray Bernays, chief of the Special Projects Office of the Personnel Branch.[30]

The Law Takes Shape

The challenges in devising a workable legal strategy to name, try, and punish Nazi crimes were daunting. Of primary concern was formulating a plan whereby the scope and scale of Nazi crime could be acknowledged: crimes encompassing war, genocide, and unprecedented destruction, implicating thousands of perpetrators and committed against non-German and German nationals alike. What was required was a mechanism that could pierce sovereign immunity, assign individual criminal responsibility for acts traditionally identified as acts of state, and condemn those who gave orders as well as triggermen. Although Bernays intended to cast the net of indictment much wider than the Morgenthau and Simon plans envisioned, he acknowledged that no traditional judicial procedure could hold all Nazi culprits within its grasp. Therefore, he sought to formulate a legal framework that would assert the criminality of the Nazi enterprise, which in his view was far greater and more malevolent than the individuals who carried it into action. His was the most eloquent argument for trials yet articulated:

> It will never be possible to catch and convict every Axis war criminal, or even any great number of them, under the old concepts and procedures. Even if this could be done, it would not, of itself, be enough. The ultimate offense, for example, in the case of Lidice, is not the obliteration of a village, but even more, the assertion of the right to do it. . . . Behind each Axis war criminal however, lies the basic criminal instigation of the Nazi doctrine and policy. It is the guilty nature of this instigation that must be established, for only thus will the conviction and punishment of the individuals concerned achieve their true moral and juristic significance.[31]

Therefore, the objectives of Bernays's trial plan went beyond punishing as many of the guilty as possible; he hoped also that it would perform an educational and reformative role in postwar Germany. He concluded that if these objectives were not achieved,

> Germany will simply have lost another war. The German people will not know the barbarians they have supported, nor will they have any understanding of the criminal character of their conduct and the world's judgment upon it. The Fascist potential will thus remain undiminished both in Germany and elsewhere, and its scope unimpaired. If, on the other hand, the approach suggested herein is adopted, the victory can be turned to more valuable use than merely putting off the Fascist menace to another day.[32]

To achieve these didactic and redemptive goals, Bernays proposed a novel and innovative judicial solution. Nazi Party and state organizations (such as the Gestapo, S.A., and S.S.) would be charged before an international court "with *conspiracy* to commit murder, terrorism and the destruction of peaceful populations in violation of the laws of war."[33] The primary international trial would prosecute defendants considered representative of the accused organizations. The proceedings would be open to the public and widely publicized and "the evidence [w]ould be full enough to prove the guilty intent . . . as well as the criminal conduct." Upon the establishment of the criminal nature of these organizations, proof of membership alone would affix the guilt of all the other organization members brought under arrest by courts of the United Nations' member states. A second tier of proceedings would be held to determine the severity of punishment. The nature of the conspiracy charge would bring all acts done in furtherance of the conspiracy (that is, from its inception onward) within the court's jurisdiction, including even prewar crimes against German nationals.[34] Bernays's plan therefore solved the two main problems facing advocates of the trial policy: it gave access to all culprits, from the idea men to the rank-and-file perpetrators, and it brought all crimes, whether committed inside or outside Germany, before or during the war, under the court's authority. Two problems remained. The concept of criminal conspiracy was unknown to international and continental European law. Further, its combination with the criminal organization charge appeared to many as a massive invocation of collective guilt.[35]

At the end of September, McCloy submitted Bernays's proposal for evaluation to assistant executive officer Colonel Ammi Cutter. Cutter praised the plan as ingenious but hastened to add that it involved "radical departures" from existing law.[36] Stimson defended the plan to Secretary of State

Cordell Hull, arguing that the scope, scale, and unprecedented nature of the Nazis' crimes necessitated breaking new legal ground.[37] On 11 November the secretaries of war, state, and navy presented a memorandum to the president that expressed their support for the conspiracy–criminal organization plan and reaffirmed their belief in the trial's educative benefit:

> Not only will the guilty of this generation be brought to justice according to due process of law, but in addition, the conduct of the Axis will have been solemnly condemned by an international adjudication of guilt that cannot fail to impress the generations to come. The Germans will not again be able to claim, as they have been claiming with regard to the Versailles Treaty, that an admission of war guilt was exacted from them under duress.[38]

The War Department's position was now more or less fixed. Further discussion of war crimes trial policy would center on details of the Bernays plan. The only major change from within the War Department was the incorporation of the charge of aggressive war. Colonel William Chanler, Stimson's legal associate, reasoned that the charge could be prosecuted on the basis of Germany's violation of the 1928 Kellogg–Briand Pact, which had banned war as a means to settle conflicts between states, and to which Germany had been a signatory. Although untested, prosecution on the basis of this charge could, if successful, produce a powerful deterrent against future military aggression.[39]

Not all in the American government supported the War Department plan. Undersecretary of War Brigadier General Kenneth C. Royall favored traditional military trials affecting fewer defendants and modeled on existing law.[40] But the sharpest criticism originated within the Judge Advocate General's Office, which attacked the notion that aggressive war could be criminalized under international law and questioned the legitimacy of the conspiracy charge with relation to prewar acts against German nationals.[41] The main thrust of its argument was that the aggressive war–conspiracy strategy departed from international law and entered political doctrine. In a note to Attorney General (and future judge at Nuremberg) Francis Biddle, Assistant Attorney General Herbert Wechsler (a trusted advisor to Roosevelt and future counsel at Nuremberg) added further criticism, calling the War Department's plan an exercise in applying ex post facto law. Wechsler objected to the use of the conspiracy charge as an exclusively American legal concept inapplicable to the Nazi leaders. He was skeptical that a single trial could effectively and efficiently achieve its goals without devolving into a debate on the fundamental differences between the Nazi and Allied worldviews, thereby providing a forum for Nazi propaganda. His cautious and restrained recommendation called for prosecution of only those against whom evidence existed of personal participation in specific crimes.[42]

Ultimately, historical circumstance, not argumentation, rescued the Bernays plan. The Waffen S.S. First Panzer Division's murder of seventy-two American prisoners in Malmedy, Belgium, on 17 December 1944 shocked and enraged the American public and convinced senior American officials (Biddle included) that the Nazis were indeed engaged in a conspiracy to commit war crimes via criminal organizations such as the S.S.[43] Internal criticism of the conspiracy–criminal organization plan quieted and the Americans turned their efforts toward selling their plan to the Allies.

In early 1945, Judge Samuel Rosenman, Roosevelt's speechwriter and special legal counsel from 1943 to 1945, took over as the White House advisor on war crimes policy. A steadfast advocate of the Bernays plan, in early April he traveled to London along with McCloy, Cutter, and Wechsler to try to win Britain's support. Lord Simon of the British War Cabinet still insisted on summary executions but offered the concession of holding an arraignment proceeding to publicize the crimes of the accused.[44] Talks stalled. But just as outside historical forces had turned the tide of American opinion in favor of the trial program, once again, historical circumstance intervened to break the impasse in Allied negotiations. President Roosevelt's sudden and unforeseen death on 12 April opened new opportunities and provided a new impetus for proponents of the trial policy. Roosevelt had never fully committed to Bernays's design, but Harry Truman, "a man of quick and firm decision," was fully converted (with Rosenman's skillful encouragement) to the wisdom of the trial policy and determined that it held far more advantage than summary execution.[45]

Later that month, Cutter penned a memorandum intended to shame the British for promoting their "political" solution. Calling it a "primitive practice of murdering helpless prisoners," Cutter argued instead for the progressive and fundamentally moral trial program.[46] In this final plea for a trial, Cutter acknowledged that no legal proceeding could come to grips with the enormity of Nazi crime, yet he still insisted that contemporary law could be expanded to name and condemn the acts being impugned. The future of the peace depended on it:

> There can be no real trial when the real offense for which Hitler and the other Axis leaders are being tried, is the totality of what they have done to the world since 1933. . . . The very breadth of the offense, however, is not in itself argument against judicial action. It is a most important reason for a trial, for it is highly desirable that there be established and declared by actual decision . . . the principles of international law applicable to the broad,

vicious Nazi enterprise. In texture and application, this law will be novel because the scope of the Nazi activity has been broad and ruthless without precedent.... There will be world judicial condemnation of depredations so great and so violent that international security cannot exist if they should be permitted to continue unchecked.[47]

Meanwhile, Truman began looking for someone to lead the American prosecution team at the proposed international trial. The president had been greatly impressed by a recent speech by Supreme Court Justice Robert H. Jackson in which he had declared: "You must put no man on trial under the forms of judicial proceedings ... if you are not willing to see him freed if not proved guilty. If you are determined to execute a man in any case, there is no occasion for a trial, the world yields no respect to courts that are merely organized to convict."[48] On 2 May 1945, Truman appointed Robert Jackson as chief of counsel for the prosecution of Axis criminality (CCPAC). He would also lead the American team in all future negotiations with the other Allied powers over war crimes trial policy.[49] Justice Jackson's formal education in law consisted of one year at the Albany Law School, which granted him a law certificate. He earned his credentials as a clerk in his cousin's practice in Jamestown, New York. In 1913, he took over this practice and was admitted to the bar at the end of that year. He was only twenty-one years old.[50] During his twenty-year career in Jamestown, Jackson represented major industries and utilities companies, but he never lost sympathy for the common man, once defending (without pay) an indigent black man who had been accused of murdering a white farmer. He won the case.[51] Jackson began his public service in 1932, when, at Secretary of the Treasury Morgenthau's request, he accepted the post of general counsel of the Bureau of Internal Revenue. Jackson rose quickly through the ranks of the governmental legal hierarchy. In 1938 Roosevelt nominated him as solicitor general, in 1940 he became attorney general and legal advisor to the president, and in 1941 he was appointed to an associate justiceship at the Supreme Court.[52] A gifted orator and jurist, Jackson was described by a colleague at Nuremberg as a "crusader for the rule of law." He was entirely dedicated to the trial of major war criminals, seeing in this proceeding an opportunity to transform international law "from a mere collection of hopes into an effective binding set of rules to govern the behavior of nations."[53]

The London Charter

Jackson wasted no time choosing his chief associates and preparing a draft agreement for a trial to present to the Allied powers at the upcoming conference in San Francisco (although Jackson did not attend).[54] There, between 2 and 10 May, the four major Allies (France, Britain, the Soviet Union, and the United States) accepted the general principle of holding a trial and agreed upon an International Military Tribunal (IMT) to hear the case. They further agreed that each would appoint a chief of counsel to prepare the prosecution.[55] The next set of negotiations, which centered on finalizing the trial law and procedure, took place in London from June to July 1945. The basis of the American proposal consisted essentially of Bernays's plan. Reconciling the differences in legal traditions and agreeing on the role of the judges, the form of the indictment, debating the viability of the conspiracy and aggressive war charges, determining the approximate duration of the trial, settling on the number of defendants to be indicted, and establishing the venue of the proceedings filled six impassioned, if also at times tedious, weeks of negotiations. More than once the trial plan teetered on the brink of collapse.[56] At long last, the Allies signed a charter outlining the laws and processes of the international tribunal, reflecting a "crude but workable" fusion of Anglo-American and continental procedural systems.[57] The London Charter (also referred to as the Nuremberg Charter) gave the accused the right to counsel and trial in their own language. A detailed indictment summarizing the evidence against them would be presented to the defendants before proceedings began, a practice common to continental procedure. Defendants would also be permitted to testify under oath and would be subject to cross-examination, which was unusual outside Anglo-American courts. Further, they would have the opportunity to make a final statement to the court not subject to challenge and not under oath, a right foreign to Anglo-American legal culture.[58] In Jackson's view, the mixing of the two legal traditions ultimately provided more rights to the defendants than they may have had in either system alone.[59]

Ultimately, there were significant differences between the London Charter and Bernays's original vision. The first casualty was the conspiracy charge, which "endured death by a thousand cuts in the drafting sub-committee."[60] Although initially conceived to link all crimes and all culprits under one criminal charge, the imprecise wording of the charter seemed to connect the notion of conspiracy solely to the crime of planning and waging aggressive war. This effectively excluded prewar persecutions of German Jews from the tribunal's jurisdiction. The charter dealt another blow to the Bernays plan with its treatment of organizational criminality. Article 9 stated

that the tribunal "may"—not "must"—declare that the group or organization of which the individual defendant was a member was a criminal organization, and qualified this by requiring that this declaration be connected to
an act of which the individual defendant was found guilty.[61]

The charge of aggressive war, which had always been Jackson's priority
(he called it "the crime which comprehends all lesser crimes"), was duly
incorporated into the charter under the rubric of "crimes against peace."[62]
The third crime named by the charter was "war crimes." Defined as violations of the laws and customs of war, the acts included under this charge
were familiar to customary international law. Jackson did not convince the
London conference that these crimes were an intended result of the war
instead of an unfortunate consequence of hostilities, but he did succeed in
his argument that Nazi leaders and officials (men who worked at desks and
who may never have personally fired a weapon) should bear responsibility
for the acts of their subordinates.[63] Consequently, article 7 of the charter
ruled out official positions or high office as a mitigating or exculpatory factor in the determination of punishment. It was with the fourth charge that
the conference broke new legal ground and gave to the trial its most significant legacy. "Crimes against humanity" encompassed the persecution of
racial, religious, and political groups as well as the enslavement of civilian
populations.[64] Although the charge was originally devised to include acts
the charge of war crimes could not (for example, the prewar persecution of
German Jews), the charter ultimately limited its scope to acts "in connection with any crime within the jurisdiction of the tribunal." This effectively
narrowed the field to persecutions connected to the war—that is, occurring
after 1 September 1939.[65] The charter of the IMT provided the framework
for the trial of Nazi leaders, but in no way did it build in a guarantee of success for the prosecution. Most of the law encoded within its pages was
untested. Indeed, the IMT was to be a trial "held by the judges—not staged
by the prosecution."[66]

The trial machinery was therefore in place. It was a remarkable achievement given the chaotic atmosphere of the time. As the historian Bradley
Smith observed, leafing through the papers of Washington officials from
the years when the war crimes judicial policy was taking shape, "one sees . . .
they were forced to make hourly hops between subjects as serious and
diverse as the atomic bomb, military strategy, inflation, postwar rationing,
occupation policies and universal military service. These men seemed
increasingly like men who, fearing they were about to drown, took to slap-
ping the water on all sides."[67] And yet from amid this confusion emerged
a plan that recognized and encompassed the Nazi criminal enterprise as a
whole, avoiding the "wilderness of single instances" and meeting the chal-

lenge of embracing "a multitude of crimes committed in several countries and participated in by thousands of actors over a decade of time."[68] The imagination of Bernays, the political acumen of Stimson, the unwavering devotion of Jackson, and the tireless work of scores of others made the punishment of Nazi leaders by trial a reality.

The International Military Tribunal Begins

Proceedings opened at Nuremberg on 21 November 1945, less than seven months after the guns had fallen silent.[69] Nuremberg was not the obvious choice of venue. Allied bombing had destroyed about 90 percent of the city center.[70] The rubble reeked with the stench of the thousands of bombing victims still buried beneath.[71] But the outskirts and suburbs were livable, and more importantly, the massive Palace of Justice (described by one observer as "an extreme example of the German tendency to overbuild") was reparable, and had extensive office space, a courtroom that could be enlarged, and an adjacent jail.[72] Nuremberg also possessed great symbolic value. As the site of the former Nazi Party rallies and the home of the 1935 race laws, bringing the Nazi leaders to trial here denoted a certain poetic justice. Not least of all it was located in the American occupation zone, and American rations were rumored to be better than anyone else's. Further, they had the personnel, equipment, money, and determination to complete the construction work and provide the essential comforts to the staffs of participating nations. Although the Russians pushed doggedly to hold the proceedings in Berlin, Western Allied reluctance to embed themselves in the heart of the Soviet zone (four-power administration of the city notwithstanding), combined with the Russians' reputation for inefficiency and proletarian-style living (indeed, Soviet delegate Nikitchenko had waved off the need for central heating in the early winter), greatly added to Nuremberg's appeal.[73]

The choice of defendants was perhaps the least contentious issue the prosecutors faced. In effect, most of the defendants had "chose[n] themselves," having occupied some of the most notorious positions and representing some of the most despised organizations in the Nazi hierarchy.[74] The list included Hitler's successor-designate Hermann Göring; the chief of the operations staff of the Wehrmacht High Command, Alfred Jodl; the chief administrator of the concentration camp system, Ernst Kaltenbrunner; Albert Speer, the head of armaments and war production; and twenty more. To everyone's surprise, when these former "heroes of Leni Riefenstahl films" filed into the defendants' box, they appeared "elderly [and] sallow.

... They were all so much smaller than anyone had imagined ... so insignificant you wouldn't notice them on the tube."[75]

The courtroom smelled of fresh paint and new wood, and on the first day, it possessed all the anticipation and excitement "of a theatrical opening night."[76] Proceedings began with the dignity and eloquence for which Jackson's oratory was known. His opening statement was solemn and stirring:

> The privilege of opening the first trial in history for crimes against the peace of the world imposes a grave responsibility. The wrongs which we seek to condemn and punish have been so calculated, so malignant, and so devastating, that civilization cannot tolerate their being ignored, because it cannot survive their being repeated. That four great nations, flushed with victory and stung with injury stay the hand of vengeance and voluntarily submit their captive enemies to the judgment of the law is one of the most significant tributes that Power has ever paid to Reason.[77]

Despite the drama of this first moment, the day-to-day reality of Nuremberg was characterized by numbing boredom. Although IBM's ingenious device, which transmitted four simultaneous translations from interpreters to listeners, worked remarkably well, the need of the translator to hear and understand required a slowed pace.[78] Further, an early ruling on procedure required that all the documentary evidence be read into the record. It certainly was not all riveting material. Together with the overlap in evidence and argumentation between the Allies' cases and the tribunal's willingness to grant extreme latitude to the defense to digress, Nuremberg devolved into what Rebecca West famously called "a citadel of boredom."[79] In her articles for *The New Yorker*, West was struck by the "extreme tedium" of the proceedings, and she described how the lawyers and secretaries "sagged in their seats," how the guards' faces were "puffy with boredom," and how the eight judges "were plainly dragging the proceedings over the threshold of their consciousness by sheer force of will. . . . All these people," she added for emphasis, "wanted to leave Nuremberg as urgently as a dental patient enduring the drill wants to up and leave the chair."[80] She was not unique in her impressions. In his memoir of the trial, Sir Hartley Shawcross, the British chief prosecutor, recalled the day that one of the French aides snored so loudly that the judges had to halt proceedings.[81] And yet this "water-torture, boredom falling drop by drop on the same spot on the soul," was punctuated by flashes of intense drama and emotion, such as the day Einsatzgruppe D leader Otto Ohlendorf admitted to having shot 90,000 Jewish civilians, and when the former commandant at Auschwitz, Rudolf Hess, estimated that two and a half million people had been murdered there.[82] The courtroom bristled when Göring bested Jackson in the verbal duel of cross-examination, and the chief prosecutor was left dangling by the tribunal, which refused to rein in the former Reischsmarschall from his diatribe.[83] The French submitted the most documents: 800 of the final 2,100.[84] But it was the Russians' case that elicited the deepest revulsion. Their film on the liberation of the Maidanek death camp sent the American alternate judge John Parker to bed for three days. Searing evidence and witness testimony of Nazi atrocities in the East finally quieted the tribunal's complaints that the trial was taking too long. They recognized that the proceedings were as much about emotional release as they were about legal adjudication.[85]

West noted that at the trial's conclusion, an unexpected gloom fell over the lawyers. Although there was ample evidence that the men sentenced to death were "abscesses of cruelty," still it was awful that the time had come to kill them—or, more accurately, that the former Allied powers had to do it themselves.[86] And yet the feeling was that it had to be done. The men who would ascend the gallows were themselves no longer a threat, and certainly their deaths could not redeem the misery that they had caused. But in them existed the symbol of all that was evil about Nazism, and that now was to be extinguished. Perhaps Jackson anticipated this penultimate moment of ambivalence when in his opening statement he emphasized the symbolic aspect of the judicial exercise:

> In the prisoners' dock sit twenty-odd broken men. . . . Their personal capacity for evil is forever past. It is hard now to perceive in these men as captives the power by which as Nazi leaders they once dominated much of the world and terrified most of it. Merely as individuals their fate is of little consequence to the world. What makes this inquest significant is that these prisoners *represent* sinister influences that will lurk in the world long after their bodies have returned to dust. We will show them to be living *symbols* of racial hatreds, of terrorism and violence, and of the arrogance and cruelty of power. They are *symbols* of fierce nationalisms and militarism, of intrigue and war-making which have embroiled Europe generation after generation, crushing its manhood, destroying its homes, and impoverishing its life. . . . Civilization can afford no compromise with the social forces which would gain renewed strength if we deal ambiguously or indecisively with the men in whom those forces now precariously survive.[87]

This trial of Nazi war criminals was only the first step in the fulfillment of the United States' commitment to trials. The American vision for Germany's rehabilitation and reeducation required the continued prosecution and punishment of criminals who came into their custody. But as will be shown, the path to the subsequent trials was nearly as difficult as that to the first.

Toward the Subsequent Nuremberg Proceedings

It is perhaps helpful to think of American judicial policy as having developed along parallel, and sometimes intersecting, tracks. In late summer and early fall of 1944, while the War Department was formulating the arguments in favor of a trial pursuant to the Moscow Declaration, the Joint Chiefs of Staff of the American military were also considering a plan of action for the war criminals problem. Propelled by the Supreme Headquarters Allied Expeditionary Force's and Eisenhower's expectation that the war would end sooner than Washington anticipated, the Joint Chiefs of Staff issued a directive to theater commanders for the arrest of suspected war criminals and the collection of relevant evidence.[88] Marked by the as yet still-raw conception of war crimes, the directive concerned "violations of the laws and customs of war which constitute offenses against person or property, committed in connection with military operations or occupation, which outrage common justice or involve moral turpitude."[89]

In the meantime, the focus of war crimes policy making had shifted to other levels and offices of the government. As shown above, during the preceding few months, attitudes toward the prosecution of Nazi criminality had significantly broadened in scope among leaders of the War, State, and Navy departments. The conspiracy–criminal organization program that grew out of the recent debates temporarily put a stop on the Joint Chiefs of Staff initiative regarding war crimes judicial policy.[90]

Upon Germany's unconditional surrender, the Combined Chiefs of Staff directed the theater commanders in Germany and the Mediterranean to arrest and detain war crimes suspects; however, they withheld authorization to conduct trials. The focus of war crimes trial planning was in the hands of the recently appointed American representative in matters of Allied war crimes policy and American chief of counsel for the prosecution of Axis criminality Robert Jackson. Within a few weeks, Jackson presented an interim report to the president that mapped out the general outlines for U.S. war crimes policy. Besides the international tribunal already taking shape, he noted that there were still three classes of crimes outside the jurisdiction of his CCPAC office: crimes committed against American military personnel, crimes with a geographical location (that is, crimes against persons or property in former Nazi-occupied territories), and cases of treason by nations against their own citizens.

Regarding the first category, Jackson proposed that the army carry out these proceedings, so long as there was no conflict of interest with the international tribunal's requirements. That is, Jackson wanted to ensure that no army-convicted defendant of potential witness value to the IMT would be executed before he could testify. Jackson established a liaison office with the theater judge advocate's staff. On 19 June 1945, the Combined Chiefs of Staff formally lifted prior restrictions and authorized the theater commanders to proceed with trials of suspected war criminals other than those who held the highest political, military, and civil positions, lest they be selected to appear in Nuremberg.[91] In Germany, the theater judge advocate went ahead with cases involving crimes against U.S. nationals (mainly military personnel) and crimes committed in concentration camps liberated by U.S. forces. In fact, the judge advocate general had already conducted its first trial on 2 June 1945, which involved the prosecution of three German nationals for their killing of an American airman. It had been tried before a military commission appointed by the local area commander. However, after the Combined Chiefs of Staff directive, further trials were directed into a centralized program. These trials came to be called the Dachau trials because the army conducted most of them on the grounds of the former concentration camp at Dachau. General or intermediate special military government courts established solely for these war crimes proceedings heard the cases. The deputy judge advocate for war crimes oversaw the cases' preparation, prosecution, defense, and review. The military government courts that conducted these trials were not as firmly bound to standard civilian legal protocol as the Nuremberg tribunals were. Indeed, the procedural guide put forward in June 1945 stated that the basic purpose of military government courts was the protection of Allied forces and the advancement of their military objectives, and further, that "it is important therefore, that when an offense against the Allied forces has been established, appropriate punishment should be imposed with a view to the prevention of further offenses. A technical and legalistic viewpoint must not be allowed to interfere with such a result."[92]

Although the accused were usually ground-level perpetrators (as opposed to top-level planners), the charges were vaguely articulated and centered on the assertion of the existence of a "common design" to commit the criminal acts alleged.[93] The indictments rarely charged individual defendants with individual crimes, and the courts relied on witness testimony rather than on documentary evidence.[94] In just over two years, 1,672 defendants in 462 cases had been prosecuted, and 426 death sentences had been imposed.

Three hundred eleven of the cases were "flyer" cases—that is, they concerned killings of downed airmen. There were eight "mass atrocity" cases, which tried the personnel of the Dachau, Buchenwald, Mauthausen, Flossenburg, Nordhausen, and Muehldorf camps and of the Hadamar euthanasia center. This category also included the perpetrators of the infamous Malmedy massacre. There were another 170 smaller concentration camp cases. In all, 854 Americans and 310 screened German nationals had been employed in the trials.[95] Although these trials attracted far less attention than the IMT, two cases—the Malmedy and Ilse Koch proceedings—earned condemnation in Germany and the United States amid accusations of American mistreatment of interrogation subjects and sentencing discrepancies. More will be said on this in chapter 2.

Jackson's interim report acted as impetus for the continued formulation of a basic war crimes policy directive for the American occupational administration of Germany. Apart from the international tribunal then being prepared, the Americans would have to deal with the many thousands of suspected war criminals who had recently come under their authority as supreme commander in their occupational zone. On 15 July 1945, the Joint Chiefs of Staff endorsed a directive, called JCS 1023/10, for the identification, apprehension, and trial of persons suspected of war crimes.[96] The instructions in this directive reflected the recent developments in American war crimes thinking. In fact, its definitions of crimes were lifted almost verbatim from Jackson's aggressive war–criminal organization proposal then being discussed at the London conference. That is, this directive named as crimes the initiation of invasions of other countries and wars of aggression, violations of the laws and customs of war, atrocities and persecutions on racial, religious, or political grounds committed after 30 January 1933, and extended to principles, accessories, and individuals connected to plans involving these offenses and who had been members of organizations or groups connected with the commission of these crimes.[97]

Although the directive authorized the immediate initiation of proceedings by military courts, persons suspected of being major offenders were to be withheld from trial until a decision was made whether they would appear in the international tribunal or in the court of another occupying power or European state. As supreme commander of American forces in Europe, General Eisenhower was responsible for implementing the directive. He in turn assigned Brigadier General Edward Betts, the theater judge advocate, the task of carrying it out. Betts looked to Jackson for advice. In a letter dated 19 October 1945, Betts remarked that the trials being prepared and prosecuted by the Theater Judge Advocate (that is, the Dachau trials) and the Office of the Chief of Counsel for the Prosecution of Axis Criminality

(OCCPAC; that is, the IMT at Nuremberg) only partially fulfilled the enormous mandate of JCS 1023/10. He recommended that the OCCPAC be carried forward to deal with the remaining war criminals in U.S. custody who would be tried before military government courts in the U.S. zone.[98]

Jackson's feelings on the matter were mixed. On the one hand, he believed that a failure to follow through with trials of members of convicted organizations and other major criminals "would discredit the whole [trial] effort." On the other hand, he himself had no interest in accepting responsibility for these proceedings. He noted that the United States presently had over 100,000 men in custody, all of whom were potential defendants. His main concern over the feasibility of the trials was the acquisition of qualified staff to carry them out. Living conditions in Nuremberg and the tedium of trial work had already caused a high turnover in personnel, and Jackson admitted that the situation as it now stood "frankly frightens me."[99]

Who from the OCCPAC would be willing to take on the enormous task of organizing these trials? Charles Fahy, the legal advisor to the Office of the Military Government, U.S. (OMGUS), approached the thirty-seven-year-old Colonel Telford Taylor, a Harvard-trained lawyer and former special assistant to the U.S. attorney general, who in the later years of the war was chief of the military intelligence service in London.[100] After the war, he was invited to take part in the IMT as assistant counsel in the OCC-PAC. Taylor accepted Fahy's request, and concurrently with his work on the IMT (he led the organization case against the Oberkommando der Wehrmacht [OKW]), he began the enormous task of recruiting personnel, sorting and cataloging evidence, and determining the size and number of what would be the Subsequent Nuremberg Proceedings (SNP).

Control Council Law No. 10

Meanwhile, American officials had to secure the legal and jurisdictional basis for the planned future trials. Upon Germany's surrender, the country had been divided among the major Allies into four zones of occupation. Each Allied zone commander exercised supreme authority over the military government in his respective zone, but a four-member Allied Control Council was simultaneously established in order to coordinate matters affecting Germany as a whole.[101] Fahy presented JCS 1023/10 to the Allied Control Council in the hopes of securing a quadripartite jurisdictional basis for the conduct of zonal trials. Coordination was needed to settle matters of extradition of defendants and transfer of witnesses between zones. The

Americans also hoped that the other Allied powers would prosecute more trials of criminals in their custody. The council approved a draft law on 1 November, which came into force on 20 December 1945 under the name Control Council Law No. 10. The purposes of the law were to give effect to the Moscow Declaration and the London Agreement and Charter, and to establish a uniform legal basis in Germany for the Allied prosecution of war criminals and other similar offenders, other than those dealt with by the international tribunal.[102]

Control Council Law No. 10 authorized each occupational power to establish its own tribunals for the trial of major war criminals in its custody. The definitions of crimes set out therein reflected Jackson's June report and the London Charter, with a few notable changes. Crimes against peace now included invasions (so as to bring the campaigns against Austria and Czechoslovakia within judicial reach), the formulation of the crimes against humanity charge dropped the qualifying phrase that these offenses be connected to another crime within the tribunals' jurisdiction, and last, membership in organizations declared criminal by the IMT was added as a new charge. The formal establishment of tribunals and the procedure by which they would function were left to each individual occupational zone commander. These matters were resolved in the American zone by Military Government Ordinance No. 7. Enacted on 18 October 1946, this law retained the procedural provisions of the London Charter, with some modifications in light of experience at the international tribunal. In addition, the ordinance declared that the findings of the IMT were binding on the American tribunals and ruled that none of the resulting judgments would be subject to review.[103]

Unfortunately, the other Allied powers in Germany either did not dedicate equal time and resources to the further prosecution of war criminals in their custody, or were not of the same mind-set regarding the goals these trials were designated to achieve. The French conducted one major trial at Rastatt of the Saar iron, coal, and steel magnate Hermann Roechling and four of his colleagues for having increased the Third Reich's war potential and contributing to the conduct of aggressive war, their enslavement and treatment of civilian and POW forced laborers, and the economic spoliation of occupied territories. Ultimately four of the defendants were sentenced to prison terms of between three and ten years. Sometimes referred to as the thirteenth subsequent proceeding at Nuremberg, the Roechling trial indictment and judgment are included in the United States–published so-called Green Series, the fifteen-volume set of excerpts from the trials, so named for the color of their covers. The French held other proceedings of "lesser" criminals, which focused mainly on crimes committed in camps and prisons against forced laborers.[104]

Regarding the Soviets, at first, Telford Taylor believed that the Russians had not done anything to fulfill Control Council Law No. 10's mandate in their zone, because Soviet prosecutors and judges at Nuremberg broke off all communications with the other Allied powers once the IMT ended.[105] Recent research has revealed, however, that in fact the Soviets tried 14,080 defendants under Control Council Law No. 10 and imprisoned (without trial) tens of thousands more in Soviet secret police prisons and camps.[106] However, the political and propagandistic aims of these measures are clear. Therefore, these proceedings cannot be described as having advanced the objectives the Americans had outlined for the war crimes trials. The British elected to hold trials before strictly military courts under the Royal Warrant in which the charges were limited to violations of the laws of war, a much narrower construction than, for example, crimes against humanity. Telford Taylor deeply regretted this turn of events, particularly with relation to the planned trial of military leaders. Almost half of these defendants identified by the Americans as major offenders were in British custody, who in turn showed little inclination to try them.[107] Taylor greatly feared that the lack of consistency in the prosecution of the generals would confuse the German people and damage the integrity of the Allied trial program. Indeed, Taylor even took steps to have the British-held generals extradited to the American zone to stand trial there. Much to Taylor's chagrin, General Lucius Clay (the deputy military governor for Germany) intervened and insisted that the British take responsibility for their own prisoners.[108] In general, it is clear that the Americans were the most dedicated to completing the process begun with the IMT.

Now that the trial machinery was in place, the Americans had to prepare individual cases. Telford Taylor took over the newly created Subsequent Proceedings Division within OCCPAC, and it was decided that Jackson would name him deputy chief of counsel for the prosecution of Axis criminality. Upon Jackson's resignation, he would assume the leadership of the Office of the Chief of Counsel for War Crimes (OCCWC), and this office would come under the direction of the Office for Military Government, U.S.

The first major question to resolve was what was actually feasible with this second round of proceedings. General Joseph McNarney, the American military governor of Germany, addressed a memorandum to the chief of staff of the War Department in Washington in which he declared that "it has become evident that the occupational authorities cannot by their own means seek out and punish all the countless offenses committed within Germany since 1933 . . . a literal compliance with JCS 1023/10 is, in practice *out of the question.*"[109] Indeed, as prodigious an effort as the Americans were prepared to expend, they openly admitted that responsibility for prosecutions would have to be shared with the German people themselves, but that an even greater symbolic value attached to the trials that the Americans would prosecute. And so it was decided that the majority of so-called organizational case trials of former members of organizations declared criminal by the IMT would be conducted through a denazification program. Conceived with a view to preventing the reentry of former Nazis into the German government, economy, or major social and cultural institutions, the denazification program used German courts and German prosecutors and judges "free from Nazi taint" to review the histories of these lower-level war criminals and to pass sentence.[110]

There was one last obstacle to overcome before the Americans could formally sever ties with the other Allied powers and proceed alone in the prosecution of war criminals in their custody. Early on in the preparation of the IMT, the issue of holding a second international trial had been raised. The immediate cause was the so-called Krupp incident. Gustav Krupp, head of the well-known and much feared Krupp mining, steelmaking, munitions-producing, and shipbuilding industrial concern, was named under the Nuremberg indictment. Although he had suffered a debilitating stroke in 1941 and his son, Alfried, had taken over the company in 1943, it was not until after the list of defendants had been announced publicly that the elder Gustav was discovered to be unfit to stand trial. Jackson moved to add other major industrialists to the indictment but was defeated by a three-to-one vote of the chief prosecutors. The French, with the Americans' and Russians' support, suggested adding Alfried Krupp, but the tribunal denied the motion in order not to delay the opening of the trial or prolong its duration.[111] At the time of their vote against the motion, the British issued a joint press release with the French stating their intention to hold a second international trial of leading German industrialists, including Alfried Krupp.[112] The French were deeply interested in bringing German industrialists to trial, as their citizens had comprised a vast number of the laborers enslaved in the munitions factories during the war.[113]

By contrast, Jackson firmly opposed committing the Americans to a second trial for strategic and practical considerations. In his view, the strongest criminal case was already being presented, and he feared a second trial would be an anticlimax in public opinion. Of no less concern was the fact that the outcome of this first case was still far from predictable, and Jackson feared that if the tribunal returned acquittals, he did not want the United States to be committed to trying an even weaker case. Politically, a second trial of industrialists and financiers could be difficult to manage because it could give the impression that these defendants were being prosecuted on the sole basis of having been industrialists, an impression made more plausible by the ardent support of the Soviet Communists and the French leftists. Further, Jackson had reservations about the appearance of a prolonged attack against private industry, which could discourage its cooperation with the United States in maintaining defenses in Europe while not at all weakening the Russian position, which did not similarly depend on private industry. Moreover, a trial of industrialists, Jackson added, would no doubt highlight a weakness in the Allied joint prosecution that hitherto had been kept from becoming too embarrassing. Jackson questioned the wisdom of prosecuting German industrialists for providing tanks to invade Poland when Russian industrialists had done the same. Last were the practical considerations of holding a second trial: a four-power trial was more expensive and prolonged an undertaking, and the Americans would most likely hold the presidency in a second trial, which pointed to Nuremberg serving again as the venue, which would again endow the United States with the burden of feeding, billeting, and administering the staffs of the four nations involved.[114] Rosenman concurred with Jackson's objections, declaring, "of course, international trials are long, complicated and vexatious," but feared that the United States would be criticized if it did not cooperate in trying the former industrialists who had aided and abetted the war criminals now on trial.[115] Fahy sided with Jackson, stating that in view of the overall international situation, it would be difficult to duplicate the successful participation of four powers in a second trial.[116]

Despite initial reservations, Telford Taylor concluded that American refusal to participate in a second trial would cost more in public opinion than would have to be expended in manpower and resources. He was confident that the trial could be short—three months, involving six to eight defendants—and that there existed ample evidence to prove serious crimes: assisting in Hitler's rise to power, waging aggressive war, plunder of occupied countries, and deportations of civilians for slave labor.[117] By contrast, in his final report submitted to President Truman in October 1946, Jackson reminded the president that the United States had no legal or moral obligation to undertake another international trial and that the "quickest and most satisfactory results" would be obtained from the immediate commencement of the subsequent cases prepared by Taylor as deputy chief of counsel. The matter was left to rest. When several months later the French suggested a reconvening of the chief prosecutors to plan a second IMT, American ambassadors quietly informed their French, Soviet, and British hosts that the United States intended only to proceed with their own zonal trials.[118]

The Subsequent Nuremberg Proceedings

Meanwhile, the planning of the SNP had long made significant progress. Despite the challenges of recruiting adequate staff for judging, prosecuting, interrogating; gathering, analyzing, and organizing evidence; determining the scope of the trial program; defining the trial procedure; and securing the material resources to accommodate the trial participants, the chief of counsel entered the first indictment less than a month after the IMT had closed. Although Taylor had originally envisioned eighteen trials, time, funds, and energy eventually whittled this number to twelve. One hundred eighty-five defendants representing the medical, judicial, S.S. and police, industrial and financial, economic and diplomatic, and military institutions of the Third Reich were brought before the bar.[119] The breakdown can be seen in Table 1.1.

Within the SNP, the cases against the German military were a priority in Taylor's plans. Perhaps stemming in part from his work on the OKW case for the IMT, which had failed to secure a conviction, his emphasis on the prosecution of German militarists was undoubtedly also fed by his conviction that a trial constituted the best defense against a revisionist German history of the war then, he observed, already under way.[120] In an address delivered to the International Association of Democratic Lawyers in Paris in April 1947, he remarked:

> The first steps toward the revival of German militarism have already been taken. The German militarists know that their future strength depends on re-establishing the faith of the German people in their military prowess and in disassociating themselves from the atrocities which they committed in the service of the Third Reich. Why did the Wehrmacht meet with defeat? Hitler interfered too much in military affairs, says Manstein. What about atrocities? The Wehrmacht committed none. Hitler's criminal orders were disregarded by the generals. Any atrocities which did occur were committed by other men such as Himmler and other agencies such as the SS. Did not an SS general say that the field marshals could have prevented many of the excesses and atrocities? The reaction is one of superiority and scorn: "I think it is impertinent for an SS man to make such statements about a field marshal," said Rundstedt. The documents and testimony show that these are transparent fabrications. But here, in embryo, are the myths and legends which the German militarists will seek to propagate in the German mind. These lies must be stamped and labeled for what they are, now while the proof is fresh.[121]

Table 1.1. The Subsequent Nuremberg Proceedings, 1946–1948

Case No.	U.S. v.	Popular Name	No. of Defendants
1	Karl Brandt et al.	Medical case (medicine)	23
2	Erhard Milch	Milch case (Luftwaffe and slave labor)	1
3	Josef Altstoetter et al.	Justice case (judiciary)	16
4	Oswald Pohl et al.	Pohl case (S.S.)	18
5	Friedrich Flick et al.	Flick case (industrialists)	6
6	Carl Krauch et al.	IG Farben case (industrialists)	24
7	Wilhelm List et al.	Hostage case (military)	12
8	Ulrich Greifelt et al.	RuSHA case (S.S.)	14
9	Otto Ohlendorf et al.	Einsatzgruppen case (S.S.)	24
10	Alfried Krupp et al.	Krupp case (industrialists)	12
11	Ernst von Weizsäcker et al.	Ministries case (government ministries)	21
12	Wilhelm von Leeb et al.	High Command case (military)	14

Source: "Introduction," National Archives Microfilm Publication 898, Roll 1.

The evidence and arguments used to write an accurate history of the Wehrmacht in the war, and the defendants' attempts to distort and refute that composition, will be the subject of two following chapters.

The first few rumblings about punishing Nazi criminals had, in three short and hectic years, given way to a vast program of war crimes proceedings. The United States was and remained unmatched in its dedication to the war crimes trial initiative and its objectives, devoting incalculable sums in personnel, resources, and energy to the endeavor. Ultimately, it became involved in five separate trial programs: the IMT, the Dachau trials, the denazification program, the SNP, and also the IMT for the Far East.[122] Not all of these trials have as admirable a record as the Americans would have hoped. But the trials held at and governed by the law of Nuremberg were unified in the founding conviction that trials could be progressive and edifying, and they denoted an optimistic outlook for Germany's political future and its future relations with the democratic West.

In his final report on the IMT, Jackson appraised the proceedings' foremost successes as having recorded Nazi aggressions, persecutions, and atrocities "with such authenticity and in such detail that there can be no responsible denial of these crimes in the future." Having submitted these crimes to the rule of law, he added, the laws of war now had the power of the precedent. In sum, the value of the Nuremberg trial would be judged by its impact on public consciousness and its legacy in future war crimes adjudication. The Subsequent Nuremberg Proceedings, the first trials administered by the United States alone, would be the first test to determine whether indeed the Nuremberg ideals had taken root. Further, of the defendant groups that remained, soldiers were one of the most contentious. The challenges involved in and raised against holding Wehrmacht field marshals and generals responsible for war crimes would test whether the Americans' commitment to the goals enunciated at the start of the trial program (justice, education, and democratization) were honored until its end.

2

The Response to the Trials: Attacks on All Sides, 1946 to 1949

It would render a great service to pacification and [be] a wise policy of occupation, if the methods used hitherto in punishing war criminals and Nazis were done away with altogether.
—Bishop Theophil Wurm, 3 May 1949

BY CONDUCTING WAR CRIMES TRIALS, American occupation authorities hoped not only to achieve justice in the face of unprecedented crime, but also to educate the German people, reconcile them with their past, and open the way toward democracy. Whether these goals succeeded depended in part on what occurred in the Nuremberg courtrooms, but also in great measure on the German response to the proceedings. This book is primarily concerned with the High Command case's success or failure as a didactic trial; however, public impressions of this trial did not begin to form when the lawyers read their closing statements. Indeed, even before the tribunal rendered its judgment in October 1948, the fabric of the entire American war crimes trial program began to fray. In the preceding years, several trial-related scandals and increasingly vocal Catholic and Protestant church–led campaigns to discredit the proceedings eroded the public's initial confidence in the legitimacy of United States war crimes adjudication. Although the decision to grant premature release to all remaining Landsberg inmates was still almost a decade away, the final disposition of the war crimes convicts had its origins in these early controversies. It was in these years that the terms were set that rejected collective responsibility for Nazi crime, and further, denied the identification of convicted war criminals as criminals. Instead, the men put to trial by the Americans were depicted as victims of unfair proceedings and Allied vengeance. But apart from the events that directly affected the war crimes trials, we must consider the overall atmosphere in Germany that contributed to undermining the judicial enterprise.

Early German Responses to the Nuremberg Trials

U.S. authorities did their best to inform themselves about the prevailing postwar German mood. Responsible not only for the physical reconstruction of their zone in Germany but also for the political and cultural reorientation of its inhabitants, they cared deeply about public opinion. Social psychologists employed in the Intelligence Branch of the Information Control Office conducted seventy-two major surveys in four years to track German attitudes to occupation policies such as economic and educational reform, the disposition of expellees and displaced persons, rationing, and, importantly, war crimes trials.[1] American authorities were pleased with the initial German response to the International Military Tribunal (IMT). About midway through, indications were that the trial was having the desired effect. Interest in the proceedings was high (in January 1946, 78 percent of respondents had read newspaper articles on the trial), and the German people were learning from them. In December 1945, 84 percent of respondents said that they had learned something new (for example, the truth about how the war began and about the existence and purpose of camps in the East). When the trial ended, 76 percent of those surveyed believed that the sentences were either fair or too mild, and 78 percent thought that the proceedings as a whole had been just.[2]

Analysts were circumspect, however, cautioning that these results lent themselves to several interpretations. On the one hand, it seemed as though the German people largely supported the punishment of Nazi leaders. On the other hand, officials wondered if perhaps this support masked a deeper desire to place all responsibility on the defendants, thereby exonerating themselves.[3] Unfortunately, there were other indications that this first trial was not fulfilling the reformative, reconciliatory, and educational functions it had been designed to achieve. Toward the end of the trial, surveyors noted a steep decline in interest. Far fewer Germans were reading press accounts, and fewer still were reading articles in their entirety.[4] In spring 1947, subsequent public opinion data revealed even more disturbing results. Asked whether they believed "National Socialism was a good idea, badly carried out," in August of that year, 55 percent of respondents said yes. Furthermore, the number of respondents who believed that Nazism was a bad idea dropped from 48 percent (July 1946) to 35 percent (August 1947).[5] This led intelligence analysts to conclude that two years of occupation had "not made much progress in shaking many Germans loose from the past."[6] Even U.S. trial attorneys lamented the little effect their work seemed to be making on German consciousness. Benjamin Ferencz, prosecutor in the 1947 to 1948 Einsatzgruppen trial, wrote dejectedly: "The German public has little interest in American trials."[7]

The following spring, occupation authorities initiated a campaign to reengage Germans with the proceedings. George S. Martin of the Nuremberg Public Relations Office embarked on a tour of the American zone, showing a film of the Nazi People's Court trials of the participants in the 20 July 1944 assassination attempt against Hitler. Presenting it as an example of "Nazi justice at work," Martin hoped not only to bring attention to the American proceedings, but also to restore trust in their legitimacy. Martin was not alone in this effort. The lead prosecutor in the IG Farben case, Robert Kempner, also undertook a lecture tour before the start of that trial.[8]

Possible explanations for the Germans' declining interest in the trials are many. First, Germans simply had other matters on their minds. The geographical and psychological dislocation and familial and material losses wrought by war and defeat were not easily overcome. Indeed, 20 percent of the population in the American zone consisted of displaced persons: ethnic German expellees from the East, Germans fleeing Soviet occupation in East Germany, and displaced persons of other nationalities.[9] Urban centers were still heavily damaged from wartime bombing. Infrastructure was fragile, and housing was scarce. Even by August 1948, over three years since the war ended, the average city dweller was underfed, which, apart from the damaging physical effects, compromised overall morale.[10] Further, there was a general sense that the German people wanted an escape from the dreary realities of everyday life, and certainly few cared to rehash the crimes of the Nazi era.

As part of their mission to reeducate and democratize the Germans under their charge, the United States established the Amerika Haus program in the regional capitals and major towns of their zone. These public centers offered lectures, films, classes, books, concerts, and youth and adult hobby clubs, through which American officials hoped to acquaint the German people with (and thereby attract and convert them to) average American "democratic" ways of life. Officials closely monitored which materials and events were most popular. Notably, and to the Americans indicative of contemporary German priorities, *Snow White* attracted the largest film audience. Fictional volumes were twice as popular as books on history and biography, and from seven to ten times more popular than works of philosophy, religion, or politics.[11]

Another source of general discontent was the denazification process. After the war, occupation officials sought to root out all traces of National Socialism from German society. Those seeking employment above manual labor, as well as all professionals and civil and public servants, were required to complete an extensive questionnaire detailing their wartime activities. In the American zone, one could not obtain a ration card or a travel permit without filling out one of these *Fragebogen*.[12] Upon examination of the form, if there was any doubt as to the individual's political sympathies, he or she would appear before a denazification tribunal. The tribunal would examine evidence, hear testimony, and pass a verdict, classifying the individual into one of five categories, from "main offender" to "exonerated." Atonement measures included fines, restrictions on employment, and imprisonment. These sometimes applied to the person's family as well.

The Americans showed the greatest ambition and expended the greatest effort to fulfill the program. By Christmas 1945, their offices were overflowing with 13 million completed *Fragebogen* forms.[13] But the process was beset by problems almost from the beginning. There were no fixed criteria for judgment, and differing levels of commitment to the program between occupation zones led to anomalous (and seemingly arbitrary) judgments.[14] Throughout Germany, denazification was "universally criticized."[15] Many Germans lost faith because officials did not seem to discriminate between nominal Nazis—people who had joined the party simply to retain their jobs—and the true believers who had joined out of genuine ideological commitment.[16] Others deeply resented that minor party members were forced into destitution pending judgment while formerly powerful or wealthy Nazis were acquitted or managed to evade examination altogether.[17]

Widespread criticism aside, as a result of American staff shortages and the sheer volume of cases to be adjudicated, the process soon devolved into an "overly complex and unwieldy bureaucratic quagmire."[18] In an attempt to restore order, Military Governor General Lucius Clay handed denazification over to the Germans. There was little improvement. At the program's height (in the American zone), 22,000 Germans worked full time to assist 545 tribunals hearing up to 50,000 cases a month.[19] However, there was no grassroots support. The Catholic Church ordered its members not to work in the tribunals or provide testimony.[20] Local priests offered themselves as witnesses for the accused and issued countless certificates attesting to the irreproachable character of the defendant.[21] In any case, the German tribunals were inefficient, corrupt, and in effect (if not also in intent) pro-Nazi, returning far fewer convictions than the Americans had estimated as appropriate.[22] When the Americans abruptly ended the program in 1948, Protestant leaders used the opportunity to tell General Clay that the Nuremberg trials were thus also merely "an anachronism."[23]

Most importantly for public reception of the war crimes trials, despite early positive (or at least disinterested) responses to the IMT, later impressions created by scandals connected to the Subsequent Nuremberg Proceedings and the Dachau proceedings badly damaged the overall view of the American trials as legally constituted and fairly prosecuted. Added to this was a negative public campaign by religious leaders (and later the West German government and veterans' associations, all of whom used the press), designed to discredit the American occupation authorities and their disposition of the war criminals issue. These factors will be explored more fully below. In the end, an increasingly hostile and disengaged public proved ever more receptive to allegations that the trials were flawed and their prosecutors unethical. Unfortunately, the basis for these allegations was many times rooted in reprehensible American conduct.

The Wennerstrum Scandal

On 19 February 1948, the Nuremberg tribunal hearing the only other war crimes trial of military men, the Hostage case, so called because of its emphasis on the murder of hostages in the Balkans, delivered its guilty verdicts. The following day, and only hours before departing the continent, presiding judge Charles Wennerstrum of the Iowa Supreme Court granted a confidential interview to a Germany-based correspondent for the *Chicago Tribune*. In declarations that resounded on both sides of the Atlantic, Wennerstrum denounced the Nuremberg proceedings' integrity: "The victor in any war is not the best judge of the war crime guilt. . . . The high ideals announced as the motives for creating these tribunals have not been evident. . . . The prosecution has failed to maintain objectivity aloof from vindictiveness, aloof from personal ambitions for convictions. . . . The lack of appeal leaves me with a feeling that justice has been denied."[24] Wennerstrum also accused Chief Prosecutor Telford Taylor of having attempted to interfere with the defense team's access to evidence documents. Taylor publicly struck back at the judge for his "subversive" remarks and "baseless slanders," concluding that they would "do grave harm to our country and your own court. They will be used by all the worst elements in Germany against the best."[25] The U.S. Army largely ignored Wennerstrum's remarks, and the judge himself, while refusing a retraction, withheld elaboration.[26] But the damage had been done. Within days, citing the Iowa judge's recent criticisms, defense counsel from three Subsequent Nuremberg Proceedings cases (the High Command case included) cabled President Truman emphasizing that their "misgivings" had been confirmed and requesting his personal intervention to ensure fair trials.[27]

The Wennerstrum scandal is representative of a pattern that would repeat itself several more times before the U.S. war crimes trial program was brought to a close. As will be explained, over the next ten years, prominent West German religious, government, and civilian representatives exploited American misconduct and a regrettable series of judicial reversals to gain the ever-increasing political capital that helped gradually to unravel the threads these proceedings had so laboriously woven together.

The German Clergy and the War Crimes Trials

In the immediate postwar years, the most concentrated and well-organized source of criticism of the American war crimes trials was the German clergy, prompting one historian to declare: "the German Churches were the most effective helpers of National Socialist war criminals."[28] Their opposition to occupation justice stemmed from a perception of the trials as unjust and from a broader rejection of collective responsibility for Nazi crime. Originally, U.S. occupation authorities had hoped that the churches might be a valuable ally in their efforts to reeducate German society. It is important to note that neither the U.S. military government nor prosecutors of war crimes trials intended to castigate the German people as collectively guilty for the Nazi regime's atrocities. However, they did seek to instill in them a sense of collective responsibility for Nazism.[29] As one of the few surviving formal institutions, and moreover one that long preceded Hitler's rise to power, the Americans viewed the Catholic Church in particular as well suited to the reconstruction of the German nation, in large part through an honest confrontation with the past.[30]

To be sure, some Catholics were willing to confront their recent history candidly. In the summer of 1945, a group of Rhineland faithful composed a statement of contrition declaring that "only honesty before God and a courageous, open recognition of our guilt will make possible an inner renewal." They requested that this statement be forwarded to occupation officials via the Vatican. However, the German bishops attending the annual conference at Fulda that summer were not as forthcoming. Although they unequivocally supported the punishment of those who committed atrocities, within a few months, these same bishops began appealing for leniency for war criminals, challenging the trials' assertions of guilt.[31] Attitudes were not much different in Protestant circles. In October 1945, the Council of the Evangelical Church of Germany issued a Declaration of Guilt from Stuttgart. It also was vague on the issue of responsibility. On the one hand, it acknowledged that Germany had brought "endless suffering" to "many peoples and countries," but the church was depicted as having only committed sins of omission. They accused themselves not of having supported the Nazi regime or any of its ideologies, but of "not witnessing more courageously, for not praying more faithfully, for not believing more joyously, and for not loving more ardently."[32] Even Pastor Martin Niemöller, who had endured imprisonment in a concentration camp for his opposition to the Nazis, reflected the church's equivocation. In an interview with American occupation officials, he asserted that "to some extent the whole world is responsible for the German disaster," and he refused to acknowledge German collective guilt "in the political sense."[33]

Rather than using the immediate postwar years to lead Germans in confronting the recent past and the question of their responsibility, the church believed that the end of the war presented the opportunity for breaking with this history and moving forward in closer union with God. Only in this way would those who had suffered be restored. As the Stuttgart Declaration asserted:

> Now a new beginning can be made in our churches. Grounded in the Holy Scriptures . . . they now proceed to cleanse themselves from influences alien to the faith and to set themselves in order. . . . We hope in God that through the common service of the churches the spirit of violence . . . may be brought under control in the whole world, and that the spirit of peace and love may gain the mastery, wherein alone tortured humanity can find healing.[34]

Church attitudes toward the Nazi past were not limited to evasive statements about guilt and responsibility. As early as 1946, Christian leaders in Germany attacked the war crimes trials. That spring, Bishop August Graf von Galen, the "Lion of Münster," who had during the Nazi years so bravely protested the euthanasia program, denounced the IMT, calling it a "show trial" that denied justice and only defamed the German people. He went so far as to claim that the accused war criminals in Allied custody suffered conditions worse than those that had prevailed in the Nazi camps.[35] In mid-March, American intelligence analysts expressed their concern over the "unique role the German Protestant, and especially, the Catholic Church is playing in favoring the cause of interned Nazis." A report from one of the prison camps noted:

We have, of late, been swamped by letters from internees' home communities testifying to the innocence, general sweetness and democratic tendencies of some former active Nazi office holders at present detained in this camp. Invariably the "pièce de resistance" of these petitions is a letter from the local priest which states that the detainee was never a Nazi, visited church regularly (the selfsame church, to be sure, which offered prayer "for our leaders") and was in general a benefactor of mankind. No doubt, at times such petitions are justified, but if they are submitted in such large numbers, they begin to point to a political trend and turn into a reflection upon the petitioner rather than the petitionee.[36]

This attitude was not limited to the German clergy. Significantly, the Vatican published von Galen's critique. Further, the pope himself called upon former Allied leaders essentially to "forget the past, and give the Germans ... the hope of a better future in the sign of love."[37] In the postwar years, Pius XII consistently characterized German Catholics as resisters and/or victims of the Nazi state.[38]

Remarkably, a prominent American bishop also encouraged German Catholics in this position. In spring 1946, Aloisius Muench of North Dakota, later Vatican representative in occupied Germany between 1946 and 1959, delivered a pastoral letter entitled "One World in Charity." In it, Muench equated Nazi crimes with Allied "crimes" (for example, comparing the bombing of Hiroshima and Nagasaki with the Nazi death camps), condemned the Allied bombing of civilians and the expulsion of ethnic Germans from Eastern Europe, excluded Jews from the litany of war victims, instead presenting them as current "harbingers of revenge," and repudiated German collective guilt.[39] As an expert on Bishop Muench writes, the circulation of "One World" around Germany by the end of that year supported the view that German Catholics required no examination of conscience, and contributed to them evading any remembrance of, or reconciliation with, their nation's crimes.[40]

On the issue of war criminals, German bishops as well as top leaders of the Evangelical Church were unrelenting. Some of the most active and best-known figures in this campaign were Johann Neuhäusler (Catholic auxiliary bishop of Munich and overseer of spiritual affairs at Landsberg prison), Theophil Wurm (bishop of Württemberg and chairman of the Council of the Evangelical Church in Germany), Hans Meiser (bishop of Bavaria), and Martin Niemöller (president of the Evangelical Church).[41] Early criticism was limited to fairly general protests that the men being tried at Nuremberg (who, admittedly, had "lacked moral heroism") were being imprisoned for crimes that leaders of other nations had also committed, and that overall the proceedings were unfair and biased against the vanquished.[42] However, critiques and accusations soon became more pointed and more concrete. But before examining the bases of their opposition, we must explain the procedure of the Dachau proceedings and the allegations stemming from one particular case: the Malmedy trial.

The Malmedy Trial Scandal

Between June 1945 and December 1947, the U.S. Army, via the Office of the Judge Advocate for War Crimes, tried 1,672 individuals in 462 cases for crimes committed against American nationals and in concentration camps liberated by American forces.[43] Compared with the Subsequent Nuremberg Proceedings that encompassed the prosecution of only 185 individuals in twelve cases, proceedings at Dachau were expeditious. The cases were tried before U.S. Forces, European Theater (USFET)–appointed special military commissions. These courts were composed of seven to nine senior officers (men with twenty-five to thirty years of service), all of whom had to have experience sitting on courts-martial. Still, only one had to be trained in law, and he advised the rest of the court on legal matters.[44] American officers and civilians acted as prosecutors and some defense counsel. German attorneys also participated in the defense.[45] Trial procedure was laxer than that applied in civil courts, in courts-martial, and at Nuremberg. The special military courts at Dachau were bound only to the rules prescribed by the Deputy Judge Advocate for War Crimes. They differed most notably from regular courts in the admissibility of evidence. In general a Dachau court could accept any evidence that "in its opinion, would be of assistance in proving or disproving the charge, or [that] would have probative value in the mind of a reasonable man." Hearsay evidence was accepted, its worth determined at the court's discretion. The Dachau cases also relied heavily on witness testimony—a stark difference from the "trial by document" approach at Nuremberg. The basis of the charges was drawn largely from the Geneva and The Hague conventions on the laws and customs of war, although USFET sought to expand their parameters by defining war crimes as "including acts in contravention of treaties and conventions dealing with the conduct of war, *as well as other offenses against persons or property which outrage common justice or involve moral turpitude.*"[46] This capacious definition of war crimes allowed for the prosecution of offenses that had not hitherto been brought before a court. All in all, the rules of procedure were designed to make the process as expedient as possible.

As with the Nuremberg proceedings, there was no appellate process in place; however, the Offices of the Deputy Judge Advocate for War Crimes and the Judge Advocate, EUCOM (headquarters of the U.S. Army, European Command, successor to USFET) were required to review and make recommendations for each sentence, especially death sentences, before they could be carried out.[47] Final confirmation of sentences rested with the theater commander of U.S. forces, General Lucius Clay, a responsibility that, he later wrote, weighed more heavily on him than any other in his position as commander in chief.[48] Accordingly, in August 1947, the Office of the Judge Advocate, EUCOM, established a War Crimes Board of Review in order to process all war crimes trial records and submit recommendations. The board consisted of three experienced lawyers, both military and civilian. They had to prepare a report in each case on whether the court was properly constituted and possessed jurisdiction, whether any error or irregularity in the conduct of the trial had disadvantaged the defendant, whether the evidence supported the judgment, and whether the sentence imposed was "legal, fair and just."[49]

Immediately after the announcement of sentences, representatives of the convicted filed numerous petitions for clemency with the Office of the Deputy Judge Advocate for War Crimes and with the headquarters of U.S. military forces. Added to these petitions, which asked for clemency or for stays of execution for prisoners whose sentences had been confirmed, were a number of writs of habeas corpus, which German attorneys filed in U.S. courts in order to challenge the jurisdiction (and by extension, the findings) of the war crimes courts. American occupation authorities considered instituting a clemency program to hear requests for sentence reduction, but concluded that beginning such a process before the conclusion of the trial program would only complicate future sentencing in pending cases. The matter was thus postponed until the projected end of the war crimes trials.[50] An elaborate (if hurried) review process was therefore already functioning when a scandal about the conduct and conclusion of the Malmedy trial erupted in the early spring of 1948.

The two-month 1946 Malmedy trial charged seventy-four S.S. men with participating in the shooting of seventy-two surrendered American troops at the Baugnez crossroads near the Belgian town of Malmedy during the Battle of the Bulge on 17 December 1944. (It will be remembered that it was the Malmedy massacre that broke the impasse in American intragovernmental discussion over war crimes trials, providing the final impetus to go ahead with the trial program.) The court at Dachau sentenced forty-three of the defendants to death.[51] This was controversial given that during the trial, defendants and their attorneys had made passionate claims of U.S. misconduct in the preparation and prosecution of the case. Defendants alleged that U.S. investigators had used physical and psychological torture to extort confessions and accusations against fellow suspects. They also criticized the use of so-called professional witnesses: former camp inmates who remained at Dachau, "housed, fed, clothed and so on" by U.S. authorities, and whose testimony was used in the trials to secure death sentences against the accused.[52]

The lead defense attorney in the Malmedy trial was an American lawyer, Willis Everett. His strategy was to admit that German troops had committed the massacre, but to argue that it was a product of the "heat of battle" and not of a Nazi criminal conspiracy or policy. Second, he attempted to discredit the evidence statements by attacking the methods used to obtain them. Everett lost his case, but he never accepted the judgment. In a 228-page critique of the investigation and trial, Everett alleged that American troops had committed similar crimes (for which they received no punishment) and described the trial as an act of vengeance predicated on illegally elicited confessions. Aside from submitting this report to the Deputy Judge Advocate for War Crimes to be included in the routine review process, Everett leaked it to the press. Splashy headlines soon appeared in the *New York Times*.[53]

The various heads of offices responsible for case reviews generally relied on their staffs for assessments and recommendations, but they were not bound by them. So it was that when the lawyer assigned to the Deputy Judge Advocate for War Crimes office's review of the Malmedy records expressed general uneasiness about the trial (citing the use of mock trials, hoods, and false witnesses), he was quietly relieved of his post and the review was reassigned to someone else.[54] Ultimately the Deputy Judge Advocate for War Crimes, Lieutenant Colonel Clio Straight, confirmed only twenty-five of forty-three death sentences and recommended reductions in the prison terms meted out to the other defendants. But his decisions did not address the allegations of wrongdoing or the Americans' supposed perpetration of similar offenses. Rather, he justified them by citing the defendants' youth: the average age of the defendants was twenty-two.[55]

In any case, Straight did not have the final word. His review proceeded to Judge Advocate (EUCOM) James Harbaugh. Harbaugh's review staff found evidence of improper pretrial investigation methods and believed the court had favored the prosecution during the proceedings. They recommended confirmation of only twelve death sentences, involving defendants who had been in command positions and who were over twenty years of age at the time of the shooting. Final confirmation rested with Military Governor Lucius Clay, who on 20 March 1948 confirmed only twelve death sentences and released thirteen others from the war criminals prison at Landsberg. The evidence of American misconduct and the reversals of the court's findings left the Dachau trial judgment "in a shambles."[56] And even then the matter was not allowed to rest.

The law permitted sixty days for the Malmedy defendants to file an appeal with the U.S. Supreme Court. Everett again prepared a lengthy and detailed writ of habeas corpus repeating claims of U.S. wrongdoing. Supreme Court Justice Robert Jackson recused himself from deliberation of the petition, claiming a conflict of interest given his intimate connection with the war crimes trials. Without his vote, the court narrowly decided (four to four against) to deny jurisdiction over this (and subsequently over all) appeals. Not satisfied with appealing to the judiciary alone, Everett brought his concerns to numerous congressmen and senators, who used their connections in Washington and to Bishop Muench and the German clergy (and ultimately also to the Associated Press and the American Bar Association) to bring pressure to bear on the military government in Germany.[57]

The German clergy seized the moment. On 23 March 1948, Bishop Johann Neuhäusler wrote to several members of the U.S. Congress expressing his "great anxiety about the proceedings at Dachau." Citing allegations of confessions coerced through torture and threats, he urged these politicians to postpone the executions pending a full reexamination of the proceedings. He attached several affidavits to support his appeal and asked his readers to share it with others so that together, "they might find a way leading to truth and charity and justice."[58]

On 5 May 1948, Bishop Wurm wrote an open letter to Nuremberg prosecutor Robert Kempner (which the German press and radio publicized) alleging American criminal conduct in the preparation of the Dachau cases that had "shake[n] the legal and moral authority" of the proceedings and degraded them to "an act of legal revenge . . . clad in sham forms of law."[59] Wurm bolstered these accusations later that spring, when he submitted a collection of petitions, affidavits, and letters to Secretary of the Army Kenneth Royall, which detailed "serious criminal irregularities" in the pretrial investigations for and conduct of the Dachau trials. Sworn statements recounted instances of torture and coercion while the suspects were in detention camps at Schwäbisch Hall and Zuffenhausen. They alleged that while interned there and in the course of interrogations, they were beaten; placed in solitary confinement; deprived of food, sleep, light, medical care, and spiritual guidance; put through mock trials; threatened with extradition to the East and/or hanging; and told that their families would have their ration cards confiscated or that they had been killed. After weeks and months of this treatment, they claimed, they signed false confessions and submitted false accusations against former comrades.[60] Wurm also presented a series of statements contesting the legitimacy of the Malmedy proceedings, asserting that, among other matters, the defense had insufficient time to prepare their case, the court admitted into evidence confessions that were recanted during the trial, the prosecution witnesses admitted their statements were false, defense witnesses withheld exculpatory testimony for fear of reprisals, defense papers were stolen, and defendants were impeded from testifying on their own behalf.[61]

Given the very public and contentious state of affairs, Secretary of the Army Kenneth Royall ordered a stay of execution on the pending death sentences and directed Governor Clay to investigate Everett's and Wurm's allegations.[62] Not stopping at an internal review, in July 1948 Royall created a second review panel, named for its chairman, Gordon Simpson of the Texas Supreme Court. The Simpson Commission, which included Judge Leroy van Roden (of Pennsylvania) and Lieutenant Colonel Charles Lawrence (of the Judge Advocate General Department), was charged with reviewing the records not only of the Malmedy case, but also of all 139 cases in which death sentences were pending. In the course of their deliberations, they examined all previous case reviews and recommendations, and in the Malmedy case, they reread the original trial records.[63]

The Simpson Commission completed its report in mid-September 1948, but the army withheld publicizing its decisions until January 1949. In the intervening months, however, Judge van Roden openly criticized the pretrial investigations for and evidence in the Malmedy case. By the end of October, he was on the lecture circuit to Rotary Clubs, veterans' associations, and church groups "doing [his] best to spread the gospel of what was done in these cases." In a private letter to Everett (longtime friends, they had served together during the war), van Roden admitted that the commission had wanted to commute all the Malmedy death sentences, given that the massacre was a "heat of battle" offense for which no American guilty of a similar crime would have been put to death.[64]

The Ilse Koch Scandal

Adding to the Americans' great embarrassment over the Malmedy case was yet another Dachau-related scandal that caused further damage to the already beleaguered public image of the U.S. war crimes program. In mid-September 1948, American authorities announced that they had reduced the life sentence of Ilse Koch, the notorious "beast of Buchenwald," to a term of only four years. Ilse Koch, the former wife of the Buchenwald camp commandant, S.S. Colonel Karl Koch, was tried between April and August 1947, along with twenty-nine other former camp personnel and one prisoner, for their participation in the "common design" to commit murder, torture, and ill-treatment in service of the camp.[65] The trial of Ilse Koch had attracted international notoriety because it included lurid testimony of her alleged moral depravity and sexual perversity. Former prisoners accused Koch of having prisoners beaten for looking at her, or beating them herself, which sometimes caused death, and perhaps most shocking of all, of commissioning and having in her possession lampshades, a photo album, and a pair of gloves made from prisoners' tattooed skin.[66] The Dachau court sentenced Ilse Koch to life imprisonment. As with all other Dachau cases, the army reviewed the records before the sentence was confirmed. Between November 1947 and June 1948, the case made its way through four rounds of review, all of which questioned the evidence suggesting a level of participation in the camp crimes commensurate with the life sentence, as well as her possession of articles made of human skin. Ultimately General Clay reduced her sentence to four years. Although American officials immediately notified Koch and the other inmates whose sentences were reduced, they made no public announcement. The Judge Advocate Office later denied any attempt at having suppressed the reversal, blaming instead "an administrative error of omission."[67]

Predictably, on publication of the sentence reduction months later in mid-September 1948, U.S. officers involved in her prosecution, former camp inmates, and ordinary American citizens expressed their outrage at the perceived betrayal.[68] President Truman himself demanded an immediate report explaining the discrepancy.[69] There was commotion in Washington, and the *New York News* reflected a growing suspicion among some American politicians that these trials were a failure:

> This noisy and bloodthirsty uproar in the capital over cutting down to four years the life sentence imposed on German war criminal Ilse Koch . . . may well lead to a healthy end. And this end will be the realization by the American people here that these so-called trials in Germany were a sadistic farce by any standards of justice, and that in our conduct of them we failed utterly in the proclaimed attempt to so run them as to set before the former followers of Hitler an example of impartial, even-handed American justice and fair play.[70]

With the stated goal of bringing Ilse Koch to justice, Senator Homer Ferguson struck a Senate subcommittee to investigate the trial and the revisions.

The Ferguson Subcommittee's report on the Koch case did not reflect well on the American review process. First, it found that Koch had indeed played a sufficiently prominent role in the camp deserving of a life term.[71] They cited trial testimony from Dr. Konrad Morgen, a German judge who had investigated (and found guilty) both Koch and her husband for corruption and criminality in 1943. At the trial, he had called her "a wholly incurable moral degenerate . . . a perverted, nymphomaniacal, hysterical, power-mad demon."[72] The subcommittee believed that when the American reviewers reassessed the evidence, they had overstepped their mandate, and insisted that weighing the value of witness statements was the exclusive domain of the court. At the same time, the subcommittee noted that the regulations guiding the review process did not specify what should be considered. The subcommittee concluded that the reduction in sentence was unjustified but chose not to contest General Clay's final decision for fear that it would set a dangerous precedent, extending the possibilities of redress indefinitely and further complicating the war crimes trial program:

> One of the primary concepts which distinguishes our judicial system from those of totalitarian nations is this guarantee to the accused of the immutability of the decision of the court of last resort. This finality of decision is a very effective safeguard against persecution. . . . To violate [it] . . . would bring disrepute on our military government authorities in Germany. . . . A reopening of the final order by the reviewing authority in violation of established principles of our system of jurisprudence because of an error in judgment or because of adverse public opinion could be a mistake of greater consequence than the injustice resulting from this single case.[73]

The subcommittee added a stinging reproach to the authorities overseeing the review process then in place for Dachau convicts: "the basic defect in the conduct of the Ilse Koch case was the failure of the responsible authorities to coordinate properly the policies of the program and the functions of the officers assigned to it." That is, poor instructions and a lack of foresight had caused the present public relations mess. Despite the injustice of the final decision, the subcommittee concluded that the United States could not bring any additional charges against Koch without violating the principle of double jeopardy.[74] All in all, the Ferguson report attempted to protect the integrity of the American judicial process in two ways. First, it affirmed the original trial by backing up its verdict. Second, it reflected the democratic spirit that was supposed to undergird the trial program by putting the United States' own processes to review and concluding in favor of the defendants' rights. What the public took away from the whole process, however, was simply that there was something wrong with occupation government trials.

Concurrent with the Americans' scrambling over the Malmedy and Koch cases, the German clergy maintained their pressure upon U.S. authorities. On 26 August 1948, Catholic bishops convened a conference at Fulda and issued a public statement formally objecting to the trials' alleged application of ex post facto law and victor's justice, and demanding the establishment of an appellate court.[75] In mid-November 1948, Bishop Meiser, of the Bavarian Lutheran Church, met with the judge advocate general and submitted a collection of articles, petitions, and sworn statements critical of tribunal processes, individual cases, and the American treatment of prisoners. At the request of the judge advocate, one of the war crimes boards of review appraised these documents. The board readily admitted that "some errors were made in the conduct of the trials," but wrote that these "few" errors had been exaggerated and exploited in order to pique the interest of church officials so that they would use their influence on behalf of convicted war criminals. The board added that the cases passed through seven separate levels of review, and that if mistakes were noted, they were corrected. Regretfully, however, the admission of error had caused church leaders to believe that "all of the trials are bad and must be held for naught." With regard to the documents describing the conduct and findings of the trials, the board did not think that they contained any actionable substance: "the papers have value only as propaganda and they are intended to arouse sympathy and incide [sic] suspicion among those who have no access to the trial records and who do not know the facts."[76]

On the other hand, the board believed that the statements alleging American mistreatment in pretrial preparations had merit. Although they did not think that this mistreatment affected the outcome of any trial, the sheer mass of affidavits claiming physical harm showed "almost conclusively that much unlawful, vicious, inhumane and sadistic practice was engaged in by American personnel of certain internment camps where suspected war criminals . . . were interned. That some of the victims . . . were later convicted of war crimes is no justification for the mistreatment." The board asserted that to allow such crimes to go unpunished would bring "serious discredit" to the army and to the United States and recommended criminal proceedings against the perpetrators.[77] Although there is no indication that the board's comments were publicized, their assessment added to the already troubled and increasingly besieged war crimes trial program. And it was about to get worse.

In January 1949, the Department of the Army released the Simpson Commission's report. The three judges had concluded that the trials were "essentially fair" and that "there was no general or systematic use of improper methods to secure prosecution evidence."[78] Still, they commuted seventeen death sentences to life terms in cases other than Malmedy. Regarding the Malmedy case, the commission asserted that it was "distinguishable from all other war crimes cases tried at Dachau [because] these offenses were committed in the heat of one of the most furious battles of the war." Although deserving of "stern retribution," the judges continued, it was doubtful that an American court-martial would impose any penalty more severe than a life sentence against American troops guilty of "like offenses in the heat of battle." The commission noted that crucial evidence had been obtained through mock trials, black hoods, and other "highly questionable" methods, which cast doubt on the entire proceedings. Accordingly, the judges believed it was unwise to proceed with the executions and so commuted the remaining twelve death sentences. At the same time, the commission believed that there was sufficient evidence to warrant guilty verdicts. Ultimately, and in a surprising twist, they concluded "that any injustice done to the accused against whom death sentences have been approved will be adequately removed by commutation of the sentences to imprisonment for life."[79]

Technically, the final decision was still Military Governor Clay's prerogative. After consulting the Simpson Commission and his own administration of justice review board reports, and eager to dispose of this political irritation before the end of military government, in March 1949, Clay announced his verdict. From his papers, it is clear that he was deeply troubled that the Malmedy case had caused so much damage. With regret, he admitted that in the emotional aftermath of the war, American investigators had used "measures to obtain evidence that we would not have employed later," and that this had given rise to much-exaggerated German propaganda. Nonetheless, Clay was firm in insisting that those who had been sentenced ("tough, hard-bitten fanatics of Nazism") were indeed responsible "for the brutal and cold-blooded murder of innocent civilians and unarmed American prisoners of war."[80] Ultimately, General Clay confirmed six death sentences and commuted six.[81] However, Secretary of the Army Royall refused to lift the stay of execution, and the Malmedy debacle dragged on.

Notwithstanding the latest pronouncements from occupied Germany, the Malmedy trial had long before transformed into a "domestic political cause célèbre" in America.[82] Earlier that winter, Senator William Langer of North Dakota introduced a resolution to investigate U.S. military justice in occupied Europe, going so far as to enter Everett's Supreme Court petition into the congressional record.[83] Around the time of Clay's decision, the Senate struck another subcommittee. Senator Raymond Baldwin chaired. Estes

Kefauver, Lester Hunt, and Joseph McCarthy joined him. They conducted hearings in the United States and Germany, interviewed participants, and analyzed the trial records. Midway through their work, Senator McCarthy withdrew from the subcommittee with a dramatic flourish, accusing them of attempting "to whitewash a shameful episode in the history of our glorious armed forces."[84] The final report, a weighty 1,700-plus pages, aimed to quiet the barrage of accusations and condemnations and salvage the image of the war crimes trial program. Although the subcommittee did condemn the use of trickery because it was "an unnecessary complication of the investigative process that could be misinterpreted or misrepresented by critics," they rejected the allegations that physical force had been used to induce confessions. All in all, they found little reason for substantive criticism of the pretrial investigation, and the six death sentences were permitted to stand. Ultimately, however, the Americans never carried them out.

As in the decision for the Ilse Koch case, the men who passed final judgment on the Malmedy scandal, though readily admitting varying levels of misconduct, were aware that the cost of righting these wrongs had perhaps become too dear. "More was at stake than the army's conduct in this particular matter," they warned, because "attacks on the war crimes trials in general and the Malmedy case in particular were meant to revive German nationalism and to cast doubt upon the U.S. occupation of Germany as a whole."[85] Moreover, a retrial, which Everett had consistently demanded, by opening the proceedings to "even more damaging scrutiny," might lead to the readjudication of other cases, a possibility that the United States was unwilling to contemplate.[86]

It bears emphasizing that the most damaging scandals attached to the American war crimes trial program originated with the army trials at Dachau. Although the individuals who lobbied on behalf of the Dachau convicts often included the Nuremberg trials in their complaints, there was no comparable evidence of misconduct between the two. Nonetheless, the accusations surrounding the Dachau trials made some Nuremberg personnel nervous that they also would be marked with the same taint. Drexel Sprecher, a prosecutor at both the IMT and the Subsequent Nuremberg Proceedings (SNP), wrote to Telford Taylor in October 1948: "There seems to be a growing attempt to discredit the trials during the last stages. . . . I suspect that certain defense counsel and some of our other long-standing opponents feel that the Dachau matter led to great discredit of the war crimes program generally—and that if they can get an investigation stirred up on Nurnberg, by a slander campaign in the press, they will have adopted a good strategy."[87] Regarding the SNP, the most common criticism rested on the overall demeanor of the prosecutors and the interpretation of the law.

We have already discussed Judge Wennerstrum's indiscreet remarks. Unfortunately, he was not unique. In April 1949, the last sitting tribunal at Nuremberg submitted its verdict in the case of *U.S. v. Ernst von Weizsäcker et al.* (known as the Ministries case), and it was not unanimous. Judge Leon Powers (like Wennerstrum, a member of the Iowa Supreme Court) filed a dissenting opinion. His disagreement centered on how he believed the tribunal had established guilt. That is, he objected to the prosecution's assertion, and the judges' confirmation, that gaining knowledge of a crime (concurrent or after the fact) and still remaining in office made one guilty of that crime. In Powers's words, such a conception of criminality "makes proof easy and guilt almost universal."[88]

These assertions played directly into the hands of religious leaders who had long contested the notion of widespread knowledge of and diffuse responsibility for Nazi crime. Although Judge Powers did not present his dissenting opinion publicly (instead, he submitted it in writing to the secretary general), within weeks, Bishops Wurm and Meiser appealed to the American authorities on behalf of the convicted von Weizsäcker and Schwerin von Krosigk, confronting them with Powers's statements.[89]

Church-Sponsored Organizations for Aiding Convicted War Criminals

Just as the American trials became ever more strained, so German church officials gained allies in their efforts to nullify the American trials completely. As early as 1948, defense counsel from the SNP had aligned themselves with powerful forces in the Protestant and Catholic churches in an attempt to repeal or reduce sentences passed against individuals at Nuremberg and Dachau. In the first months after the SNP, Dr. Georg Froeschmann, a former Nazi and S.A. member and defense counsel at the IMT and in the Ministries, Medical, and Race and Settlement Main Office–S.S. (RuSHA) cases had advised prisoners at Landsberg on the available clemency and review processes. Soon finding himself with an overwhelming caseload, Froeschmann asked Dr. Rudolf Aschenauer, whom, in his words, he admired more for his energy than his skill, for help. Aschenauer, a thirty-five-year-old attorney from Munich, had extensive knowledge of the American trials, having worked at the IMT and represented S.S. leader Otto Ohlendorf in the Einsatzgruppen trial.[90] Because most defendants could not pay for their services, Aschenauer suggested asking both churches for funds. With the churches' approval, the two men established the Kirchliche Gefangenenhilfe (Committee for Church Aid for Prisoners, or CCAP) in November 1949.[91] The membership of the CCAP denoted its dual function as legal counsel and public lobbyist for war criminals. Johann Neuhäusler was the chairman, there was one representative each from the Caritasverband (a Catholic relief organization) and the Innere Mission (a Protestant relief organization focused on community service), a delegate from the Bavarian State Secretariat, two representatives from the Justice Faculty, and, significantly, one representative of the press. In April, Aschenauer, who ran the CCAP office, was designated the chief counsel for Landsberg prisoners. Shortly thereafter, he and Froeschmann parted ways over disagreements about the financial management of the organization. In the assessment of American intelligence gatherers charged with investigating Aschenauer and the CCAP, he did not act from ulterior motives, "other than he may be a bit over-zealous in an attempt to make a name for himself in the legal field."[92] Nonetheless, he proved himself an unwavering advocate on behalf of convicted war criminals and a fierce opponent of the American trials. He was the author of at least three published pamphlets: the eighty-page "Zur Frage einer Revision der Kriegsverbrecherprozesse" (On the Question of a Revision of the War Criminals' Trials), which discussed the alleged legal and procedural problems inherent in the Dachau and Nuremberg trials; "Um Recht und Wahrheit im Malmedy-Fall" (Of Law and Truth in the Malmedy Case), which detailed the U.S. Senate investigation into alleged mistreatment of German prisoners in the preparation of the Malmedy case and which criticized Lucius Clay's revisions; and "Der Malmedy-Fall 7 Jahre nach dem Urteil" (The Malmedy Case Seven Years after the Judgment), another piece on the Malmedy trial.[93] He eventually represented all Landsberg prisoners who submitted bids for clemency and/or sentence revision. His and the church organizations' activities on behalf of the convicted at Landsberg will be discussed in chapter 7.

Although the American war crimes trials succeeded in arousing the consciousness of ordinary Germans, their first impressions, on balance, were negative. Moreover, while the Americans had hoped to enjoin the churches (the only intact German institutions in the immediate postwar years) in their attempt to educate the German people about their nation's responsibility for the war and its crimes, this, too, met largely with failure. A rearrangement of occupation authority and the establishment of a West German government in the summer and fall of 1949 further aggravated the already passionately contested war crimes issue. In chapters 6 and 7 I will explain the second half of the story of the dismantling of the American war crimes trial program, or perhaps more accurately, the American war crimes punishment program, with special focus on the particular and decisive role the High Command case convicts played in the surrounding debate. How a fledgling government of a recently defeated and occupied nation so quickly achieved the release of so many of its most culpable criminal leaders is startling—and significant. Although much of the explanation for this turn of events must be rooted in the scandals and reversals that battered and bruised the trials in the late 1940s, to this must be added the layers of the identity of some of the convicts as soldiers and the gathering tensions of the Cold War. However, in order to join these threads, we must first explore the High Command case.

3

Prosecuting Hitler's High Command: *U.S. v. Wilhelm von Leeb et al.*

The evidence of criminality is overwhelming.
—Chief of Counsel Telford Taylor

GIVEN THE AMERICANS' ALLEGATION that "German militarism" was the root cause of the world conflict and their belief that the war crimes and crimes against humanity identified in the indictment were perpetrated in service of the war, this trial of three German field marshals and eleven generals was seen as one of the most significant of the postwar trials of Nazi leaders. It posed many legal and rhetorical challenges. Because international law recognized the legitimacy and justifiability of an army's duty to fight, kill, and occupy, the prosecution of these soldiers required definitions of murder and abuse that had to be disengaged from the dreadful necessities and awful realities of war. In doing so, the trial demanded a rigorous exposition of the formulation and dissemination of criminal orders, the limits to military officers' initiative and responsibility, the doctrine of superior orders, and the military's participation in Nazi ideological crimes. The Americans faced an uphill battle in convincing the German people of the defendants' wrongdoing. The officer corps had long been one of the most revered institutions in German society, and there was some truth to the oft-repeated and much exaggerated protestations that these men were not Nazis. Reflecting on the challenges involved in bringing these officers to trial, the American chief of counsel, Telford Taylor, commented:

> Field Marshals such as von Leeb . . . were men of the highest standing in Germany; they were not Nazis in any party or political sense, and no doubt they were repelled by some facets of the Nazi regime. The "respectability" and "nonpolitical" appearance of these men no doubt lie at the root of the

protests which were raised against their indictment and trial. It proved exceedingly difficult to "get it across" to the Germans (and, indeed, to some others) that it was not the purpose of Nuernberg to try Nazis who might or might not be criminals, but to try suspected criminals who might or might not also be Nazis.[1]

Accordingly, the prosecution devoted most of its energy to proving the defendants' commission of crimes, and less to surmising their motivations. As the evidence mounted, it became increasingly difficult to separate the defendants from the ideological goals their criminal acts undoubtedly served. However, the prosecution maintained its focus on the acts themselves. This chapter will introduce the defendants of the High Command case, explain the basic strategy of the prosecution, summarize the crimes charged, and provide an overview of the form and content of the evidence submitted for judgment.

Overview of the Prosecution's Case

Telford Taylor opened the prosecution's case on 5 February 1948. Five of the other nine prosecutors also read sections of the opening statement. Some of the High Command case prosecutors held top positions in the Nuremberg War Crimes Office, such as Paul Niederman, who was the director of the military and S.S. division, and Walter Rapp, who was the director of the evidence division; however, little of the lawyers' individual personalities came through during proceedings. As will be shown, the prosecution's case consisted mainly of the rather mechanical entering of documents into evidence. Counsel did not even read these exhibits into the record, as at the International Military Tribunal (IMT). The lawyers merely described, in a phrase or two, what each document's contents were. It was common for the prosecution to enter more than a hundred exhibits in a single day of proceedings. Although undoubtedly committed to the present case and to the larger goals of justice and education that they sought to achieve, several of these prosecutors had served in other Subsequent Nuremberg Proceedings (SNP), and this trial came at the end of a long, tedious, and exhausting process. At times, the prosecutors gave the impression of being just plain tired. By contrast, they showed more emotion in their cross-examinations of the defendants, frequently revealing their contempt and frustration at the latter's intransigence.

In his portion of the opening statement, Taylor framed the whole spectrum of crimes as springing from a deep-seated and long-standing aggressively ambitious German militarism. Offering a history lesson in German warmongering, Taylor drew a line connecting the seventeenth-century Thirty Years' War to the Wehrmacht's support for rearmament and for Hitler's aggressive aims during the interwar years as alleged proof of the Germans' militarist tradition. Although Taylor referenced this issue again briefly in the prosecution's summation, it was not developed in great depth beyond the opening statement. It seems to have served more as a rhetorical tool, setting the context justifying the United States' targeting of this group for criminal prosecution. Undoubtedly, it grew out of the Americans' preoccupation with the aggressive war charge, so vehemently advocated during the organization of the war crimes trial program and so passionately emphasized at the IMT.

Ultimately, the issue of "German militarism" was too broadly referenced here—that is, the prosecution did not individualize it as a motivating factor, applying it instead to the officer corps as a whole. It did not contribute to the case against any single defendant. The judges never commented on it, and it did not appear to have influenced their interpretation of evidence. Nonetheless, in the opening statement, Taylor expressed the hope that exposing the military's misdeeds might act as a cure for the Germans' alleged penchant for war. It was the High Command case's potential rehabilitative function that for Taylor gave this case its particular and distinctive significance: "It is because of the dominant part which military matters have played in the life and thought of Germany . . . that this twelfth and last case before the Nuremberg Military Tribunals may well prove of greater importance to Germany than any other case heard in this courtroom."[2]

Even though the documentary evidence was not read aloud in court, the day-to-day proceedings against the armed forces High Command did not escape the sometimes grinding monotony and repetitiveness that characterized its parent trial. The prosecution called twenty-nine witnesses, including a former French slave laborer, a prisoner functionary from Auschwitz, an Einsatzgruppen leader (the Einsatzgruppen were the S.S. formations that followed the army into the East to round up and shoot all political and racial "enemies"), and various German military field and staff officers. The rather modest number of witnesses (by contrast, the defense called sixty-six) was in keeping with Justice Jackson's strategy at the IMT to build the case on a documentary foundation. No witnesses said anything that could not be established by the 1,778 exhibits the prosecution entered into evidence.[3] On the whole, the witnesses' presence in court seemed rather to confirm what counsel alleged to be proven by these records. Certainly, the testimony of a couple of these witnesses (for example, Kazimierz Smolen's and Otto

Telford Taylor, chief prosecutor at the Subsequent Nuremberg Proceedings. Courtesy of the U.S. Holocaust Memorial Museum, Photo Reference Collection 16824.

Ohlendorf's, noted below) stood out as some of the most dramatic moments in the trial, but their words were not the deciding evidence in the case.

At court, the prosecution did not present a chronological narration of the crimes of the Wehrmacht. During the twenty-six days that they introduced evidence, the lawyers skipped around the indictment, one day discussing the army's cooperation with the Einsatzgruppen, the next day explaining Oberkommando der Wehrmacht (OKW) staff organization, then on to the Commissar Order, followed by the treatment of POWs, then cooperation with the Einsatzgruppen again, then the interwar renunciation of the Versailles Treaty, back to POWs, and so on. By contrast, the prosecution's memoranda on particular charges and the briefs detailing the criminal activities of the defendants, all of which quoted extensively from the evidence, were much more systematic and evocative. Staggering in scope and horrifying in detail, the prosecution exhibits chronicled the armed forces' planning of aggressive war, the deliberate abuse and liquidation of millions of Soviet prisoners of war, the murder of Western Allied soldiers and airmen, the extermination of Polish and Soviet civilians (particularly Jews, the intelligentsia, and political leadership), the retaliation killing of civilian hostages, reprisals against "partisans" and "partisan-suspects," deportation and exploitation of civilians and prisoners of war for the slave labor program, and numerous other offenses.[4]

The OKW

What was the OKW, and how had its members come to be targeted for trial? Hitler created this organization after the February 1938 crisis in relations between himself and the army, in which both the commander in chief of the armed forces, Field Marshal Werner von Blomberg, and the commander in chief of the army, Field Marshal Werner von Fritsch, were forced into retirement amid charges of scandal, one of which had been entirely fabricated.[5] The Oberkommando der Wehrmacht was the High Command of the three branches of the German armed forces.[6] Its function in peacetime was to make all preparations for national defense, and during the war, it coordinated the overall conduct of military operations. Hitler assumed the title of commander in chief of the armed forces, and the OKW essentially became his personal staff for the coordination and direction of the army, navy, and air force.[7] From the time of its creation until Germany's unconditional surrender, approximately 130 officers held posts in the OKW.[8]

The General Staff of the High Command was one of the groups charged at the IMT as being a criminal organization. Telford Taylor, later chief of counsel for the SNP, led the case. To his disappointment, the tribunal did not believe that the OKW constituted an "organization" or "group" within the meaning of the charter, and so refrained from declaring it criminal. However, in its judgment, the tribunal emphasized that there was "clear and convincing" evidence that OKW officers had planned and waged an aggressive war and had committed war crimes and crimes against humanity. Further, the tribunal continued,

> they have been responsible in large measure for the miseries and suffering that have fallen on millions of men, women and children. They have been a disgrace to the honorable profession of arms. Without their military guidance the aggressive ambitions of Hitler and his fellow Nazis would have been academic and sterile. . . . The truth is they actively participated in all

these crimes, or sat silent and acquiescent, witnessing the commission of crimes on a scale larger and more shocking than the world has ever had the misfortune to know. This must be said.[9]

The tribunal recommended that separate trials should be arranged so that those within the OKW guilty of crimes "should not escape punishment."[10] Accordingly, the United States organized the High Command case. It was not the Americans' only trial of military leaders, but it was the most comprehensive in its investigation of the military's complicity and participation in ideologically motivated political and racial crimes. The other two cases were *U.S. v. Erhard Milch*, which concerned slave labor and medical experiments, and *U.S. v. Wilhelm List et al.* (also known as the Hostage case), which emphasized the army's draconian hostage reprisal policy in the Balkans.[11] By contrast, American officials organized the High Command case to include the field marshals and generals who were "in the closest planning relationship with Hitler," who organized aggressive wars and who issued and distributed orders resulting in the whole spectrum of war crimes and crimes against humanity.[12]

Where did those accused in this proceeding fit in the organization and administration of the Wehrmacht? Three of the High Command case defendants—Lieutenant Generals Walter Warlimont, Hermann Reinecke, and Rudolf Lehmann—were OKW staff officers. Walter Warlimont was chief of the Department of National Defense, immediately subordinate to General Alfred Jodl. In January 1942, Warlimont also assumed the title of deputy chief of the Armed Forces Operations Staff. From this position Warlimont took a leading role in the development and dissemination of some of the OKW's most egregious criminal orders, such as the Commissar Order and the Barbarossa Jurisdiction Order. Hermann Reinecke was chief of the General Armed Forces Office (Allgemeines Wehrmachtamt, AWA) from December 1939 until Germany's surrender. The AWA supervised several independent branches of the OKW, one of the most important of which was the Office of Prisoner of War Affairs, which oversaw all matters relating to German and Allied POWs.[13] From within the AWA, Reinecke also headed the National Socialist Guidance Staff. Established in December 1943, this office oversaw the political education of the armed forces. Reinecke was indicted for the formative role he played in the definition and enforcement of POW policy and for indoctrinating troops with Nazi racial and political hatred. Rudolf Lehmann acted as chief of the Armed Forces Legal Branch from 1938 to 1945 and accordingly was in charge of preparing legal opinions of interest to all three branches of the service, as well as drafting orders that transformed Hitler's general directives into concrete instructions.[14]

The trial organizers were equally interested in prosecuting field commanders—the officers who put the orders, directives, and policies formulated by the staff officers into action. Although most of the defendants were members of the army, prosecutors included two representatives of the air force and navy. Field Marshal Hugo Sperrle commanded one of the Air Fleets, the largest unit of the air force. Between 1938 and 1941, Admiral Otto Schniewind acted as chief of the Naval War Staff in the Office of the High Command of the Navy (Oberkommando der Marine, OKM), where he was directly subordinate to Admiral Erich Raeder, who was tried and convicted at the IMT. From 1941 to 1944, Schniewind assumed command of the High Seas Fleet. The cases against them concerned mainly the charge of crimes against peace—that is, their knowledge of and contributions to the preparations for various invasions and campaigns. As will be shown, most war crimes and crimes against humanity comprised offenses against soldiers and civilians by army personnel.

Of all three branches of the Wehrmacht, the army was by far the largest and most complex. Field Marshal Walter von Brauchitsch was commander in chief of the High Command of the Army (Oberkommando des Heeres, OKH) from 1938 until December 1941. His chief of staff was General Franz Halder.[15] (Halder provided important testimony during the trial.) The largest army field formation was the army group, which was composed of two or more armies. During a campaign, the army group exercised tactical control over its armies. An army headquarters directed its subordinate units and acted as field headquarters for matters of administration, supply, and so on. In any given campaign, the operational area comprised that territory where fighting units engaged the enemy, either on their own or on enemy soil. It was divided into the battle zone and rear area. Both army groups and armies had designated rear areas that could be anywhere from a few dozen to a few hundred miles in breadth. The rear areas came under the command of officers directly responsible to the commander in chief of the army or army group, respectively. The mandate of the rear area commanders was to administer and maintain peace and security in the occupied area. The distinction between battle zones and rear areas is important, because many of the army's crimes, particularly against POWs and civilians, took place in the latter.[16]

The High Command case defendants included commanders and staff officers of all the highest army field formations. They fought the war from Norway to Greece and from the interior of France to the outskirts of

Moscow. Their most important commands are listed in Appendix 3. Apart from their high rank and extensive staff and field command experience, the defendants had many other attributes in common. None were members of the Nazi Party; in fact, it had long been German military tradition that officers did not even vote, in order to preserve at least the outward appearance of being apolitical and loyal to the nation irrespective of its current government.[17] All of the defendants had entered the military at a young age. Hermann Hoth was only ten years old when his mother sent him to cadet boarding school. Most of the others began their training immediately after their graduation from gymnasium. Only one, Otto Woehler, worked briefly on a family farm before joining the army.[18] Nearly all had been in continuous military service through the mid-1940s.[19] Accordingly, they had all fought or served in staff positions during World War I, several on the eastern front. They became members of Germany's interwar 100,000-man army and had closely observed the rise of Nazism, Hitler, the rearmament program, and the Reich's ever-increasing territorial ambitions. The average age of the defendants at the outbreak of World War II was fifty-three years. Wilhelm von Leeb was the oldest at sixty-three years, and Woehler was the youngest, at forty-five. All were married and had children. Two of the accused lost sons in the war: Woehler's son was confirmed killed in action, and Hoth's son went missing on the eastern front in 1943.[20]

The Prosecution's Objectives and Strategy

The American war crimes trial program's interconnected goals of justice and education found expression in the High Command case as well. The justice sought in the trial was not simply a reflection on the past, passing judgment and imposing punishment for crimes already committed, nor would it be measured only by the number and severity of the sentences. The trial's success would also be assessed by its effect on German (and world) attitudes toward the most recent and future wars. In his opening statement for the prosecution, American Chief of Counsel Telford Taylor reminded the tribunal of former secretary of war Henry Stimson's assertion that trial—and indeed punishment—were the only means to bring the law in line with the broadly shared intuitive rejection of Nazi crime, and thereby change and develop the law that would govern future conflict: "The Second World War brought it home to us that our repugnance to aggressive war was incomplete without a moral judgment of its leaders. What we had called a crime demanded punishment; we must bring our law in balance with the universal moral judgment of mankind."[21]

Therefore, the prosecution carefully constructed, on a foundation of the military's own records, an image of the war that they hoped would impress itself upon the German imagination. From its conception, planning, initiation, and waging, U.S. prosecutors sought to prove that the war had been a criminal enterprise to its core. The evidence showed that the various military campaigns were not preemptive, defensive, or retaliatory. Rather, documents proved that they had been criminally contrived from the start and criminally waged until the end. This criminality pervaded all levels and all theaters, from the OKW offices in Berlin to the most remote military outposts in the East. Atrocities accompanied all operations and targeted combatants and civilians alike.

The prosecution was eager to show that the crimes charged contravened formal laws and conventions, such as the 1919 League of Nations Covenant (Germany joined the League of Nations in 1926), the 1925 Treaty of Locarno, and the 1928 Kellogg–Briand Pact, which bound adherents to respect the territorial integrity and post–World War I borders of member states, reaffirmed the Versailles Treaty conditions regarding disarmament and banned aggressive war, and the 1907 The Hague and the 1929 Geneva Conventions, which governed the treatment of enemy civilians and POWs in wartime. Germany had been a signatory of these international agreements and yet had viciously trespassed against them all. However, the prosecution was equally intent on proving that the defendants' actions were so patently reprehensible that no prohibitive legislation was necessary to support their legal characterization as criminal. That is, the defendants' offenses were not simply criminal in letter, but also, and significantly, criminal in spirit. Indeed, the words used to describe their actions were very plain: murder, abuse, torture.

During the proceedings, the prosecution was not markedly concerned with exploring any individual defendant's personal motivations. In essence, Taylor postulated that the German officer corps had thrown its lot in with Hitler because of his commitment to restore Germany's military strength and honor.[22] They were no less attracted by the promotions he bestowed and the "realistic" foreign policy objectives he promised. Their shared desire to put the Wehrmacht "to use" cemented the military's allegiance to the Führer, and their alliance constituted, Taylor argued, the "keystone in the arch of the Third Reich," enabling Hitler to attempt his most ambitious and pernicious aims.[23] Taylor reminded the tribunal that this alliance was strong enough to withstand the murders of the Roehm purge, and the slander and forced retirements of the von Blomberg–von Fritsch affair.[24] When at times relations between the officers and Hitler were strained, these disagreements, Taylor contended, turned on strategic issues of method and timing, but never purpose.

Interestingly, although the prosecution never labeled these defendants Nazis, the evidence showed that under their military leadership, "millions had died in pursuit of Nazi racial and social myths."[25] During the proceedings, there were suggestions that it was the defendants' unscrupulous but apolitical ambition that fueled their participation in Nazi crimes. At other times, the prosecution presented evidence indicating certain defendants' overt support for and agreement with the principles guiding anti-Jewish and anti-Communist offenses. In any case, the vaguely articulated issue of the defendants' personal motivations was of secondary importance. Undeniably, their actions were criminal. Accordingly, the prosecution built its case around the evidence of these actions: the defendants' criminal orders and directives and the countless ground-level reports from areas under the defendants' command that demonstrated their implementation. This material was, in Taylor's words, "quite compelling enough" and "provide[d] its own eloquence."[26] The prosecution was confident that it could secure convictions on that basis alone. Moreover, an exhaustive accounting of personal motivations was not required to prove individual liability for the crimes charged. Technically, on the issue of criminal responsibility, Control Council Law No. 10 declared that "an individual shall be found guilty of the crimes defined in Law No. 10 if he was (a) principal, or (b) an accessory, or if he (c) took a consenting part therein, or (d) was connected with plans or enterprises involving the commission of the crime, or (e) was a member of an organization or groups connected with the commission of the crime."[27]

In view of the law that emphasized action, consent, and knowledge, and in order to connect these defendants to the crimes, the prosecution devised an overall "theory of responsibility." It was expressed first in the indictment and opening statement, and then more finely tuned in the individual briefs and memoranda pertaining to the particular charges and to each defendant.

The prosecution's theory of responsibility centered largely on the defendants' positions, ranks, and corresponding influence on military policies and operations. Although the defendants were not direct participants in the atrocities that claimed the lives of hundreds of thousands of POWs and civilians on both fronts, Taylor declared that they bore primary responsibility for the murders. Having codified such measures in orders and directives, the men in the dock had "deliberately contrived" the policy of mass slaughter made manifest by their subordinates.[28] The prosecution contended further that the commanders bore a greater measure of guilt than their ground-level troops because their opposition to criminal orders would have had far greater effect than the opposition of a single soldier.[29]

For staff officers, guilt was relatively simple to identify: these were the men who composed and disseminated flagrantly criminal orders, or shaped the policies, for example, for the treatment of prisoners of war, which contravened international agreements, not to mention basic moral precepts. As for field commanders, as previously mentioned, they did not enact these orders themselves. However, by virtue of their rank, they were held responsible for these crimes and many more. In some instances, guilt was clear-cut. In the prosecution's view, a commander who consciously and deliberately passed on an unlawful order (that is, an order that was criminal on its face) had committed a crime, irrespective of whether the order was subsequently implemented or not.[30] Certain evidence exhibits proved the defendants' personal orders for unlawful acts, and accordingly they were guilty, not only of issuing the criminal order but also of the crimes committed by their subordinates in fulfillment of it.[31]

In other cases, criminal guilt was inferred. The sheer scope and scale of the crimes and the corresponding number of culprits rendered impossible the prosecution of each individual offense and each individual offender. Therefore the trial organizers, and accordingly the prosecution, sought to determine "where the deepest individual responsibility lay."[32] Some of the defendants in the dock had been army group commanders, and they had wielded authority over entire army group areas (battle zones and rear areas). Where evidence revealed systematic and pervasive perpetration of crimes, the prosecution deemed the commanding officer, by virtue of his position, accountable. This principle of command responsibility—the notion that commanding officers are generally responsible for the conduct of their subordinates—was imputed to varying degrees against all field commanders in the High Command case. It had most recently been applied in two other American-led trials against military leaders that were repeatedly cited in the indictment, the opening and closing statements, and the briefs and memoranda.

The first of these was the 1945 trial of a Japanese war criminal in Manila, General Tomoyuki Yamashita. Between October 1944 and September 1945, General Douglas MacArthur and General Yamashita fought tenaciously for control of the Philippines. During the battle, Japanese troops raped, tortured, and killed over 35,000 American prisoners of war and Filipino civilians. Soon after the cessation of hostilities, and on MacArthur's order, five U.S. generals put Yamashita to trial, charging that he had "unlawfully disregarded and failed to discharge his duty as commander to control the operations of the members of his command, permitting them to commit brutal atrocities and other high crimes."[33] The American military commission did not allege that Yamashita bore any criminal intent, or even that he had been grossly negligent.[34] During the proceedings, the prosecution produced no evidence that directly linked him through orders, directives, or reports to the atrocities before or after their occurrence. The question before the court, therefore, was whether a commander could be held responsible for the conduct of his subordinates.[35] The court answered in the affirmative, declaring: "where murder and rape and vicious, revengeful actions are widespread offenses, and there is no effective attempt by a commander to discover and control the criminal acts, such a commander may be held responsible, even criminally liable, for the actions of his troops."[36] General Yamashita was put to death on 23 February 1946, instituting the so-called Yamashita precedent for the strictest interpretation of command responsibility.

The other case was the Hostage case, one of the other Subsequent Proceedings held at Nuremberg. It focused on the murder of thousands of civilians in Greece, Albania, Yugoslavia, and Norway in accordance with the army's hostage reprisal policy. It also discussed the conduct of S.S. killing squads in the army's areas of operation.[37] One of the central assertions of the judgment was that a military commander had an affirmative duty to keep himself informed of the events in his area of command.[38] This assertion, repeatedly advanced at the High Command case, negated some defendants' claims that they could not be held responsible because they had been unaware of the crimes being committed in their areas. The judgment in the Hostage case declared: "The commanding general of occupied territory having executive authority as well as military command, will not be heard to say that a unit taking unlawful orders from someone other than himself . . . is thereby absolved from responsibility. . . . The duty and responsibility for maintaining peace and order, and the prevention of crime rests upon the commanding general. He cannot ignore obvious facts and plead ignorance as a defense."[39]

The prosecution held that it was unnecessary to prove that a defendant in fact had personal knowledge of criminal activities by his own troops or by other agencies (for example, the Einsatzgruppen) operating in his zone. Rather, the prosecution maintained that it was sufficient to show that the defendant *ought* to have known.[40] Notably, the prosecution's case against Field Marshal von Leeb consisted almost exclusively of reports by subordinate units that detailed the perpetration of crimes.[41] U.S. attorneys were unable to produce a single criminal order bearing his signature.[42]

Once it was shown that a defendant should have known about the crimes being committed in his area, the prosecution further argued that these commanders had an obligation to protest or intervene against these activities. Again, with reference to their senior rank and command jurisdiction, the prosecution asserted that "theirs was the ultimate power and duty to see to it that the laws of war were observed."[43] Especially with regard to army group commanders, as bearers of the broadest reach of executive power, these officers had the authority to issue local decrees even if they deviated from existing laws.[44] As will be shown below, any nonmilitary agency (such as the Einsatzgruppen or the Economic Staff East, which drafted civilian slave labor) had to obtain permission from the army group to operate in that zone. Therefore, an army group commander had the power and duty to issue prohibitive orders preventing such agencies from committing crimes against civilians or combatants in his area.[45] Should any harm have come to them, he was personally accountable.[46] Moreover, if a commanding officer passed down a criminal order without issuing a countermanding order, or even if he did not personally pass down criminal orders but could be expected to have known that they would be passed down through alternative channels and he did nothing to intervene against them, the prosecution asserted that he was criminally responsible for the results thereof.[47] In general, the prosecution interpreted omitting to intervene as evidence of the defendant's agreement with or approval of the order's purpose.

Another guiding principle of the prosecution's conception of criminal responsibility was the exclusion of superior orders as a defense. Superior orders was a defense intended to apply to those who, bearing little command authority, had no opportunity for reflection or choice about their obedience. Logically, if the superior orders defense was to apply to everyone, only the head of state would be responsible. This, the prosecution urged, simply could not be. Somewhere a line had to be drawn demarcating the deepest responsibility. In their view, responsibility rested with the commanding officers, who, by bringing the chain of command and compulsion to obey to bear on their subordinates, made themselves criminals:

> Men in the mass, particularly when organized and disciplined in armies, must be expected to yield to prestige, authority, the power of example, and the threat of instant punishment. The standards of conduct of soldiers are bound to be powerfully influenced by the examples set by their commanders. That is why we said in our opening statement that "the only way in which the behavior of German troops in the recent war can be made comprehensible as the behavior of human beings is by full exposure of the criminal doctrines and orders which were pressed upon them from above by these defendants and others."[48]

The High Command case defendants could not appeal to superior orders as exculpation for their crimes. Still, the procedure governing the court did allow such orders to be considered in mitigation of punishment, even for top-level commanders. In assessing the extent of this mitigation, the prosecution asked the tribunal to determine three things: (1) the defendant's attitude toward the criminal order; (2) how well equipped, by rank and education, the defendant was to resist the order; and (3) whether the order's criminal character was obvious.[49] In the first place, there were instances where certain defendants were able to prove that indeed they had protested the existence of particular orders (for example, von Leeb and the Commissar Order), but who claimed that they had nonetheless been compelled to carry it out. However, the prosecution held that for a defendant to successfully plead superior orders in mitigation, his opposition had to have been constant. It was, in their opinion, insufficient for him to have been inwardly opposed but to have acquiesced in its implementation later.[50] Indeed, when all was said and done, actions counted for more than intentions. Responding to the defense's persistent claims that defendants had dissented internally from the criminal orders, the prosecution insisted that at most, these claims proved that when these generals "swallowed" these orders, they "might have tasted bad."[51]

Second, the prosecution simply did not accept that the defendants in this case were subject to the same pressures felt by their troops in the receipt of such orders. Having consistently argued that this case was not about the conduct of soldiers in "the heat and excitement of battle," the prosecution reminded the tribunal that these crimes were not committed "as a result of snap judgments in serious emergencies." Rather, as the evidence made clear, these crimes were the deliberate product of plans and policies defined months and years ahead of hostilities: "These men's orders came in writing from a distant place. They had the opportunity for full reflection on a course of action to be pursued."[52] Further, the prosecution pointed out that although the defendants claimed that they were inescapably beholden to their superiors, almost all had demonstrated numerous occasions when they had opposed, with impunity, decrees and orders handed down to them by their superiors.[53]

Last, the prosecution insisted on the unmistakable criminal intent of the orders in question. In such cases, no defendant could claim that his obedience was required. Indeed, the prosecution's position with respect to superior orders was entirely in keeping with the interpretation of the law by German courts before the Nuremberg trials. The issue of *respondeat superior* had long posed a legal dilemma because jurists commonly accepted that nations require armies that are founded on discipline and that military discipline requires unflinching compliance with orders. But they recognized too that in the case of criminal orders, the soldier is caught in a bind: he could face civilian prosecution for obeying it or court-martial if he did not. To deepen the dilemma, legal scholars conceded that it is not in society's interest that a soldier should get away with either committing illegal acts under orders or defying military orders with impunity. The general rule among jurists in dealing with this dilemma had been that a soldier committing an offense in obedience to superior orders was relieved of responsibility for wrongdoing unless the illegality of the order was made clear on its face. In such a case, the law held that it is incumbent on the soldier to refuse obedience or face penalty. This criterion for judgment became known as the manifest illegality principle. Significantly, the German Supreme Court applied the manifest illegality principle in the 1921 Leipzig trials. Three cases in particular dealt with this issue, and in all three cases, the German court, drawing on the existing German military penal code, concluded that despite the existence of superior orders, the subordinate ought to have known that the orders constituted crimes against military and civilian law, and so was guilty of those crimes. However, the Nuremberg court did accept the existence of superior orders as a factor to be taken in mitigation when determining sentence.[54]

Nonetheless, the defense consistently argued that obedience was beyond question. In defending the OKW at the IMT and Wilhelm von Leeb during the High Command case, defense attorney Hans Laternser asserted: "a military man is not allowed to decide for himself whether the cause for which he fights is good or bad.... It is his duty to obey and to ask no questions." The prosecution soundly rejected this contention. They emphasized that granting immunity to the defendants on that basis would be tantamount to denying them their humanity.[55] These were, after all, thinking human beings who were on trial. If protest, intervention, and impediments all failed, these commanders should at least have resigned their posts. Legislated or not, ordered by superiors or not, as individuals with consciences, they had to have recognized the criminal nature of what they were being asked to do. Moreover, they were in a position to refuse their participation in such egregious crimes. As General Franz Halder testified at the trial, Hitler would have been unable to replace even the generals he mistrusted because at least until 1941 or early 1942, many months after the issuance of some of the most savage orders, he could not have done without their expertise.[56] It was, the prosecution insisted, within the defendants' power to say: "This we will not do." That they did not "take the honorable course open to them" constituted, the prosecution concluded, "a tragedy of immeasurable consequence."[57]

The Indictment

The prosecution filed the indictment on 26 November 1947, and the arraignment was held one month later. When Telford Taylor opened the case on 5 February 1948, he estimated that the prosecution would need only twenty days to present its arguments and evidence.[58] (They used twenty-six.) The charges in the indictment differed slightly in scope and organization from the charges laid before the IMT. Count 1, crimes against peace, now included invasions and acts of aggression as well as aggressive wars, so as to bring the annexations of Austria and Czechoslovakia under the tribunal's jurisdiction.[59] Count 2 comprised war crimes and crimes against humanity related to crimes committed against enemy belligerents and prisoners of war. Count 3 encompassed war crimes and crimes against humanity related to crimes committed against civilians. Count 4, the common plan or conspiracy, applied to all three of the foregoing charges.

COUNT 1: CRIMES AGAINST PEACE

The charge anchoring the indictment was crimes against peace. Taylor, quoting at length from Henry Stimson's 1947 article "The Nuremberg Trial: Landmark in Law" in the prosecution's opening statement, emphasized to the tribunal that one could not "moderate the excesses of war without controlling war itself," and that recent experience had proven that the problem of war crimes had to be attacked at its root: aggressive war.[60] Clearly, this approach was shaped by the priorities of the American trial planners and Justice Jackson's efforts to establish before the IMT that "launching . . . a war of aggression is the supreme international crime . . . in that it contains within itself the accumulated evil of the whole." The prosecution contended that crimes against peace involved both action and state of mind, meaning the defendants' knowledge of Hitler's aggressive aims toward other countries.[61] Even if individual defendants were not directly involved in every campaign, Taylor and the rest of the prosecution team sought to prove the defendants' awareness of and consent to plans and preparations for the invasions. Inspired by the judgment of the IMT, the prosecution built their case around the defendants' connections to four secret meetings with Hitler in which he made his military ambitions clear. They added a fifth meeting of which the IMT had been unaware.[62]

The first of these took place on 5 November 1937, when Hitler announced to the commanders in chief of the three branches of the military, the foreign minister, and the war minister his intention to attack Austria and Czechoslovakia. Colonel Friedrich Hossbach recorded the minutes

The prosecution counsel's table during the High Command case. Telford Taylor is seated at the top left. Photograph taken by the U.S. Army Signal Corps, courtesy of the Harry S. Truman Library, Judge John C. Young Photo Collection.

of the meeting in his now famous memorandum. Hitler declared: "The question for Germany is where the greatest possible conquest can be made at the lowest cost. . . . The German question can be solved only by way of force, and this is never without risk. . . . For the improvement of our military-political position, it must be our first aim in every case of entanglement by war to conquer Czechoslovakia and Austria simultaneously in order to remove any threat from the flanks of a possible advance westwards."[63]

In the intervening months between the meeting and the Anschluss, through speeches and written assurances, Germany declared its respect for Austria's independence, even while military leaders were preparing for an attack. In February 1938, Hitler summoned Austrian chancellor Schuschnigg to his home at Obersalzburg demanding special concessions for Austrian Nazis and making open political and military threats. Shortly thereafter, Sperrle conducted intimidating Luftwaffe maneuvers on the Bavarian border. In response to Schuschnigg's call for a plebiscite on Austrian independence, Hitler threatened invasion. Schuschnigg resigned, and Hitler sent in his forces. By 13 March, the annexation was complete. Two and a half months later, again in spite of repeated German assurances and treaties guaranteeing Czechoslovakia's territorial integrity, on 30 May 1938, Hitler issued a directive to the high commands of the army, air force, and navy, stating: "It is my unalterable decision to smash Czechoslovakia by military action in the near future."[64] Field Marshal von Leeb returned from retirement to become commander in chief of the 12th Army and to assist in the planning of the assault on Czechoslovakia.

General Franz Halder's diary proved an invaluable source for the prosecution on the inner workings of the OKW and the sequence and circumstances for major military decisions leading up to and including the first years of the war. From 1938 to 1942, Halder was chief of staff to von Brauchitsch, the commander in chief of the army. Accordingly, he attended countless conferences and meetings with Hitler and was intimately involved with all the major decisions.[65] In the time immediately before the annexation of the Sudetenland, Halder noted disagreement between Hitler and his generals over these plans. In fact, General Ludwig Beck, chief of the army general staff between 1933 and 1938, wrote a memorandum, which he circulated to all commanding generals, warning that if Germany pursued the Sudeten question, then it would result in world war.[66] The prosecuting attorneys interpreted the disagreement as proof that the generals knew of Hitler's aggressive intentions. Unfortunately, the memorandum did not elicit the requisite support from other generals, nor did it deter Hitler from his course. Although eleventh-hour negotiations in Munich preserved the peace, the Führer's ambitions were not satisfied. A few months later, from

Warlimont's department, came the formulation of a Hitler order regarding the rest of Czechoslovakia: "To the outside world too it must clearly appear that it is merely an action of pacification and not a warlike undertaking." Exploiting the secessionist unrest by Slovaks in March 1939, Hitler marched on Prague and created the Protectorate of Bohemia and Moravia.[67]

The annexations of Austria and Czechoslovakia facilitated the attack on Poland. In an affidavit prepared for the IMT, defendant Johannes Blaskowitz made clear that there was no disagreement in principle with Hitler's designs on Poland:

> A war to wipe out the political and economic loss resulting from the creation of the Polish Corridor and to lessen the threat to separated East Prussia surrounded by Poland and Lithuania was regarded as a sacred duty though a sad necessity. The at first (1933–35) secret and later unconceded [sic] rearmament of Germany was welcomed by me. All officers of the army shared this attitude and therefore had no reason to oppose Hitler. Hitler produced the results which all of us warmly desired.[68]

Just as Hitler's territorial ambitions were increasing, so too were the planned campaigns to be increasingly brutal in outcome. To von Brauchitsch, Hitler emphasized that Poland should be knocked out so completely that it need not be taken into account as a political force for decades.[69] At a conference on 23 May 1939, which Admiral Schniewind and General Warlimont attended, Hitler announced his decision to invade Poland in order to enlarge Germany's living space and secure its food supplies, fully conscious of the consequences:

> A mass of 80 million people has solved the ideological problems. So, too, must the economic problems be solved. . . . This is impossible without invasion of foreign states or attacks upon foreign property. . . . The national political unity of the Germans has been achieved. . . . Further successes cannot be attained without the shedding of blood. . . . It is a question of expanding our living space in the East and of securing our food supplies, of the settlement of the Baltic problem. . . . There is therefore no question of sparing Poland, and we are left with the decision: To attack Poland at the first suitable opportunity. We cannot expect a repetition of the Czech affair. There will be war.[70]

Three months later, Hitler convened another meeting, this one attended by von Leeb, von Kuechler, Schniewind, Salmuth, and Warlimont, in which he elaborated on his intentions for Poland. He announced that he would provide "a propagandist cause for starting the war," whether credible or not.

Confident of victory, Hitler declared that no one would question the start of the war, because "the victor shall not be asked later on whether we told the truth or not."[71] Generals Hoth, Reinhardt, von Kuechler, and von Salmuth participated in the invasion. Von Leeb held the west with Army Group C, in conjunction with Sperrle's Air Fleet Three.[72]

Fully aware that war with Poland would lead to war with France and England (who had guaranteed Poland's borders after the Munich Agreement), at these same May and August 1939 meetings in which he discussed the Polish campaign, Hitler reasoned that Germany would also have to invade and occupy the Low Countries. Despite a long series of treaties and statements between 1926 and 1939 in which Germany had assured Belgium, the Netherlands, and Luxembourg of its peaceful intentions and respect for their neutrality, in conferring with his generals, Hitler declared:

> Declarations of neutrality must be ignored. If England and France intend the war between Germany and Poland to lead to a conflict, they will support Holland and Belgium in their neutrality and make them build fortifications, in order to finally force them into cooperation. . . . Therefore . . . we must occupy Holland with lightning speed. . . . An effort must be made to deal the enemy a significant or the final decisive blow. . . . *Considerations of right or wrong, or treaties, do not enter into the matter.* . . . If Holland and Belgium are successfully occupied and held, and if France is also defeated, the fundamental conditions for a successful war against England will have been secured.[73]

The prosecution argued that it had to have been plain to the defendants who attended either of these meetings that the attack on the Low Countries was illegal (that is, in contravention of international agreements), and further, that it would perpetuate war, in that the reason for the invasions was to secure bases for future operations.[74] In fact, on October 1939, von Leeb wrote to von Brauchitsch to warn against the coming invasions, stating: "If Germany, by forcing the issue, should violate the neutrality of Holland, Belgium, and Luxemburg, a neutrality which has been solemnly recognized and vouched for by the German government, this action will necessarily cause even those neutral states to reverse their declared policy towards the Reich, which up till now showed some measure of sympathy for the German cause."[75] The prosecution declared that "no document in the entire record [was] more damning," in that it indisputably proved that the generals on trial knew that what they did was wrong.[76]

On 23 November 1939, Hitler called another meeting with his military leaders that von Leeb, von Kuechler, Schniewind, Warlimont, Hoth, and von Salmuth attended. The prosecution emphasized this conference to show that top commanders and staff officers could have had no illusions as to the aggressive intentions behind these campaigns. Hitler began the conference by reviewing his political goals and achievements since 1919, and he reminded his listeners that he had not built up the armed forces to be idle, but had always intended to strike. Repeating again the rationale for occupying Holland and Belgium, Hitler promised that at the earliest favorable moment, he would attack France and England as well.[77] General Hoth's notes from the conference illustrated the officers' willing rejection of peace for war:

> Improvement of positions for naval warfare and of naval bases obtainable only by the invasion of Luxembourg, Belgium and Holland. The Führer has made up his mind to this effect. . . . Is there any need at all for an attack? . . . There is a general conviction that great changes in history can be brought about only by the sword. . . . Why not peace? Law of nature. Self preservation. . . . The Führer is resolved to make a lordly decision—to fight. . . . Never before was the situation as favorable as it is now. It would be a crime not to exploit it.[78]

On 10 May 1940, German forces, led, in part, by Reinhardt, von Salmuth, Hoth, von Leeb, von Kuechler, and Sperrle, invaded Holland, Belgium, and Luxembourg. France fell soon after.[79]

The most significant campaign for the High Command case was Operation Barbarossa, the attack on the USSR. From its inception, this war in the East was to be unlike all campaigns that preceded it. It was to be a total war of destruction—a *Vernichtungskrieg*.[80] On 30 March 1941, Hitler held a conference attended by von Leeb, von Kuechler, Warlimont, Hoth, and others, in which he reviewed the course of events since France's defeat and told them of his resolution to destroy Russia.[81] Hitler described the campaign as a preventive war, but evidence showed that it was launched to gain resources and living space (*Lebensraum*), and to bring England "to her knees." As Hitler noted, with no opposition from Britain, he could be master of Europe and the Balkans.[82] Hitler insisted to his generals that the obliteration of Bolshevism and the Communist intelligentsia was as much a part of their duties as leading their troops in battle. In his diary entry of the meeting, Halder described the coming war in the following terms:

> Clash of two ideologies. Crushing denunciation of Bolshevism, identified with asocial criminality. . . . We must forget the comradeship between soldiers. A Communist is no comrade before nor after the battle. This is a war of extermination. . . . We do not wage war to preserve the enemy. . . . War

against Russia: Extermination of the Bolshevist Commissars and of the Communist intelligentsia. . . . This is no job for military courts. The individual troop commanders must know the issues at stake. They must be leaders in the fight. . . . This war will be very different from war in the West. In the East harshness today means leniency in the future. Commanders must make the sacrifice of overcoming their personal scruples.[83]

That these objectives were understood and pursued by the men on trial was illustrated by the defendant General Reinhardt's 11 May 1941 combat directives for Operation Barbarossa:

The war in Russia is the inevitable result of the struggle for survival forced upon us, especially the struggle for the economic independence of greater Germany and the European territory under its rule. It is the old fight of the Germanic race against the Slavs, the defense of the European culture against a Muscovite–Asiatic flood, the thrusting-back of Jewish Bolshevism. The aim of this fight must be to smash the present Russia, and it must therefore be conducted with utter ruthlessness. The complete merciless annihilation of the enemy must be the inflexible purpose of the planning and execution of every combat operation. In particular no mercy must be shown to the followers of the present Russian–Bolshevist system.[84]

By the end of May, the OKW finalized the date for the invasion. Halder remarked in his diary: "OKW insists that the date for Barbarossa be kept. No objections on the part of the army."[85] On 22 June 1941, without a declaration of war and in contravention of the August 1939 Non-Aggression Pact, German forces invaded the USSR.

COUNT 2: WAR CRIMES AND CRIMES AGAINST HUMANITY:
CRIMES AGAINST ENEMY BELLIGERENTS AND PRISONERS OF WAR

With regard to count 2, Taylor sought to distinguish between the awful realities of all wars and the exceptionally heinous conduct of the Wehrmacht in this one. In the opening statement he declared: "Any war means pain and death and grief. . . . It will be said that in time of war such crimes must occur in every army." Nonetheless, he continued, quoting Justice Jackson, "it is not because they yielded to the normal frailties of human beings that we accuse them. It is their abnormal and inhuman conduct which brings them to this bar."[86] Having already established that the campaign was being waged for ideological as much as for territorial or strategic reasons, the prosecution outlined how OKW officers formulated and distributed (before and after the fighting broke out) orders that aimed at the total annihilation of the Soviet Communist leadership and fighting force. One of the most startlingly vicious of these, and indeed, a cornerstone in the prosecution of the High Command case, was the June 1941 Commissar Order.[87]

Political commissars were Red Army soldiers entrusted with the ideological indoctrination and morale of their comrades. Like regular soldiers, they wore military uniforms, carried weapons, and fought at the front. Months before Germany invaded the USSR, the highest-level military leaders discussed and drafted an order stipulating that they were not to be taken prisoner if captured in battle. Rather, German combat troops were to kill them immediately and to the last man.[88] On 6 June 1941, Walter Warlimont issued the order entitled "Directive for the Treatment of Political Commissars" to the supreme commands of the army and air force. Two days later, Commander in Chief of the Army von Brauchitsch transmitted the order, with a few amendments, to the army groups and armies in the East, with the request that they make further distribution.[89] The latest version stipulated that commissars were to be dealt with "unobtrusively outside the actual battle zone, by order of an officer."[90] In no way, however, was the order's harshness mitigated. The preamble to the order declared:

> The troops must realize: 1) In this fight treating such elements with consideration to leniency and international law is completely wrong. They are a menace to our own safety and to the rapid pacification of the conquered territories. 2) The political commissars are the originators of the Asiatic barbaric methods of fighting. They must be dealt with promptly and with the utmost severity. Therefore, if taken while fighting or offering resistance, they must, on principle, be taken care of immediately with weapons [that is, shot].[91]

The order continued that commissars were not to be recognized as soldiers, and therefore, the protections codified by international law regarding prisoners of war were not to apply. If commissars were detected in the rear areas, the order stipulated that they were to be handed over to the Einsatzgruppen or Einsatzkommandos (a subdivision of the Einsatzgruppen) of the Security Service. Last, subordinate units were requested to submit regular reports on the execution of the order.[92] The prosecution entered scores of these reports into evidence that detailed the places, dates, and numbers of commissars killed.[93] Related to the Commissar Order, in fall 1942, Hitler asked Warlimont to prepare an order for the killing of all Allied soldiers captured when they were engaged in special missions against German forces. Issued on 18 October 1942 from the OKW to all armed forces branches, in all theaters, it directed: "all enemies on so-called commando missions in Europe or Africa challenged by German troops, even if they are to all appearances soldiers in uniform . . . either armed or unarmed, in battle or in flight, are to be slaughtered to the last man . . . even if these individuals . . . should be prepared to give themselves up, no pardon is to be granted them on principle."[94] The prosecution evidence showed that von Kuechler, Reinhardt, von Salmuth, and Reinecke passed on this Commando Order, and that American, Canadian, British, and Greek soldiers were murdered in fulfillment of it in France, Italy, Austria, and Norway.[95]

It is impossible to communicate, in a few pages, the plight of POWs under the German army. At trial, the prosecution declared, "The treatment of Russian prisoners of war was a crime of incalculable proportions."[96] Aside from the commissars and commandos identified for immediate execution, various military staff and field officers outlined a broad program, through orders and directives, for the exploitation, abuse, neglect, and murder of POWs. It is estimated that 3.3 million Soviet POWs perished at the Germans' hands.[97] The OKW and the High Commands of the three branches of the military shared jurisdiction over POW matters. The chief of prisoner of war matters in the OKW was defendant Hermann Reinecke. Subordinate only to Hitler and Wilhelm Keitel, Hitler's chief military advisor, Reinecke was responsible for formulating the armed forces' general policy with regard to prisoners of war.[98] However, jurisdiction over individual prisoner of war camps was divided between the OKW and the army depending on their locations. POW camps in the operational area fell under the control of the OKH, whereas POW camps in the General Government (the southwestern area of Poland occupied by Germany but not directly incorporated into the Reich) and outside the operation area (including the Reich) were administered by the OKW.[99]

As noted by the prosecution, shortly after the issuance of the Commissar Order, Reinecke formulated and disseminated a number of decrees for the identifying of commissars among Soviet POWs, and for transferring them to concentration camps for execution. (It will be recalled that the Commissar Order called for the immediate liquidation of any commissars from among captured Red Army soldiers. Reinecke's decrees aimed at identifying and eliminating any commissars who had not been discovered earlier.) Reinecke's directives went further, however, in identifying several additional categories of prisoners for "special treatment"—that is, execution. The screening, segregation, and elimination program was possible only through the cooperation of the military with the civilian agencies of the Security Police (SIPO), Security Service (S.D.), and Gestapo.[100] On 17 July 1941, Reinhard Heydrich issued Operational Order No. 8 to SIPO, S.D., and Gestapo commanders and to Einsatzgruppen A, B, C, and D, which assigned Einsatzkommandos to POW camps in the General Government and East Prussia for the screening, segregation, and disposition of "suspicious" elements among the POW populations of the eastern campaign. Consisting of five to seven S.S. men, these Kommandos would be used "for the purging of the prisoner camps which contain Soviet Russians." Significantly, the order noted that the procedure had been determined in tandem with the OKW Prisoner of War Department, and that the commanders of POW and transit camps (known as Stalags and Dulags, respectively) were "duty bound" to cooperate closely with the Einsatzkommandos.[101] Categories of prisoners to be identified were as follows:

> Professional revolutionaries; the officials of the Comintern; all influential party officials of the Communist Party of the Soviet Union and its subdivisions in the central committees, the regional and district committees; all people's commissars and their deputies; all former commissars in the Red Army; the leading personalities on the central and intermediate level of the state administration; the leading personalities of the economy; the Soviet Russian intellectuals; all Jews; all persons found to be agitators or fanatical Communists.[102]

Executions of particular prisoners were not to be carried out in or near the camps, but away from view. If the camps (for example, in the General Government) were too close to the German border, prisoners were to be deported to former Soviet territory to be shot.[103]

Shortly thereafter, on 24 July 1941, the OKH issued a similar order to all army groups, armies, and army group rear areas with instructions for the treatment of "intolerable elements" in POW camps in the operational zone. In contrast to Heydrich's Order No. 8, this later order prevented the SIPO and S.D. from operating within the camps themselves. Instead, Wehrmacht personnel were to screen and segregate POWs into the following groups: "1) Ethnic Germans, Ukrainians, Lithuanians, Latvians, Estonians; 2) Asiatics, Jews, German-speaking Russians; 3) politically intolerable and suspicious elements, commissars and agitators."[104] Prisoners in the first category were used as army auxiliaries. Of the second category, Jews were handed over to the Einsatzgruppen for execution, while the others were to be used for forced labor outside the Reich or to man antiaircraft guns in the combat zone. Prisoners in the last category were kept alive in the camps until a firing squad arrived and could dispose of them, or until their deportation to other camps could be arranged.[105] In practice, army authorities themselves sometimes carried out the executions in the theater of operations.[106]

As reinforcement of the order, and indicative of the OKW's overall attitude toward Soviet POWs, Reinecke issued instructions to the army, air force, and navy on 8 September 1941, for the treatment of Russian prisoners of war, in which he declared: "The Bolshevist soldier has therefore lost all claim to the treatment as an honorable opponent, in accordance with the Geneva Convention. . . . The order for ruthless and energetic action must be given at the slightest indication of insubordination, especially in the case of Bolshevist fanatics. Insubordination, active or passive resistance, must be broken immediately by force of arms (bayonets, butts and forearms)."[107] Reinecke's instructions further repeated the provisions in Operational Order No. 8 and the OKH's 24 July 1941 order for the segregation of civilians and prisoners of war of the eastern campaign who were deemed "politically undesirable."[108] He also acknowledged that the fate of prisoners of war, although technically still under military jurisdiction, was to be decided by the Einsatzkommandos of the SIPO and S.D. civilian agencies. Urging Wehrmacht POW camp commanders to cooperate with the Einsatzkommandos, the order stipulated: "The fate of those segregated as 'politically undesirable' is being decided upon by the Einsatzkommandos of the Security Police and SD. Should any of the persons suspected later turn out to be unobjectionable they are to be returned to the PW camps. If the Einsatzkommando demands the handing over of further persons, this request must be granted. Officers will often be segregated as 'politically undesireable.'"[109] Himmler subsequently distributed these instructions to Heydrich and all four Einsatzgruppen.[110]

Admiral Wilhelm Canaris, head of counterintelligence in the OKW, vigorously rejected Reinecke's directives of 8 September and set forth his objections in a memorandum submitted to Reinecke and Keitel a week later, on 15 September 1941:

> The principles of general international law on the treatment of prisoners of war apply. . . . War captivity is neither revenge nor punishment, but solely protective custody, the only purpose of which is to prevent the prisoners of war from a further participation in the war. This principle was developed in accordance with the view held by all armies that it is contrary to military tradition to kill or injure helpless people; this is also in the interest of all belligerents in order to prevent mistreatment of their own soldiers in case of capture. The decrees for the treatment of Soviet prisoners of war . . . are based on a fundamentally different viewpoint. . . . According to this viewpoint, military services for the Soviets is not considered military duty but . . . is characterized in its totality as a crime. . . . The expressly approved measures will result in arbitrary mistreatments and killings.[111]

The memo's significance was great, the prosecution argued, because it incontrovertibly showed that even senior OKW officers recognized the illegality of their policy toward Soviet POWs. Unfortunately, Canaris's objection made no impression.

In keeping with the overall attitude toward the treatment of Soviet prisoners of war, the military made wholly insufficient preparations to shelter, clothe, feed, and care medically for the vast numbers of troops who surrendered to German forces in the first months of Operation Barbarossa. Described as a fate that "would stagger the most comprehensive imaginations," the prosecution presented countless documents and called witnesses to testify who outlined the conditions these unfortunate captives faced.[112] If not refused quarter and shot outright, surrendered soldiers were herded into barbed wire enclosures with no shelter, extra clothing, or even cooking facilities.[113] Luckier prisoners were housed in unheated sheds. In some places, basic sanitation could not be maintained, which, in combination with the lack of nutrition, exhaustion, and cramped quarters, soon resulted in epidemics—particularly of tuberculosis, typhus, and typhoid. Those who died were buried naked, and camp officials redistributed their clothing to the prisoner population, perpetuating the spread of disease.[114] The absence of food routinely reduced camp inmates to cannibalism, for which they were immediately shot. With the army's awareness and permission, as noted above, the S.S. had free rein in the camps to select the politically or racially undesirable for execution. The army also used Soviet POWs to clear mines "in order to spare German blood," and housed them in buildings slated for German occupancy, so that booby traps might be discovered. These prisoners were used at the front to build fortifications, to dig trenches and anti-tank ditches, and to try to encourage other Red Army soldiers to surrender. Prisoners who fled and were recaptured were immediately shot.[115]

The evidence against General Hans von Roques contained some of the most shocking descriptions of the Soviet prisoners' plight. As commander in chief of the rear area of Army Group South, he exercised jurisdiction over dozens of transit and permanent POW camps. A report submitted to his headquarters in December 1941 revealed that in only three months, four camps registered mortality rates of 28, 87, 82, and 80 percent. Notably, these figures did not include those who had died in a typhoid epidemic. The POWs' condition, the prosecution emphasized, proved the Wehrmacht officials' deliberate policy of neglect.[116]

In October 1941, General Erwin Lahousen visited Army Group North headquarters, about which he was called to testify in court. While in transit, he had noticed thousands of Soviet prisoners of war being led to various camps: "Towards us marched endless columns of half-starved and frozen

prisoners; every thousand yards or so some would collapse and die."[117] Prisoners of war were frequently deported to concentration camps to be executed or used there for forced labor. A witness named Kazimierz Smolen, a
Polish soldier who had been deported to Auschwitz in April 1940 and was
employed in the Political Reception Department there from mid-1941 until
January 1945, testified about the arrival of 10,000 Soviet POWs at that
camp in October 1941. Their identifying marks indicated that they had been
transferred from a Wehrmacht POW camp. Furthermore, the OKW had
furnished Auschwitz personnel with record cards for each prisoner, to be
filled out upon their death and returned to the Wehrmacht Information
Office under Reinecke. Smolen described how, apart from ill-treatment and
starvation, a detachment of the nearby Kattowitz Gestapo screened and
selected these prisoners for execution. Divided into categories of "fanatic
Communists," "politically intolerable," "politically non-suspect," and "suitable for reconstruction work," camp personnel branded these prisoners and
killed certain groups (the first and second) outright. In letters to the OKW,
Smolen's office informed them of those prisoners who had received "special
treatment." He recalled making particular reference to the fact that some of
them had been killed by way of a new experimental gas. Smolen was most
likely referring to the introduction of Zyklon B. In the fall of 1941, in
attempts to find a more efficient means of killing, Auschwitz personnel conducted experiments on Russian POWs with this chemical, which had been
used for decades in Germany for fumigation and disinfection. This gas was
subsequently used in Auschwitz, Birkenau (part of the Auschwitz complex,
where the vast majority of killings in gas chambers took place), and other
camps for the mass killing of Jews and other deportees and prisoners.[118]

   The scope of German abuse of Soviet war prisoners was devastating. In
a letter to OKW chief Keitel on 28 February 1942, an official of the Ministry for the Occupied Territories lamented:

> The fate of the Soviet prisoners of war in Germany is a tragedy of the great-
> est extent. Of 3.6 million prisoners of war, only several hundred thousand
> are still able to work fully. . . . Death and deterioration to the extent
> described could have been avoided. In the Soviet Union, for example . . . the
> indigenous population wanted to place food at the prisoners' disposal. . . . In
> the majority of cases, the camp commanders have forbidden [this] and they
> have rather let them starve to death. . . . In numerous cases, no shelter for
> prisoners was provided at all. They lay under the open sky during rain or
> snow. . . . Utterances such as these have been heard: "The more these pris-
> oners die, the better it is for us."[119]

This critique of the overall policy toward Soviet POWs did not spring from the official's sympathy for the victims. Rather, the goal of his report was to point out the consequences of the treatment of Russian prisoners for the German economy and armaments production.[120] Indeed, the army's December 1941 setback outside Moscow had caused some German officials to rethink their policy toward POWs. Concerned now with obtaining sufficient manpower to operate armaments and munitions industries in the Reich and to aid in the fortifications and defenses of the battle zones (all of which was, it should be noted, prohibited labor according to international law) for what was now shaping up to be a prolonged engagement in the East, German authorities mitigated certain measures. Contrary to former policy, prisoners who escaped were not automatically shot upon recapture.[121] Nonetheless, the "politically eligible" prisoners (that is, non-Jews, non-Asiatics, non-commissars and non-German-speaking Russians) deported to the Reich for labor still endured horrific conditions in the camps. Rations were insufficient. The prosecution cited one memorandum to the chief of armaments attesting that the POW laborers' diet had hitherto consisted only of horses and cats.[122] POW camp commanders allowed the sick to starve or identified them to the Gestapo to be killed. German forces executed without trial all POWs in the Reich who had sexual relations with German women.[123] The IG Farben, the Flick, and especially the Krupp cases, the three SNP trials of industrialists, exposed in great detail the conditions endured by prisoners of war (notably also French, Serbian, Belgian, and Polish POWs) exploited in the Reich armaments factories. Prosecutors in the High Command case frequently cited their findings.

COUNT 3: WAR CRIMES AND CRIMES AGAINST HUMANITY:
CRIMES AGAINST CIVILIANS

The category of crimes against civilians included army measures that were intended to terrorize and intimidate the populations of occupied areas, and policies that aimed at the destruction of racial and political "enemies." Military leadership and personnel often conceived and perpetrated the terror and intimidation actions. In the case of racial and political persecution, the military more frequently performed a supportive function, facilitating the wholesale murder of millions by other Nazi organizations. Although the Wehrmacht committed crimes against civilians in all theaters, their campaign against the Soviet Union was unequalled for the fanaticism and ferocity with which the Nazis conceived and implemented this war of conquest. The prosecution described Operation Barbarossa thus:

Hitler and the generals laid their plans for the war against Russia on the basic assumption that every Slav is sub-human and every Jew is sub-human and criminal as well. The Russians, therefore, were to be treated like beasts, and the Jews were to be killed like dangerous beasts. . . . Germany's treatment of the Jews of Europe and the Slavs of Eastern Europe is the blackest page in the history of civilization.[124]

We have already seen the consequences of this view for Soviet POWs. The most far-reaching and devastating criminal order in its consequences for *civilians* in the East was the Barbarossa Jurisdiction Order. Drafted by the defendants Warlimont and Lehmann, on 13 May 1941, Keitel issued the "Decree on the Exercising of Jurisdiction by Military Courts in the Area 'Barbarossa' and Special Measures by Troops," which legalized the killing of Soviet civilians suspected of hostile activities toward German forces. It bears quoting from at length:

I.   Treatment of Crimes by Enemy Civilians
   1.   Until further order the military courts and the courts martial will not be competent for crimes committed by enemy civilians.
   2.   Franctireurs will be liquidated ruthlessly by the troops in combat or while fleeing.
   3.   Also all other attacks by enemy civilians against the armed forces, its members and auxiliaries will be suppressed on the spot by troops with the most rigorous methods until the assailants are destroyed.
   4.   Where such measures were not taken or at least were not possible, persons suspected of the act will be brought before an officer at once. This officer will decide whether they are to be shot. Against localities from which troops have been attacked in a deceitful or treacherous manner, collective coercive measures will be applied immediately upon the order of an officer of the rank of at least battalion, etc. commander, if the circumstances do not permit a quick identification of individual perpetrators.
II.   Handling of Crimes by Members of the Wehrmacht
   1.   [For cases of] offenses committed against enemy civilians by troops of the Wehrmacht or by its auxiliaries, prosecution is not obligatory, even where it is at the same time a military crime or misdemeanor.[125]

Attached to the order were supplements composed by von Brauchitsch, which subsequently became known as the Brauchitsch Disciplinary Order. It emphasized that it was the senior officers' duty to prevent "arbitrary excesses of individual members of the army" and that soldiers could not exercise their own judgment in such matters but were to follow the orders of their superiors. The prosecution argued that, notwithstanding von Brauchitsch's supplements to it, the order was baldly criminal on its face because it abolished trials for enemy civilians and German soldiers who were suspected of committing an offense, it expressly provided that mere suspicion was adequate grounds for execution, and it exempted troops from prosecution for their illegal acts.[126]

The Barbarossa Jurisdiction Order had the overall effect, the prosecution continued, of driving Russian civilians to join the partisans. Apparently Hitler welcomed this consequence, because he announced on 16 July 1941: "The Russians have now ordered partisan warfare behind the front. This partisan warfare has some advantages for us; it enables us to eradicate everyone who opposes us."[127] Accordingly, and in the same vein as the Barbarossa Jurisdiction Order, the OKW instituted a hostage reprisal policy to be applied wherever the Wehrmacht encountered resistance, insisting "only terror will deter . . . the population from resistance."[128] For example, Warlimont's office in the OKW issued the directive "Treatment of Enemy Civilians and Russian Prisoners of War in the Rear Areas of the Army Groups" on 25 July 1941, which was distributed to the rear area commanders of Army Groups North, Center, and South. It ordered in part:

> In view of the great expanse of the areas of operation in the East and the treachery and peculiarity of the Bolshevik enemy especially extensive and effective measures are called for from the start.
> I. Treatment of Enemy Civilians:
> . . . The necessary speedy pacification of the country can be achieved only if every mere threat by the enemy civilian population is ruthlessly stopped.
> The proposed allocation of partisan detachments in the rear of the army, the call for the formation of bands from among youths, and altogether the whole insidious actions of the supporters of the Jewish–Bolshevik system indicate that guerilla warfare will revive even in the areas hitherto quiet. . . . Attacks and all kinds of acts of violence against persons and objects, as well as all attempts, are to be beaten down ruthlessly by use of arms until the enemy is annihilated. In cases of passive resistance or if, in cases of road blocks, shootings, raids or other acts of sabotage the culprits cannot be determined at once and taken care of in the already ordered manner, *collective forcible measures* are to be carried out without delay. . . . The population is held responsible for order in their areas even without special previous announcement and arrest. . . . Suspected elements, who *although they cannot be proved guilty* of a serious crime, seem dangerous because of their atti-

tude and behavior are to be handed over to the Einsatzgruppen or the Kommandos of the S.P. (S.D.).[129]

The OKW supplemented this order with another on 16 September 1941, which detailed to what extent and in what manner the army was to apply such measures. As above, the conflation of alleged military security necessities with ideological preconceptions was clear:

> It should be inferred *in every case* of resistance to the German occupying forces, no matter the individual circumstances, that it is of Communist origin. . . . In this connection it should be remembered that a human life in unsettled countries frequently counts for nothing, and a deterrent effect can be obtained only by unusual severity. The death penalty for 50 to 100 Communists is generally to be regarded in these cases as suitable atonement for one German soldier's life. The way in which the sentence is carried out should still further increase the deterrent effect.[130]

The order further specified that the victims should be leading members of families and of their communities, that their names should be published, and that any of the culprit's associates who were already in custody should be shot. The army applied the order with particular ferocity in the Balkans, but General Blaskowitz used it against resistance fighters in France as well.[131]

The prosecution entered into evidence scores of field reports demonstrating how broadly subordinate units interpreted and how frequently they implemented the foregoing orders. The following examples were selected from the activity reports submitted by secret field police, counterintelligence units, and regular troops to Army Group North headquarters between July 1941 and February 1942, while von Leeb and later von Kuechler were commanders in chief. They describe Russian civilians being shot or hanged because "they made anti-German remarks during a village meeting"; because "the man could not disprove that he had been employed as a spy"; because two men had "anti-German tendencies"; because a man had "a stubborn character"; because a man "gave an impression of cunning"; because five civilians "listened to Radio Moscow"; because a woman had "Communist tendencies"; because a distiller, his wife, and his two children were suspected of "making preparations for distributing Schnapps to partisans."[132]

The OKW issued further orders to perpetuate and encourage the directives laid out by the Barbarossa Jurisdiction Order. The following Keitel order dated 16 December 1942 was found in the records of Reinhardt's Third Panzer Army:

The enemy employs fanatical Communist-trained fighters in partisan warfare, who do not shrink from any acts of violence. More than ever before,
this is a question of existing or perishing. This battle has nothing at all to
do with soldierly chivalry, or with the Geneva Convention. Unless this battle against the partisans in the East, as well as in the Balkans, is conducted
with the utmost brutality, the available forces will soon not suffice to master
this pestilence. The troops are therefore entitled and even obliged to employ
whatever means in this fight without any restraint, also against women and
children, as long as it leads to success. No German who is committed in the
fight against partisans must be called to account in disciplinary action or
before a court martial for his actions in the fight against partisans and their
followers.[133]

Not surprisingly, such partisan-combating methods extended at times to the
destruction of entire communities. Note the following excerpt from a report
submitted in February 1943 by troops under Reinhardt's command: "in
order to keep bands from resettling in this territory the population of villages and farms in this area were killed without exception to the last baby.
All homes were burned down."[134]
  The army did not always immediately impose sweeping and collective
punishments. Under General Reinhardt, the Third Panzer Army communicated a March 1942 OKW order that demanded that "band supporters and
band suspects . . . provided that they have not been shot immediately, . . . [or]
hung," were to be handed over to S.S. and police leaders for deportation to a
concentration camp.[135] Accordingly, between September and December
1943, the same Panzer Army arranged with the S.D. for a large-scale evacuation of 3,808 civilians from the area of Witebsk to Auschwitz because that
population was suspected of helping "bands." Army personnel guarded them
in a military transit camp and supervised their transport to S.D. custody. The
witness Smolen, who testified about the murder of Russian POWs at
Auschwitz, recalled that the Witebsk evacuees were housed in a separate
camp at Birkenau, which was referred to as the Russian family camp. There
they received the same paltry rations and same brutal treatment as other
inmates of the camp. Camp records produced at court revealed that approximately 300 of the Witebsk children, including babies who were born in the
camp, were gassed in spring 1944. The adults who did not die from starvation, ill-treatment, and disease were later also gassed.[136] On Reinhardt's personal responsibility for the deaths, the prosecution declared:

  It is entirely immaterial, for the determination of Reinhardt's guilt, whether
  the Witebsk deportees were driven to the gas chambers at Auschwitz one

day or one year after he had deported them there; the children were exterminated shortly after their arrival, their parents sometime later. One must expect any human being of mediocre decency and standards of morality to consider it a crime to deport children to a concentration camp. General Reinhardt's intimate knowledge of the practices of the S.D. put him in a position to judge better than anybody else what an enormous risk threatened every human life against whom the S.D. murderers were turned loose.[137]

Yet another measure instituted to combat resistance movements was the Night and Fog Decree. Conceived by Hitler but composed by Lehmann (whom the prosecution described as its "guiding spirit"), this 7 December 1941 order stipulated that civilians accused of crimes or resistance activities could be seized from their homes and taken for trial before special courts in the German Ministry of Justice. Whether sentenced to a prison term or acquitted, the accused were then handed over to the Gestapo for protective custody for the duration of the war. Some received no trial but were deported immediately to the Mauthausen, Auschwitz, Flossenburg, Dachau, Ravensbrück, or Buchenwald camp. Thousands suffered torture, neglect, and death because of this policy. The victims' whereabouts, trial, and fate were kept secret in order to deliberately terrorize his or her family and associates. The decree's cover letter read: "Efficient and enduring intimidation can only be achieved, either by capital punishment or by measures whereby the relatives of the criminal and the population do not know the fate of the criminal." Wehrmacht troops applied the order in France, Holland, Norway, Bohemia and Moravia, and Ukraine.[138] The foregoing orders and a multitude of others resulted in an overall policy of unprecedented brutality.

Crimes against Jews, Romani, and "Inferiors"

The orders regarding the treatment of racial "enemies" blurred and overlapped with the orders and policies related to political and military opponents. Because the language of the orders and the ideology that inspired them equated Jews with Bolshevists/Communists and partisans, Jews could be killed outright on a number of pretexts. Still, the prosecution produced evidence showing that Wehrmacht actions against Jews had a specifically racial element. Moreover, the prosecution argued that the officer corps was aware of the regime's racial goals from its earliest days and was kept apprised of the ever-expanding policies to achieve them. Their role in the state's program to eliminate these racial "inferiors" exceeded simple awareness, however, spanning both active participation in killings and, more often, the facilitation of these programs.[139] It went without saying that the war presented the opportunity to bring racial, particularly antisemitic, ideology to its "logical" conclusion, and that without the military's conquest and occupation of vast territories in the West and East, organizations such as the S.S., S.D., SIPO, and Gestapo would not have had access to Europe's largest populations of Jews and Romani, or indeed the territory on which to perpetrate the murders. Even before the army's formal agreement with the Einsatzgruppen to shelter, supply, and feed these units while they did their work, the prosecution demonstrated how Wehrmacht officers prepared their troops psychologically for the extraordinary tasks ahead. They produced an order that von Kuechler issued in August 1940, in which he addressed soldiers who had recently been transferred from the western to eastern theater: "The final ethnical solution of the ethnical struggle which has been raging on the eastern border for centuries calls for one-time harsh measures. Certain units and departments of the party and the state have been charged with the carrying out of this ethnical struggle in the East. Soldiers must keep out of these tasks of other units. They also must not interfere with these concerns by criticism."[140]

As the prosecution had explained above, the triggermen in the anti-Jewish campaign consisted mainly of the S.S. Einsatzgruppen, but the relationship between them and the armed forces was close. In implementation of an agreement reached among the OKW, OKH (represented by Quartermaster General Eduard Wagner), and chief of the SIPO and S.D. Reinhard Heydrich one month earlier, on 28 April 1941, Commander in Chief of the Army von Brauchitsch issued an order to all army groups and armies that informed their commanders of the Einsatzgruppen's tasks and defined the relationship between the two organizations. It began: "The carrying out of certain security police tasks requires the employment of Sonderkommandos of the SIPO and S.D. in the operational area."[141] According to the order, the military commanders would still possess a great deal of control. Although these Sonderkommandos would receive their tactical orders from Heydrich, they would be dependent on the armies for logistical support. Further, if the commander in chief so decided, he could exclude them from operating in army territory:

[The Einsatzgruppen] are subordinate to the armies with reference to order of march, rations and quarters. . . . They receive their technical instructions from the Chief of the S.P. and S.D. and if occasion should arise are subordinate to restrictive orders of the armies with reference to their activities.

... [A commissioner of the security police and S.D.] is required to bring to
the attention of the commander-in-chief of the army, promptly, the instructions sent to him by the chief of the Security Police and S.D. The military
commander is empowered to issue the commissioner instructions which are
necessary to avoid an interruption in operations; they take precedence over
all other instructions.[142]

In summarizing this relationship, the prosecution described the power of
the army group commander as "the blazing glory of the noon-day sun" and
the power of the Einsatzgruppe leader as "the tiny flicker of the firefly."[143]
Indeed, one of the most dramatic moments of the trial occurred when Otto
Ohlendorf, head of Einsatzgruppe D, whom one of the other Subsequent
Proceedings tribunals had recently condemned to death for his participation in the mass killings of Jews and others, took the stand for the prosecution. Counsel had called him on rebuttal because all of the defendants had
denied that they could give orders to the Einsatzgruppen. Ohlendorf testified that the Einsatzgruppen reported all of their tasks to the army commanders, and that together, they and the army agreed on the time, place,
and possible support of the troops for particular "liquidation action[s]."[144]
    Although the defendants vigorously denied it at trial, the prosecution
repeatedly insisted that no army officer or soldier could have avoided learning about the Einsatzgruppen's murderous tasks. On this the prosecution
called the witness Hans Freuchte, who had been a medical officer in one of
the POW transit camps in General von Roques's Army Group South rear
area:

> For every officer and for every enlisted man it was, at that time, a matter of
> course that every Jew was shot. . . . This subject was discussed with almost
> everybody with whom one talked for more than three minutes. At least it
> was brought up, and I have not talked to anyone who said: "That is com-
> pletely new to me. I don't know anything about it. What are you telling me?"
> It was a completed fact for everyone.[145]

The connection between the Einsatzgruppen and the army, which the
prosecution called "a model of complicity in crime," went far beyond awareness and formal logistical support.[146] Einsatzgruppe A, composed of 990
men under the leadership of S.S. Gruppenführer Walter Stahlecker, began
collaboration with Army Group North on the second day of Operation Barbarossa.[147] In a report summarizing the Einsatzgruppe's activities up to 15
October 1941, which the prosecution submitted into evidence, Stahlecker
commented: "In accordance with the basic orders received . . . the clearing

activities of the Security Police had to aim at a complete annihilation of the Jews, Sonderkommandos reinforced by selected units . . . therefore performed extensive executions both in the towns and in rural areas. The actions of the execution Kommandos were performed smoothly."[148]

He estimated that since operations began, his group had shot 135,567 people, mostly Jews. Regarding his relationship with military authorities (Army Group North was at that time under General von Leeb; General von Kuechler commanded the 18th Army within Army Group North), he wrote that from the beginning, cooperation with the army "was generally good, in some cases . . . it was very close, almost cordial." He remarked further that it had soon become clear that they would have to carry out their work at the front lines as well as in the rear areas. Accordingly, police detachments "always" entered large towns with the first army units.[149] Apart from carrying out the killings themselves, the Einsatzgruppen strove to exploit indigenous antisemitism by provoking pogroms against local Jewish populations. In these cases as well, the army proved itself a knowing accomplice:

> Native antisemitic forces were induced to start pogroms against Jews during the first hours after capture. . . . During the first pogrom . . . the Lithuanian partisans did away with more than 1500 Jews, set fire to several synagogues or destroyed them by other means and burned down a Jewish dwelling district consisting of about sixty houses. . . . These self-clearing actions went smoothly because the army authorities who had been informed showed understanding for this procedure.[150]

The prosecution noted that strong relations and close cooperation between the Einsatzgruppen and the army were noticeable in Army Group South as well. An Einsatzgruppe report of 20 August 1941 recounting the murder of Jews in Zhitomir, in Volhynia, USSR, which at that time was within General von Roques's rear area, explained:

> Above all, Wehrmacht circles now show an ever-growing interest and understanding for the tasks and the importance of security police work. This could be observed to a particular extent at the time of the executions. In addition, the Wehrmacht itself is anxious to further the tasks of the security police. Thus, at the present time, the Wehrmacht continually sends reports to all the offices of the Einsatzgruppe informing the latter of located Communist functionaries and Jews.[151]

The prosecution produced several orders originating with the army showing that the military leadership went beyond simply fulfilling their

agreed-on obligations to these police organizations and that the field commanders exceeded their instructions for practical support. General von
Roques issued decrees in July 1941 in his area requiring, on penalty of death,
that all Jews over fourteen years of age wear identifying armbands marked
with the Star of David. He also established ghettos and prohibited Jewish
religious observance. All these measures, the prosecution noted, exposed the
Jews to ill-treatment and ultimately execution by the Einsatzgruppen.[152] In
the shooting of Jews at Zhitomir, referred to above, the Einsatzgruppe report
noted that among the killers, "the Wehrmacht was also represented in great
numbers."[153] The prosecution submitted documents revealing similar measures in other army group areas, notably in Army Group North, where one
infantry regiment reported that they not only had marked Jews (this time
with a large yellow dot), but had removed and suspended them from their
trades and professions and confined them in a concentration camp.[154] These
and other orders suggested the military's agreement with the ideology motivating the crimes against particular racial and political groups. On 10 October 1941, General von Reichenau issued his infamous order calling for
"revenge on subhuman Jewry," and in unmistakable terms, he demanded the
full cooperation of ordinary troops:

> The most essential aim of war against the Jewish–Bolshevistic system is a
> complete destruction of their means of power and the elimination of Asi-
> atic influence from the European culture. In this connection the troops are
> facing tasks which exceed the one-sided routine of soldiering. The soldier
> in the Eastern territories is not merely a fighter according to the rule of the
> art of war but also a bearer of ruthless national ideology and the avenger of
> bestialities which had been inflicted upon German and racially related
> nations. Therefore the soldier must have full understanding for the neces-
> sity of a severe but just revenge on subhuman Jewry. The army has to aim
> at another purpose, i.e. the annihilation of revolts in the hinterland, which as
> experience proves, have always been caused by Jews.... This is the only way
> to fulfill our historic task to liberate the German people forever from the
> Asiatic–Jewish danger.[155]

In furtherance of the Reichenau Order, General Hoth issued his own
instructions to his troops on 17 November 1941:

> Every trace of active or passive resistance or of any kind of machinations by
> Bolshevik–Jewish agitators are [sic] to be immediately and pitilessly rooted
> out. The necessity of severe measures against elements foreign to people and
> kind, must be understood precisely by the soldiers. These circles are the spir-

itual pillars of Bolshevism, the tablebearers [priests] of its murder organization, the helpers of the partisans. It consists of the same Jewish class of people which has done so much harm to our Fatherland and by its hostile activity ... and anti-culture, which promotes anti-German currents in the whole world and which wants to be the bearer of revenge. Their annihilation is a law of self-preservation. Any soldier criticizing these measures has no memory for the former demoralizing traitorous activity lasting for years carried on among our own people by Jewish–Marxist elements.[156]

The prosecution revealed how the Wehrmacht similarly targeted Romani for extermination. Commonly identified with partisans in military correspondence, reports showed that units in Army Group North and South systematically killed Romani or handed them over to the S.D. as "a political measure."[157] The army was also involved in the elimination of so-called mental inferiors in the occupied territories. In fall 1941, General Wagner (the same Wagner who, along with Heydrich, worked out the details for the army's cooperation with the Einsatzgruppen) presided over a number of meetings in OKH headquarters during which the army defined its policy toward mental patients in newly conquered territories. Halder noted in his diary that on 20 September, Wagner declared, "Russians look on the feeble-minded as sacred beings. Killing them is necessary nonetheless."[158] Related to this, the prosecution produced evidence of two of the defendants' direct involvement in the murder of the mentally disabled. Tracing the correspondence between von Kuechler's 18th Army in Army Group North and the S.D., the prosecution detailed how on 24 December 1941, the S.D., with the army's express consent, shot 240 women patients (who were mentally ill or who had epilepsy or syphilis) at the monastery of Makawerawskaja-Pustinj.[159] In November 1941, army troops under General Reinhardt murdered ten inmates of an asylum at Kalinin. Reports produced at trial revealed that they had been killed on the pretext that they "posed a danger," but also, and significantly, because the army could not house or feed them.[160]

The Civilian Slave Labor Program

Described by the prosecution as "the revolting offspring of the aggressive wars and invasions," the civilian slave labor program was "designed to keep the German war machine rolling at the frightful expense of the freedom and lives of millions of persons." All of the defendants who held field commands in the East, the prosecution demonstrated, made huge numbers of prisoners available for prohibited labor.[161] According to the evidence, they used civilians at the front, indeed at times even while under fire, for illegal labor such as clearing mines, digging trenches, and building fortifications. At least 5 million workers were deported to Germany. The army conscripted men, women, and children alike, through decrees demanding "voluntary" service or by kidnapping them off the street or from their homes in the night. Deportation and conditions of work were cruel and inhumane. Documents revealed how the army completely disregarded the conscripts' most elementary needs, and failed to protect the integrity of families or the basic rights of individuals. The guiding principle was that slave laborers and prisoners of war should be housed, fed, and treated in such a way as to exploit them to the greatest possible extent at the lowest possible expense. All but Schniewind took part in this program.[162] For example, on 7 October 1943, the commander in chief of the 18th Army wrote to General von Kuechler, then commander in chief of Army Group North, warning against proceeding with a planned forced evacuation of 150,000 civilians requisitioned elsewhere for forced labor: "One must keep clearly in mind that these treks will be trains of misery. . . . Already up to the collection camps Luga and Jamburg the treks will have to cover up to 150 kilometres. Therefore they will be on their way up to two weeks. Considering the state of the clothing, especially the shoes, of the population and the expected weather, the participants of these marches will soon be in an indescribable state, especially the women and children."[163] Von Kuechler took no heed of the warning.

Those civilians who survived the deportation to work camps endured horrifying living conditions. Enclosed in barbed wire, often cut off from their families, denied food in order to compel labor, the young and old, healthy and sick, were pressed into service. The prosecution produced a report that had been sent to the army under Reinhardt:

> Men and women were assigned for work from Labor Camp Witebsk, which had been unable to work for quite some time. They were told they would be taken to a hospital. Among them were people seventy-eight years of age, blind, paralytics and people with heart diseases who collapsed at the slightest amount of work, women pregnant in the last stages up to the ninth month, people sick with bad abscesses, out of whose shoes pus ran, and some with frozen limbs.[164]

The Prosecution Closes Its Case

Telford Taylor and the other prosecutors took turns reading their closing statement on 10 August 1948, after the defense had presented their cases, but before the defendants' final pleas. They reviewed the indictment and addressed some of the most common defense arguments raised in this and other Nuremberg cases, such as the superior orders defense and the criticism of Control Council Law No. 10. They then briefly summarized which defendants could be most closely associated with which crimes and reiterated the prosecution's arguments regarding command responsibility. One can detect the prosecutors' fatigue with the trial and frustration at some of the defense's more outlandish claims, as in places they described the defense cases with sarcasm and contempt.[165]

Looking at the case as a whole, the prosecution had offered a detailed and comprehensive exposition of the "staggering enormity" of Wehrmacht crime.[166] Their theories of the defendants' individual responsibilities were similarly broad: action, knowledge, and position all linked the defendants to the foregoing crimes. Notably, at the conclusion of "this long and profoundly important trial," the prosecution emphasized that the defendants should be held accountable not only for their professional failings, but for their moral failings as well.[167] It was in the generals' sometimes ambiguous relationship to the Führer that the American prosecutors had identified the defendants' most damning dereliction. This was one of the most interesting aspects of the prosecution's case. There were several instances in the course of presenting evidence that the prosecutors admitted that both some defendants (for example, von Leeb) and other Wehrmacht leaders (for example, Beck and Canaris) clearly and openly protested against particular policies and orders. However, they consistently interpreted these instances simply as proof of the defendants' awareness that these orders and policies were indeed criminal. Interestingly, although the defense raised it several times, the prosecution never mentioned the 20 July 1944 assassination attempt against Hitler, which was mainly planned and carried out by army officers. One can surmise, however, that it would have been similarly presented as yet further evidence of the military's recognition of Hitler's patent criminality.

Therefore, while the prosecution conceded that at times the accused may not have trusted Hitler, they reminded the tribunal that these soldiers had nonetheless "lent him their active and energetic collaboration and put their talents at his disposal."[168] Moreover, none had shown any remorse during the proceedings for their participation in Hitler's criminal enterprise. The prosecution drew the tribunal's attention to the fact that throughout the trial, the defendants had resorted to inconsistent and implausible excuses and had "denied knowledge of things which must have truly assailed all their seven senses." Insisting that these were neither unintelligent nor insensitive men, the prosecution contended that they had always been capable of exercising moral judgment about their actions, for which they were now being called to account.[169] Although so much of the prosecution's conception of criminality had hinged on the defendants' ranks and overall legal definition of command responsibility, with this insistence on the moral dimension of their acts, the prosecution sought to personalize the guilt shared by many. Indeed, while the evidence presented at trial implicated the institution of the Wehrmacht as a whole, the prosecution endeavored to put individual faces to these crimes. In the end, after all, this trial was a trial of thirteen individuals.[170] However, the prosecution did not always clearly draw the lines demarcating individual responsibility. They left it to the judges to sift through the avalanche of documentation to determine the specifics of the defendants' actions and affix the boundaries of personal liability. Ultimately, the judges were much narrower in their conception of criminal responsibility than the prosecution would have hoped. However, before explaining the judgment, we must first examine the arguments raised by the defense.

4

The Soldiers' Defense

It is a strange wrangling over words and phrases which we will have to develop before the tribunal.
—Opening Statement for Walter Warlimont

A MERE SIX MONTHS after Germany's surrender, on 19 November 1945, five Wehrmacht field marshals and generals, including the future High Command case defendant Walter Warlimont, submitted a memorandum to the International Military Tribunal (IMT) "to give testimony on behalf of the entire German army."[1] Aiming to provide the Allies with "as clear a picture in this area as possible," they considered it their duty to all soldiers to advise the prosecuting powers that the army had stood against the party and the S.S., that it had disapproved of nearly all of Hitler's decisions, and that it had opposed the perpetration of war crimes.[2] These were men whose senior ranks and leading positions had provided them with a privileged view of events as they actually unfolded. General Warlimont was the Oberkommando der Wehrmacht (OKW) chief of the Department of National Defense, Field Marshal Walter von Brauchitsch was commander in chief of the High Command of the Army until Hitler took over this post in late 1941, Field Marshal Erich von Manstein was commander of Army Group South until March 1944, General Franz Halder was chief of the Army General Staff until September 1942, and General Siegfried Westphal was chief of the General Staff to the commander in chief west until May 1945. Highly placed, they seemed credible witnesses. Although they had composed the memorandum from memory and appended no supporting documents, each declared that he would be willing to swear an oath to its accuracy.

In the memo, the generals asserted that they had not felt obligated to oppose Hitler because the soldier's credo was "to stay completely away from politics." They even went so far as to criticize the military men who had orchestrated the 20 July 1944 coup against Hitler, arguing: "It could not be a task of leading officers to break the army's back. Anyone who sets out to change his country's government is responsible for providing a new and better government."[3] In any case, they contended that the Führer had promised peace at home and abroad, although without mentioning the domestic violence that secured this peace. Regarding the war, they emphasized that the army had only been interested in preparing a defensive force and that its leaders had been shocked by Hitler's successive announcements of new campaigns. They had supported these campaigns only in the face of mounting threats from other nations, the generals alleged, and repudiated any shared ideological commitment to Hitler's aims.[4] They omitted, minimized, or blamed on others all of the military's violations of the laws and customs of war. Glossing over the army's indigenous antisemitism, they denied all knowledge of the concentration camps and claimed ignorance of the S.S. and Security Service's (S.D.'s) "political tasks" in the East.[5] The generals insisted that all army leaders were outraged by Hitler's racial and political goals once they learned of them. Regarding the army's brutal antipartisan campaign, the memorandum maintained that the partisans' cruelty toward German forces justified their actions, but that Wehrmacht officers uniformly ignored Hitler's harshest orders for reprisal.[6] Each one of these claims could be soundly disproved by evidence in Allied possession, prompting one historian to describe the memorandum as an "unscrupulous falsifying of history and a clean conscience."[7] Indeed, although each of the authors could be connected to the foregoing offenses either by knowledge or participation, none accepted any responsibility for his actions or his failure to act.[8]

It is difficult, on the basis of the available evidence, to make a claim as to a deliberate and concerted conspiracy among senior Wehrmacht officers to distort the truth about their motivations, goals, and conduct during World War II. On the one hand, less than 1 percent of German generals and admirals wrote their memoirs. On the other hand, those who did write their memoirs left records that are generally unreliable as to the political dimensions of their activities.[9] The issue is further complicated by the fact that, as shown in the High Command case, the language of military directives blurred the lines between civilian and combatant, Jew and partisan, unlawful belligerent and ideological foe. Frequently, the state leadership co-opted formerly valid principles such as "military necessity" in order to provide unmistakably racial and political policies (such as the targeting of Jews and Communists as part of the antipartisan campaign) with a veneer of legitimacy. When, under judicial examination, the High Command case defendants parroted back these same justifications, it is sometimes difficult to ascertain whether they were using these excuses consciously and expediently, aware of their inaccuracy, or whether they had deceived themselves into believing the rhetoric, either at the time or after the fact.[10]

The Memorandum of the Generals is significant because it represents

The High Command case defendants listen to the proceedings. Back row, left to right: Walter Warlimont, Otto Woehler, Rudolf Lehmann. Front row, left to right: Wilhelm von Leeb, Hugo Sperrle, Georg von Kuechler, Hermann Hoth, Hans Reinhardt. Photograph taken by the U.S. Army Signal Corps, courtesy of the Harry S. Truman Library, Judge John C. Young Photo Collection.

the pattern of defense arguments used by military officers at the International Military Tribunal, the Subsequent Nuremberg Proceedings, and throughout the posttrial years by West German veterans, private citizens, and institutions in their efforts to win clemency for soldiers convicted of war crimes. Together, these claims created an alternate image of the attitudes and actions of the Wehrmacht to the one advanced by the prosecution at Nuremberg. Drawing on the defendants' opening statements, closing briefs, evidence, and testimony, this chapter will explain the defense strategy used in the High Command case. The similarities between this early statement of innocence and the claims set forth in the 1948 trial of the accused field marshals and generals will emerge with striking consistency.

The chapter focuses on the arguments of five of the defendants: Hermann Hoth, Georg von Kuechler, Hans Reinhardt, Walter Warlimont, and

Hermann Reinecke, for several reasons. They represented both staff officers and field commanders, their testimony was the most evocative and provided a representation of the spectrum of explanations offered during proceedings, and ultimately they earned some of the trial's most severe sentences. The chapter also concentrates on four crimes of the indictment: the transmission and implementation of the Commissar Order, the antipartisan campaign, the Wehrmacht's treatment of Jews, and the Wehrmacht's treatment of Soviet prisoners of war. These were the four pillars of Wehrmacht criminality.

Hans Laternser Opens the Defense for the High Command Case

The defense commenced arguments on 12 April 1948. Each defendant's attorney read his client's opening statement in succession. During the weeks that followed, each of the accused and his witnesses took the stand and were examined by their own and prosecution counsel. The case for each defendant lasted an average of one week. Although each of the field marshals and generals, in conjunction with his attorney, mounted a separate defense, Wilhelm von Leeb's attorney, Hans Laternser, frequently acted as spokesman for the entire group. Laternser had become somewhat of an expert in defending soldiers in Allied war crimes trials. He led the defense of the OKW at the IMT, pleaded for Albert Kesselring before a British military court in Rome in 1947, and represented Wilhelm List during the Nuremberg Hostage case. In later years, he made a career out of defending some of Germany's most notorious war criminals. During the 1960s, he represented defendants in both Auschwitz trials and the euthanasia trial. A historian of the 1963 Auschwitz trial, where Laternser represented five of the accused, describes him as the "most right wing" of the defense attorneys there.[11] However, his past affiliation with the Nazi Party was ambiguous. Investigations related to his 1948 denazification hearing revealed that while a young clerk at the Cologne district court, he had applied to join the Nazi Party. Strangely, however, his status never changed from that of membership candidate, and he insisted during his hearing that he had been a staunch opponent of the regime. He even claimed that he had been connected to the 20 July assassination plot. Laternser described his activity for the Nuremberg courts as proof only that he was "a seeker and servant of truth and justice." The denazification tribunal ultimately categorized him as a "fellow-traveler" (*Mitläufer*) of the regime, concluding that his opposi-

tion never exceeded the level of listening to prohibited foreign radio broad-
casts and privately uttering anti-Nazi insults. Therefore, he did not meet the
threshold stipulated by law to be categorized as "exonerated."[12]

Laternser affected a theatrical courtroom style. A former colleague from
the IMT attributed it to his early training as an opera singer.[13] On the day
of the arraignment, setting the tone for the High Command case, he presented a detailed motion denying the jurisdiction of the court. Indeed, he
outpaced his fellow counselors in lodging objections and noticeably tested
the tribunal's and prosecuting attorneys' patience with his frequent inter-
ruptions. However, his skills as a lawyer earned him the respect of his peers.
Throughout proceedings, the other defense attorneys often deferred to his
briefs on matters such as the crimes against peace and conspiracy charges.

Laternser began the defense phase of the High Command case when
he read the opening statement for von Leeb. The other defense cases were
remarkably similar to this one, as well as to the 1945 Memorandum of the
Generals. A summary of Laternser's statement therefore provides an
overview of the scope, direction, and tone of all the others. In general, his
strategy can be described as both offensive and defensive. He attacked the
validity of the law and the jurisdiction of the court, and he defended the
Wehrmacht as an institution and the particular activities and attitudes of
his client.

Laternser began by refuting the prosecution's "caricature" of the German
officer corps—that is, their depiction of this group's "craving for war" and
"contempt for international law."[14] He argued that throughout the nineteenth century, the German army had only been involved in wars of national
unification, and thereafter had built up its military forces solely because of
the country's vulnerable position on the continent.[15] He claimed that Germany's war literature had never glorified combat, quoting the revered Count
Alfried von Schlieffen, who declared that "even a victorious war is a national
disaster."[16] Last, he contended that the German profession of arms had been
dedicated exclusively to defense and cited von Leeb's book on defensive
strategy.[17]

As a whole, Laternser continued, the officer corps had always been
"dominated by decency" and displayed respect for the laws of war.[18] It was
only when their opponent had erased the line separating civilian from belligerent (a reference to Soviet partisan warfare) that the German officers
"were reproached for their actions."[19] In any case, Laternser added, the
army's policies on antipartisan fighting (and civilian labor, hostage reprisals,
and so on) were required by battle conditions, he contended that military
necessity was still an accepted principle in law. By way of illustration, he referenced the Allied bombing of German cities and the Americans' release of

the atomic bomb in Japan.[20] Further, the tribunal adjudicating the recent Hostage case had recently ruled that partisans could legally be shot, and anyway, he concluded, the Soviet partisans' particular cruelty amply justified the severity of the Wehrmacht's antipartisan campaign.[21]

Laternser argued that the army had not been blind followers of Hitler, citing as proof the 20 July coup and a long list of senior officers who had either been relieved of duty or dishonorably discharged for their opposition to the Führer's aims. He contended that the men in the dock had been brought to trial solely because of their rank and the inescapable duties of their position. He pleaded for the tribunal to consider the conditions under which they had been called to act, which had been created by "a dictator of the worst kind . . . who placed these decent people of the best families into tragic situations." He insisted that no prosecutor could understand the context of their conduct, and consequently "could play no part in the objective recording of history."[22]

Regarding the law and procedure of the court, Laternser insisted that the crimes against peace charge was new law and therefore violated the axiom "nullum crimen sine lege, nulla poena sine lege," the commonly cited defense claim at Nuremberg that law cannot be applied retroactively.[23] At the same time, he disputed the characterization of Germany as aggressive, arguing that the invasion of France was retaliatory because that country had declared war on Germany first, and that Operation Barbarossa was a preemptive strike in anticipation of imminent attack.[24] Driving his point home, he referenced the contemporary situation: "Since the end of the war we have seen Russia extend its political and military sphere of power . . . we can only imagine the next steps."[25] Arguing that Germany had long recognized that violent expansion was an inherent feature of Communist ideology, it alone had undertaken the "life and death" struggle in order to forestall the Soviet takeover of the continent.[26]

In response to the prosecution's evidence of army-implemented orders and policies constituting war crimes and crimes against humanity, Laternser offered denials. He maintained that von Leeb was an honorable and humane soldier who had not seen, issued, transmitted, approved, or abetted such orders. He insisted that it had been impossible to issue oral or written countermanding orders. Documents reporting the killing of commissars, he claimed, were wrongly interpreted. Von Leeb knew nothing of the Einsatzgruppen's anti-Jewish activities, nor did he possess the judicial, executive, or territorial authority required to halt them. When, by circumstance, he learned of one particular massacre, he believed this to be an isolated "excess" and lodged a protest with the appropriate authorities.[27] Von Leeb, Laternser asserted, was unaware of the state's plan to destroy the Jews until he arrived at Nuremberg for trial.[28]

Laternser concluded the opening statement by listing the numerous disadvantages the defense staff had allegedly encountered in preparing their cases. He contended that the prosecution had had more time, larger staffs, and better resources. Once proceedings began, Laternser continued, because the prosecution's evidence was not read into the record, the defendants and their attorneys struggled to keep up. He ended by declaring that none of the defense attorneys had been able to fulfill their responsibilities satisfactorily.[29]

Laternser's opening statement contained all the elements that the other lawyers would repeat and develop throughout proceedings: the attack on the Nuremberg trials' law and procedure, the refutation of German militarism, allegations regarding the misinterpretation of the evidence, the denial of criminality, the appeal to soldierly duty and superior orders, the justification and rationalization of the defendants' conduct in war, and an emphasis on the good character of the accused. Each of these elements will be explored in greater depth in the following pages.

Elements of the Defense Strategy: The Attack on the Nuremberg Trial

Each of the High Command defense cases sought to undermine the validity of the Nuremberg process. Defense attorneys argued that Control Council Law No. 10, which outlined the charges and procedure of the court, was ex post facto law and therefore could not legally be applied. They focused particular attention on crimes against peace. In an effort to buttress the enforceability of this charge, the prosecution had cited various prewar treaties and conventions, particularly the 1928 Kellogg–Briand Pact, as evidence that German officers were well aware of the prohibition against aggressive war. The defense countered that this pact bestowed no criminal responsibility on individual violators and therefore the defendants could not have been cognizant of the repercussions of their participation in these campaigns.[30] Moreover, the defense argued that the charge was tainted by the Soviets' own wartime actions. Citing the principle of tu quoque, meaning literally "you as well," the defense insisted that German defendants could not be held accountable for an offense of which another nation's leaders were also guilty. Therefore, they urged, having the Soviets as signatories of Control Council Law No. 10 and the crimes against peace charge despite their own invasions of Poland and Finland undermined the integrity of these laws and prevented their legal application to Germany.[31]

Apart from the alleged invalid law, the defense attorneys in the High Command trial also cited various practical impediments to the preparation of their cases. In keeping with the overall depiction of the proceedings as victor's justice, they claimed that the Americans had provided them with insufficient space and time in which to work, that they had had unequal access to the archives from which to draw their exhibits, that the prosecution had withheld exonerating documents, and that the English translations of the documents contained numerous misleading errors.[32] These complaints were largely unfounded. Although the High Command case began to take shape during the researching and presentation of the OKW case for the IMT, the prosecution had not devoted the entire intervening period to preparing its case. The Office of the Chief of Counsel for War Crimes was, after all, prosecuting eleven other trials. At any rate, seven of the thirteen defense attorneys in the High Command case were familiar with the procedure applied and Wehrmacht-related evidence submitted at Nuremberg, having served either at the IMT or other Subsequent Nuremberg Proceedings, or both. Laternser, as mentioned above, served at the IMT and on the Hostage case. The others had also served at one or more of the IMT, Hostage, Race and Settlement Office–S.S. (RuSHA), Krupp, Einsatzgruppen, Justice, Pohl, and Ministries trials.[33]

The defense teams had ample time to prepare their cases. Attorneys had been able to begin work from the moment of the arraignment on 30 December 1947. In addition, after the trial commenced in February 1948, the defendants and their attorneys, upon request, were excused from proceedings to finalize their cases. They were able to keep abreast of developments through the written transcriptions of the daily proceedings provided to them. Moreover, the trial recessed for one month after the prosecution completed its case to provide the defense with extra time to prepare their arguments. Regarding the availability of evidence, the tribunal granted the defense equal access to the Washington, D.C., archives from which to draw exhibits.[34] Further, the prosecution's document books were translated in full and provided to the defense. Complete copies of the original documents were also available.

It should be noted here how the trial evidence was organized. The prosecution and defense counsel assembled their exhibits into document books. Apart from witness affidavits, these books consisted of translated excerpts from the original documents, with a notation summarizing each exhibit's contents and indicating for which defendant the exhibit was intended to speak for or against. Although some of these excerpts extended into hundreds of pages, generally, the whole document was not translated for the document books. However, copies of the original German documents were available for consultation and included in the trial records. Over the course of proceedings, defense counsel frequently raised concerns that an excerpt might be taken out of context and reentered the same document in its complete version, which was duly translated for the tribunal. In all cases where the defense identified translation errors, the corrections were entered into the record. Further, within the Nuremberg Palace of Justice, the Americans created an office, called the Defense Center, that was devoted to supporting the defense attorneys in all aspects of their work. This included running a document room from which counsel could obtain transcripts and copies of the evidence and document books of all past and current Nuremberg trials.[35]

In terms of practical support, the Americans salaried, billeted, and fed the defense attorneys and financed their travel to Nuremberg, as well as the transport of their assistants and witnesses. They obtained affidavits from foreign countries and scheduled interrogations. They furnished defense counsel with secretarial staff, office space, and office supplies. Even their laundry soap and cigarettes were provided free of charge.[36] It should be noted that despite their protestations, the defense attorneys in the High Command case managed to submit 2,122 evidence exhibits, called sixty-six witnesses to the stand, and used eighty-five trial days—over three times as many as the prosecution—in which to present arguments.[37]

The real challenges confronting the defense were neither office space nor the nascent status of laws being applied in court. Indeed, the attorneys' largest hurdle was that of the overwhelming mass of incriminating evidence against their clients. The prosecution had already produced the orders, policies, and reports signed, approved, and transmitted by the men in the dock. As a result, defense counsel were forced to attack the form and substance of the evidence itself. These efforts would consume the bulk of their energy for the remaining trial days.

The Problems with Evidence

As the prosecution had focused on documents, the defense declared that its own case would rest on the proper "interpretation" and "correct reading" of this evidence.[38] This defense strategy worked in three ways. First, the defendants attempted to attribute alternative meanings to the terminology of these exhibits. Next, they argued that the documents had to be understood within the context of their creation—that is, the circumstances of Hitler's dictatorship and the conditions of battle in the East. Finally, the defendants claimed that exculpatory evidence had either disappeared or, alternatively, could never have existed in documentary form.

Defendants and their representatives insisted that much of the prosecution's evidence, such as army activity and counterintelligence reports, could not be taken at face value. They argued that because the documents in question had been written hurriedly during mobile warfare, their authors had kept them brief and had had no time to include important details about the circumstances prompting the action described.[39] Further, they claimed that many military reports were deliberately incorrect and reported the execution of an order on which higher authorities had insisted, but which was not actually carried out, because it was seen to be wrong or inexpedient.[40] Counterintelligence reports, they maintained, could also be misleading. For instance, many of these reports detailed the killing of civilians, but very few took the time to note the circumstances and details "that alone make the events comprehensible," such as the preceding judicial investigation that "undoubtedly" ascertained their guilt and justified the measure.[41] For all these reasons, Hoth's attorney declared that "military reports made in time of war ... have only a very limited probative value."[42]

The defense also disputed the prosecution's interpretation of specific words and phrases. Several attorneys insisted, for example, that the army's use of the term "special treatment," a notorious designation of murder, referred only to segregation, not to killing.[43] Reinhardt contested the prosecution's translation of an order dealing with the shooting of civilian slave laborers who attempted to escape, insisting that the order intended only that they be fired upon but not shot dead.[44] Hoth's representative contended that it was only an unfortunate coincidence that the army's expression "concentration camp" was the same as that used by the S.S. to describe the camps they established and administered because by no means did the same conditions prevail in both.[45] He and others also maintained that "partisan suspect" referred only to persons who had been suspected of partisan activity and whose activities were later confirmed by thorough interrogations and investigations.[46]

These explanations provided a partial refutation of some of the prosecution's most damaging evidence. In view of the foregoing claims about the deceptive appearance of the prosecution's exhibits, the defense could argue, for instance, that an army activity report describing the "special treatment of commissars" proved nothing, for several reasons. It meant only that they were segregated from other captured prisoners, which was not illegal. Or, if the surrounding language denoted that they had actually been killed, then this still suggested no crime, because the report had simply omitted the fact that the commissars had been proven to have been involved in sabotage and therefore their executions were justifiable. Alternatively, the defense could claim that the report was, in fact, a deliberate falsification of the events, in an attempt to make authorities believe that the Commissar Order was indeed implemented.

Another way that the defense attempted to undermine the probative value of the prosecution's evidence was by emphasizing context. Indeed, it was one challenge, the defense insisted, for the prosecution to properly translate and understand the language of their orders and reports. However, as Reinecke's attorney eloquently (if unconvincingly) suggested, the documents also spoke "a language of time and circumstance" that no prosecuting attorney or court interpreter could adequately and successfully express.[47] This elusive language had mainly to do, so the argument went, with the circumstances of the Nazi state and the conditions of battle in the East.

The Importance of Context: The Dictatorship and Soldierly Duty

The prosecution had presented scores of documents purporting to show the defendants' willing support for and implementation of Hitler's aggressive military aims and racial and political policies. The defense countered that the prosecution had not taken sufficient account of the context of the Nazi rise to power and the circumstances imposed by the dictatorship. By this omission, they stressed, the prosecution had mistaken the defendants' exercise of duty and obedience for manifestations of acquiescence and approval.

The defendants and their representatives clearly bristled at the prosecution's allegations regarding "German militarism" and their unquestioning support for Hitler. All of the defendants emphasized the supposed strict division between the military and political spheres, reminding the tribunal that because they could not vote, they could not influence government. That said, even from their outsider perspective, they contended that there seemed to have been no cause for opposition to Hitler. In fact, during the early years of the regime, there appeared to be good reason to support the new Führer. As Warlimont's representative argued, Hitler seemed to have come to power legally and democratically, and the army could see the good done in Germany by the National Socialist government. Moreover, Hitler's diplomatic triumph at Munich in September 1938 only confirmed his prestige and legitimacy as a national leader.[48]

In a pretrial interrogation, Reinecke admitted that he had become attracted to National Socialism out of a sincere belief that the creation of a "people's community [was] the only salvation for Germany from the state of confusion which reigned before 1933."[49] In his opening statement, Hoth admitted to having been taken in by the propaganda message that Germany faced an unavoidable choice between Nazism and Communism.[50] In any case, whether they agreed with Hitler or not, the defendants maintained, they were bound by the constitution and by their oath to obey his directives.[51]

The generals insisted that their outward cooperation with Hitler's policies by no means signaled their inward agreement with these policies' underlying aims. Regarding their support for rearmament, several of the accused contended that it was within Germany's rights to ensure its defensive capabilities. Moreover, they asserted, the western nations' tolerance of Hitler's repudiation of the Versailles Treaty's disarmament clauses was evidence of their tacit concession to these rights.[52] None of the accused admitted to having had any inkling of the war that lay ahead. In general, all the defendants emphasized Hitler's Basic Order No. 1, which declared that "nobody must know, nobody must know more, nobody must know in advance, unless Hitler so wills."[53] In effect, all claimed ignorance of Hitler's nefarious intentions until it was too late. Against the prosecution's evidence that these defendants had been present at key conferences in which Hitler had announced his criminal plans for invasion and the murderous policies that would accompany them, the defendants argued that they had had no control or influence over Hitler's aims. Referring to these conferences as "one-sided manifestations of intentions," the defendants insisted that there was nothing they could do to reason with him or dissuade him from his goals.[54]

When asked why they did not resign their posts, the accused emphasized the circumstances of the dictatorship that severely restricted their freedom of action. Reinecke and Reinhardt argued, respectively, that no "free citizen of the United States" could understand what it was like to live in Nazi Germany, nor could any "non-military court thinking according to a democratic worldview understand the commander's predicament at the time."[55] The "omnipresent coercion of the state," they and others alleged, controlled their free will and personal expression, creating a situation they could not change, as Warlimont asserted, "without becoming traitors or violators of their oath."[56] Open resistance was futile or suicide, they claimed, and resignation would only have aggravated the situation, as others, perhaps more compliant members of the party or S.S., would simply have taken their place.[57]

One of the most reflective defendants on his allegiance to the state was

Georg von Kuechler. Under examination during the trial, he adamantly insisted that his military career had served the German nation alone, never Hitler and the Nazi Party. He had considered resignation several times before the war broke out, given his alleged political differences with Hitler and especially the Fritsch affair, but each time he had concluded that it was his duty to remain in his position out of loyalty to the Fatherland. Once hostilities began, von Kuechler stated, resignation would have been tantamount to desertion: "If millions of Germans had to fight and give their lives and blood for the fight in World War II, I, being an old soldier, was obliged to do my duty as long as there were tasks given to me."[58] He couched these claims almost in self-sacrificial terms: he had set aside, under great moral strain, personal political convictions in order to serve the greater good. Having made the decision to remain at his post, von Kuechler continued, he had recognized that there would be a conflict of conscience. He professed that there was tension between his duty of obedience to orders issued by the head of state and his superior officers, his duty toward his subordinates and soldiers, and his conscience. He could not satisfy all three.[59] The underlying contention, however, was clear: neither blind obedience to the Führer nor craven lust for war, and least of all approval of Hitler's ideological aims, had motivated his activities.[60]

The Reality of Combat in the East

The defense discussion of conditions in the East served both to explain the conditions under which certain policies and actions came about and to justify the severity of these policies and actions as militarily necessary. Because most of the prosecution evidence pertaining to the war crimes and crimes against humanity counts concerned events in the East, the defense argued that "the basic facts and conditions which were decisive for the conduct of the war must have been completely different" in that theater.[61] Indeed, the defendants were unanimous that "the battle in the East had its own character" and that "war in Russia had its own methods."[62] This was due in part to the physical conditions of the eastern front. The vastness of the territory, the harsh winter, and the muddy season severed communications, strangled supply lines, and defeated efforts at maintaining adequate shelter. All of these conditions had repercussions, they claimed, for the monitoring of other state agencies' activities with regard to their treatment of Soviet civilians and for the care of Russian prisoners of war.

However, the uniqueness of the eastern theater was most pronounced, the defendants attested, in the "character" of the eastern opponent. As von Kuechler's counsel declared: "The difference in the conduct of the war, when compared to that customary up to that time, was solely and exclusively due to the adversary who now opposed them. It was a political adversary, a soldier who for decades had been instructed politically in the Bolshevist principles and who had been turned into a fanatic by the high-ranking leaders."[63] Hoth's attorney added:

> Inasmuch as [the Russian] is European, he is in general, good-natured, loyal and, as he lacks initiative to take individual action, tends to be led, and in fact needs leadership. . . . The Russian man is deeply rooted in nature and has strongly developed instincts. If his emotions are roused by external forces, they can result in extremely cruel excesses. . . . The Communist government which, in full awareness of this fact, at the time used above all Asiatic types, knew how to incite these instincts again and again and to exploit them in the interest of its military plans. This also explains the institution of the partisans and the political commissars. Both were something essentially strange to the German soldier. He was used to fac[ing] an enemy in open combat, an opponent who knew to respect the laws and customs of international law. Thus, all these artificially engendered difficulties were added to the natural difficulties encountered in the East.[64]

Given the physical conditions of the battlefront and the nature of the opponent, which, it was emphasized, only those who had actually experienced combat in the East could comprehend, the defense insisted that "the language of the then issued orders and the severity of the executed measures [could] be understood" and, by extension, condoned.[65]

The foregoing arguments were concerned with responding to the prosecution's evidence. However, the defense was also intent on explaining why they could not prove their claims to innocence with evidence of their own. They raised several excuses. Quite simply, some argued that exonerating witnesses and former allies in their alleged resistance efforts were dead, or were being held prisoner in Russia.[66] They also pointed out that by the very nature of their opposition activity, no records were ever created. As Warlimont's representative argued, his client's resistance had been guarded and clandestine, and "what was secret and discreet is hard to prove now."[67] There was a problem, too, with the defendants' own memories. Throughout the trial, the defense insisted that guilt could only be assigned after entering the innermost thoughts of the accused at the moment in which he made the decision producing the event in question. However, "the abundance and the dynamics of the impressions which overwhelmed him at the time, sometimes with the speed of lightning," were nearly impossible to reconstruct, even for the men who had participated in the act themselves, let alone on the basis of written records.[68]

The Defense Evidence

The defense drew on a wide variety of material to support their case. There were fragments of speeches by Hitler and other German statesmen, copies of Hitler's decrees, and excerpts from German newspapers such as the *Völkische Beobachter*, which purported to prove the compelling nature of the propaganda on the need to combat Communism, the justifiability of war with the East, and the general conditions of life under the dictatorship. Articles by legal scholars in Germany and abroad challenged the legitimacy of various parts of the indictment, especially the crimes against peace and conspiracy charges. The defense cited judgments of other Nuremberg trials, particularly the Hostage case, to reinforce their contentions as to the legality of killing hostages and partisans. Army organization charts on the chain of command and service records of the accused were submitted to make the case that certain orders could have been transmitted through alternative channels, or that on the particular date of a particular event, the defendant was on leave or occupied elsewhere. Attorneys also submitted army activity and situation reports, letters and teletypes from field commanders, secret field police and counterintelligence reports, and interrogation records of partisans, prisoners of war, and saboteurs that illustrated the severity of battle conditions and proved partisan activity, as well as bolstered their claims that no executions of civilians were carried out before thorough investigations into their suspected hostile activities.[69]

One of the key collections of documents consisted of seventy-eight excerpts from a book entitled *Bolshevik Crimes against the Laws of Warfare and Humanity*, compiled by defense attorneys at Nuremberg, which described, in lurid detail, atrocities committed by the Russians against German combatants and Soviet nationals. The defense also resubmitted certain prosecution exhibits with additional pages, in order, they argued, to better explain the context of the events they discussed. Notably, Reinhardt's documentary defense consisted exclusively of expanded versions of prosecution exhibits.[70] Among the largest categories of evidence was the witness affidavit. Although many witnesses appeared in court to confirm the defendants' claims, scores more recorded their testimony in witness statements. For example, Hermann Hoth's attorney alone submitted ninety-two affidavits along with his closing brief. These declarations affirmed, citing past conversations with him or personal observations, that Hoth believed that the war against Russia was only a preventive strike; that the Commissar Order was not executed in strict adherence to its wording in his area of command; that he had attempted to improve the conditions for POWs; that although he had passed on the Barbarossa Jurisdiction Order to his troops, they had not complied with it because Hoth ordered reprisals against German soldiers who unjustly killed Soviet civilians; and that he had expressed his indignation over the liquidation of the Jews in the East.[71]

Significantly, and in stark contrast to the prosecution, the defense rarely quoted from their evidence in the presentation of their case or in their opening and closing statements or briefs. The defense lawyers relied almost exclusively on the testimony of the defendants and witnesses. Moreover, they spent most of this time responding to particular prosecution exhibits, using the strategies outlined above—that is, emphasizing context and wording. Whereas the prosecution's case was mainly documentary, the defense case was more rhetorical.

The defendants' protestations over the problems with the trial evidence did not challenge all the evidence of their individual contributions to the crimes outlined in the indictment. When confronted with the specifics of these exhibits, the accused resorted to two other general strategies: denial (of knowledge, of participation, of illegality, of memory) and justification. What follow are representative excerpts of the lines of argumentation the defendants used in their briefs and courtroom testimony to respond to four key elements of the indictment.

Responding to the Crimes in the Indictment: The Commissar Order

The Commissar Order was the cornerstone in the prosecution's case against the Wehrmacht leaders. As discussed in chapter 3, it called for the immediate execution of all Red Army commissars, the ideological overseers of Soviet troops, whom German forces caught in battle. Walter Warlimont, who in his capacity as chief of the OKW Department of National Defense had been closely involved in drafting the order, issued it on 6 June 1941. Two days later, Commander in Chief of the Army von Brauchitsch reissued it, with a few amendments, including a directive that executions only be carried out by order of an officer.[72] Despite his direct connection with the order, Warlimont insisted that for all intents and purposes, Hitler had issued it himself during the 30 March 1941 conference in which he announced his intention to unleash a "war of extermination" on the USSR.[73] Warlimont maintained that although he had participated in drafting the order, he had hoped to prevent it from being released. But, he added, a colleague, General Wagner (who later brokered the agreement among the army, the S.D., and Security Police [SIPO] for cooperation in anti-Jewish policy), had convinced him otherwise. Wagner allegedly argued that if the army did not submit the order, then Hitler would simply use the S.D. at the front lines in order to implement it and the army would lose complete control.[74]

The only alternative, Warlimont asserted, was to distribute some kind of letter or statement limiting potential "excesses." Von Brauchitsch accomplished this, he maintained, when he formulated his amendments. Because, Warlimont's attorney attested, he was satisfied that the army commander in chief's anticipated additions would guarantee that no commissars would be killed, he saw no reason to change the wording of the Commissar Order or to hesitate in its distribution. When confronted by the prosecution's copious evidence that commissars were indeed executed, Warlimont answered that these reports must either have been fabricated or referred to commissars killed in combat.[75] Warlimont's brief provided the tribunal with a view of the order from the perspective of the staff officer. Von Kuechler and Hoth discussed it from their points of view as field commanders.

At trial, von Kuechler admitted that although von Brauchitsch had made amendments to "soften it," the Commissar Order still conflicted with his views on warfare. Nonetheless, he had passed it on to his subordinates, but he had simultaneously expressed his repudiation of it on ethical and disciplinary grounds.[76] He stated that he had believed that his expression of opposition would prevent it from being carried out. He had not been able, he insisted, simply to ignore it:

> Between the devil and the deep blue sea I had to find a way through. On the one hand I did not want to be endangered by being regarded as a disobedient commander, because it was quite obvious that it would become known and that it would be said the commander-in-chief did not carry out an order. On the other hand, however, I did want to express my own opinion in regard to this order that it wasn't to be followed. That was my position.[77]

He declared that he believed that his verbal intervention had been successful. On his trips to the front line, he claimed, he never heard about commissars being shot, and he alleged that reports and division and corps diaries that mentioned the shooting of commissars were never communicated to him. In any case, he surmised, the reports presented here in court showing that commissars were shot could have been referring to commissars shot in battle.[78]

Hoth's defense took a somewhat different, and not altogether consistent, approach. He maintained that although the commissar was a "blood-thirsty beast," he too disapproved of the order, believing that it "asked very much of the troops," who would have expected to treat the commissars according to the laws governing the custody of any prisoners of war.[79] Still, Hoth emphasized, he had to pass it on; otherwise, he would have been discharged and another commander would have taken his place, over whom Hitler would have exercised even stricter supervision.[80] Interestingly, he added that he had also felt obliged to transmit the order because it would inevitably have become known to his troops one way or another, and at least if he announced it, he could make his opposition to it known to his men. When prodded on what he said to his soldiers to mitigate the order, Hoth responded that he could no longer remember, but that certainly he had added nothing, such as, perhaps, a remark insisting on the soldiers' "strictest observance" of it.[81]

The examining attorney reminded Hoth that the German military penal code prohibited the execution of orders with "criminal intent." Hoth answered that he never considered that it might have been illegal, arguing that Hitler, the legal head of state, had issued it, and that at that time he had had full confidence in him. "Even today I think that . . . [Hitler's] intention really was to protect the troops against the commissars. I do not think that Hitler had any criminal intent," Hoth concluded. As the other defendants testified before and after him, Hoth claimed that the reports attesting to the execution of commissars in the field referred to commissars who had been shot in combat and/or that the reports were designed to mislead higher authorities into believing the order was carried out.[82]

Antipartisan Warfare

The Wehrmacht's campaign to destroy Soviet partisan resistance included measures such as the May 1941 Barbarossa Jurisdiction Order and hostage reprisals. As explained in chapter 3, the Barbarossa Jurisdiction Order suspended courts-martial for civilians suspected of sabotage or guerilla warfare, allowed and encouraged the summary killing of these individuals and collective reprisals against whole communities, and explicitly relieved the army of the obligation to punish German soldiers who had committed crimes against civilians. The prosecution had submitted numerous documents that they alleged demonstrated that the order was implemented, not only to combat partisans, but as pretext for the wholesale slaughter of racial and political enemies, such as Communists and Jews. The prosecution also cited the infamous September 1941 Hostage Reprisal Order, which called for the execution of fifty to one hundred Communists for every German life lost to insurrection in the occupied territories. Both these policies, the prosecution contended, had provoked and prolonged the partisan movement.

Hoth testified that "this pest of decent warfare" in Russia did not result from atrocities committed by German soldiers, nor was it "a desperate battle of the tortured Russian population." Hoth claimed that Russian civilians were friendly toward the Germans, declaring that when he and his troops arrived in new towns in the East, Russians greeted them with gifts of bread and sang songs of welcome.[83] He attributed the development of the partisan movement exclusively to Stalin's 3 July 1941 radio address (delivered after the distribution of the Barbarossa Jurisdiction Order), which called for the formation of partisan detachments in order to wage war "without mercy" and to pursue every German and annihilate him everywhere.[84]

When he received the Barbarossa Jurisdiction Order, Hoth explained, he suspected no criminal intent behind it and duly transmitted it to his troops. He declared that the order "made sense" because it took Russian conditions into account.[85] In this connection, he made repeated references to the "cruel fury of the partisans," as depicted in the defense document book on Soviet atrocities.[86] In answer to prosecution exhibits on reprisal measures related to the Barbarossa Jurisdiction Order, he argued, alternatively, that he had no recollection of some of these events, that these measures could not be proven to have been illegal (because partisans had forfeited the legal protections afforded to lawful belligerents), and that these excesses might have occurred anyway, without his transmittal of the Barbarossa Jurisdiction Order.[87] In general, Hoth insisted that suspected partisans were always conclusively interrogated and their guilt confirmed before their execution, and that these investigations "were conducted so carefully" that no mistakes occurred.[88]

Reinhardt elaborated on the antipartisan campaign as a "bitter necessity, in genuine self-defense."[89] He explained that in his army area in 1943, partisan bands blew up thousands of railway lines in a single night, destroyed army property and vehicles, murdered sleeping troops, attacked hospital trains, and raided whole villages for food and supplies on which his troops depended for their lives.[90] He too stressed the atrocity reports of partisan strikes against Germans, drawing particular attention to an account of a

"Jewish-led" partisan band that allegedly ate German soldiers alive.[91] Despite provocation of this kind, Reinhardt maintained that investigations of suspected partisans were thorough and "infallible," and that only the truly guilty "received their well-earned punishment."[92] Neither political enmity nor Hitler's policy of extermination had motivated the measures, he assured the court:

> My troops were compelled to conduct antipartisan warfare in order to defend themselves; purely military self-defense; they had to fight against this band warfare which had been forced upon us from which we could suffer severely and which we had to defend ourselves against, and if this band warfare cost lives, I expressly state very great sacrifices and victims on both sides resulted, and the guilt is attached to those organizations which initiated this band warfare and not to my soldiers who defended themselves against this type of warfare. The struggle was hard, bitter and serious; it was conducted by my soldiers only with the greatest reluctance.[93]

Von Kuechler also testified that there had been nothing wanton about this fight. He insisted that suspected partisans and partisan helpers had been interrogated at length, the activities of partisans or partisan helpers had always been proven beyond doubt, and an officer had made the final judgment.[94] Further, the activities of partisan helpers had to have been proven to be voluntary. Von Kuechler claimed that the civilian population had been duly warned against such activities via posters, their town mayors, and other public announcements.[95] Von Kuechler freely admitted that he had transmitted a request to the commander of the rear area that everyone without identification was to be viewed as a partisan and shot, but he argued that decent, honest members of the population would not have been affected by such a measure. Anyway, he said, even in these cases, connections to partisans still had to be proven. Von Kuechler reflected that he had never experienced such morale-destroying measures at the hands of any other civilian population, and he conceded that excesses did occur.[96] After all, he seemed to suggest, "war is hell":

> You just have to visualize how these battles took their course; how we had to fight for every strong point and every house; how our soldiers found mutilated comrades of theirs . . . and in this battle rage, and in this passion, in this indignation, about such offenses on the other side, actions might well have occurred which would have certainly not happened in a calmer situation. But I suppose that will be the same in every battle. . . . When you see the white in the enemy's eyes, and when it is a question of his life or mine,

then passions run away with you and many things happen which might have better remained undone.[97]

Nonetheless, von Kuechler was adamant: some arbitrary actions may have occurred, but in no way did they prevail.[98]

The Wehrmacht's Treatment of Jews

The prosecution described the cooperation between the Wehrmacht and the Einsatzgruppen in their persecution of the Jews as a "model of complicity in crime," in that the army trapped, identified, and confined Jews, and then handed them over to the S.D., who merely struck the final blow. As discussed in chapter 3, the High Command of the Army (Oberkommando des Heeres, or OKH) and OKW, represented by General Wagner, and chief of the SIPO and S.D. Heydrich struck an agreement in April 1941 calling for the army's logistical support (rations, shelter, supplies, movement) of the Einsatzgruppen in order for them to perform their political/security tasks of eliminating so-called racial and ideological enemies of the state. The prosecution produced additional evidence of the army's direct participation with them in mass shootings of Jews, Romani, and other "undesirable elements."

During the preparation of the High Command case, the defendant Otto Woehler, who had been chief of staff of the 11th Army where Einsatzgruppe D chief Otto Ohlendorf did his work, was interrogated (interestingly, with Ohlendorf present) on the army's connection to this organization. Woehler admitted that his commander Field Marshal Erich von Manstein had awarded iron crosses and army merit crosses to Einsatzgruppen men, adding that he would not have done so had he been ignorant or disapproving of their activities. Although he tried to avoid implicating the army in the actual killings by saying that the Einsatzgruppen's tasks were carried out on special orders from Heinrich Himmler, he conceded that "cooperation with the Einsatzgruppen was generally free of friction."[99] Needless to say, there was no trace of this openness at trial. Rather, all the defendants who had been implicated in the anti-Jewish actions denied categorically that they had known of the Einsatzgruppen's political-racial functions, let alone that they had helped carry them out.

In rebuttal, the prosecution called Otto Ohlendorf to the stand, where he testified that the Einsatzgruppen had regularly informed the army of all their tasks and that frequently the two organizations coordinated participation in "liquidation actions."[100] It is telling of the damaging impact of Ohlendorf's testimony that, more than any other prosecution witness, he elicited the strongest reaction from the defendants. They called him a liar, or declared simply that he was wrong.[101] Perhaps more imaginatively, War-limont argued that no witness possessing the "double-track morality of the S.S." could be trusted to speak the truth about German generals.[102]

When confronted with specific evidence regarding their individual con-nections to anti-Jewish actions, the accused responded with various expla-nations. Von Kuechler insisted that he had known nothing of the S.D. and their atrocities during the war in Russia and that he had heard of the Ein-satzgruppen for the first time at Nuremberg.[103] He could not remember having received orders regarding the actions of the S.D. and S.S., and he denied having received reports of their activities.[104] He surmised that the cooperation between the Wehrmacht and the Einsatzgruppen mentioned in these reports had to do only with their helping in fighting at the front, antipartisan activities, and interrogations.[105] Orders for army cooperation with the S.D. produced at trial had been transmitted, he declared, without his knowledge or consent. In any case, he continued, all police and political measures had fallen outside his executive power.[106] He explained:

> If I may give you an example and if I may describe executive power as a cake or a pudding it would mean that a lot of pieces were cut off this cake or out of this pudding. . . . If one had got the whole cake it would mean that one would reign supreme in one's area—but as it happened one was only a par-tial master of one's area. . . . I was the commander-in-chief of the army group and it was really my only task to wage operations and there was urgent need all the time all over this front. . . . Throughout all these years when I was commander-in-chief of the army group, there were constantly heavy defensive battles raging which used up the whole strength of the com-mander-in-chief. . . . It was only natural therefore, that concerning those events which were further remote, further to the rear . . . one could not con-cern oneself much. . . . I did not have to concern myself with the S.D.—and police channels were entirely on their own responsibility.[107]

Von Kuechler claimed never to have heard during the war about the shooting of Jews as a political measure, and his only explanation for their separate listing in field reports was that this had been the whim of the reporter.[108] Underlying all these claims, the constant refrain was that Jews were not shot because of their race, but because of their role in the war: "Jews were not shot because they were Jews—they were convicted of hav-ing helped or participated in partisan warfare"; "Jews were not shot because they were Jews but because they had participated somehow with partisans"; and "I don't think the Wehrmacht troops would shoot them simply because they were Jews—they had to have been partisans."[109]

Hermann Hoth's testimony regarding these crimes is interesting because he had been personally implicated in inciting anti-Jewish violence among his troops. In October 1941, General von Reichenau issued an order calling for the army's "revenge on sub-human Jewry." In furtherance of this order, Hoth issued his own instructions to his men a month later, requiring the immediate and pitiless rooting out of every trace of active and passive "Bolshevik–Jewish" resistance.[110] Linking them to the "same Jewish class of people which has done so much harm to our Fatherland," he called the annihilation of Bolshevik Jews "a law of self-preservation."[111] Hoth offered a lengthy explanation for the language he used and sought to clarify his actual intentions in issuing this order.

First, he declared that he had issued this order exclusively to his regimental commanders, not directly to the soldiers. It was up to these commanders to explain its contents to officers, who would transmit the message "in such a form as was suitable for them."[112] He insisted that his objective in issuing this order was simply to encourage his troops to be vigilant about the emerging partisan movement in Ukraine, where they were posted. "The German soldier," he explained, "in his good nature . . . easily forgot that he was still in the enemy's territory."[113] He wished to remind them of their task to "break the power of Bolshevism."[114] He said that he had in mind "the bestial cruelty of the Red Army soldiers against our prisoners and atrocities . . . committed by individual civilians," and he wished to remind the German soldier of these things in order to shore up his fighting morale.[115]

He denied that Hitler's racial theory played any role in the formulation of this order and declared that he personally was not opposed to race mixing between Germans and Slavs, and that he had never been an antisemite.[116] At the same time, he believed that the large influx of eastern Jews into Berlin during the interwar years and "their influence in Germany's economy, in German literature, in the German press, in the theater, in certain professions . . . brought about a strong tension in Germany."[117] Because of this tension, Hoth explained, he wasn't "a friend to the Jews," but he nonetheless felt that the Nazis' "coercive measures" were wrong.[118] It was, he surmised, because of the Nazis' treatment of the Jews in Germany that Jewish opinion turned against the Germans, particularly in Russia.[119] Once deployed to the eastern front, he believed that it was his duty to explain "the mood of the Russian Jew" to his troops. However, he emphasized, he never intended for his order to result in any physical harm, and he maintained that his soldiers "carried out [their] hard profession with clean hands."[120]

Hoth claimed to have known nothing about the so-called Führer Order calling for the extermination of Jews because they were Jews.[121] He consistently claimed, as had von Kuechler, that all liquidations of Jews were carried out because they had committed some crime (duly investigated and proven) against German forces. That Jews were implicated so frequently in this connection was no surprise, Hoth volunteered, because "it was a matter of common knowledge in Russia that it was the Jews in particular who participated to a very large extent in sabotage, espionage, etc."[122]

The Wehrmacht's Treatment of Soviet Prisoners of War

Hermann Reinecke's testimony on this count was important because as chief of the General Armed Forces Office (Allgemeines Wehrmachtamt) in the OKW, he had supervised all POW affairs. The prosecution had shown that he had formulated policies for the screening, segregation, and elimination of certain categories of Soviet POWs. In practice, the army cooperated closely with the SIPO, S.D., and Gestapo in carrying out these policies. Reports from the prisoner camps themselves revealed that POWs suffered abuse and neglect on an unprecedented scale. The army pressed them into illegal and dangerous labor, and confined them in primitive enclosures without sufficient shelter, clothing, food, or medical care. Death rates exceeded 80 percent in some of the camps under the defendants' jurisdiction.

Reinecke admitted that he had participated in the composition and issuance of decrees that "were contrary to international law," but he insisted that he was only an accessory acting under superior orders. Indeed, he claimed that he had suggested only positive and helpful measures for prisoners, and that all policies to the detriment of the captives, such as the directives for the "special treatment" of Russian POWs, came directly and exclusively from Hitler or Keitel.[123] He emphasized that he had possessed no criminal intent, and he had attempted to forestall certain measures by delaying or mitigating particular decrees. He added that open resistance was senseless, in that he only would have been removed without influencing the course of events at all. So, he concluded, he remained at his post, "using a minor evil as a tactical means to prevent great evil."[124]

On the other hand, he attempted to defend some of the Wehrmacht's policies toward Soviet POWs. He repeatedly made reference to Russia's nonadherence to the Geneva Convention, which released Germany of all legal obligations to treat their prisoners of war according to its standards.[125]

Further, he explained, the Soviets' cruel treatment of German prisoners and the conduct of Soviet prisoners toward their German captors justified the particularly severe measures.[126] His attorney declared, "Many a military preventive measure is explained by the character of the Russian POWs, in particular those of Asiatic stock. Given the opportunity, the Russian POW has a tendency towards uncontrolled conduct. Consequently, it happened repeatedly that Russian POWs attacked and killed guards who had been too careless or trusting. It was, furthermore, common knowledge that escaped Russian POWs committed any kind of outrage, especially robbery, assault and murder."[127]

Testimony from field commanders also denied the existence of any ill will toward their Russian prisoners. Hoth declared that on his numerous trips among the troops, he observed that they treated their captives as humanely as possible under the circumstances. He claimed that the prisoners felt so genuinely grateful for their treatment by German forces that one could have granted them a furlough and they would have returned. He emphasized that they never called their prisoners by a pejorative name "such as the word 'Boche' [that] applied to German prisoners of war." Indeed, his men's nickname for their prisoners was the friendly "Ivan"—indicative, he insisted, "of the family-like relationship that our soldiers had to the Russian prisoners of war."[128]

Von Kuechler ventured a little further in his testimony, admitting that POWs endured great hardships during their internment. But, he insisted that they had been in distress because they were in very poor condition when they were captured: weak, diseased, half-starved, and without winter clothing. The field marshal stated that he personally had visited all the POW camps and had ordered improvements whenever and wherever possible. For example, he claimed, horses that had died near the camps were butchered and the meat was distributed among the POWs; he had permitted bonfires to be lit when there was no danger of air raids; and he had established hospitals staffed by Russian doctors and supplied by the army with equipment and medicine. He claimed always to have cut his own troops' rations when forced to reduce the POWs' food allotment.[129] He asserted further that army staff had deliberately exaggerated mortality rates in the camps in order to impress upon the superior agencies the desperate need for supplies.[130] The other key condition causing the POWs such grief, von Kuechler added, was the harsh winter of 1941 to 1942, which he called an "act of God." Von Kuechler categorically denied that the prisoners' poor condition was due to malicious intent or deliberate neglect. As for the report that alleged the 16th Army (then part of his Army Group North) had killed wounded POWs, he explained that that must have been a clerical error.[131]

The Appeal to Character

At some point in almost all their cases, the defendants raised the issue of their character. They intended this to apply to the tribunal's overall assessment of their alleged criminal intent. In general, they claimed that they had done all that was within their power to oppose, mitigate, delay, and offset the negative consequences of Hitler's aims. Here especially witness testimony and affidavits played a crucial role. For instance, a witness appearing on behalf of Reinhardt emphasized the general's kindness and goodwill toward the Soviet civilians. Upon his regular trips to German-supervised labor columns of civilian workers, the witness explained, he inquired into the laborers' state of health, as well as their accommodations and supply, ending always with the inquiry: "What is lacking?"[132] Reinhardt himself lived a modest life, taking quarters in only two rooms of a peasant's house. He was alleged to have stated that he didn't want anyone driven from his home because of his needs.[133]

Another witness attested to Reinhardt's faith: "he in a very rare manner combined the best soldierly traditions with the highest principles of humanity. War and its many crises and dangers has torn all masks from our faces. I think that everybody got to know the other fellow as he really was. We all knew that the general used all his force; that he derived all his energy from his deep, profound belief in God." His "irreproachable conduct" and "chivalrous attitude" were guided by a sense of the coming final reckoning with God, the witness affirmed.[134] All of his troops, he concluded, revered Reinhardt as a father because of the kindness and care he showed them.[135] In his closing brief, Reinhardt's attorney conceded that "during a war, wrong decisions cannot always be avoided."[136] However, he cautioned, one could not put oneself in his place, and to pass judgment on him required that one consider his personality: "a high sense of responsibility, deeply religious feelings, the straight line of humanity, justice and chivalry, and his unerringly humane attitude." Reinhardt, his counsel concluded, did not deny all mistakes; "he only claims that he acted as a soldier . . . as uprightly, as justly and as humanely as his conscience bade him and as the situation of his soldiers allowed."[137]

The content of witness affidavits submitted on behalf of Reinhardt overlapped with those for Georg von Kuechler. The areas on which they agreed consisted of examples of von Kuechler's efforts to restore economic stability, as well as medical and religious services for the civilians in the zones of occupation. Many depicted him as having an empathetic personality: conscious of the consequences of his decisions and constantly seeking to avoid unnecessary hardships on civilian populations. They asserted that he had always helped civilians and prisoners of war whenever he could. Most of the statements declared that he had been a fierce and outspoken critic of Hitler and the party and had a high sense of honor. They described him as warm-hearted, kind, and humanitarian in outlook. Given his character, they could not believe that he could have committed any crimes.

Although there were undoubtedly numerous cases of criminal behavior among the defendants, one cannot conclude that they acted criminally in all instances. Here too von Kuechler offers a striking example. He and wit-nesses testified to two personal interventions in response to anti-Jewish measures in Poland at the beginning of the war. In the town of Wlawa, he had heard that a police detachment had taken measures against the Jews there. In response, he claims, he canceled all anti-Jewish decrees and had his troops disarm the detachment. He had then ensured that the policemen were returned to East Prussia and that court-martial investigations were ini-tiated against them. In the second incident, a Waffen–S.S. artillery regiment had instigated a pogrom against the Jews of Roczan. Von Kuechler alleged that he reproached the S.S. commanders for these crimes and that they were court-martialed. However, dissatisfied with the verdict and sentence, he had ordered a retrial. At that point, von Kuechler stated, Himmler took steps to have an independent S.S. court-martial assume jurisdiction. As punishment for his interference, von Kuechler stressed, he was the only senior officer participating in the Polish campaign to be passed over for promotion.[138] It is likely that Johannes Blaskowitz, who was indicted in the High Command case but who committed suicide shortly after proceedings began, also protested S.S. atrocities against Jews in Poland and was denied promotion in return.[139] Because of his suicide, the court never investigated the issue. Regarding von Kuechler's claims, interestingly, the prosecution never dis-puted his intercession on behalf of Jews in Poland. At the same time, the tribunal later convicted him of the widespread application of the Barbarossa Jurisdiction Order—that is, the murder of civilians, including Jews, some-times on the flimsiest of pretexts, in his area of command in the Soviet Union. All we can conclude is that these defendants were not always con-sistent in their actions, and that their motivations were complex. In any case, as explained in chapter 3, the defendants' motivations were not of great con-cern to the prosecutors. Ultimately, their actions mattered more than their intentions in the assignment of responsibility and guilt.

The prosecution's image of Wehrmacht crime possessed a compelling coherence. First, they identified specific Nazi ideological aims; then they described the invasions, orders, and policies in furtherance of those aims; and last they produced ground-level reports showing the fulfillment of these orders and policies. The evidence they submitted in court showed that the targets and victims of these plans and directives matched ideological pre-conceptions with such consistency and in such numbers that one could not deny the true aims underlying the military's actions.

The defense constructed their alternative image of the Wehrmacht's conduct in the war with a variety of elements: context, justification, denials, and the officers' character. They used similar explanations for different crimes; at other times, they offered several excuses for the same event. Their case lacked the logical consistency and coherence offered by the opposing side. Therefore, even though they submitted more exhibits than the prosecution, they did not match the latter's impact. It is significant that the defense did not quote extensively from their evidence in their briefs, relying instead on witness testimony and affidavits, which were as dubious and unverifiable as the defendants' own versions of events.

A fascinating aspect of the defendants' testimony is their Janus-faced relationship with the Nazi state's ideological goals. The defendants never denied that Hitler and the S.S. formulated and executed racial and political policies. At certain moments in their defense, the accused even used some of the same ideological tropes that infused these policies, such as equating Jews with Bolsheviks, and citing the "inhuman fanaticism and cruelty of the Asiatic Russian." Nonetheless, in all instances of the army's involvement in killing Jews, Romani, and Communists, they insisted that these persons were not persecuted for ideological reasons, but that they had been caught in the act or had been proven to have violated the military code of conduct between belligerents and civilians.[140] Never did they admit the indispensable connection between their function as soldiers—as conquerors, pacifiers, and occupiers—and the achievement of Nazi goals. Instead, they viewed their being implicated in these crimes as merely the product of historical circumstance, for which they could be pitied. They certainly showed no remorse.

The tribunal granted the defendants the final word in the High Command case. They in turn elected to have Wilhelm von Leeb, the most senior officer, present a closing statement on their behalf. Von Leeb was brief. Insisting that the accused never compromised their soldierly qualities of loyalty, obedience, duty, unselfishness, and gallantry, he contended that the only thing that had changed under the Nazi regime was what was demanded of them. With deep regret and profound sadness, he concluded that they had been victims of history: "No soldier in all the world has ever yet had to fight under such a load and tragedy. . . . We are soldiers who have upheld their soldierly honor even in this Second World War amidst turmoil and dictatorial violence."[141] Von Leeb's final plea was both reflective of and anticipatory of a larger trend among the West German public to remember the war from a perspective of, and using a vocabulary of, victimization. The wartime bombing of German cities, along with the expulsion of millions of ethnic Germans from eastern borderlands at the war's end, and the German POWs' prolonged captivity in the Soviet Union contributed significantly to the rhetoric of German victimization, which some have argued was both necessary for West Germany's reconstruction and a lasting impediment to its honest coming to terms with the past. Indeed, West Germans, in their search for a new national identity and in view of newly forming relations with the West, found it awkward and unpleasant to accept the history of the war in the East as an ideologically motivated campaign, and one that was instrumental in facilitating Hitler's plan for the final solution of the "Jewish problem." As one historian commented, "the view of the war adopted in West Germany was characterized by avoidance and denial of the true intentions of the campaign and the devastation it wrought." It took generations for this view to change.[142]

The continuity in the defense strategies of military men from 1945 to 1948 and beyond is another one of the most interesting aspects of the High Command case. The following chapters on the debate over imprisoned soldiers and West German efforts to free these war criminals reveal that broad sections of the public believed these claims. Advocates for the convicts insisted that these men had only done their duty, asserted that waging war in the East was not only justified but necessary, denied their contributions to Hitler's racial and political programs, and maintained that these individuals had never compromised their personal integrity, either as professional soldiers or as human beings. However, before revisiting the issue of the defense arguments' lasting resonance in German society, we must turn to the judgment and examine how the tribunal contended with the mountains of evidence and weighed the merits of the two diametrically opposed representations of these Wehrmacht leaders' actions.

5

Presiding Judge John Carlton Young
and the High Command Case
Judgment

> There isn't as much glamour to this as there appeared to be from a
> distance of 8000 miles.
> It's gosh awful work.
> —Presiding Judge John Carlton Young, 14 March 1948

WHEN IT CAME TO RENDERING JUDGMENT in the High Com-
mand case, the tribunal confronted an unenviable challenge. During 111
trial days, they had heard 89 witnesses, accepted 3,900 documents into evidence, and accumulated 10,000 transcript pages of proceedings. In addition
to contending with this massive record, they would have to adjudicate
unprecedented issues of law and fact, and weigh the merits and deficiencies
of fervently pleaded prosecution and defense arguments for thirteen individual defendants. The prosecution had presented devastating evidence of
criminal policies and orders conceived and implemented by the men in the
dock. Overlaying this was their far-reaching interpretation of command
responsibility, which, in essence, connected the criminality of a whole institution to the field marshals and generals brought to this trial. The defense
used all possible excuses and explanations to refute the defendants' knowledge of and participation in these crimes. At the same time, they juxtaposed
this strategy of denial with various arguments that sought to justify the brutal measures imposed in the East and gain understanding of the particular
predicament of the officer in combat. Last, in efforts to disengage the individual from the crime, the defense attempted to draw a distinction between
the grandfatherly defendant in the courtroom, the otherwise God-fearing,
compassionate, and upright citizen, and the soldier of whom Hitler, during
his war, had made dreadful, but inescapable, demands. The judges faced a

tremendous task, and they possessed only the most rudimentary guidelines with which to fulfill it.

Indeed, when the Allies created Control Council Law No. 10, they were rather vague about who actually would judge the war crimes proceedings it mandated. This law provided only that the accused should be brought before "an appropriate tribunal." Each individual occupation zone commander was responsible for determining the nature of the tribunal and its rules and procedures. There was some question among the occupation authorities as to whether these trials should use military officers or civilian judges to adjudicate the cases. Whereas the British opted to form courts-martial staffed by military officers, the Americans believed that the judgments would command more prestige in Germany and abroad if they came from civilian jurists. In addition, always with a view to the trial's didactic function, they wanted professionals experienced in judging complicated issues of law and fact who would set forth their decisions in detailed judicial opinions, which was not customary practice in courts-martial.

On 18 October 1946, the Office of the Military Government, U.S. (OMGUS), and the Subsequent Proceedings Division issued Military Government Ordinance No. 7, which stipulated that the judges would be drawn from the highest courts in the individual states or from the U.S. Supreme Court. They were recruited by the U.S. War Department, and once nominated, the U.S. military governor approved their selection and appointed them to a particular tribunal. Each tribunal comprised three judges, of which one was named presiding judge. U.S. Supreme Court Chief Justice Harlan Stone prohibited the nomination of Supreme Court judges because Robert Jackson's absence during the International Military Tribunal (IMT) proceedings had caused problems and delays in the adjudication of their cases. Ultimately thirty men—twenty-five state supreme court justices and five law school deans and prominent practicing attorneys—served in the twelve Subsequent Nuremberg Proceedings (SNP). Some of them served in more than one trial.

The tribunals were subordinate to OMGUS only in administrative matters. As for the day-to-day workings of the court, the tribunals were responsible to themselves. All three members of the individual tribunals attended proceedings. Each could ask questions of the defendants and witnesses, and they worked jointly on the judgments. For example, in the High Command case, the judges met several times to agree on their decisions and opinions, and then wrote various sections of the judgment separately. The presiding judge led proceedings and ruled on defense and prosecution motions and objections. He also sat on the Supervisory Committee of Presiding Judges, which assigned the cases among the tribunals and acted for all the judges in various administrative and executive matters. The presiding judge performed one other important function. Soon after the SNP got under way (six tribunals sat simultaneously), the concern arose that several tribunals might render inconsistent rulings on questions of law or procedure. To avoid this, OMGUS made a provision for a joint session of all tribunals (represented by their presidents) to meet and review such conflicts and render decisions that would thereafter be binding on all tribunals.[1]

Presiding Judge John Carlton Young

At first glance, little in John Carlton Young's background seemed to presage the momentous task entrusted to him as presiding judge in the High Command case. He was born in 1886 in Iowa, moved to Missouri as a boy, and worked there as a schoolteacher to fund his legal education. Called to the Missouri bar in 1912, he gained admission to the bars of Colorado and California over the following two years. He briefly taught at a military school in New Mexico before opening a law practice in Colorado Springs in 1914. He married Irene Xetah Lawrence one year before, and they eventually had two sons: John Jr. and Rush, both of whom served in World War II. John Jr., in fact, was in Nuremberg during the last days of the war. Described by Rush as "straight as a string," Young served as Pikes Peak region district attorney from 1925 to 1931. In 1931, he won a seat as district judge, no small victory given that he was a Democrat in a strongly Republican area. His predecessor described him as a "fair, fearless and impartial judge." He was elected to the Colorado Supreme Court in 1935, and he served as its chief justice from 1942 to 1945.[2] He had no formal training in international law, and throughout his time in Nuremberg, he was rather bemused that he should have been chosen to adjudicate an international law case. He never boasted about his prestigious role. Referring to the army-supplied letterhead identifying him as an "international jurist," in a note written from Nuremberg to a friend in Colorado Springs, he quipped: "I try to be reasonably humble in my arrogance over my new attainments and to bear in mind Aesop's story of the frog in the pool that wanted to be as big as the bull in the pasture, of course, with disastrous results."[3]

After the war, he surmised that he had been selected, aside from the fact that "no other Colorado Justices were free," because of an answer he gave in a preliminary interview. Asked to define a war crime, he replied: "it could be defined by putting an acetate overlay on the lists of crimes in the civilized countries of the world and determining which types most frequently

The High Command case tribunal. From left to right: Winfield Hale, John
Young, Justin Harding. Photograph taken by the U.S. Army Signal Corps,
courtesy of the Harry S. Truman Library, Judge John C. Young Photo Collection.

appeared. Those crimes such as murder, rape and assault should be defined
as war crimes because there would be near to unanimous agreement that
these things were criminal conduct."[4] Young's emphasis on those offenses
that could be universally declared criminal guided his judgment of the High
Command case. Suspicious of the looser procedures and new categories of
law applied at Nuremberg, Young interpreted the exhibits and founded his
judgment on what he believed to be internationally accepted legal standards
of conduct at the time of the events in question. As will be elaborated upon
below, he was much narrower in his construction of criminality and his consideration of evidence than the prosecution had wanted. As much as he
believed in the momentous historical implications of his decision, he held
fast to his role as a careful interpreter of the law, and he resisted the call of
using the trial to write a sweeping history of Wehrmacht criminality.

In temperament, Young was patriotic and perhaps somewhat isolation-
ist: his wariness of the United States becoming entangled in Europe's ongoing conflicts intensified the longer he remained in Germany. Still, being a

Freemason and a Lions' Club member, he also had a charitable spirit. In fact, he put great effort into aiding the immigration of his Nuremberg driver and cook to Canada and the United States, going so far as to call in a personal favor from a contact in Washington. He was a scholar as well as a lawyer, with abiding interests in philosophy, literature, religion, and medicine. He loved his family deeply. Always with a twinkle in his eye, he had a keen and often self-deprecating sense of humor.

Of the three members of the High Command case tribunal, Judge Winfield Hale of the Tennessee Court of Appeals was the most outspoken during proceedings. He used his role to interject questions of the defendants and witnesses that he thought would benefit the history books. He frequently asked for detailed insider views of leading personalities and major events, whether or not they had any legal bearing on the case. The third member of the tribunal, Justin Harding, district judge in Alaska, whom Young described as "a wiry little shrimp," was quieter, interrupting now and then only for points of clarification.[5] Young also was not an imposing presence during the High Command case proceedings. However, although he disclosed little of his personality at court, in scores of letters written from Nuremberg to his family, friends, and colleagues in the United States, with sharp perception and biting wit, he revealed his thoughts and opinions of the trial, its participants, and his contribution, and he provided a detailed account of the life of a Nuremberg judge.

The Life of an American Judge in Nuremberg

At Nuremberg, Young cut the figure of the quintessential American westerner. The army misplaced his and his wife's baggage on the journey overseas, so for the first six weeks, he sported a cowboy hat and sweater from home, most often paired with G.I. shoes and army pants (their acquisition, he remarked later, having been no mean feat, given his forty-four-inch waist).[6] During his year in Europe, Young was preoccupied by his ranch in Pikes Peak, Colorado. Indeed, a good portion of the letters to his sons was marked by concerns over whether his cattle were all accounted for and fat enough, speculations on what prices he might receive for them, the condition of his tractor, whether he should plant alfalfa or oats (or both) next season, and so on.[7]

He arrived in Nuremberg in time to preside over the arraignment of the defendants on 30 December 1947. However, no courtroom was available to accommodate the proceedings until 5 February.[8] The couple spent the intervening weeks traveling around Europe, visiting Switzerland, Luxembourg, and Prague. They went sightseeing in Berlin, and Young related with awe the eeriness of touring the Chancellery, Propaganda Ministry, and Reichstag, once the seats of so much power, and now empty, looted, and in shambles. Shocked and impressed by the devastation of the urban landscapes, he was saddened by the destruction, but not altogether sympathetic with the German people. He observed: "The old biblical quotation that the way of the transgressor as hard is borne out in these German cities."[9] While in Berlin, he met with General Lucius Clay, whom he portrayed as having "a dynamic personality and giv[ing] one the impression that any matters in his hands will not be neglected but intelligently looked after."[10]

Not all of his time could be spent touring, however, and daily life in Nuremberg left much to be desired. Even the presiding judge of a major war crimes trial had to send home for a stapler, drive eight miles to obtain a pan to fry his bacon, and rely on coffee as currency. He declared to John Jr.: "My conviction is that even a general in this area would go hungry and ragged if he had to live off the country unless he could speak profanity fluently and had the persistence of a bull terrier."[11] Feeling out of his depth regarding the local language and history, he ordered two books from New York that promised to teach German quickly and asked that his son dig out an old volume on European history from the basement of his home, in order that he might "camouflage [his] colossal ignorance with at least a thin veneer."[12] To his chagrin, the conditions of everyday living too often overpowered these early efforts at acclimatization. Describing his army-issue socks, he remarked to Rush: "[they] necessitate my speaking profanity when I ought to be concentrating on speaking German."[13]

While awaiting the start of the trial, Young also passed the time hunting wild boar with Judge Hale and preparing for the case—or as he put it, "trying to veneer my ignorance of international law with a smattering of information concerning what has been done in the Nuremberg trials."[14] He read over the IG Farben and Hostage case records, and he visited the ongoing Krupp proceedings.[15] He was not always comfortable with what he found. To a colleague in Colorado Springs, he declared:

I am glad you are not over here with your fixed and definite ideas of relevancy, hearsay, ex post facto and all the other foundations of the law on which you stand, for some of the things that are done to these ancient principles would make you "as crazy," to use an expression I heard the other day, "as a blind dog in a meat house." No man whose legal ideas show any arthritic tendencies has any business dabbling in international jurisprudence.[16]

Young seemed particularly perturbed by the rules of evidence applied at Nuremberg. Article VII of Control Council Law No. 10 stipulated: "The tribunal shall not be bound by technical rules of evidence. It shall adopt and apply to the greatest possible extent expeditious and non-technical procedure, and shall admit any evidence which it deems to have probative value." Referring to this in a letter to John Jr., he remarked doubtfully: "I think this means if it makes it look like what someone is trying to prove is so or isn't so it goes in."[17] Although ultimately Young was confident that the High Command case tribunal gave the defendants a fair hearing, his reservations and frustrations with international law never fully abated. He later likened his experience with it to surviving the Bataan death march.[18]

The Trial Begins

At first, Judge Young depicted the proceedings as both exciting and challenging: "I described coming here as being like having a ring-side seat at the development of the common law. It probably is but it also has characteristics of a ring-side seat at [a] Roman chariot race, a Spanish bull fight and a Rose Bowl game all going on simultaneously in the same arena. And one man tries to referee the performance."[19] However, the masses of documentary evidence and the plodding pace soon wore him down. By the end of the first month, he characterized the trial as a "grind," made even more arduous by Judge Wennerstrum's recent indiscretions at the conclusion of the Hostage case in February 1948. As explained in chapter 2, soon after his tribunal rendered judgment, Wennerstrum gave an interview in which he accused the prosecution of bias and Telford Taylor of blocking the defense's access to evidence, and criticized the Nuremberg trial system's lack of an appeal process. Of his diatribe, Young remarked: "He has given marvelous example of the value of the prayer 'Dear God please help me to keep my damn mouth shut.' A judge last of all should start effervescing. His judgment should speak his views. . . . This was a tough assignment and too much talk has not made it easier."[20] Indeed, as the trial progressed, Judge Young seldom discussed the day-to-day occurrences at court in detail and on the rare occasion when he did, he always prefaced his remarks with the reminder: "Private—Not for Publication."

Certain events demanded comment, however. Initially, Young was profoundly shocked by the Nazi crimes revealed to him during the proceedings. In mid-March 1948, he and his wife visited the Dachau concentration camp. To his sons, he professed: "You can't believe it when you are on the scene of such colossal horrors. Makes one wonder what if anything civilization means."[21] As time wore on, however, the very scale of the crimes and the monotony of the proceedings seemed to dull his earlier dismay. Toward the end of the trial, after having listened to one witness testify for seven days on the activities of the Einsatzgruppen, he remarked irreverently: "it is getting like the story Johnny [his grandson] likes—'Along came a locust and took another grain of corn.'—only it is 'Along came an S.D. and killed another bunch of Jews.'"[22]

From time to time, Young also touched on the defendants. Although Judge Hale viewed them rather generously, describing their attitude at court as "impeccable—neither defiant nor fawning" and admitted to feeling sympathetic toward von Leeb, that "salty old character," Young was without pity.[23] He referred to Blaskowitz as the "balcony hurdler" (as he had committed suicide after the arraignment by throwing himself over the prison's third-story catwalk), and, noting that Sperrle was gravely ill and could die and that Karl Hollidt might have cancer, he concluded: "Don't mind if either occurs."[24] Warlimont frustrated him to no end by never providing a simple and straight answer to the prosecutors' questions: "When I know he was fourth from Hitler not over fifth then I know he must have been in accord with most of Hitler's plans. . . . He himself is cagy, never could answer a question in precision, always go all the way around Robbin-hood's barn, alibi—alibi—alibi."[25] Over time, however, he viewed these officers with a curious fascination, and remarked to his sons: "It is certainly a queer sensation to see the pages of history turned by men who were there when the pages were written." Moreover, not all of them, he thought, were equally guilty. Of von Leeb and Halder, he declared that "both were very able men and anti-Hitler I am sure. They were in a hard box to get out of." He even suggested that there were three cases whose potential political value did not seem to justify their prosecution.[26] Although he never specified which defendants he had in mind, from the judgment we can deduce that he was referring to Wilhelm von Leeb, Otto Schniewind, and Hugo Sperrle. However, by the end of the proceedings, Young was convinced that the men before him were neither "dumb" nor "unobserving," and their continued allegiance to the Führer before and during the war represented a lapse in moral and professional judgment that no circumstance could mitigate. This belief was reinforced by Halder's impromptu characterization of Hitler, which was the highlight of the entire trial for Judges Young and Hale. Hale, in the interests of history, had asked for Halder's impressions of the Führer. Young included a copy of Halder's testimony in a letter to his sons. It read:

The picture which I gained of Hitler is as follows: An unusual power of intellect; an amazingly quick comprehension; but not a trained person who could adapt himself to logical lines of thought; a person with very strong emotional tendencies; his decisions were conditioned by what he called intuition, that is his emotions, but no clear logically thought-out considerations; his intellect also included an amazing power of imagination and fantasy which in an astonishing degree had its repercussion in his lines of thought or events; substantial parts of his character were a tremendous tenacity and energy of will-power which also enabled him to surmount all obstacles, even in minor matters. The thing that most impressed me about Hitler was the complete absence of any ethical or moral obligation; a man for whom there were no limits which he could not transcend by his action or his will; he knew only his purpose and the advantage that he pursued; that for him was the imperative call.[27]

It was plain enough to Young that following such a man into world war was utterly contemptible.

During the many long months in Nuremberg, the only nontrial issue that preoccupied him more than his ranch was the strain of the international situation. The Russians—or, as he referred to them, "those damn cusses"— were to him an imposing threat. He considered Communism "a hellish thing ... like a cancer" for which there was no cure, and the solidifying battle lines of the Cold War, indeed so close to his own position near the eastern border, together with the Soviet posturing over Berlin, left him feeling nervous and vulnerable. Likening the Americans' situation to that of "a bunch of sitting ducks," he declared repeatedly that he "never wanted to get away from anything so bad in my life."[28] He even visited Clay personally for assurances about American preparedness should relations collapse entirely.[29] The tension between the West and the Soviets, palpable "like an ever present tornado cloud," depressed him.[30] Eventually his view of the menacing "Rooskies" seeped into his overall view of trial: "most of the things were done to the Russians and I am getting so that doesn't seem so bad to me." For Young, there was a certain irony to the case's portrayal of the Soviets as victims: "It is certainly a peculiar situation to be trying men for aggressive war against a nation whose aggressive tactics have the world now in a state of turmoil and alarm. Just like trying one gangster for killing another gangster from a gang that is on a rampage while the trial is going on."[31]

There is no evidence from the judgment that his antipathy toward the Russians influenced his evaluation of the evidence. The longing for home, however, never diminished. "Hell to be a judge when it keeps you from seeing your own cattle," he lamented.[32] Indeed, almost from the time the trial began, Young was constantly making projections about when it would end and he could come home. He was nearly always wrong. Ultimately, he stayed six months longer than he anticipated when he accepted the job. Although he never wavered in his dedication to see his duties to completion, he considered the time away from family a sacrifice.[33] For consolation, he surrounded himself with photos of his sons, his grandchildren, and of course his ranch.

As the trial wound its weary way to a close, Young's trepidation about the upcoming task of writing the judgment became more pronounced: "Sometimes I wish I had remained a hay pitcher. I really excelled in that and a man should excel in something."[34] To be sure, writing the judgment posed several challenges. The first was the sheer volume of evidence and length of the transcript (10,000 pages) that had to be digested, analyzed, and evaluated. "However to classify the rubble dumped on us is to me a mystery," Young wondered.[35] The second challenge was the realization that the tribunal's verdict would be a statement of new international law, with the power of precedent over the conduct of all countries. Calling it "a damn serious business," Young expressed his acute awareness that "international law cannot be written for dictatorships alone but must be applicable to the whole family of nations and must spring from the composite thought of the nations."[36] He often doubted that he was up to the task, admitting, rather vulnerably, "when God makes little peas he makes an awful mistake to let them get in big pods."[37]

Composing the Judgment

Among Young's papers are the notes he took during proceedings, annotated copies of the evidence and transcript, and early drafts of his verdict. Leafing through the pages, one gets a sense of how he navigated the massive record and developed the basic principles on which his judgment was built. In a notebook, whose cover bore Young's inscription, "Some Suggestions and Bright Ideas in Here," he had sections on legal issues arising from the case, reminders to himself to read particular trials (such as the IG Farben, Hostage, and Yamashita cases), summaries of various defense lawyers' arguments, a list of issues to be addressed in the judgment, as well as lines and phrases encapsulating his opinion on fundamental points of contention: "Policy makers ones chargeable aggressive war," "a commander with knowledge at his peril carries out a criminal national policy," and so on.[38]

In a couple of letters, Young complained about the prosecution's strategy, which presented an overall environment of criminality (criminal orders producing criminal acts over a vast territory in which the defendants were located), which left him to sift through the mountains of exhibits for proof of individual wrongdoing: "In these cases we have corpus delicti to burn."[39] And:

> When it comes to tying things down I am simply appalled at the loose ends in the case. The rule has apparently been thoroughly established that individual responsibility must be shown, as in any ordinary criminal case, but there are many, as is always the case, who feel that if the corpus delicti is sufficiently atrocious that every person in the neighborhood is ipso facto connected criminally with it. It would be very easy to handle one of these cases under the principles of jurisprudence set forth in the Barbarossa Decree.[40]

But of course that wouldn't do. The judgment would be no blanket declaration of guilt, but a complex and differentiated appraisal of individual culpability. This took time. His work was complicated by the sudden death of Judge Hale's wife in early September, leaving two judges to do the work of three.[41] Young and Harding met to agree on basic principles, then wrote sections of the judgment independently.[42] In a letter home, Mrs. Young noted that her husband was "working harder than in all his life," laboring long into the night and on weekends. His nerves wore thin.[43] Ultimately, Young, ever humble about his contribution to the end product, hoped simply that it would be remembered "that I did the best I could in the place where I was with the things I had at my disposal."[44] He was confident that the tribunal had run a fair and impartial trial, and he contented himself with the knowledge that the soundness of their verdict would be left to posterity to assess:

> So far we have a record nobody can find fault with. We have from a judicial standpoint made a record in one of the most important cases in which there can be found no error, the only place for error is what we do on it. And that can be judged by history if we have a proper basis. After all it is all any of us do to become parcel and part of history.[45]

The Judgment

Anticipating worldwide interest, the American Public Information Office ventured that aside from the Berlin airlift, "no occupation story likely will compete with the decision of the [High Command case] tribunal . . . for

View of the mimeograph room at the Nuremberg Palace of Justice after the transcripts on the sentencing of the High Command case defendants had been run off. Courtesy of the Stadtarchiv Nürnberg, Photo A65-RA-121-D.

prominent news space."[46] Indeed, reporters from all the major news wire services and from as far away as Spain, Turkey, and Czechoslovakia appeared in the courtroom to hear the judgment.[47] Released on 27 October, Judge Young had requested that Hale return to Nuremberg for the two-day reading because he "never liked to sentence defendants," and he preferred to shoulder one-third over one-half of that task.[48]

The judgment, which had taken two and a half months to compose and which filled 316 transcript pages, began with a detailed exposition of the indictment, a review of the procedures applied at court, and a brief summary of the chronology of events. It outlined the primary governing laws, specifically Control Council Law No. 10 and the IMT judgment, which, according to Control Council Law No. 10, was to be regarded as a statement of international law by the SNP tribunals. It reviewed rulings on the tribunal's jurisdiction and defense arguments regarding ex post facto law and the tu quoque principle. In responding to the defense's claims that Control Council Law No. 10 represented new law and therefore violated the maxim "nulla poena sine lege," the tribunal declared that the contention was without merit.[49] Indeed, the validity of the basic laws of the court had so frequently been ruled on by the IMT and the other SNP that the tribunal did not see the need to repeat the exercise. The defense had also objected that the USSR was also guilty of aggressive war and therefore had no standing to accuse Germany of the same charge through its promulgation of the Nuremberg Charter and Control Council Law No. 10. The tribunal ruled simply that "an accused does not exculpate himself from a crime by showing that another committed a similar crime," and further, that both these laws were approved by nineteen nations other than its four principal signatories and therefore could be seen as a statement of international law.[50] After laying this foundation, the judgment moved swiftly toward addressing the individual charges.

The tribunal struck the conspiracy charge from the indictment, arguing that it brought no evidence or information to light not already raised by the other three charges. That is, because the defendants were already indicted as principals and/or accessories to war crimes, crimes against peace, and crimes against humanity (defined as having ordered or abetted an offense, taken a consenting part therein, or being connected to any plans or enterprises related to their commission), there appeared to be no separate basis for an additional charge. The tribunal was quick to add, however, that their opinion on the conspiracy count referred only to the facts in the case before them, and noted that the charge certainly might have merit in other cases.[51] As it turned out, however, the conspiracy count succeeded in only half of the SNP.

The conspiracy charge having been disposed of, the tribunal moved to a discussion of the so-called Controlling Principles in Trial—that is, the basic premises that governed their approach to the case, the evidence, and the defendants. The tribunal had taken its inspiration from Judge Hu Anderson's concurring opinion in the Krupp case. (It will be recalled that Judge Young spent a fair amount of time visiting those proceedings.) The first of these principles was that the judges considered that the tribunal had been formed to administer the law, separate from the political power of the Allies. Second, neither the identity of the defendants as former enemies nor the political priorities of the U.S. government had any bearing on their consideration of the case. The tribunal had been concerned solely with what the law (customary or codified) was at the time that the crimes had been committed, and whether the evidence showed that the defendants violated it. Related to this, the defendants were presumed innocent until proven guilty. Next, criminal statutes were interpreted restrictively: criminal responsibility was to be considered an individual matter, and criminal guilt had to be personal. Last, the tribunal rejected any application of ex post facto laws, arguing that to do so was tantamount to a denial of justice in international law. The tribunal also declared that the burden of proof had rested squarely with the prosecution, and in instances of ambiguity, the defendant had enjoyed the benefit of the doubt.[52]

The judgment next addressed the count of crimes against peace. Surprisingly, the tribunal issued no convictions on this count in the High Command case. The judges' reasoning offers an excellent example of how narrowly they interpreted the law. Beginning with the definition of war as "the implementation of a political policy by means of violence," the tribunal hastened to add that war in itself was not criminal. War could be justified, and armed forces retained internationally legitimate functions. Rather, it was the criminal intent of the initiator of war that gave it its illegal status. To their view, the essence of the crimes against peace charge was therefore participation in the initiation of invasions and in the planning, preparation, and waging of aggressive wars. Accordingly, criminality was to be confined to those who took part in the decision for war at the policy-making level and, still at the policy-making level, those who decided to continue or extend the war. The question then became one of where the boundary between policy makers and non–policy makers was located. It was clear that somewhere between Hitler and the common soldier lay the difference between the criminal and the excusable. However, Control Council Law No. 10, the tribunal continued, did not specify where that boundary lay, nor had any other Nuremberg trial drawn that line judicially.

It was obvious that the defendants, all of whom were high-ranking officers, had known Hitler's intentions to launch aggressive war; but, the tribunal concluded, neither their knowledge of his plans nor their rank made their subsequent participation criminal. The definition of a policy maker, according to the tribunal, was the capacity to shape or influence policy, which none of the defendants could be proven to have possessed. Undoubtedly, they had acted as the instruments of the policy makers, but the tribunal did not find that at the time of the events in question, international law criminalized those who acted as the executors of policy makers' plans. "We do not hesitate to state," the tribunal added,

> that it would have been eminently desireable had the commanders of the German Armed Forces refused to implement the policy of the Third Reich by means of aggressive war. It would have been creditable to them not to contribute to the cataclysmic catastrophe. This would have been the honorable and righteous thing to do, it would have been in the interest of their state. Had they done so they would have served their fatherland and humanity also.[53]

As the judges saw it, however, the failure of the accused was moral, not legal. Not having occupied a policy-making position at the moment war was initiated meant they could not be held responsible for crimes against peace. To be sure, the manner in which they waged war could be deemed criminal, and was to be dealt with in the last two remaining charges: war crimes and crimes against humanity.[54]

Proceeding from the IMT judgment, which was quoted at great length throughout the judgment, the tribunal was able to enter on record the vast spectrum of Wehrmacht crimes. That is, that judgment had already done the work of establishing the illegality of the Commissar and Commando orders, the treatment of prisoners of war, the Night and Fog Decree, the hostage reprisal policy, the enslavement of civilians, and the activities of the Einsatzgruppen.[55] "The record in the instant case," the tribunal declared, "is replete with horror. . . . No nation, no army and its leaders, of any time, civilized or uncivilized, and its leaders, labor under so great a load of guilt as do Hitler's Germany, its army, and its leaders."[56] The task before the High Command case tribunal was therefore limited to assessing which defendants could be individually connected to the foregoing crimes and criminal policies.[57] How that connection was made and what factors mitigated that connection were shaped by several issues: superior orders, the illegality of orders, the limits of command responsibility, the defendants' responsibilities as commanders of occupied territories, and their relationship with Hitler. All of these elements were discussed in turn and provide explanation of how the tribunal obtained the final guilty verdicts.

Although repeatedly raised as a defense, the tribunal did not accept the existence of superior orders as an excuse for participation in illegal orders or policies. Not only had the defendants failed to prove coercion (defined as "such imminent physical peril as to deprive [the defendant] of freedom to choose the right and refrain from the wrong"), but the tribunal reminded the court that it was a cardinal point that international law superseded national laws or directives. No state order could set aside the prohibition against murder, assault, abuse, and so on.[58] Moreover, the German Military Penal Code of 1872, still in force during World War II, declared that "the obeying subordinate shall be punished as an accomplice to an illegal order— if he exceeded it or if he knew the order was criminal." The tribunal noted that even Josef Goebbels himself, in the 28 May 1944 edition of the *Völkische Beobachter*, stated, "It is not provided in any military law that a soldier in the case of a despicable crime is exempt from punishment because he passes the responsibility to his superior, especially if orders of the latter are in evident contradiction to all human morality and every international usage of warfare."[59]

Both the military penal code and Goebbels's injunction placed importance on the criminality of the order being obvious. The tribunal emphasized this as well. Acknowledging that armies are built on discipline, wherein
orders must be obeyed, the tribunal declared that it is not the subordinate's
responsibility to screen superior orders for questionable points of legality.
To an extent, the judges conceded, the soldier has the right to believe that
the orders he receives are legal. Recognizing that many of the defendants in
this case were field commanders with "heavy responsibilities in active combat," the tribunal did not expect them to have assessed each order as a lawyer
might.[60] The tribunal concluded, therefore, that a defendant should only be
held accountable for implementing superior orders that were criminal "on
their face," or that the defendant could be presumed to have known were
criminal. Related to this, there was some question as to the limits of a commander's criminal responsibility for transmitting the illegal orders of his
superiors. Although the prosecution argued that a commander was responsible for the communication of a criminal order "in any manner whatsoever,"
the tribunal deemed this too far-reaching. For example, the record revealed
instances where the transmitting of orders was conducted by an army's staff,
bypassing the commander altogether. The principle applied for a finding of
guilt, then, was that there had to be evidence that the defendant personally
passed an order that was criminal on its face into the chain of command.[61]
    Discussion proceeded to one such criminal order. The tribunal noted
that no defendant had disputed the illegality of the Commissar Order.
Although the tribunal believed that some defendants did try to sabotage the
order, and some figures of commissars killed may have been exaggerated, the
record still showed that it was implemented throughout the army and that
many commissars were shot by units under the defendants' command.[62] The
judges held all defendants who could be shown to have known about the
order, to have passed it on to subordinates, and/or to have been aware that
it was implemented in their area of command criminally liable for its implementation.
    By contrast, dealing with another alleged criminal order, the Barbarossa
Jurisdiction Order, presented a challenge, and is an example of the tribunal's
view that commanders would only be held accountable for orders that were
criminal on their face.[63] This May 1941 Oberkommando der Wehrmacht
(OKW) order allowed for the murder of Soviet civilians suspected of any
activity considered hostile to German forces. The tribunal had reviewed the
order meticulously: it was quoted at length in the judgment, and pertinent
lines of the text were underlined and emphasized. The judges broke it down
into its two component parts. The order (1) called for the suspension of
courts-martial for the accused civilians, and (2) relieved commanders of the

obligation to try soldiers who committed crimes against enemy civilians.[64] The tribunal found that international law did not necessarily mandate courts-martial for offenses by civilians in occupied territories, nor did it clearly oblige commanders to prosecute delinquent soldiers. However, it did find that the practices of leaving summary proceedings to the discretion of a junior officer, shooting mere suspects, and killing whole groups in reprisal actions were criminal acts. In conclusion, then, the tribunal ruled that the Barbarossa Jurisdiction Order was not entirely illegal "on its face." The defendants' criminality therefore hinged on proof of their having transmitted the order without sufficient safeguards to prevent its illegal application and evidence of its misapplication by subordinate troops.[65]

The judges ruled similarly with regard to hostages and reprisals. The Hostage case had declared that hostages (even reprisal hostages) could legally be taken and killed, if done in strict compliance with certain preconditions, and as a last, desperate remedy against insurrection.[66] The High Command case judges were uncomfortable with this ruling, however, finding that international law was actually still hazy on this issue. Rather than rule on the legality or illegality of the hostage reprisal policy as a whole, the tribunal concluded that in this case, international legal safeguards had clearly been abused or ignored and that the killings of hostages amounted to plain murder.[67] In a similar vein, with regard to antipartisan warfare, the tribunal agreed that not all partisans met the The Hague Convention requirements for their recognition as lawful belligerents. However, the judges noted, the evidence clearly showed that entire groups had been classified as "partisans" before hostilities, suggesting that antipartisan measures were simply a pretext for the wholesale execution of state "enemies."[68] In practice, the definition of partisan was too broad, and the policy allowing for the execution of mere partisan suspects ("the most vicious classification") signified a "monstrous proposition," opening the way for large-scale abuse.[69] For their license to kill partisans without proof of their activities, the orders surrounding antipartisan warfare were deemed criminal on their face.[70] With regard to the hostage reprisal policy and the treatment of partisans and partisan suspects, where the evidence showed the defendants' support for or furtherance of the criminal application of these policies, they were deemed guilty of the charge.

Regarding the German army's treatment of prisoners of war, the tribunal referred to the Geneva and The Hague conventions' stipulations that armies owed POWs elementary care and were not to subject them to dangerous work. Although Russia, the defense had repeatedly emphasized, had not signed the Geneva Convention, the tribunal ruled that both these international treaties could be seen as expressing existing international law, and therefore binding on Germany, if not in letter, at least insofar as generally accepted custom. The tribunal was willing to concede that many Soviet POWs undoubtedly came into German custody in a deplorable state; however, the army's policies of turning prisoners over to the S.D. (with the expectation or suspicion that they would be killed), the execution of prisoners who had escaped and been recaptured, and the systemic neglect resulting in widespread famine and disease made the Wehrmacht's treatment of Russian POWs a crime under international law.[71] Where defendants could be personally linked to such abuses, they were found guilty.

The tribunal next discussed the limits of the responsibilities of commanders in occupied territories. Essentially, it was a statement on the command responsibility principle, which, in the absence of evidence clearly connecting individual defendants to particular crimes, the prosecution had cited in order to hold the defendants criminally responsible. The tribunal refused to accept that rank and position alone bestowed criminality, and, as in their discussion of commanders' culpability for transmitting illegal orders, they insisted that criminality required a personal act or deliberate omission.[72] Here too the tribunal looked for evidence of the defendants' knowledge and participation in or failure to intervene against the crimes under consideration.[73] In their defense, the field commanders on trial had argued that other state agencies (particularly Nazi economic agencies and police organizations) operating outside their executive power had committed the crimes. The tribunal did not find that the evidence sustained these claims. In fact, the record established certain defendants' voluntary cooperation in the illegal exploitation of occupied areas.

With regard to the Einsatzgruppen, which the defendants insisted functioned on separate authority, the tribunal maintained that commanders in occupied territories were responsible for the protection of the civilian population, an obligation that they could not legally abdicate. At the same time, the tribunal looked for evidence of the defendants' knowledge of the Einsatzgruppen's tasks and whether any commanders attempted to resist their activities.[74] All along, the prosecution had argued that the men in the dock had to have known of the racial policies that the S.D. and SIPO (Security Police) were pursuing. After all, 90,000 Jews had been killed in the area of the 11th Army, 40,000 were murdered in the rear area of Army Group North, and the record revealed numerous occasions when soldiers themselves had taken part in the massacres.[75] But, the tribunal retorted, it was unreasonable to expect that commanders could have been all-knowing and all-powerful with regard to the conduct of their troops.[76] Further, the Einsatzgruppen did have other legal and legitimate police functions in securing the rear areas. Some massacres, particularly early on in Operation

Barbarossa, were camouflaged as pogroms carried out by the indigenous populations, and S.D. reports detailing their own operations did not always reach the desks of the field commanders. All in all, the tribunal concluded that the timing, location, combat situation, and command structure all influenced what commanders knew about the Einsatzgruppen's activities, and these factors would have to be individually assessed for each occasion and for each defendant. The evidence, in their view, did not support any "general presumption of knowledge."[77]

The last issue the tribunal considered before coming to the verdicts against the defendants and pronouncing sentence was one of the most profound, and it set the tone with which the individual defendants were addressed. Responding to the evidence of some military leaders' "considerable" opposition to Hitler, specifically Halder's plans for a coup over the Sudeten question and von Leeb's letters to von Brauchitsch opposing the invasions of the Low Countries, the tribunal reached much the same conclusion as the prosecution. Readily admitting that there had been opposition and that this opposition had been genuine, the tribunal emphasized that its existence made the defendants' subsequent and continuing allegiance to the Führer all the more damning. The tribunal cited key testimony on the relationship between Hitler and the military given at different points in the trial by General Halder and Field Marshal von Leeb. The tribunal recalled that to von Leeb, Hitler was "a demon . . . a devil," and to Halder he had "a complete absence of any moral or ethical obligation."[78] The judges were willing to accept that many of the demands Hitler made of his officers may indeed have been "in contrast to their principle and natures" and against their "humane and soldierly feelings" (as von Leeb had solemnly declared in his final statement), but, the tribunal insisted, "the inescapable fact remains that in part at least, if not to the whole, they permitted their consciences and opinions to become subordinate to Hitler's will, and it was this which has placed such great and ineradicable shame upon the German arms."[79]

The tribunal did not end their comments there, however. Revealing some sympathy for the predicament of the soldier, the judges called attention to the overall context:

> We realize the feelings of professional pride, of ambition to succeed in their profession of arms, of fear for their personal safety or of reprisals against their families, their love of country, their soldiers' concept of obedience, and, indeed, the ingrained respect of the German for those in authority over him, were factors in their decisions. We are aware of the tendency toward degeneration of "civilized" warfare in the modern concept of "total war," and of the war madness that engulfs all people of belligerent powers.[80]

Interestingly, the tribunal seemed to suggest that the men before them were not inherently evil and allowed that in a different war, guided by different leadership, they might never have become embroiled in the crimes that brought them to Nuremberg. But, the tribunal emphasized, these considerations could not excuse the defendants for having followed Hitler into catastrophe. And for that they would be held accountable.[81]

For each defendant, the judgment included a brief biographical summary including birthplace and date, training, and military ranks and posts. Moving from crime to crime (Commissar Order, Commando Order, Barbarossa Jurisdiction Order, ill-treatment and murder of POWs, ill-treatment and murder of civilians, forcible recruitment and deportation of civilian slave laborers, use of POWs for prohibited labor, the hostage reprisal policy, antipartisan activities, cooperation with the Einsatzgruppen, persecution of Jews, and others), the tribunal quoted from pertinent documents—sometimes many for the same charge—to support each finding of guilt.

In the interests of avoiding repetition here, lists of the crimes for which each defendant was convicted are provided at the end of this chapter. There were three fairly surprising verdicts. The tribunal found Field Marshal Hugo Sperrle of the air force and Admiral Otto Schniewind of the Naval War Staff not guilty on all counts. Neither had been as deeply implicated in the same kinds and number of crimes as the OKW staff officers and army field commanders, and the tribunal did not believe that the evidence allegedly connecting them to the slave labor program and the Commando and Barbarossa Jurisdiction orders was sufficiently convincing. Their inclusion among the accused seemed to have been motivated by the Americans wanting representatives of the air force and navy at the trial, but their cases were weaker from the outset, and less important than those pertaining to the other defendants. Sperrle and Schniewind were released immediately upon the close of proceedings. They convicted Field Marshal von Leeb on the sole count of having transmitted the Barbarossa Jurisdiction Order without attaching safeguards to prevent its illegal application. The evidence had also shown that it had been illegally applied in his area of command, which meant that he was responsible for these deaths. Nonetheless, of all the defendants, von Leeb seemed closest to having earned the tribunal's respect, because, they emphasized, "He was not a friend or follower of the Nazi Party or its ideology. He was a soldier and engaged in a stupendous campaign with responsibility for hundreds of thousands of soldiers, and a large indigenous population spread over a vast area. It is not without significance that no criminal order has been introduced which bears his signature or the stamp of his approval."[82] The judges released him with time served.

All of the remaining defendants were found guilty on counts 2 and 3.

The judgment singled out Georg von Kuechler and Hermann Hoth, sentenced to twenty and fifteen years, respectively, for their particular viciousness in dealing with civilian populations in the occupied territories.[83] The judges stressed Hans Reinhardt's contribution to the civilian slave labor program, quoting his personal directives, which called for the retention of food, wages, and liberty in order to compel cooperation.[84] This and other crimes earned a sentence of fifteen years. Although many defendants were shown to have knowingly and approvingly cooperated in the murderous tasks of the Einsatzgruppen, the evidence against Karl von Roques, whom they sentenced to twenty years, "show[ed] beyond doubt the complete subservience of the Wehrmacht in [his] area to the SD and its full cooperation with the SD program, with knowledge of its debased and criminal character."[85] The tribunal reserved special contempt for OKW staffers Hermann Reinecke and Walter Warlimont, who each received a life sentence. Though neither had necessarily conceived of the criminal policies that characterized the war, both had personally contributed to molding them into their final executable form, which, once communicated through the Wehrmacht and police, "brought suffering and death to countless honorable soldiers and unfortunate civilians."[86] The tribunal expressed their regret that they could not also have found Reinecke liable under international law for his leading contribution to the Nazi Wehrmacht indoctrination program or his role as judge in the so-called People's Court, a particularly brutal instrument of Nazi terror, but asserted disdainfully that both activities reflected "his character as a trusted and supine instrument of Hitler's will in any capacity."[87]

Upon passing the sentences, all of which Military Governor Lucius Clay confirmed upon the customary review, the defendants were delivered to Landsberg prison in Bavaria to join the war criminals convicted by the army's Dachau trials and the other SNP. Interestingly, Landsberg, located about forty-five kilometers west of Munich, was the same prison where Hitler was incarcerated after his failed coup in 1924, and it was where he wrote *Mein Kampf.* Defense counsel tried once more to repudiate the jurisdiction of the tribunal, filing requests for writs of habeas corpus with the District Court for the District of Columbia and with the United States Supreme Court, challenging the validity of Control Council Law No. 10. Both petitions were denied.[88]

The High Command case judgment, reflecting Judge Young's cautious approach to international law, was conservative in many respects. It did not exploit the full scope of the crimes against peace charge stipulated by Control Council Law No. 10, nor did it go as far as the Yamashita case in defining command responsibility. In all instances of assigning guilt, the tribunal demanded documentary proof of personal initiative and/or knowing omission. As Young had remarked several times over the course of the trial and the preparation of his opinion, he strove to produce not only a judgment fitting the evidence presented in court and reflective of the contemporary state of the law, but also one that could help define a new code of conduct for all armies. The judgment was careful not to criminalize fighting war, drawing a strict line between those who initiate wars and those whose duty it is, whether on the side of the aggressor or the aggrieved, to fight them.

The judgment was marked by sensitivity to the challenges facing the soldier, bound by a command structure, operating under extreme stress, in an overall context of war: "human violence at its utmost."[89] The judges did not demand that these men be legal scholars, nor did they insist that a commander's power over his subordinates and in his territory was absolute. The tribunal sustained the guilty verdicts because the defendants' acts, at their core, were plainly and obviously criminal in the universally accepted definition of the term. The Commissar Order and Barbarossa Jurisdiction Order, draconian antipartisan measures, cooperation with the Einsatzgruppen, the enslavement of civilian populations—to modern memory, the hallmarks of the particularly Nazi style of war—were, at their root, still simply murder, abuse, and gross neglect of the people to whom the men on trial legally and morally owed protection. That these crimes carried with them the opprobrium of having advanced Nazi racial and political goals added to the defendants' shame, but not to their criminality in terms of the law.

After reading the judgment, the members of the tribunal returned home to the United States. Records contain no evidence that they involved themselves publicly in the debate over the imprisonment of soldiers, which gained in momentum and intensity upon their conviction at the High Command case. The text of the judgment itself was left to fulfill Nuremberg's educative mandate or not. One may question whether this document, with its restrictive interpretation of the evidence and the law, contributed to or detracted from the trial's didactic function. Indeed, first and foremost, this decision represented an assessment of thirteen soldiers' individual contributions to a criminal enterprise far larger than was within the tribunal's jurisdiction to assess. In that respect, the judgment did not match the scope of the prosecution's case or the documents it placed on record. However, the tribunal's findings heavily impugned the Wehrmacht as an institution. The fact that the defendants were found guilty because of the acts of their subordinates established that the numbers of ordinary Germans involved in the perpetration of racial and political war crimes and crimes against humanity extended into the millions. As the first major confrontation with the crimes of the Wehrmacht, Telford Taylor, always more concerned with the trial's educative value than Judge Young, was confident that the prosecution's and tribunals' work in this and the other Subsequent Proceedings had succeeded. Writing to Secretary of the Army Kenneth Royall in the spring of 1948, he remarked confidently: "In my opinion, the records and judgments in these ... trials constitute a ... vital source of information upon the basis of which history can be written far more truthfully and fully than would otherwise have been possible."[90] In a statement for the International News Service, Taylor declared: "I venture to predict that as time goes on we will all hear more about Nuremberg rather than less, and that in a very real sense the conclusion of the trials marks the beginning, and not the end, of Nuremberg as a force in politics, law, and morals."[91]

He was mistaken. Ultimately, the High Command case failed as a didactic trial. But this failure stemmed from the actions and decisions of the political authorities who inherited its record, and with it the responsibility to honor its verdicts. The final political disposition of the case and those sentenced in it is the subject of the next two chapters.

Summary of Verdicts and Sentences

WILHELM VON LEEB (TIME SERVED)

Guilty on count 3: transmitted the Barbarossa Jurisdiction Order without safeguards to prevent its illegal application; criminally responsible for its illegal application by subordinate units.[92]

HUGO SPERRLE

Not guilty on all counts.[93]

GEORG VON KUECHLER (TWENTY YEARS)

Guilty on counts 2 and 3: transmitted and implemented the Commissar Order; used prohibited labor of civilians and POWs; was aware of illegal executions of POWs but took no corrective action (although evidence does not prove that he transmitted orders); criminally responsible for illegal executions carried out by his subordinates; criminally guilty of neglect of POWs in his area while commander in chief of the 18th Army, but not while commander in chief of Army Group North; guilty of ruthless cooperation in the slave labor recruitment program and of widespread application of the Barbarossa Jurisdiction Order; not criminally connected to activities of Einsatzgruppe A, but guilty of distributing the von Reichenau order resulting in the persecution of Jews; had knowledge of and supported other measures persecuting Jews (especially imposition of identifying armbands and establishment of ghettos).[94]

HERMANN HOTH (FIFTEEN YEARS)

Guilty on counts 2 and 3: knowingly and approvingly transmitted the Commissar Order, which was carried out by subordinate troops; failed to provide adequate care for POWs; criminally neglected POWs; exhibited a "general attitude of ruthlessness and brutality in dealing with the [civilian] population"; issued an order similar to the von Reichenau order regarding the persecution of Jews; passed on the Barbarossa Jurisdiction Order without safeguards (it was criminally applied in his area); guilty of illegal antipartisan and hostage reprisal activities; made no effort to curb the illegal activities of the Einsatzgruppen in his area of command after learning that it was a murder organization.[95]

HANS REINHARDT (FIFTEEN YEARS)

Guilty on counts 2 and 3: transmitted the Commissar Order orally, and despite his claims that he repudiated it verbally and protested about it to his superiors, evidence showed that it was carried out by units under his command; transmitted the Commando Order; used POWs for illegal and dangerous labor in his area; evidence showed that subordinate units illegally killed POWs with his knowledge; turned POWs over to the S.D. for "special treatment"; guilty of dereliction of duty in that he did not acquaint himself with the contents of reports on these occurrences that were submitted to him; illegally seized civilians (women, children, and the elderly) for forced labor; distributed an order for coercive measures to be applied in recruitment of civilian forced labor for the Reich; deported civilians for labor in Auschwitz; not only tolerated but encouraged the forcible conscription and illegal use of civilians; passed on the Barbarossa Jurisdiction Order; applied illegal reprisal measures against civilians; promoted ruthless antipartisan fighting methods; cooperated with the S.D., especially by handing over partisan supporters and partisan suspects to the S.D., including men, women, and children, knowing that organization's function.[96]

HANS VON SALMUTH (TWENTY YEARS)

Guilty on counts 2 and 3: criminally responsible for distributing the Commissar Order, although it was not proven that he approved of it or that it was carried out by subordinate units; transmitted the Commando Order; used POWs illegally on the eastern and western fronts; transmitted orders regarding the illegal execution of POWs and partisans; handed POWs and civilians over to the S.D., at times on the basis of mere suspicion of having an anti-German attitude; knew the S.D. was a murder organization, but did not protest against or criticize their presence in his area of command; did not request the S.D.'s punishment or removal from his area of command; used civilians in prohibited labor and deported slave laborers to the Reich; issued orders for illegal antipartisan actions and collective reprisal measures against civilians and civilian hostages, although it was not proven that he passed on the Barbarossa Jurisdiction Order specifically; cooperated with the Einsatzgruppen in the persecution and execution of Jews; issued personal orders for soldiers to participate in Einsatzgruppen shootings.[97]

KARL HOLLIDT (FIVE YEARS)

Guilty on counts 2 and 3: knowingly and approvingly used POWs for prohibited labor; knowingly and approvingly used civilians in illegal labor and participated in the recruitment for slave labor in the Reich.[98]

OTTO SCHNIEWIND

Not guilty on all counts.[99]

KARL VON ROQUES (TWENTY YEARS)

Guilty on counts 2 and 3: issued personal orders for and knew of, approved, and acquiesced in acts by troops under his authority and by agencies within his area that violated the most elementary duty and obligations owed to POWs and the civilian population; implemented the Commissar Order extensively (but it was not proven that he transmitted the order); provided knowing support for S.D. in illegal executions of Jews, civilians, and POWs; tolerated S.D. screening operations in camps under his command; guilty of gross neglect and murder of POWs generally; transmitted Barbarossa Jurisdiction Order to subordinates and issued personal orders calling for mass reprisal actions where partisan activity was suspected; persecuted Jews (through the imposition of ghettos, the prohibition of religious rites, the confiscation of all valuables, and requiring identifying marks such as the Star of David); responsible for the terror killings of partisans and partisan sympathizers and the turning over of Jews and Communists to the S.D.; supplied logistical help and support to the S.D.[100]

HERMANN REINECKE (LIFE IMPRISONMENT)

Guilty on counts 2 and 3: formulated and implemented criminal orders and policies concerning the treatment of POWs in the Reich, General Government, Reich Commissariat, and other OKW areas; criminally liable for the program of segregation and execution of POWs by the S.D. and SIPO and the execution of commissars in the General Government; responsible for the illegal executions of POWs for trying to escape or having sexual intercourse with German women; ill-treatment and abuse of POWs in labor camps; criminally responsible for participation in the Third Reich's looting program.[101]

WALTER WARLIMONT (LIFE IMPRISONMENT)

Guilty on counts 2 and 3: formulated the Commissar Order; formulated and enforced the Commando Order; involved in creating the Terror Flier Order, which encouraged German civilian lynch mobs to kill downed Allied airmen; criminally participated in the deportation and enslavement of civilians; formulated the Barbarossa Jurisdiction Order; formulated the order for the illegal killing of hostages; knew of the extermination program against the Jews, although evidence did not prove his criminal connection to the program.[102]

OTTO WOEHLER (EIGHT YEARS)

Guilty on counts 2 and 3: knew of and acquiesced in the prohibited labor of POWs; implemented the Barbarossa Jurisdiction Order; guilty of compulsory recruitment of civilians and others for slave labor in the Reich; knew of and cooperated with the Einsatzgruppen (especially sheltering, feeding, and helping with shootings).[103]

RUDOLF LEHMANN (SEVEN YEARS)

Guilty on counts 2 and 3: played a pivotal role in the formulation of the Barbarossa Jurisdiction Order; involved in the formulation of the Commando Order; leading contributor to the Night and Fog Decree; involved in the formulation of the Terror and Sabotage Decree.[104]

6

The Debate over Imprisoned Soldiers and the Politics of Punishment, 1949 to 1952

We still have to look forward to some unpleasantness in this matter before it is over, but from the way things are going here it looks as if we have gotten a good start toward writing a successful end to the chapter.
—John J. McCloy, U.S. High Commissioner for Germany

The case of soldiers . . . is Landsberg's last chapter but one, not the last.
—*Frankfurter Allgemeine Zeitung*

BEGINNING WITH the International Military Tribunal and continuing through the conclusion of the Subsequent Nuremberg Proceedings (SNP), these trials in general and the High Command case in particular were dogged by persistent criticism in Germany of being no more than an application of retroactive law and an exercise in double-standard victor's justice. A constantly recurring theme in public responses to the trial was that all parties to the war, but especially the Soviets, had committed similar abuses, and that in the end, it was a soldier's duty to serve his nation and obey orders. Advocates also attested to the honorable, moral, and Christian character of the convicted, who simply could never have been party to the offenses charged against them. As well, the immediate political and social circumstances of the time proved inhospitable ground in which to root the intended lessons of the trial. The hardening battle lines of the Cold War weakened the Americans' capacity to convince the German people of the Wehrmacht's participation in Nazi crimes. Having recently sentenced German soldiers for wartime crimes against—in large part—Soviet nationals, the Allies would soon be making overtures to the Federal Republic to join in the defense of the West against the same Communist superpower. Further, convicted former field marshals and generals, languishing in Landsberg prison, still enjoyed the respect and loyalty of men who were now being asked to don uniforms in common cause with their comrades' captors.

As explained in chapter 2, early popular opposition to the judgments of the American war crimes trials centered on the evidence of American misconduct in the Malmedy and Koch cases, and the imposition of death sentences. The campaign to commute these sentences briefly eclipsed concern with the military men imprisoned at Landsberg. But their release soon became the major bargaining chip in the negotiations over West German integration in Western defense plans. For the German leaders who entered into these negotiations with the Americans, the necessary prerequisite for any Federal Republic contribution to the defense of the West was the restoration of German military honor. This required a return of all German prisoners of war still in Allied custody and, significantly, the release of all military men convicted of war crimes serving terms in occupation authorities' prisons. The incremental transformation of West Germany from occupied territory to sovereign state gave it the political leverage required to press its demands ever more forcefully.

In 1948, the Western Allies still regarded the Germans with a great deal of ambivalence. On the one hand, the atrocities revealed through the trials "marked them indelibly" as a nation responsible for unprecedented crime. Moreover, in the early postwar years, there was an abiding fear of a resurgence of aggressive nationalism, or worse, neo-Nazism. On the other hand, defeat, denazification, and decartelization had all but wrecked the nation's administrative and economic infrastructure, resulting in an enormously expensive occupation. The Americans and British alone spent about $700 million per year to run their zones. In any case, the emergence of Germany as the key Cold War European state pointed away from punitive policies toward more reconstructive ones. That is, because West Germany would be the bulwark against Communist encroachment in Central and Western Europe, it would have to possess a strong democratic government. Although officials from both East and West had argued that Germany should be reunified under a promise of neutrality and demilitarization, others had deep misgivings, first, that Germany could reemerge as a belligerent power, and second, that the Soviets might seek to incorporate the whole country under its sphere of influence. The U.S. State Department decided that it was better to live with a divided Germany than to risk losing it altogether to the Communists. It would require the end to occupation and the creation of a strong and stable parliamentary West German state. The man appointed to oversee this project was John J. McCloy.[1]

In the summer of 1949, McCloy, who replaced military commander General Lucius Clay, assumed the office of High Commissioner of the U.S.

United States High Commissioner John J. McCloy. Photograph taken by Harris & Ewing, courtesy of the Harry S. Truman Library, C.W. Jackson Files—White House Meeting Files, 67-5499, and Stock Montage Chicago.

Zone in West Germany. He and the British and French high commissioners retained authority over West Germany's security, denazification,
decartelization, reparations, and foreign affairs. All other matters of government were to be transferred to a new West German administration.
Indeed, in anticipation of the upcoming changes, Governor Clay had authorized a representative body of the state (Land) parliaments to draw up a constitution, called the Basic Law, to govern the future West German state. It
came into effect at the end of May. In mid-August, McCloy and the other
high commissioners presided over the first national elections. The Christian Democratic Union, in coalition with the Free Democratic Party and the
German Party, won a slim majority, and Konrad Adenauer—by one vote—
was elected chancellor.

The dual program to strengthen democracy and achieve sovereignty
dominated Adenauer's chancellorship. The defining issue, ultimately, was
rearmament. Given the presence of Soviet forces in the East and the steady
buildup of the East German police into a quasi-military force, the question
of West German remilitarization had to be addressed. Although there were
and remained strong voices in the West German parliament opposed to
rearmament (notably from the German Socialist Party), seeing it as final
closure to the possibility of reunification, Adenauer regarded it as a sure path
to independence and thus "the essential question of our political future."[2]
As will be explained, the issue of war criminals figured prominently in all
negotiations between Germany and the Western Allied powers over the end
of occupation and rearmament. Adenauer later remarked in his memoirs
that from the time of the republic's founding, he "let slip no opportunity to
discuss this question with leading foreign personalities."[3] It should be noted,
however, that because the Americans had conducted the most extensive proceedings and possessed the largest population of convicted war criminals
(three times that of the British and French), the debate was mainly a German–American one.[4]

Shortly after the establishment of the Federal Republic of Germany in
May 1949, the Adenauer government announced its goal to "pardon . . .
offenses against the law arising from the bygone period of distress and transition" and its intention to request a general amnesty for persons sentenced
by military government courts.[5] Conceding that the request for amnesty
had nothing to do with juridical aspects of the war criminals issue, the federal government highlighted "the importance such amnesty bears upon a
general political appeasement" and promised "a lasting echo among the population."[6] The German press and veterans soon joined their government in
this demand. Although articulated differently at different times, the intention to secure an amnesty for convicted war criminals occupied a central

place in all discussions between the Federal Republic and the Western Allies, and did not abate until the last inmate of Landsberg was set free in 1958.[7]

A New Policy for Sentence Revision

The American law devised for the Subsequent Proceedings and the Dachau trials stipulated that judgments of guilt or innocence were considered final and not subject to appeal or revision. Consequently, there was no formal appeals process through which the convicted could challenge the verdicts passed against them. Until 1950, reviews had taken place on an ad hoc basis, which, particularly in the Dachau cases, had caused widespread apprehension over the equitability of the sentences and the rights of the convicts. The United States wished to appear responsive to defendants' rights and to preserve political stability in Germany and its loyalty to the West. Accordingly, in November 1949, State Department officials instructed the recently installed U.S. High Commissioner McCloy, along with the American military commander General Thomas Handy (who retained jurisdiction over the Dachau trial convicts), "to undertake a review of sentences . . . in order to eliminate any wide disparities . . . among sentences for comparable crimes; to ensure that the punishment is reasonable for the offense; and to establish uniform standards for amnesty, pardon, clemency, parole or release."[8]

Occupation officials closely involved in war criminals matters were deeply concerned by this new policy proposal, as seen in a memorandum by the U.S. High Commission for Occupied Germany (HICOG) Administration of Justice and Prisons Division, which also reflected the thoughts of the army's judge advocate. The memo contained a warning against a literal interpretation of the foregoing directive. Although in favor of establishing a clemency process, the authors argued that the bases for these decisions should be strictly limited to compassionate grounds and to issues arising after the sentences were confirmed. Only in extraordinary cases, such as mistaken identity, they urged, should any clemency action reverse original convictions.[9]

They based their advice on their interpretation of the German attitude toward war criminals as displayed by the countless petitions that had been sent to the military governor and the high commissioner. These appeals came from the prisoners themselves, their counsel, their relatives and friends, their business and professional associates, public officials, and even "persons and organizations bearing no apparent relationship to the individuals or proceedings." The "frequently striking and suspicious ... similarity of their arguments" suggested a determined and organized campaign. On the surface, the petitions sought to elicit sympathy for the convicts. Upon examination, however, they revealed "an attack upon the original war crimes program as a whole, its underlying philosophies and theses." The appeals consistently aimed at relitigating the issues that were adjudicated at the trials and confirmed during the automatic posttrial review, such as the defenses of "superior orders, tu quoque, ex post facto law, [and] the fairness of the trial." It was obvious to those who received these petitions that they intended to abrogate the war crimes program as a whole, and by implication undermine the Allied assertion of German responsibility for the war. The authors of this memo were adamant that these efforts should not succeed:

> In our judgment nothing should be done which even remotely suggests a departure from the firmly established position of the United States that these criminals merited trial and conviction, that the defenses raised and asserted by them (all of which were given careful consideration, both in the course of the original proceedings and upon review) are meretricious, and that the penalties visited upon them represent the measured condemnation of civilized society for the offenses of which they stand convicted.[10]

At the same time, occupation authorities did not wish to appear wholly dismissive of legitimate bases for clemency, such as a convict's medical condition or family hardship, and agreed that these should be accorded due consideration. But the directive had also called for a reassessment of the propriety of the sentences in order to ensure that comparable sentences had been meted out for comparable offenses. Here again the memo's authors expressed reservations. In their view, this could only be achieved if the original bases for conviction were reexamined—that is, if the trial records were reopened. Doing so, they feared, would "open the door to an endless rehash of the very arguments which have already been fully adjudicated by courts of competent jurisdiction, and [will] cast doubt upon the validity of the findings, conclusions, judgments, and sentences of these courts. It would undermine not only the judicial determinations in the cases, but the policy and position of the United States in sponsoring and undertaking the program as a whole."[11] Clearly, it was not a lack of confidence in the trials' findings that led occupation officials to keep the records of the proceedings closed. Rather a sense of protectiveness and an insistence that the decisions reached at Nuremberg be respected led them to recommend a clemency program that would be tightly limited in scope. HICOG and the army followed their advice, but it brought vexing complications.

The Advisory Board on Clemency
for War Criminals

As a first measure, in December 1949, McCloy instituted a system of credits for "good conduct time," wherein convicts were ultimately granted remission of one third of their sentence for good behavior, the same formula that applied in U.S. prisons.[12] Although the good conduct time credit drastically reduced the amount of time yet to be served by all convicts other than those facing life terms or execution, the implicit insistence on the validity of the trials' conclusions irritated German groups seeking sweeping pardons.

More importantly, in accordance with the recommendations of the December 1949 memorandum, McCloy created an Advisory Board on Clemency for War Criminals in March 1950.[13] Named for its chairman, David Peck, presiding judge of the New York Supreme Court's Appellate Division, the Peck Panel had a mandate to consider clemency petitions from SNP convicts and to submit recommendations to the high commissioner for sentence modification. Judge Peck was joined by two others: Brigadier General Conrad Snow of the State Department legal staff, and Frederick Moran, chairman of the New York State Board of Parole.[14] McCloy appointed each member, and none had had any prior contact with, or had publicly expressed any opinion about, the war crimes trials.[15] In conformity with the foundational law of the Subsequent Proceedings, and in view of the warnings from the December 1949 memo, procedural guidelines prohibited the Peck Panel from reviewing the tribunals' decisions with regard to law or fact. Beyond this, however, the board's instructions were imprecise. It was to rectify disparities among sentences imposed for similar offenses, and it was permitted to take the health and family conditions of the defendant into account. Further, the panel could consider other "pertinent facts tending to warrant mitigation of the sentence," although these facts were not defined. The form and procedure of the hearings were left to the board's discretion.[16] The army also created a War Crimes Modification Board to revise the Dachau trial convicts' sentences. The two boards had different staffs and worked independently of each other, although they endeavored to harmonize the factors considered in the clemency recommendations. The army also applied the same good conduct time remission as the HICOG authorities.[17]

There was much work for the Peck Panel to do. Moran traveled to Germany in April to retrieve the tribunals' judgments, which he brought to Washington for the panel to study. The three men convened in Munich in July to complete their research and read individual petitions and their supporting documents. Moran interviewed each SNP convict at Landsberg.[18] A planning memo projected that the board would conduct 105 hearings over eleven days in August.[19] They would unfold at a dizzying pace. Lawyers for the convicts were allowed to speak for thirty minutes each, although no prisoners or members of their family were permitted to appear before the board.[20] Anxious to provide the German people with a reasonable chance to present their views on the clemency program, McCloy arranged, via the West German federal Ministry of Justice, for a panel of eight German consultants to present arguments and petitions on behalf of the individual prisoners and permitted them access to the same records viewed by the board. However, they could only make recommendations.[21] Significantly, not a single representative of the Nuremberg prosecution staff was invited to take part in the proceedings, despite at least one offer to lend expertise on the details of the individual cases.[22] After each hearing, the board took fifteen minutes for deliberation. The panel conducted all proceedings orally and made no transcriptions.[23]

In their applications to the board, none of the High Command case convicts expressed any remorse or uttered any apology. Rather, they repeated the same defense claims raised in court: they were bound by an oath of obedience but had clandestinely subverted certain orders; they had been apolitical servants of the state, and their relationships with Hitler and Nazism had been jagged and strained; as soldiers, they faced a unique predicament that no one acquainted with fighting in the East would condemn. Interestingly, not all of them denied wrongdoing, but those who did admit to participating in the implementation of orders that were now deemed criminal strove to justify these policies and their cooperation with them. Hans Reinhardt defended Germany's wartime behavior as a legitimate defense against the "Bolshevist danger for our people," and admitted that if he could not avoid "certain harsh measures," this had to be understood in the context of that dire struggle.[24] Indeed, several High Command case convicts felt vindicated by the continuing tension between East and West. Rudolf Lehmann declared that since the time of his conviction, "the whole world has increasingly realized that—in war and in peace—relations with the East are not governed by normal principles."[25] Hoth's attorney was even more direct, stating: "the Korean War has shown the Americans what the Soviet methods of warfare are and the extension of the term 'military emergency.'"[26] All the claimants agreed that they had acted in the belief that their conduct was right and necessary.

The High Command case generals were not alone in their efforts to secure early release, and they benefited from the energy and resources of the government, churches, and other organizations, as well as their communities. At the time that the clemency board did its work, the federal Ministry of Justice prepared summary sheets on all the men held at Landsberg that detailed their family's financial circumstances. Almost all of the High Command case convicts had lost all of their property at the war's end. The Allies had confiscated their homes, land (most of which was situated in what was now East Germany or Poland), savings, and personal effects. Pensions were canceled. The wives and children of the convicted were left with little means to survive and depended on the generosity of local churches and veterans' charities and on intermittent handouts from their husbands' former subordinates, as well as on the small sums that middle-aged women could earn in postwar West Germany. These summary sheets emphasized the family's financial straits and, by extension, their frequently drab living quarters and menial work, to bolster claims that these men were badly needed at home.[27]

Another important source of aid was the Zentrale Rechtsschutzstelle (the Central Office for Legal Protection). This agency, which began functioning in March 1950, was a division of the federal Ministry of Justice and coordinated the work of the International Red Cross and Protestant and Catholic organizations, such as the Hilfswerk der Evangelischen Kirche in Deutschland and the Deutscher Caritasverband, to protect the legal rights of Germans in foreign custody. It devoted considerable effort to those sentenced for war crimes in occupation courts. Through its component organizations, it evaluated the Nuremberg trial material, gathered "new" and allegedly exculpatory evidence, and furnished necessary documents to present to the current and future clemency boards.[28] In addition, the Zentrale Rechtsschutzstelle provided funds for the High Command case convicts' legal representation before the Peck Panel.[29]

Private citizens, veterans, and even whole communities voiced their support for the generals' applications and offered to act as sponsors upon their release. Retired general Gustav Harteneck distributed a circular criticizing the High Command case and established an account for donations to fund visits to Landsberg by the convicts' families.[30] Appeals on behalf of individual convicts described them as Christian men, family men, kind and compassionate, well-meaning and honorable, used and abused by Hitler, who had exploited the "chaotic times" and their sense of soldierly duty.[31]

The Advisory Board's Recommendations

The Peck Panel's report on their decisions, which was later published for German consumption, outlined the main criminal programs of the Nazi state, such as the mass murder of Jews, Romani, partisans, and hostages, and the enslavement of civilian populations. Of the convicts, they noted that all now claimed to have hated their work but felt inextricably bound by superior orders to carry out the tasks assigned to them. The board explicitly rejected this defense: "So long as there was an order which trickled down from the top, everyone in the wash of it enjoyed an immunity bath. It may be a consoling philosophy as it is a blind philosophy. But if it is to be negated, and there is to be a world of law and justice, individuals in positions of some authority at least must be held answerable for their acts."[32] Further, they declared that "a mistaken tenderness toward the perpetrators of mass murder would be a mockery, undoing what Nuremberg had accomplished."[33] But for all the board's insistence on holding convicts answerable for their crimes, they were quite generous in the revisions they recommended. In a conference with McCloy in early August, Peck remarked that the board had felt that the sentences, generally speaking, were excessive.[34] In their published report, they concluded that they had made "all possible allowances" and that if they erred, it was "on the side of leniency."[35]

In formulating their recommendations, the Peck Panel, contrary to their instructions (however vague), departed from the tribunals' conclusions. That is, they proclaimed that they had felt themselves bound only by the facts established by the evidence, but not by the conclusions drawn from them. Significantly, they contended that they had guarded against confusing the "enormity of the program in which a defendant was engaged" with the degree of the individual's responsibility for it. The implication, of course, was that they felt that the tribunals had punished the defendants for the acts of the group. The board defended their sometimes "sharp reductions" as being "due and proper recognition of differences in authority and action among defendants" and their relation to each other and to the programs in which they participated.[36] Altogether, the board reviewed 105 sentences and recommended commutations or reductions in 84 of them: the commutation of 7 of the 15 death sentences, and the reduction of 77 of the 90 prison sentences.[37]

The HICOG legal staff were deeply troubled by the board's lenient recommendations, and they communicated their concerns to McCloy before his final decisions. Robert Bowie, HICOG general counsel, declared flatly that in twenty-four cases, these recommendations were invalid, having taken insufficient recognition of the seriousness of the crimes prompting the sentences. Further, he stated that the board had been too lenient in another twenty-two cases. Bowie charged that the board appeared to have overstepped its mandate in second-guessing some of the tribunals' original findings, and that it "seem[ed] to have concluded that the facts as stated in the judgments do not establish beyond a reasonable doubt the defendant's responsibility for specific crimes."[38] Bowie suspected that the board's doubt originated from having read only the judgments, which did not include reference to all of the incriminating evidence presented at court. Further, the board had insisted on proof connecting individual defendants with specific crimes. But, Bowie argued, it was a basic strategy of the prosecution, in the High Command case and in others, to affix guilt by "showing that the defendant held a responsible staff or executive position in an organization ... which engaged in mass atrocities." Bowie was most troubled by the board's revision of several sentences imposed in the High Command case against

> three generals who appear to be universally regarded as particularly evil. They were all directly implicated in the program which encompassed the murder of commandos, commissars and captured Allied airmen as well as in the brutal mistreatment of prisoners of war. The grounds advanced for clemency are the alleged subordinate positions of the generals. However one of them, von Kuechler, was a Field Marshall and the two others, Reinecke and Warlimont were Lt. Generals.[39]

In Bowie's view, not only had the board acted against instructions, but by not taking the full trial records into account, they had misunderstood the enormity of the acts impugned. This contributed to an incomplete perception of the convicts and their crimes. In any case, however, the Peck Panel's work was complete. It was now up to McCloy to confirm or reject their recommendations. But before exploring the high commissioner's decisions and the reasons that sustained them, we must examine the pressures that McCloy faced at this time.

Imprisoned Soldiers and the Rearmament Debate

The eruption of the Korean War in late June 1950 heightened East–West tensions and highlighted the need for a West German military force.[40] Only five years since Germany had been told it must never again possess weapons, Cold War considerations prompted the abandonment of this policy. The dilemma, of course, was how to make West Germany simultaneously strong enough to deter the Soviets, but not so strong as to pose a threat to the West. The French, understandably the most apprehensive of Germany's neighbors, devised a plan that would both rearm and contain West Germany. The brainchild of French prime minister André Pleven, the Pleven

Plan, later known as the European Defense Community, or EDC, envisioned a West European army in which the military forces of various states would be integrated under one amalgamated command structure. That is, no single state would be able to deploy troops independently. The EDC met with broad approval. From Adenauer's point of view, rearmament under any guise meant increased national sovereignty. From the American perspective, the EDC more closely unified Western Europe and created a military force whose strength and resources no single state would have been able to muster.[41] Although formal negotiations over the EDC were still some months away, the intensification of the rearmament debate created an entrée for individuals seeking leverage in the matter of imprisoned soldiers.

Not surprisingly, during the period of the Peck Panel's work and before McCloy's final decisions, the high commissioner received hundreds of letters on behalf of the military men in prison, many of which were written by former soldiers and colleagues. Many of these communications began by reminding McCloy of the West's desire and need for a German contribution to defense plans.[42] They stated plainly that no German soldier could be expected to join such a force after "six years of defamation."[43] Retired admiral Gottfried Hansen, later head of the largest German veterans' association, declared, "An end [must] be put to defamation by releasing the numerous innocent German soldiers who are still being held in confinement."[44] General Heinz Guderian explained, "The former German soldiers cannot understand that the United States of America emphatically demand a German contribution to the defense of Western Europe, while at the same time many of their comrades are languishing in prisons. . . . If the United States are interested in preparing the Germans for a contribution to the defense of Western Europe, I, in concurrence with all my comrades, consider it an urgent necessity that first the so-called 'war criminals' question' be settled."[45]

The enormous number of petitions from former German officers and ordinary German citizens alike convinced McCloy that the German people did not understand what the trials had been about or what the defendants had done.[46] Having carefully studied the trial records and personally being particularly interested in the cases involving soldiers, the high commissioner was at pains to communicate the truth of the situation to the men and women who appealed to him. To Hansen he wrote:

No one aware of the facts can possibly say that these men observed either the ethics of their profession or the fundamental principles of humanity and law. . . . I cannot believe that allowance should be made for a professional soldier who either connived or participated in . . . [the] slaughter of Jews because they were Jews, Communists, parachutists, aviators, commandos, and other "undesireables." Such connivance and participation took place and there can be no doubt of it.[47]

McCloy's frustration and distress at the German public's ignorance of their recent past and the facts revealed by the trials were made clear in a January 1951 meeting with a Bundestag delegation, during which a member of parliament requested "that the excesses of the Nazis should be cancelled by a great gesture of clemency." The high commissioner insisted that the trials had been "provoked by a spasm of criminality" that demanded judicial confrontation. In some cases, there simply was no justifiable reason for clemency, because in view of the crimes, he "could hardly believe that the men who perpetrated [them] were human." McCloy expressed his indignation at the Germans' "tendency to put things under the carpet and refus[al] to acknowledge what actually happened." In his view, the Germans should "face the issue squarely and understand the enormity of what had been done." Political considerations could in no way shape his clemency decisions, he continued, because this would elicit cynicism and disillusion or be construed as condoning the crimes.[48]

At the same time, in all his communications, McCloy was careful to emphasize that the honor of the regular German soldier was in no way impugned by the trials' findings, because those who had been convicted were not condemned for what they had done on the battlefield, but for having supported and participated in Nazi racial and political policies.[49] McCloy's efforts to assuage the bitterness expressed over the imprisonment of soldiers were no doubt linked to the reemergence of the rearmament question over the last few months. The American forces' military reversals in Korea in December meant German rearmament had become HICOG's "number one priority."[50] Indeed, the new commander of NATO forces, General Dwight Eisenhower, was invited to Frankfurt to meet with two of Adenauer's defense advisors—both former Wehrmacht generals—in order to smooth some ruffled military feathers. The encounter possessed great significance because Eisenhower had been openly contemptuous of the German officer corps during the war. Contrary to military tradition and etiquette, Eisenhower had refused to receive a single captured German general during battle, and he would not shake General Jodl's hand at the Germans' official surrender in Rheims. Not to risk any confusion about his true feelings on the matter, years later, he wrote that he considered his former foes "a completely evil conspiracy with which no compromise could be tolerated."[51]

However, when brought together with Chancellor Adenauer and the former lieutenant generals Hans Speidel and Adolf Heusinger during a reception at the McCloy residence, Eisenhower extended his hand, smiled broadly, and declared that he had "never intended to challenge the honor of the German soldier and officer."[52] Upon his departure from Germany, the general announced his willingness to let "by-gones be by-gones" and released a statement widely published in that country and abroad: "There is a real difference between the regular German soldier and Hitler and his criminal group. For my part, I do not believe that the German soldier as such has lost his honor. The fact that certain individuals committed, in war, dishonorable and despicable acts reflects on the individuals concerned and not the great majority of German soldiers and officers."[53] Adenauer, Speidel, and Heusinger expressed their delight and satisfaction at this statement and declared that they had "shed completely their reluctance to participate in military negotiations caused by reproaches of former Wehrmacht colleagues."[54] The sudden warm and conciliatory attitude showed how directly the American treatment of former soldiers dictated German feelings about military integration with the West. Unfortunately for the Germans, however, Eisenhower, who by his statements himself appeared unaware of (or willing to overlook) the depth and breadth of Wehrmacht culpability for Nazi crime, did not have final say over the fate of soldiers at Landsberg. McCloy was not as forgiving.

The Landsberg Decisions

At the end of January 1951, in order to make the final clemency decisions, McCloy sequestered himself in his home for days to read and reread the Peck Panel's recommendations and the original Nuremberg judgments, "wrestling with his soul and his heart."[55] His political liaison in Bonn, Charles Thayer, described the mood: "From all over Germany wives, fathers, mothers and children of the Landsberg prisoners sent petitions, pleas and outright threats against McCloy and his family. . . . As the deadline for the final decision approached, newspaper editors raised the tension still higher with editorials denouncing the war crimes trials."[56] The night before the decisions were to be announced, an official from the German Defense Office pleaded with Thayer to intercede with McCloy, professing that "it would be impossible to persuade any German ever again to bear arms for any cause" if the death sentences were upheld. Later that same evening, Speidel and Heusinger appeared at McCloy's home to plead for mercy.[57]

In the end, McCloy commuted the executions of ten of the fifteen prisoners under sentence of death and further reduced prison sentences for the vast majority (sixty-seven of seventy-three) of convicts serving jail terms. Almost one third were granted immediate release. Notably, he reduced the sentences of only three of the remaining six High Command case convicts still at Landsberg. At this time, only von Kuechler, Reinhardt, Hoth, Reinecke, von Salmuth, and Warlimont remained in prison, the others having died or been scheduled for imminent release in accordance with the good conduct time credit. Reinecke's, Hoth's, and Reinhardt's sentences remained unchanged. Warlimont's sentence was reduced from life to eighteen years and von Kuechler's and von Salmuth's from twenty to twelve years each. It is significant to note that the three High Command case reductions were to shorter prison terms; none were to time served, as in many other cases. In all, McCloy's decisions applied to eighty-eight prisoners. Convicts in the IG Farben and Flick cases were not affected because they had either already been released or were scheduled for release in the time since the Peck Panel conducted their deliberations. McCloy also released one prisoner on medical parole.[58] The remaining death sentences were carried out amidst great protest in June 1951.

In the January 1951 précis of his decisions, entitled "Landsberg: A Documentary Report," 500,000 copies of which were distributed among German political, religious, and institutional leaders and interested members of the public, McCloy made a special point of explaining his position vis-à-vis the military men in his custody.[59] Contrary to the common impression that the sentences against former soldiers maligned the German military profession as a whole, McCloy insisted that the judgments rendered at Nuremberg were based on charges of excess far surpassing anything that could be considered militarily necessary. He declared that he understood the bitter realities of partisan warfare and that when "the heat of battle" or "true military considerations" could be convincingly argued, he moderated the sentences. Regarding the High Command case convicts, he concluded that there remained "an area of real guilt which . . . a professional soldier . . . cannot countenance."[60] In a letter of thanks to Judge Peck and the other members of the clemency board, McCloy stated that the revision process had thrown "new light in Germany on the Nuremberg trials and is again giving the people an appreciation of the horrors of the Nazi regime." Although aware that the battle for public opinion had not yet been won, he concluded hopefully: "it looks as if we have gotten a good start toward writing a successful end to the chapter."[61] McCloy's optimism was misplaced.

The Response to McCloy's Landsberg Decisions

The response in the West German press to the Landsberg decisions was mixed. Most papers devoted considerable space (an average of a full page) to detailed analyses of the results. They mentioned each prisoner by name and quoted at length from McCloy's statements in the Landsberg report. Newspapers described the report as evidence of the high commissioner's "thoroughness" and "conscientiousness" in reviewing the cases. Indeed, papers emphasized the term "clemency" and referred to the American authorities' "goodwill," "impartiality," and readiness to grant prisoners "the benefit of the doubt."[62] Through its Press Information Office, the federal government praised the obvious "care and consideration" that had been devoted to each case. Predictably, the government, church officials, and many papers expressed regret that seven death sentences had been confirmed. This included two army cases over which General Handy had jurisdiction. Articles commonly referred to the fact that the death penalty had been abolished in West Germany, and that by now too much time had elapsed since the sentences were first imposed for the penalty still to be valid. However, other editorialists admitted that, particularly in regard to the SNP convicts, these sentences had applied only to "Nazi beasts," although one commentator called them "the last of Hitler's victims."[63]

Criticism of the Landsberg decisions tended to settle on issues of the Malmedy case and the confirmation of soldiers' sentences. As explained in chapter 2, the resentment about the Malmedy trial's conduct was profound. Even though General Handy commuted the death sentences of six of the S.S. officers involved, lingering doubts about their culpability made even their prison terms impossible to accept.[64] The federal government's military advisors criticized the decisions regarding their former colleagues, and an association of former German soldiers published a statement declaring that the Landsberg decisions "prove that the discrimination of the victors against the vanquished continues to exist."[65] Another report opined that the cases of the generals remained "a serious psychological burden for the German rearmament problem."[66] On the other hand, several articles praised the reduction of sentences for soldiers who had merely "followed orders." Perhaps the most telling piece appeared in an editorial in the *Frankfurter Allgemeine Zeitung*, entitled "Landsberg—Not the Last Chapter." The author praised McCloy's courage to "break with the dogma of the infallibility of the Nuremberg courts" but reproached his decisions on soldiers as misunderstanding contemporary realities: "It seems that the main argument for the approval of the hard sentences imposed on German generals is out of place in modern wars. . . . The case of soldiers shows clearly that Mr. McCloy's action of January 31 cannot mean the last word. It is Landsberg's last chapter but one, not the last."[67]

German opponents were unmoved by the Landsberg revisions. Analyzing over 1,000 letters written to McCloy in response to the clemency action, HICOG officials noted that most writers regarded the prisoners as Germans first, and as war criminals only second, if at all. Over 95 percent favored further sentence revisions, and half of these advocated a total abrogation of their terms. Of those who wrote, 60 percent were former soldiers or family members of soldiers. Significantly, a full 60 percent of correspondents cited the influence of press reports in having shaped their opinions.[68] That is, certainly the pre-Landsberg criticism of the press played its part in shaping opinion, although the post-Landsberg positive media assessments did not appear to have had much impact.[69] These letters represented all genders, ages, and institutions. Pastors wrote on behalf of their congregations, and men's and women's groups, youth groups, and local chapters of political organizations made appeals. Particularly striking were the letters from primary- to university-level students that emphasized that the handling of the Landsberg cases would have a decisive effect on their attitude toward cooperating in the defense of the West.[70]

The bases for their clemency requests tended to fall along several common lines of argumentation. They appealed to the principle of Christian charity, especially with regard to those facing the death penalty. Letters also cited the potential positive effects on German–American relations. They referred to Soviet crimes committed before and after the war, and they argued that a favorable disposition of the prisoners in American custody would have a positive influence on Soviet treatment of the German POWs still under their control.[71] The last set of appeals for amnesty or clemency centered on "legal" reasons for setting the sentences aside. They claimed irregularities in the conduct of the trials (the process that governed proceedings, the evidence used and the methods by which it was obtained, and the application of ex post facto law by victors over the vanquished). They emphasized that the new West German constitution had abolished the death penalty and concluded that it could not be enforced against the Landsberg prisoners. Frequently, they declared that the existence of superior orders ought to have been extenuating in the tribunals' assessments of defendants' activities.[72] That this correspondence contained, on the whole, a few standard arguments and at times even identical phrasing suggested that these letters were part of a well-organized campaign. Indeed, HICOG analysts noted that the provenance of letters clustered around certain geographical areas—for example, Munich, the home of Princess Isenburg's Arbeitung für Wahrheit und Gerechtigkeit

(Working Group for Truth and Righteousness), and Baden-Württemberg, where Bishop Wurm was most active.[73]

Several letters referred to the High Command case convicts by name. Heinz-Joachim Schmidt, a veteran of the eastern front as a commanding officer of a bomber wing and former General Staff officer, wrote to express his regret that McCloy's decisions had not extended to "most of the generals still suffering prisonership in Landsberg."[74] He protested that not even the most earnest prosecutors could understand the reality of war in the East or the situations with which generals had been confronted. He admitted that the Nazi civilian administration had caused great harm to occupied populations, but he added that "women and even children among the partisans" had caused great losses to the army before the commanding officers issued "actions" against the Russian population. He declared: "I consider it quite impossible that men such as . . . Reinhardt, Hoth or von Salmuth issued their orders against the partisans and their accomplices in a criminal way of thinking."[75] Similarly, Lieutenant Colonel Gerhard Matzky, German liaison director of the Labor Services Division of the U.S. Army European Command, who wrote on behalf of the largest group of former German soldiers who were at that time in service of the U.S. Army, expressed his disappointment over the situation of soldiers at Landsberg. In no uncertain terms Matzky concluded that the former officer corps's readiness for new military sacrifices was tenuous because their cooperation with rearmament depended on the "just revision of the Nurnberg verdicts against former German soldiers."[76] In support of this, Matzky reiterated that despite the brutal reality of war in the East, former High Command generals had committed no crime:

we former German soldiers know from our own experience with how much conscientiousness and seriousness our former higher troop leaders, as for example the former Field Marshals List and von Kuechler as well as General Reinhardt and others have been seeing to it that in the areas under their command the war was fought according to the general rules of international and human law, in spite of opposing criminal orders of their supreme commander Hitler and in spite of the fact that the Bolshevistic enemy, whom we at the time already had recognized as World Enemy No. 1 kept by no means whatsoever to the above rules.[77]

Like Schmidt, Matzky insisted that the "non–war experienced" judges had not taken account of the battle necessities of the time, perhaps because they "were lacking experience with an enemy whose complete recklessness they only very recently had an opportunity to feel for themselves."[78] This last statement was a veiled reference to the American experience in Korea. Other letters were explicit in comparing the German antipartisan fighting of World War II to measures allegedly used by the Americans against Communist partisans in the Korean War. Many even cited the "wisdom of German methods of dealing with partisans" as having been "confirmed in Korea."[79] Bishop Theophil Wurm took this approach when he wrote to McCloy, "The military commanders have profited less from the review than have other groups. Reports on the warfare in Korea raise the question in many instances whether the first sentences passed upon the generals were not perhaps based on insufficient knowledge of present-day partisan warfare, and whether therefore the sentences should not have been reduced to a greater extent."[80] To this, McCloy replied,

> There was no military reason behind the slaughter of Jews as such, or Gypsies, or other entirely non-military characters, where they had no relation whatever to incidents against German troops. And where men by their own orders countenanced or were responsible for such things I did not feel I could grant clemency. . . . Perhaps, although I have never seen any evidence to support the charge, which appeared first in certain Communist circles, severe counter-action had been taken in Korea against partisans. But of one thing you can be certain, no "Fuehrer" order was issued in Korea. There was not and there never will be any transmission of an order to kill all people of a certain religious belief and there is no one hundred to one reprisal order, and there never will be.[81]

Although untrue, the equation of the Wehrmacht's actions in the East with the Americans' experiences in the Far East fortified the German public's belief that atrocities were simply part of modern warfare. Nearly two years after the Landsberg decisions were handed down, press editorials were still referring to accusations of Western nations' misconduct in Korea and elsewhere. The *Frankfurter Allgemeine Zeitung* averred:

> In clashing with the notorious methods of Communism, the West kept its reputation no more unblemished than did the Germans. The unusual nature of guerilla warfare and the viciousness of ambush attacks, and the instinct for self-preservation, which can drive men to unleash uncontrollable passions, have harden [*sic*] the laws of war. Court proceedings can not change this. Above all, one should avoid making generalizations without knowledge of the local situation and when authentic eyewitnesses are lacking. Would it not be best to strike out the term "war criminals" in Germany and open the prisons?[82]

McCloy's numerous patient and impassioned responses to criticism of his decisions repeated two basic principles: that in his rulings on former soldiers he had differentiated between military necessity and crime, and that he had not been, nor would he be in the future, influenced by the political ramifications of his decisions.[83] To Baron Alexander von Falkenhausen, he declared, "I gave heavy consideration and thought to the cases of the generals, [and] the motivation for my decisions . . . was to distinguish . . . between action, even though it was drastic, which was related to military security and that which was merely carrying on a racial or political policy of peculiarly brutal character."[84] To Eleanor Roosevelt, who questioned his motives in having released so many from Landsberg, he contended, "Neither the clemency board nor I for one moment permitted political pressure inside or outside Germany to affect our decisions. . . . In Germany, as you may know, there has been considerable agitation that we should release the imprisoned generals at Landsberg and it was argued that such action would be helpful in achieving wide public support in Germany for participation in European defense. I repeat that such arguments had no effect on me. . . . You will notice that the chief German generals in Landsberg will remain there."[85]

McCloy expended much energy to convince individuals of the legitimacy of his Landsberg decisions and the legal and evidentiary records on which they were based. However, the sheer volume of dissent and its implied threat to future military cooperation between the United States and West Germany convinced HICOG officials that a more broad-reaching and ongoing response was required. But there was a split in the interpretation of the Germans' intercessions for war criminals and in the proposed remedies for this increasingly bothersome political problem. Because many analysts believed that the appeals on behalf of war criminals were the result of "confusion or ignorance of the facts," there was some reason to suppose that the publication of more information about the trials would undercut these requests. Accordingly, some HICOG officials emphasized that greater effort was required "to expose the motives and faulty reasoning of those who actively campaigned on behalf of the Landsberg prisoners."[86] They recommended an education program via the quasi-official American mouthpiece, *Die Neue Zeitung,* or through their newsreel material.[87]

By contrast, there were those who believed that the clemency appeals and requests for other concessions sprang from a deep-seated and conscious attempt to deny the assertions of the trials, which an information campaign alone would not likely reverse. From a pragmatic point of view, then, some American officials searched for a way to defuse the situation while still protecting the integrity of the proceedings. In a memo entitled "Comments on

Concessions to War Criminals," HICOG records officer Richard Hagan declared that the continuing agitation on behalf of imprisoned soldiers "is an attempt to wring from the Allied powers concessions which will lay the foundation for white-washing the German General Staff and officers corps. . . . So long as these ex-officers stand convicted as war criminals such objectives can not be achieved with ease."[88] He predicted that the Germans would eventually be brought around to Western defense plans, but under no circumstances should the integrity of the trials be compromised to hasten their reconciliation: "Former German officer corps members and ordinary soldiers will flock to Western defense without these concessions the moment the concrete political road is opened for them. Allied objectives in the war crimes program and trials cannot be defeated by adoption of these unsound suggestions."[89]

Nonetheless, perhaps recognizing that some gesture was required to achieve progress, Hagan recommended establishing a program whereby war criminals could apply annually to HICOG for sentence revisions or medical parole.[90] It is critical to note here again that, as with the 1950 clemency revisions, the American conception of parole and clemency entailed early release from prison, but on the basis of extenuating circumstances that neither negated the original sentences that had been imposed nor questioned the judicial conclusions upon which they had been based. In other words, despite early release, the men involved would still "stand convicted of war crimes."

Meanwhile, West German officials began working with the Allied High Commissions (that is, the American, British, and French) on an agreement to end occupation law and to iron out the details for the proposed West German contribution to the planned European Defense Community (EDC). The 1952 negotiations over the "Convention on the Settlement of Matters Arising out of the War and Occupation Treaty," which outlined Germany's future participation in the EDC, included discussion of the war criminals question. Exploiting the former Allies' desire to secure West German commitment to membership in the planned supranational West European army, Chancellor Adenauer, with the backing of almost the entire Bundestag and at the insistence of many veterans' associations, demanded the general release of prisoners convicted of war crimes.[91] Erich Mende, the chairman of the Foreign Policy Committee of the Free Democratic Party (part of Adenauer's coalition), had written to McCloy in November 1951: "If our common purpose of keeping Germany in the Western orbit . . . is to be achieved, it is essential to make further visible progress toward getting rid of the *rankling complex* of Landsberg."[92] During talks, the Allies offered to transfer jurisdiction over their war crimes prisoners to the Federal Repub-

THE DEBATE OVER IMPRISONED SOLDIERS   175

lic, provided that it promise to enforce the sentences as then in effect or as provided by a new clemency board.[93] Alternatively, the Allies proposed establishing a mixed board (including Allied and German members) to consider appeals and advise on clemency. Ultimately, because the German government refused to acknowledge the legitimacy of the trial judgments, when the Western occupation powers and Germany signed the Bonn Settlement Convention on 26 May 1952, they dropped the proposal for the transference of custody, but retained the plan for the institution of a mixed board.

Although recognized by a few individuals as progress on the issue, many more from the Bundestag, veterans' associations, and the press were displeased. They saw the proposed board not as a solution to the war criminals problem but rather as an institutionalization of it. That is, as the Foreign Ministry shamelessly noted, this was no onetime total *Endlösung* ("final solution") of the war criminals problem; rather, it entailed a procedure whereby convicts would only be dealt with individually through a process that affirmed the propriety of the original judgments and sentences.[94] Irrespective of immediate German opinion on the proposed plan, however, the mixed board could not begin its work until the Bundestag's ratification of the convention. Ten months of energetic campaigns in parliament, in veterans' associations, and in the press for the securing of a general amnesty followed. All three groups openly demanded release of war criminals in exchange for their support of the Bonn Convention, and more importantly, for the EDC.

It should be noted that by May 1952, only thirty-five men convicted by the SNP remained at Landsberg.[95] The rhetoric used by groups lobbying for their release obscured the fact that even fewer of them were actually soldiers. In the first place, all incarcerated war criminals were referred to as soldiers, even though many had had no connection to the Wehrmacht at all. Second, the term "war criminals" appeared only in quotation marks or preceded by the qualifier "so-called." Last, lobbyists conflated the category of "war criminals" with prisoners of war, identifying them with the POWs still held in foreign (particularly Soviet) territory. Discussion within the Bundestag perpetuated the view that the trials were simply acts of political retribution without valid legal foundation. In each of the debates on the subject of war criminals, "speakers from every German political party except the Communists attacked the theory of the trials—or the continued imprisonment of convicts—or both" and called for a single sweeping amnesty.[96]

Writing as chairman of the Verband deutscher Soldaten (Association of German Soldiers) and the Bund der ehemaliger versorgungsberechtigter Soldaten und Hinterbliebenen (Association of the Formerly Support-Entitled Soldiers and Their Heirs), which altogether represented, he claimed,

2 million veterans (the Americans estimated 80,000), and backed by another ten POW and veterans' associations, retired admiral Gottfried Hansen forwarded a resolution to the American High Commission that declared, "no German can be expected to don a military uniform again until the question of 'war criminals' has been satisfactorily settled."[97] The resolution rejected the remedy proposed by the Bonn Convention and urged the speedy granting of a general amnesty. The letter concluded by announcing the various veterans' associations' expectation that the federal government and Bundestag would insist on a solution, such as a general amnesty, as a prerequisite for ratification of the Bonn Treaty.[98] Through its journal *Der Heimkehrer* (*The Returnee*), another veterans' group organized a write-in campaign that elicited 40,000 postcards from German citizens demanding amnesty.[99]

The German press echoed and encouraged these sentiments and demands. HICOG officials noted the almost daily appearance of articles campaigning for the release of war criminals, focusing particular attention on former soldiers. In August 1952, the *Frankfurter Allgemeine Zeitung* printed an editorial that mentioned the cases of two High Command case convicts and its representation of them, their circumstances, and their crimes. It illustrates the style and tone of press coverage that sought to elicit sympathy for the prisoners, and to mislead the public about the scope of and personal responsibility for their wartime crimes. It read in part:

> Reinhardt had been sentenced severely on the ground that a patrol of a unit under his command brought in two prisoners who were not alive. At that time, General Reinhardt was on vacation. . . . And how is Mr. Donnelly [the new High Commissioner for Germany] going to deal with the case of Colonel General von Salmuth, whose wife has to earn her living as a cloakroom attendant? Salmuth is still imprisoned at Landsberg for offences committed on orders of his chief of staff.[100]

Overall, press arguments regarding Nuremberg tended to fall along the following lines: there were no war crimes and therefore no basis for trials; the Allies had applied victor's justice and ex post facto law; and soldiers had only followed orders. Moreover, the newspapers rarely referenced facts, and because they lumped all prisoners into the category of soldiers and all common crimes into the now dubious category of "war crimes," American analysts concluded that they had been able to "thoroughly mislead and confuse the German public."[101] Indeed, a 1952 poll revealed that 63 percent of respondents did not believe that German generals held as war criminals were actually guilty, and only 10 percent supported the war crimes program as a whole.[102]

Initially, as in 1951, High Commissioner McCloy held firm, stating plainly that a general or indiscriminate release of prisoners was simply too high a price to pay for confirmation of the Bonn Treaty. A HICOG Public Affairs Office guidance memo attempted to restore some much-needed perspective on the situation: "In no modern army except that of National Socialist Germany have orders that certain categories of prisoners of war and of civilians unconnected with combat or resistance be killed merely on grounds of their political, racial, or religious characteristics been issued by the supreme command, transmitted by army commanders and other high-ranking officers, and executed sweepingly. . . . Prisoners still in U.S. custody are those in whose cases no justifiable reason for release could be found."[103] Accordingly, American officials repeatedly insisted that these men had been found culpable for offenses ranging from assault to murder and therefore could be classified as common criminals. They tried striking back at the apparent West German consensus that sought to trade military support for the release of war criminals through their newspaper, *Die Neue Zeitung*. In an article entitled "A Necessary Clarification," U.S. authorities warned Germans not to make the war criminals question a political issue and declared that "during World War II things took place in the German Wehrmacht that until then had been absent from the armies of all civilized countries." They announced that neither the United States nor any other future partner of West Germany in the European Defense Community was prepared to purchase its military commitment with political concessions on the issue of war criminals.[104] Privately, however, U.S. occupation authorities realized that the continued incarceration of ten Wehrmacht generals (five of whom had been convicted in the High Command case) ensured the persistence of "a war criminals problem."[105]

Interestingly, American authorities were willing to accept a share of the responsibility for the failure of the German press, politicians, and citizens to understand the reasons for and findings of their war crimes trials. A July 1952 memorandum prepared for Eli Whitney Debevoise, deputy general counsel with HICOG, lamented that a lack of trial records available to the German people (as well as to HICOG officials themselves) had caused the "grief" experienced with the present "contract flap" and other prior war criminals issues, and had prevented these problems from having been more satisfactorily resolved. Frederick Hulse, the memo's author, reminded Debevoise that the original purpose of the trials "was to document the Nazi period and bring before the world generally and the Germans particularly a working knowledge of the Nazi state, what it was designed to accomplish, [and] the methods employed." Hulse stated pointedly that had American authorities honored their goal of education by ensuring the timely availability of the trial materials, then the present "scandalous deterioration" in the German public's understanding of war criminals and their crimes might have been avoided.[106] Debevoise communicated these sentiments to Assistant High Commissioner Samuel Reber, pointing out that at that time there were fewer than ten sets (actually there were seven, none of which were complete) of the trial records available in German in all of Germany. "As the German public is not informed," Debevoise explained, "unfriendly newspapers, unfriendly members of the legislature and unfriendly officials are able to focus attention on the prisoners without revealing any facts and as we have not made the facts available. . . . [We] are and will continue to be at a disadvantage for many years to come."[107]

The Failed German Publication Project

What explains this "scandalous" state of affairs? From the start, the Americans believed that they could control the situation. As the Subsequent Proceedings were drawing to a close, Chief Prosecutor Telford Taylor admonished his superiors against lapsing in their educational efforts. Recommending that significant excerpts of the trials be published in English and German, he reasoned, "The United States government has made a heavy moral investment in these trials, and this investment will not show a favorable rate of return if the records are left in the dust on the top shelf out of reach. . . . The Nuernberg record is a good one. We must not provide an excuse for ill-informed discussion of the Nuernberg trials by making access to the truth difficult."[108] He insisted that a publicly accessible record that documented the Nazi era constituted one of the most effective tools in the democratization of Germany:

> The re-education of Germany in order to provide a sound basis for a democratic government is a crucial objective, but it is far from easy to take effective steps in pursuance of this purpose. But one thing we can do is make the facts available to German historians, so that future generations of Germans will be able to grasp the full and malignant import of the Third Reich, and understand why it proved such a terrible engine of destruction for the world and for Germany herself.[109]

He further warned that without publication, the whole war crimes trials program would be left "truncated and incomplete."[110]

At first, Taylor's advice was followed, but from the outset, the English edition was clearly privileged over the German in terms of staff, budget, and page spread. The army controlled the purse strings. Their original plan allocated $317,000 for the publication in English of a fifteen-volume set of 1,000 pages per volume.[111] By contrast, the army dictated that the German edition should be only half as long, limited to 2,500 sets total, and moreover, that its publication was to be made dependent on the paper supply in Germany.[112] The men Taylor designated to oversee the publication project lobbied persistently for an increase in their budget to allow for 4,000 German sets so that 2,000 could be donated to universities and other interested institutions and the other 2,000 could be sold.[113] They argued that this project would only require a third of the amount allocated to the English edition and pointed out that the sale of these sets would allow the army to recoup half of its publication costs.[114] Although a minimally sufficient budget was granted for the preparation of the German manuscripts, no funds were promised for the actual printing of these volumes.[115]

At various times, Taylor, his former deputy chief of counsel, Drexel Sprecher (who was also in charge of the publication project), and Paul Gantt, director of the publications division for the German edition within the Office of the Chief of Counsel, War Crimes, all wrote to appeal for more generous support of the German project. They struggled to keep the preparation of the manuscripts progressing, enduring unending difficulties in obtaining and retaining qualified staff for the organizing and editing of the German volumes, and in full awareness that the German edition "[might] never see the light of day."[116] To the army, they forwarded correspondence from German scholars and citizens alike who asked about access to trial records to demonstrate the level of interest in Germany for these records.[117] They approached various publishing houses to negotiate deals that would help defray the costs to the army, either by profit sharing or guaranteed sales.[118] They reasoned that compared with the costs incurred by the proceedings, the publication project was insignificant, and yet bore such important implications: "a number of articles on the Nurnberg trials are being written in Germany, but there is nothing approaching an objective record or objective publication—and there will be none."[119] And further: "A failure to publish these proceedings in German will be regarded, especially by the Germans, as a sign of timidity and uncertainty in our occupation policy. Nurnberg has been too large a project, and its announced objectives too important and too closely associated with the occupation of Germany, to justify its deactivation without its activities being made a matter of record in the German language."[120]

Answering the critique that the proceedings should not be published because they constituted a "sore spot" in German–American relations and the advice that they should simply be "played down" and permitted to "sink into oblivion," Taylor argued that they were already too important in German history to be forgotten. The fact that they were being "bitterly attacked" in the press and journals meant that they were already the flash point of controversy in Germany. But, he added, the records of the proceedings were the necessary ammunition to end the dispute and rebuild a democratic German society.[121] Thomas Carson, who was in charge of the Office of the Military Government, U.S., Control Office, was unmoved by Taylor's plea, and expressed his doubt that the publication of the trial records "would reach the German masses and leave an imprint on the German mind."[122] For a while, the army remained open to having a German publishing firm underwrite the entire project, but in June 1949, they made clear that from their point of view, the "printing of completed German manuscripts cannot be assured."[123]

In the conclusion to his August 1949 final report, Taylor expressed his profound disappointment with the American authorities' disposition of the trial materials and again tried to impress upon his superiors the crucial importance of this issue:

> It seems to me that there has been an unfortunate lack of planned effort to utilize the documents and other evidence disclosed at the trials so as to advance the purposes of the occupation of Germany. Nowhere can these records be put to more immediate or better use than in German schools and universities, and in German books and magazines. . . . The least we can do is to insure that the documents which expose the true nature of the Third Reich are circulated throughout Germany. The Nuernberg documents must be used to the full . . . if the Germans of today are to grasp the truth about the past.[124]

Apparently, Taylor's arguments and warnings were unconvincing. In late October 1949, Secretary of the Army Gordon Gray revealed that the military regarded the trial reports "of insufficient value to the military to warrant their publication" and had suspended work on both editions. Although under pressure from the State Department and with funds granted by Congress efforts resumed on the English version, the German edition was never resuscitated.[125] Major Abraham Hyman, acting advisor on Jewish affairs at European Command headquarters, took up the matter with McCloy in December 1949: "There is . . . little room for doubt that the records of the major war crimes trials have inestimable value in the re-education of the German people. If the English edition can serve a purpose worthy of congressional support, it is . . . patently more important that Germans . . . should have ready access to an authentic account of Nazism at work." Requesting a revival of the German publication project, Hyman contended that "unless the U.S. authorities take the initiative in this matter . . . material which should be within easy reach of the Germans, will be either relegated to the museums or fall into the hands of those who may be interested in suppressing the facts the trials revealed."[126]

Time passed, and nothing was done to advance the German publication project, despite the fact that public ignorance and/or denial of the trials' findings had greatly complicated the debate over imprisoned war criminals. As it was, the only document on the trials issued by the American High Commission was the Landsberg report, which explained McCloy's January 1951 clemency decisions. A mere eight pages of this publication was dedicated to summarizing all twelve Subsequent Proceedings. Described as "only a good newspaper article," it had undeservedly become the "authoritative" German document on the trials.[127] Soon after this document was released, and in view of the fact that occupation headquarters continued to be bombarded by criticisms and appeals, there was some discussion about whether there would be any benefit in disseminating additional material. But even at this point, certain occupation officials advised against this strategy. One HICOG advisor told McCloy that releasing justifications "had the tendency to keep issues alive and to invite further counter-blasts to the point where it became a form of scab-picking," and that he would do well to let the matter "die down."[128] Although this advisor was aware of the strong reasons for keeping the matter alive, he believed that the publication of trial material would have the opposite effect intended: "The more we ourselves publish or release the more rebuttal material we invite. Furthermore, there is the danger that every statement that will be issued will be put under a microscope and examined not with respect to its genuine merits and broad implications but merely for the purpose of seeking either technical flaws or areas in which legitimate differences of opinion may exist. We have been through this mill enough times so that we may fairly know what to expect."[129]

However, withholding trial documents had not allowed the matter to die down. Rather, as HICOG staffers Debevoise and Hulse noted, it was the absence of available court records from both the Germans and American authorities in Germany that had, they believed, unnecessarily complicated negotiations over the end to occupation and future military cooperation and had, moreover, disadvantaged the U.S. position.[130] Hulse wrote: "It is now apparent that had the records been published and *even if bound records had been available to us,* the grief experienced with the clemency decisions of January 1951 . . . and the contract flap of 1952 would have been more easily, satisfactorily and convincingly dealt with by referring to them."[131] It was all the more frustrating given that, as Debevoise explained, it had been his and other HICOG officials' experience that Germans' attitudes changed once they found out what the Subsequent Proceedings actually involved.[132]

Assistant High Commissioner Reber summarized the situation as it stood in late July 1952. Given that individuals from German military and political circles were staking ratification of the EDC on the "solution" of the war criminals problem, there was a need to remind American authorities in Germany of the crimes that had been committed. Accordingly, HICOG sent out summaries of the records of prisoners still in U.S. custody. Reber declared that the United States had no reason to doubt the convictions and sentencing of the men held in Landsberg, but in the same breath he added, "It is our primary purpose at this time to prevent this issue from becoming an obstacle to ratification of the Bonn Agreements and European Defense Treaty and to forestall its developing into a serious impediment to future military cooperation." He argued that they must not "tamper with the judgments" or give in to indiscriminate release. He concluded that the mixed clemency board outlined in the contractual agreements posed the most promising solution. However, because ratification was still months away, the question of what to do at the moment to quell continued opposition had to be resolved.[133]

The mixed clemency board was envisioned for the future, but American authorities began exploring the possibilities and potential benefits of a publication campaign. On 19 August, the HICOG Office of Public Affairs inquired about the condition and use of German SNP records held at Göttingen and Heidelberg. The Institut für Völkerrecht in Göttingen had one complete set of the twelve trials' records. Despite being unbound and lacking complete indexes, the director of the institute reported that they were very much in use by graduate students, professors, lawyers, and writers. Although no copies had been made for sale or general use, the institute received constant inquiries for reproductions of particular sections.[134]

Heidelberg's university library possessed a partial record of the trials—about 75 percent of the transcripts and evidence exhibits. About three quarters of these were in German. Although none of the documents had arrived bound, the university had spent 26,000 deutsche marks to bind them itself. At the time of HICOG's inquiry, they had no indexes but were handwriting their own, as well as tables of contents. However, the completion of this modest project was dependent on securing additional funds that library staff doubted would materialize. Because the university did not want to publicize their possession of the records until they were fully processed, only twenty-three students had thus far consulted them. Further, the university planned to reserve the documents for research only and would not open them to general use by the public. Beyond what existed at Heidelberg and Göttingen, no university in Germany possessed a complete set of trial materials.[135]

Because trial records in German existed only in an unorganized and mostly inaccessible state, HICOG officials leaned toward publication and wide distribution of German-language copies of the indictments and judgments pertaining to the prisoners in their custody.[136] This might, some thought, go some way toward correcting the contemporary situation whereby complainants and respondents dealt with "a handful of prisoners on subsidiary matters which are so troublesome that . . . both the Allies and the Germans have forgotten why the trials were held."[137] Taking the High Command case in point, one observer noted that the generals were "usually described as the innocent soldiers illegally imprisoned, or . . . too old or too sick to serve their sentences," instead of men convicted of egregious war crimes amply and convincingly documented in a court of law. Even the *Frankfurter Allgemeine Zeitung* had recently suggested publishing extracts from the judgments "in order to help reach an understanding."[138]

Once again, HICOG deputy counsel Debevoise made an impassioned and comprehensively argued plea for the publication project. He began by explaining how German politicians and the press had made the subject of war criminals a central concern through daily newspaper articles and speeches inside and outside the Bundestag. Although by September 1952 only 35 men of the original 142 convicted in the SNP remained at Landsberg, the presence among them of career generals ensured that HICOG would continue to have an "unliquidated" war criminals problem. He emphasized that criticism centered on the military leaders because the general public thought "that whatever they did was done as a military matter and in a military manner and no blame attaches."[139] Debevoise did not think that the situation was likely to improve. He concluded, "The German campaign is aimed at unraveling loose threads in the fabric of action taken by the Allies on war criminals, and thus progressively unraveling the whole fabric." Moreover, the campaign was narrowing in focus. Debevoise explained that "the spearhead of the approach is directed at freeing the 'upright' military men," whose cases could be depicted "more sympathetically . . . and in ways which are difficult to refute propagandistically." Furthermore, prior granting of clemency had only opened the way for further appeals and had placed the American authorities on the defensive.[140]

Debevoise remarked that occupation authorities were "faced with . . . a long haul" but recognized that steps had to be taken immediately. These included consulting with the army in order to "reduce the problem to something less conceptual and more tangible" and to make accurate information available to the German public, press, and politicians. In the longer term, he advocated the publication, in German, of the entire judgments and opinions. He ended his memo with a prediction that the United States would eventually be forced into negotiations over the war criminals issue with the German government—that is, that they had lost the initiative and authority. America would be at a disadvantage, he added angrily, because "no concerted effort has been made to clarify the questions in any way and no single unit or national element is in a position to deal with the whole question with full knowledge of the facts."[141]

Not everyone shared Debevoise's conviction that a publication campaign was the solution. Questioning the wisdom of releasing the case summaries that HICOG had prepared, Secretary of State Dean Acheson was concerned that such large amounts of "raw material" would merely "increase the heat of discussion; would be unpersuasive and would create the probability that we be dragged into discussion of individual cases" and pressed for release of additional documents without any positive effects on the EDC and Bonn Convention ratification.[142] At the same time, however, he conceded that the State Department believed that German sympathy for war criminals could be traced back to their not having understood their crimes. However, rather than issuing material from the trials, Acheson suggested a different approach. He argued in favor of educating the German public (through politicians and the press, particularly *Die Neue Zeitung*) about the true nature of the crimes committed by relating war crimes, whenever possible, to common-law crimes or violation of ordinary (and familiar) law codes. Because it was clear that in West Germany a general attitude had emerged that equated "war crimes" with acts that "any soldier might commit in time of war," Acheson hoped simple references to murder, as opposed to references to violations of the Geneva Convention and The Hague Convention, might "divest war crimes and war criminals of military aura which carries the implication that punishment is unjust."[143] His recommendation is significant because it demonstrates that United States–German relations with respect to war criminals had so regressed that not only were the Americans reluctant to put the trial records before the public, but even the very terms "war crime" and "war criminal" were to be removed from dialogue. Two weeks later, occupation officials in Germany confirmed that although they remained concerned about "meeting the pressure of German public opinion," they did not intend to open the publication campaign. In the short term, they wished to avoid being "dragged into unprofitable discussions of individual cases." In the longer term, they did not believe that such a strategy would pose any "lasting . . . remedy for a problem which to Germans is essentially political and emotional."[144]

By the end of 1952, belief in the possibility of winning over German public opinion vis-à-vis war criminals had so diminished that the HICOG Office of Political Affairs undertook to devise a solution that would leave the verdicts untouched but would, from a practical point of view, solve the problem. Noting that both the Protestant and Catholic churches and political parties of all stripes had not relaxed their campaigns for release, analysts believed that if German public opinion on this issue did not change soon, then the EDC, the Bonn Convention Treaty, and even the Adenauer government were in danger of failing.[145] A telegram to the State Department reported:

> It is clear that Ger[man] agitation for release of war criminals has gained considerable momentum and it can be predicted that the increase will continue over the coming months. Problem will undoubtedly cause chancellor difficulty in ratification process and may cut his majority by enough coalition votes to cast doubt on validity and finality of ratification vote. But the problem will not end with ratification. On the contrary, it will affect both the wholeheartedness of the Ger[man] defense effort and the chancellor's chances of success at the polls in early summer 1953 unless problem has been both rapidly and finally solved after EDC comes into effect.[146]

Indeed, opposition to the continued imprisonment of soldiers showed no signs of relenting.[147] The German Ministry of Defense officials informed occupation authorities that they had been receiving a "flood of letters" from former colleagues and veterans' associations stating that they would "never volunteer for service until the war criminals problem had been solved."[148] The idea that military men were guilty of war crimes had simply not penetrated public consciousness, and careful explanation and education were by now seen to be pointless. As one HICOG commentator explained,

> With regard to . . . those convicted of shooting hostages and partisans, there is real disagreement as to their guilt. [Germans] insist that similar actions have been taken by United Nations troops in Korea or British troops in Malaya, often producing detailed accounts . . . which cannot be refuted without more accurate facts about the same incidents. Even when every argument has been met, as we have attempted to do through a study of all case records available to this office, and the protest dies down from want of further fuel, it has been found that within a week the same protest will be made again by the same person, who apparently feels that he was argued down but not proved wrong.[149]

Ultimately, HICOG concluded, with regret, that the United States was now in two unavoidable yet fundamentally contradictory roles: "occupier

and executor of occupation justice" and "Germany's ally and friend." Added
to this realization was the belief that there was no time left to coax the Germans around to seeing the legitimacy of the trials' conclusions. With the
Bonn Treaty ratification and a federal election looming large, American
authorities noted that the crucial time to resolve the war criminals issue was
now—and could not wait for the mixed board envisioned by the Bonn Convention to come into existence, let alone for prisoners' sentences to expire.[150]
Disappointed by their own failings, worn down by the uncertainty of its military security combined with relentless pressure from the West German
public, and worn out by what was now the eighth year of occupation, the
HICOG Offices of Political Affairs and Public Affairs recommended the
disposition of the war criminals problem via a jointly (American and German) administered process that would implement "a more lenient system of
sentence reduction and parole."[151] Concluding that "a solution cannot be
brought about ... by the refusal to see the problem in its political ... light,"
they proposed to the State Department that the situation be resolved in six
to nine months, advising that the United States should first release those
prisoners "whose retention will continue to occasion major outcry."[152] At
the top of the list were the High Command case generals. This new policy
in the disposition of the war criminals issue, the memorandum's authors
admitted, ignored the juridical and moral aspects of the problem. Indeed, it
represented a departure from the American war crimes trial program's
founding goals of justice and education.[153] Nevertheless, the new course had
been set. The final disposition of the High Command case convicts is the
subject of the next chapter.

In one way, the American war crimes trial of representatives of the German High Command was a success: prosecutors meticulously cataloged and
judges confirmed the criminal activities of the Wehrmacht during the war.
Considering that even the most conservative estimates of the Wehrmacht's
total victims numbered in the millions, the sentences imposed on the guilty
field marshals and generals were symbolic of a greater guilt and responsibility shared by thousands more perpetrators. Unfortunately, the political
authorities who were entrusted with the trial record and the responsibility
to honor its conclusions by enforcing even these meager sentences failed in
their task. By not having communicated the substance of the proceedings
in a timely and effective way, American authorities squandered whatever
opportunity they had possessed to convince the German people under their
administration of the legitimacy of the trials' judgments and reconcile them
to their recent traumatic past. Particularly in the case of imprisoned soldiers,
this omission was deliberately exploited by the Bundestag, the press, the
churches, and veterans' associations, who, with little grounding in the facts,

mounted and sustained a campaign to empty Landsberg of its inmates. The German government strengthened the offensive by using its increasing political weight and military indispensability to pry convicted war criminals loose from American custody. The "resolution" of the war criminals problem raises pressing questions about the limitations on the court's ability to make its work relevant to public understanding and memory. Although organized and prosecuted with a view to their educational function, the American Subsequent Proceedings at Nuremberg required strong political commitments to carry their lessons beyond the bench. In the context of the nascent Cold War, commitments to education were, regretfully, politically inopportune.

7

Setting the War Criminals Free: The Interim and Mixed Clemency and Parole Boards, 1953 to 1958

> May I extend to you my personal congratulations on the successful outcome of your petition for parole. We all wish you happiness, good health, and all success for the future.
> —Colonel W. S. Nye, chief of the Historical Division, U.S. Army, Europe, to General Walter Warlimont, 16 June 1954

BY THE END OF 1952, the Americans capitulated to German pressure for a resolution of the war criminals problem, which had been exacerbated by the political exigencies of the Cold War and compounded by the United States' failure to legitimize the trials to the German public. They now had to devise the mechanism by which to release the remaining prisoners at Landsberg. The Bonn Convention to end occupation, which the Allies and West Germany negotiated in May 1952, envisioned a mixed board including British, French, American, and German members who would consider clemency appeals from war criminals convicted in Allied courts. However, this mixed board would not come into effect until the convention's ratification, still a projected two to three years in the future. Concluding that they had to act on the war criminals issue immediately, the Americans created the Interim Mixed Parole and Clemency Board, composed of U.S. and German representatives, to evaluate applications and recommend actions to the appropriate U.S. High Commission for Occupied Germany (HICOG) and army officials. Established on 31 August 1953 by joint order of High Commissioner James Conant and commander in chief, U.S. Army, Europe, General Charles Bolte, the Interim Mixed Board included three Americans and two Germans. HICOG had suggested that the three Americans consist of a civilian judge or lawyer, a representative of the State Department, and a general—"men of real stature"—who had in no way been connected to the war crimes trials.[1] Accordingly, U.S. officials appointed Henry Shattuck, a Boston lawyer and former treasurer of Harvard University, as the chairman of the board. Edwin Plitt, a career foreign service officer, and Major General Walter Muller of the U.S. Army completed the American contingent. The German Ministry for Foreign Affairs nominated Dr. Emil Lersch, a retired justice of the federal Supreme Court, and Dr. Hans Meuschel, president of the Bavarian State Court, and they were duly appointed.[2]

Although it was clear that the board had been created for the very purpose of granting early release to the convicted, HICOG and the army took pains (if only on paper) to protect the integrity of the war crimes trial program. By provision of the joint order, they insisted that neither parole nor clemency represented a reappraisal of the propriety or legality of the trials, and they prohibited the board from questioning the applicant's guilt and sentence, which were to be considered "final and incontestable."[3] Instead, their decisions would be predicated on the overall context of the crime or crimes in question. Of significance was whether the offense was a single action or repeated over a long period of time, what the position and authority of the criminal was at the time that the crime was committed, whether the individual had committed the crime on his own initiative or upon superior orders, whether there was any disparity between the criminal's sentence and other sentences imposed for similar offenses, and the convict's age, health, conduct, and overall character.[4] In practice, the question arose as to the admissibility of allegedly new evidence. The board decided that it would not use such evidence to challenge the original verdicts, but would take it into consideration if it provided "insight into the character of the applicant and the likelihood of his successful reintegration into society."[5]

In principle, parole was a continuation of punishment, in that it would involve close supervision and a prohibition against political activity and public statements or writing by the parolees.[6] The parolee would have to make monthly reports and seek approval for any change in employment or travel beyond a specified area. Further, he was not to associate with "evil companions," codefendants from his trial, or anyone else convicted of war crimes, and he was to avoid "immoderate use of intoxicating liquors."[7]

When the Interim Mixed Parole and Clemency Board began its work in November 1953, there were still 313 prisoners at Landsberg or on medical parole, only 31 of whom were convicts from the Subsequent Nuremberg Proceedings (SNP). Of the original High Command case convicts, only three, Hermann Hoth, Hermann Reinecke, and Walter Warlimont, remained in prison. The others had either completed their sentences, died, or been released on medical or compassionate parole. Since the time of the Peck Panel's reviews, medical or compassionate parole was available to convicts in exceptional circumstances. For example, Georg von Kuechler was released on medical parole on 18 February 1953 on the basis of several chronic conditions, including emphysema and arteriosclerosis. While on medical parole, he was prohibited from leaving Bavaria, and he could not work, be politically active, speak publicly, or publish any material.[8]

In Hans Reinhardt's case, in November 1950, his daughter, with whom he was very close, suffered a psychotic break and attempted suicide. In her doctor's opinion, it was her distress over her father's conviction and imprisonment that prompted the crisis. Reinhardt applied for compassionate parole in order to care for her and his wife. In the March 1952 HICOG evaluation of the petition, the reviewing officer concluded that Reinhardt represented a good parole candidate because he had "only received and executed orders in the field." McCloy acquiesced, but he cautioned that "there should be no publicity" about Reinhardt's release, which he granted on 14 June 1952.[9]

Hans von Salmuth also applied for medical parole in the spring of 1951 but was refused. Although the record is patchy, it is clear that he left Landsberg sometime in the summer of 1953, most likely on good conduct release.[10] The good conduct time remission program (explained in chapter 6) continued throughout the many changes to the overall parole and clemency system. Any convict who met the requirements automatically obtained good conduct release upon having served two thirds of his sentence. If a convict had been released on parole (for which he was eligible after serving one third of his sentence) before having served two thirds of his sentence, upon reaching that date, his status was changed from "paroled" to "good conduct release." These men were still considered prisoners, however, and the convict remained subject to certain restrictions and to limited supervision by the U.S. parole officer. Only the granting of clemency ended the prisoner status.[11]

The Parole and Clemency Applications

The intensity and tenacity of German demands for the release of prisoners sentenced at Nuremberg convinced the Americans that the cases of all war criminals required swift and comprehensive action. Accordingly, U.S. officials concluded that the compassionate and medical parole program already in place was neither adequate nor equitable, and they replaced it with reviews by the Interim Mixed Board. Under the new system, prisoners serving finite terms would apply to the board for parole, and if successful, they could thereafter apply for clemency to have their sentences commuted to time served. Those serving life sentences first had to apply for clemency for a reduction in their sentence, then parole, then clemency again. To be sure, this was a complex, time-consuming, and costly program to administer.

The interim board made its decisions based solely on written records. Neither the applicant nor his attorney was permitted to appear before the board. Parole applications consisted of a variety of documents and reports, including the applicant's institutional record, the prison director's evaluation of whether the parolee was likely to adjust well to civilian life, a certificate affirming the identity and responsibilities of the appointed parole sponsor, and a summary of the case in which the applicant had been convicted.

The case summary consisted of a one-page précis specifying the name of the trial concerned, all previous clemency actions, and the projected release date. The summary devoted only two paragraphs to a description of the applicant's offenses and the extent of his participation. The HICOG records officer, who prepared the report, drew this information from the judgments as they appeared in the Green Series, the collection of excerpts from the Subsequent Proceedings, published by the U.S. government. This report for the board included no explanation of the evidence, nor did it provide any sense of the scope and scale of the suffering and lost lives involved. Despite the fact that neither verdicts nor sentences could be challenged during the parole and clemency evaluation processes, outside groups and institutions sometimes submitted material on the applicant's behalf, which purported to refute evidence in the record and/or conclusions made by the court. For example, in Hermann Hoth's case, the Zentrale Rechtsschutzstelle (Central Office for the Protection of the Law), the federal organization that advocated on behalf of imprisoned war criminals, obtained sworn statements from two veterans who disputed the date of a particular massacre of Jews discussed in Hoth's prosecution.[12] None of these submissions was sufficiently extensive to offset the verdict as a whole, let alone in part, but they did reveal the Germans' stubborn refusal to accept the judgments as final.

Members of the German public also intervened on behalf of the applicants. In Reinecke's case, thirty-seven former and current government officials, retired military officers, and leaders of veterans' associations, church representatives, a Swiss diplomat, and private citizens—all former colleagues, subordinates, and friends—submitted statements in support of his clemency application. They emphasized his "honorable," "chivalrous," "genteel, steadfast, kind and upright" disposition; his constant concern for "the welfare of his fellow man"; and his vigorous advocacy for the Geneva Convention during the war. They declared with confidence that if released, he would pose no problem politically, especially since he was still anti-Bolshevist. One admitted that he had had "a weakness for National Socialism" and that he may have made mistakes, but that his "fair and good activities done in favor of so many fellow creatures" warranted his consideration for clemency. Another argued that what he had done had only been done out of obedience to superior orders and that certain aspects of his duties had been repugnant to him.[13]

Help for the convicts came in other forms as well. Officials of religious organizations such as the Protestant Innere Mission (Inner Mission) volunteered to act as parole sponsors.[14] Government pension offices issued statements certifying the amount to which the defendants were entitled upon their release. In some cases, the wives of the convicts had already been receiving this support.[15] The veterans' and POW association Verband der Heimkehrer, Kriegsgefangenen und Vermissten–Angehörigen (Association of Returnees, Prisoners of War and Relatives of the Missing), a group encompassing a half million ex-soldiers and the family members of those who remained in foreign custody as POWs or who were still missing in action, asked its members to make known what jobs members could guarantee to potential parolees, in order to show occupation authorities that these convicts would pose no financial burden to society if let go.[16]

In the words of their captors, the three High Command case convicts seemed ideal candidates for parole. Hoth's work in the prison laundry was rated "excellent," he spent his leisure time reading, and he had conducted himself with courtesy and cooperation toward the Landsberg personnel and other prisoners. Landsberg director Colonel E. C. Moore believed that as a soldier, Hoth would feel honor-bound to carry out his duties as a good citizen, and his personal "trustworthiness" offered every reason to support his parole.[17] Moore expressed similar sentiments about Reinecke, describing him as calm, reserved, courteous, and cooperative. His work in the prison laundry, supply room, and hospital was admirable, and he spent his free time quietly working on his family tree and reading. Indeed, incarceration seemed to have had "little outward effect" on him, as he had always maintained a "high morale" and "a good sense of humor."[18] Believing him to be "a man of integrity" and possessing above-average intelligence, the Landsberg director assured the board that Reinecke would be "an asset to any community."[19] As for Warlimont, Moore depicted him as somewhat more aloof, but added that he had never caused any trouble. He preferred to spend his time, when not tending the prison garden or teaching Spanish to his fellow inmates, writing military studies for the army's historical division. In the words of its chief, Warlimont had willingly and cheerfully made a "unique contribution to the writing of military history in the national interest," filling in the many gaps in materials captured from the Germans.[20] Moore concluded that Warlimont possessed the "mental, physical and cultural background qualifications to make him an excellent citizen."[21]

In theory, one of the requirements for parole was some evidence that the convict "regretted" the acts for which he had been convicted.[22] Were the High Command case generals remorseful? The record clearly shows that they were not. Warlimont told prison officials that he believed he had to accept responsibility "for certain occurrences" because he had been a senior officer, but that he bore no personal guilt.[23] Reinecke similarly had accepted his conviction as a matter of "fate" stemming from the high position he occupied.[24] Six years after the conclusion of the trial, Hoth still did not feel that he had committed any crime.[25] Moreover, in an interview with Director Moore, he revealed his resentment toward parole. Having hoped to leave Landsberg a free man, he was disappointed that he would remain subject to the same "dishonoring and oppressive" conditions applicable to common criminals. He declared that the German public expected the stigma of crime to be removed from the Landsberg convicts, and warned that if it was not, there would be negative consequences for future military cooperation.[26] Still, the convicts' lack of contrition proved no impediment to their release. Overall, American authorities regarded these men as well behaved, peaceful, and harmless. Within thirteen months of the interim board having been established, the Americans returned these last three remaining High Command case convicts to their homes, their families, their communities, and their pensions.

The Last High Command Case Generals Return Home

Upon his release, Reinecke moved into a new apartment in the "most exclusive quarter" of Hamburg, continued the genealogical studies that he had begun in prison, and resumed his favorite sport of hunting.[27] He showed absolutely no bitterness over his conviction and imprisonment. Indeed, he expressed to his parole officer his appreciation for the treatment he had received during his incarceration and for the opportunity to be paroled, which he found to be no hardship. By contrast, Hoth remained depressed and angry and told his parole supervisor that he was still convinced of his own innocence. He insisted that he could produce witness statements "proving" that he gave no criminal orders, and that he had known nothing about the incidents for which he had been convicted. Nonetheless, he too lived a quiet life, passing the time walking in the mountains around his home in Goslar.[28] Warlimont, "the most outstanding and most intelligent parolee," also kept to himself. His parole officer had the impression that his "correct and etiquette-addicted manner" made friendships difficult. However, he did attend cultural events in his hometown and was active in his church, where he always demonstrated "an open hand and a good heart," as his priest attested.[29] He continued his work for the army historical division, for which its chief, Edward James, remained ever appreciative.[30] Only fifty-nine years old when released from Landsberg, Warlimont had expressed some interest in returning to the new West German army. Because he had demonstrated that he could be trusted, the U.S. parole officer did not see any cause for concern.[31]

All told, the interim board released 250 prisoners on parole, and reduced two convicts' sentences to time served.[32] This left forty-nine "hard core" (in the Americans' words) Landsberg prisoners for consideration by the future mixed board.[33] The ratification of the European Defense Community (EDC) Treaty in West Germany in March 1953, the restoration of German sovereignty through the ratification of the Bonn Convention and the Paris Protocols on 23 October 1954 (which went into effect on 5 May 1955), and the introduction of the first military legislation in the Bundestag reinvigorated political and public interest in the question of the remaining war criminals imprisoned in Germany. Although in August 1954 the EDC Treaty failed ratification in France (originally the plan's primary author), West Germany was invited to participate in NATO. Therefore, the main elements of the debate over the release of war criminals before any German military contribution to the defense of the West did not change significantly.[34] Representatives of all coalition parties, the press, and other organizations and institutions, such as the Verband der Heimkehrer, Deutscher Caritasverband, and the Zentrale Rechtsschutzstelle, as well as prominent leaders from the Protestant and Catholic churches, renewed appeals for release. They argued that the West German government could not recruit armed forces while soldiers remained imprisoned on German soil, that a better class of professional soldier would not serve so long as former colleagues were in jail, that "ten years in prison is enough punishment," that it would aid the release of POWs still being held in the USSR, and that it would bring right-wing nationalists into the mainstream Federal Republic fold.[35]

The Mixed Clemency and Parole Board

The mixed board, formed in August 1955, combined representatives of Britain, France, and the United States with an equal number of German members. Upon its establishment, the American embassy, which had assumed jurisdiction over former HICOG prisoners when occupation ended, declared its intention to follow the mixed board's recommendations on the release of war criminals, emphasizing, "We believe that the U.S. member of the board will be as lenient as appropriate in dealing with the remaining U.S. cases."[36] There were only forty-nine men remaining in Landsberg when the mixed board began its work in October 1955. Ten of these were SNP convicts, but none were generals convicted during the High Command case.[37] For the remaining Landsberg prisoners' parole applications, the mixed board focused less on the nature of the offense than on the convict's prison conduct record and potential for successful readjustment to society.[38] In its evaluations of applications for clemency (essentially the reduction of sentences or parole to time served), the mixed board weighed the gravity of the offense against the length of the sentence and against other sentences served or being served for similar crimes. Obviously, prior granting of parole and clemency had created an ever more moderate basis for comparison. In August 1955, Britain and France still had forty-five war criminals in their custody at the prisons of Werl and Wittlich. Between 1955 and the end of 1957, the mixed board granted them all early release, and the British and French authorities imposed no restrictions or conditions on their freedom.[39]

By contrast, the Americans retained the parole and clemency procedures instituted during the previous two years. However, as early as 1955, few of those prisoners released on parole bothered to apply for clemency from the mixed board. Their parole officers reported that the former Landsberg prisoners were confident that the West German government would force some action that would bring the whole war criminal issue to an end.[40] By the spring of 1957, close to 300 American cases remained under the board's jurisdiction, with the last sentence set to expire in 1985. In view of Britain's and France's final disposition of the cases, Spencer Phenix, the American member of the mixed board, recommended an acceleration of the clemency-granting process. In his view, parole (which was intended to facilitate reintegration into society and prevent a criminal relapse) had ceased to serve any real purpose, as recidivism was unlikely. Accordingly, the Americans gradually phased out the parole system by commuting the remaining sentences to time served.[41]

However, this still left four prisoners serving life terms at Landsberg. They were Adolf Ott, Ernst Biberstein, and Martin Sandberger, all convicts in the Nuremberg Einsatzgruppen trial, and Otto Brinkmann, a convict from the Nordhausen (a subcamp of Buchenwald) concentration camp case tried at Dachau. Interestingly, when in January 1958 the German Foreign Office submitted applications for parole on their behalf (an unprecedented step), the U.S. parole officer recommended to the mixed board that they be denied, declaring that these men would be of "no benefit to society or themselves" if released. In response, the German government applied for clemency. Given that Britain and France had already released all of their war criminals unconditionally, the mixed board did not believe they could justifiably keep them in prison. The mixed board commuted their sentences to time served, and on 9 May 1958, all were set free from Landsberg.[42] In the end, the longest any war criminal spent in Western Allied custody, aside from the International Military Tribunal convicts held at Spandau, was nearly thirteen years. Only four convicts were imprisoned this long, and they all served under American jurisdiction. It would seem that the United States was the most reluctant of the former Western Allies to "abandon the principle of punishment."[43]

One of the most striking aspects of the clemency and parole process was the existence in West Germany of resolute, well-organized, and persistent support for the High Command case generals and their fellow inmates in Landsberg. From the beginning of the first Subsequent Proceedings until the establishment of the mixed board, private citizens and public officials, clergy and veterans, friends and strangers, provided funding for their legal representation and for family visits to the prison, and circulated critiques of the trials. They intervened with occupation authorities, provided care for their families, vouched for their release on parole, and guaranteed them jobs or pensions upon their release. Appeals by these groups and individuals to occupation officials reveal an ongoing effort to justify and mitigate the prisoners' participation in the policies and actions deemed criminal by the courts, even though they never conceded that the convicted were guilty, criminally or otherwise. Once released, communities welcomed the generals with open arms. Clearly, the record of the Wehrmacht's criminal past, let alone of the convicts' personal contributions to Nazi crimes, had made virtually no impact on German public consciousness. Although the Americans never retracted the verdicts they passed against these men, the early and near-wholesale release of the convicts could not but have undermined the magnitude of the crimes that earned the sentences. Abandoning punishment was simply the final stage in the long series of actions that eroded the trials' didactic value. Although subsequent historical research ultimately vindicated the record of Wehrmacht crime created during the High Command case, generations would pass before this history gained wide acceptance.

Conclusion

There are no tidy endings following mass atrocity.
—Martha Minow

EVEN AS LATE AS THE 1990s, the notion that the Wehrmacht was guilty of war crimes and crimes against humanity during World War II had not penetrated German public consciousness. Most Germans had embraced an entirely different image of the Wehrmacht, which can be traced to the November 1945 Memorandum of the Generals: the army's first formally articulated claim to innocence. This memorandum echoed through the defense arguments raised during the High Command case and through the myriad objections to the continued imprisonment of soldiers convicted of war crimes. The basic premises of these claims were that the military had been no servant of Hitler or his racial and political policies; that it had accepted war against the Soviet Union as a preventive war, and that the Soviets, in view of their international ambitions, were a justifiable target; that the military had had no knowledge of or control over the S.S.'s destruction of the Jews; that other crimes may have occurred, but these were provoked by the enemy, whose conduct was no better and likely even worse; and that soldiers had merely done their duty and ultimately became victims of the state they reluctantly obeyed.[1] This counterimage of the German military in World War II entered the public imagination as a myth of the Wehrmacht's "clean hands." Its attraction and its longevity are not surprising. Given that 20 million "ordinary" Germans had served in the army, to accept the Nuremberg prosecution's version of events would have implicated vast portions of German society in Nazi crime.[2]

Although a handful of talented and courageous German scholars began writing about the true history of the Wehrmacht's conduct during World War II during the mid-1960s, it took another thirty years to dislodge the myth from public memory.[3] This occurred with the 1995 exhibition entitled "War of Extermination: Crimes of the Wehrmacht, 1941–1944." Sponsored by the privately funded Institute for Social Research in Hamburg, the exhibition focused on the army's conduct in Ukraine, Byelorussia, and Serbia. It detailed the army's shooting and hanging of civilians, its participation in the destruction of the Jews, the capture and starvation of POWs, and

197

the spoliation of occupied territories and terrorizing of their inhabitants. It included about 800 photographs, some of which were official army propaganda, the majority being the personal souvenirs of individual soldiers. Excerpts from military orders and reports explained the context of and motivation behind the acts these images depicted. The exhibition toured Germany and Austria, where, over four years, it attracted close to a million visitors, earning it the designation "*the* contemporary history exhibition in the Federal Republic."[4]

In the early months, quiet public debate on the exhibition and its meaning took place in the cities hosting the display. As it reached Bavaria and Austria, however, peaceful, albeit painful, reception of the exhibition turned to shock, dismay, and rage. In Munich, Vienna, and Dresden, there were riots and street demonstrations against the exhibit's opening; in Saarbrücken, the exhibition site was firebombed. Acrimonious debates about knowledge, complicity, and the responsibility of "ordinary soldiers," as well as the national heritage of the Nazi past, ignited newspapers, radio, and, notably, the Bundestag. Ultimately, the exhibition provoked a national confrontation with and refutation of the myth and made public what scholars had long accepted.[5]

The German reaction to the Wehrmacht exhibition is all the more striking in view of the High Command case, because this trial had already laid bare the truth of all of these crimes. It had done so, indeed, for a much larger geographical area than the exhibition described, on a foundation of irrefutable documentary evidence. Moreover, the trial had been organized and prosecuted with the very purpose of making these things known to the German public. What went wrong? There were some early setbacks to the American war crimes trial program as a whole. The Wennerstrum, Koch, and Malmedy scandals, upon which the German churches and others seized in their efforts to discredit American trials, shook the German public's initial confidence in the war crimes trial program. However, the merits of the High Command case record were impressive. The prosecution had presented a systematic accounting of Wehrmacht crime that connected Nazi ideological aims with military orders and directives, as well as ground-level reports that proved their execution. In turn, the defense had been given ample latitude in refuting the record and providing its own explanation of events. The tribunal had returned a nuanced judgment that interpreted the law conservatively and was sensitive to the particular dilemmas of the soldier and the reality of combat, but still unmistakably implicated the institution as a whole and confirmed the personal guilt of the men in the dock.

Nonetheless, from the time the trial record and the obligation to honor its conclusions passed to occupation officials' hands, American authorities muddied the waters that had been so painstakingly distilled in the judicial process. The High Command tribunal's stringent adjudication of individual criminality was thrown into doubt by the Americans' own appointees to the first clemency board in 1950. The Peck Panel worked at a hurried pace: they did not consult the complete trial records, nor did they solicit advice from prosecutors involved in the proceedings. In some instances, they set aside the tribunals' conclusions. Overall, they implied that sentences had been excessive and that individual convicts had unjustifiably been punished for the crimes of the group. This review process set the tone for what followed. Rather than making the trials the center of an ongoing discussion about crime and responsibility, the Americans, under unrelenting pressure from the West Germans, allowed the trials to recede ever further into the recesses of public memory. Through successive sentence modification programs and their general reluctance to make their trial records publicly accessible, U.S. officials surrendered the opportunity for educating Germans about the validity of the trials, and about the validity of the judgments against soldiers. This was not an uncontested loss. At various times, occupation officials and former trial prosecutors offered compelling arguments for an information campaign to reestablish the truth these trials had revealed. Others, including statesmen in Washington and leaders of the American army, did not believe that the results of a public education program would justify the effort. In the end, Telford Taylor's fear that the trial records would remain "on the top shelf, out of reach," came true.[6]

The absence of accessible trial records allowed the West German press, politicians, and other organizations to exploit the public's ignorance. Significantly, it also left American authorities themselves with inadequate means to respond effectively to West German demands. As Cold War divisions hardened and the United States–West German political relationship became more sensitive, it was the West Germans who increasingly defined the terms of the debate. Indeed, the Americans hesitated even to use the words "war crimes" and "war criminals" in later public discussions or communications about the war criminals issue. When they sought to inform the public at all, they spoke frequently in terms of common crimes ever more remotely connected with the war and Nazism. With the clemency and parole decisions, the focus shifted away from the convicts' wartime positions and offenses, toward the individual circumstances of these aging, ailing, well-behaved, and now harmless men, whom their impoverished families needed, and whom their communities would gladly support. During the ten years after the conclusion of the High Command case, the Americans successively scaled back the sentences for the vast majority of their war crimes convicts (those who faced the hangman in 1951 excepted), until Landsberg was empty and paroles had been canceled. While their criminal records were never withdrawn, the war criminals' early release undermined the significance of the offenses that had earned these sentences.

At the beginning of this book, I wrote that justice was only one goal of the Nuremberg trials. Transcending the boundaries of jurisprudence, the war crimes trial program initiated at Nuremberg entailed a novel social experiment. The American trial planners envisioned a process by which not only justice would be served, but also an entire nation would be educated about its traumatic and contested history. Upon a foundation of honest reconciliation with its crimes and the consequent rejection of the former political regime and worldview, democracy could take root and flourish. Or so the Americans hoped. Were any of these goals achieved?

Measuring the relevance of the war crimes trials for Germany's transition from fascism to democracy is complicated by paradox and underscores the mixed legacy of the trials. In a curious incongruity, West Germans approached the war criminals issue in a mostly "democratic" way: they did not storm the walls of Landsberg, they did not attack occupation forces, and they only rarely threatened violence. Rather, as individuals and as organizations, they wrote letters, submitted petitions, and debated in the Bundestag and in their newspapers. An official with the U.S. High Commission noted the irony of the situation when he remarked that although it would have been preferable for the Germans to focus their attention on more "important" matters than the fate of convicted war criminals, "that [they] are taking advantage of the *democratic privilege* of expressing their views on controversial issues is commendable."[7] Years earlier, West Germany's military governor, Lucius Clay, observed that American responsiveness to German criticism of the war crimes trial program was itself "another . . . valuable lesson in democracy."[8] Certainly this might be true. But war crimes trials were only one point in a much larger constellation of factors—weightier factors—that contributed to West Germany's political transformation. To be sure, the recent memory of the Weimar Republic, Germany's first fleeting experiment in democracy, the pace and success of West Germany's reconstruction and economic recovery, and the steady hands and firm convictions of various political leaders who sheltered and sustained the fledgling democracy own larger shares of West Germany's postwar political success. Let us then consider the remaining two Nuremberg goals for which the trials played a more direct role: education and justice.

Although the law, process, and results of Nuremberg were intended to shape German memory of the war, neither the Nuremberg Charter nor Control Council Law No. 10 (which governed the Subsequent Nuremberg Proceedings) contained any mechanism to communicate the findings of the court to the public. Perhaps the architects of the trials believed this would occur spontaneously and as a matter of course. Initially, the International Military Tribunal captured both domestic and international attention. It was the first trial of its kind, it took place soon after the war ended, it involved some of the Nazi state's most prominent figures, and it laid out, for the first time, the most shocking and heinous of the Nazis' crimes. But those proceedings were long, laborious, and mostly dull, and interest steadily dwindled. Twelve cases later and three years on, few still cared about war crimes trials, particularly given the West Germans' consuming preoccupation with physical, material, and emotional recovery and their hostility toward the trials' implications regarding broadly shared civil responsibility for and complicity in Nazi crime.

The absence of a specific mechanism or method to connect with German society during proceedings meant that communication of the trials' lessons rested with the heirs of the trial program—that is, American occupation and government officials. Whatever will they possessed to see this task through, it was steadily eroded by mounting political concerns to mollify West German discontent over the imprisonment of war criminals and to retain West Germany's loyalty to the West. One may well argue that the educative goal was from the beginning beyond reach—that the injured and embittered German public would have proven insurmountably unreceptive to the trials' message. However, the Americans did not exhaust the didactic potential of the rich and valuable historical record produced at Nuremberg. U.S. officials did not publish the trial records in German, nor did they furnish their own representatives in Europe with comprehensive information about the trials' findings. The United States did not establish a foundation upon which to build a productive, ongoing discussion about crime, guilt, and responsibility beyond the end of proceedings. One can only imagine where such a discussion might have led. The Nuremberg experience tells us clearly that political will must match the judicial ambition in any trial program with didactic goals. Justice will surely fail in the absence of governmental commitment to support the verdicts and reinforce the lessons they contain. Translation of trial documents, outreach to the public, and a time frame extending past the reading of the judgments are fundamental to any such project.

To understand whether Nuremberg achieved "justice," one must first consider what was meant by the term. The justice served at Nuremberg comprised three elements. The first was the development of the law to address the scope and scale of unprecedented human suffering. In recognizing the value of the lives the Nazis damaged and stole, victims were "rescued from oblivion," and the essential humanity that was denied them was restored.[9] Second, justice required the application of the law—or, more precisely, the reintroduction of the rule of law through trials, which by extension, as Lawrence Douglas has shown, signified the reintroduction of a moral order into a world evacuated of moral sense.[10] Third, justice required punishment, holding a representative sample of perpetrators accountable for their crimes.

Arguably, the trials succeeded in the first two aspects. Nuremberg was a watershed in jurisprudence. It ushered in a new culture in international criminal law, and it inspired conventions on genocide, human rights, and a host of transitional justice processes. To be sure, these have not always been obeyed or applied, but there is a foundation for international justice where before 1945 there was none. Regarding punishment, the record is disappointing. Of the 185 defendants indicted at the Subsequent Nuremberg Proceedings, 35 were acquitted, 8 were released from trial, and 11 were released with time served. Of the remaining convicted, 24 were sentenced to death, 20 to life imprisonment, and 87 to prison terms.[11] Most of these war criminals had their sentences commuted and/or reduced through various rounds of review. By 1958, not a single one remained in prison. But perhaps focusing on these figures misses the point. To some observers, any punishment was wholly inadequate. In writing to Karl Jaspers about her observations of the International Military Tribunal, Hannah Arendt declared that no penalty was equal to the crimes that "explode the limits of the law."[12] But in the same thought in which she decried punishment's inadequacy, Arendt also declared it essential. The punishment of Nazi criminals was surely not a function of commensurate retribution. In this and subsequent atrocity trials, judicial penalty signified and expressed something more. This is what gave it its meaning.

Years after Nuremberg, Arendt attended and commented on the Eichmann trial. Although highly critical of the proceedings, she nonetheless fully endorsed the death sentence the Israeli court passed against Eichmann.[13] His one life could not atone for the millions he helped destroy. Yet execution was the most severe and definitive statement of rejection the collective human conscience could issue against him. Upon reflecting on the same trial, the American scholar Yosal Rogat similarly articulated the very necessity of punishment: "a great crime offends nature, so that the very earth cries out for vengeance. . . . A wronged collectivity owes a duty to the moral order to punish the criminal."[14] In its opening statement, the High Command case prosecution quoted from Henry Stimson, insisting, "What we had called a crime demanded punishment; we must bring our law in balance with the . . . judgment of mankind."[15] In its broadest sense, therefore, the punishment issued in atrocity trials addresses itself to the universal and the collective.

But punishment can also serve more individualized ends. It speaks to the perpetrators and the victims, as well as to their national communities.[16] Jean Améry, the Holocaust survivor and memoirist, wrote that punishment forces a moment of confrontation between the perpetrator and his crime. For the criminal, who never saw his actions in their moral dimension, punishment is imposed "in order that the crime becomes a moral reality for the criminal—in order that he be swept into the truth of his atrocity."[17] In its judgment against Eichmann, the Israeli court ruminated on the meaning and usefulness of punishment in terms of its reflection upon the victim. Citing Grotius, the seventeenth-century Dutch philosopher and forefather of international law, it proclaimed that the failure to punish offends the honor of the victim and furthers his degradation.[18] Punishment, pronounced and enforced, carries a message for observers of trials as well. By inflicting a "publicly visible defeat" on the wrongdoer, punishment denies the perpetrator's message that the victim was "worth less than he," and reasserts the truth of the victim's value.[19] By extension, a society's greater or lesser support for punishment reflects the depth of its collective memory of the crime.[20]

These messages form the core of the lessons didactic trials aim to impart: that the world takes notice of and rejects mass crime, that the perpetrator must confront the moral implications of his actions, that a victim's worth will be honored, and that society remembers the offense. The processes of didactic trials further serve educational efforts by gathering and interpreting evidence that clarifies the historical record. They make public that which is privately mourned and irrefutable that which is maliciously denied. By respecting due process and conducting proceedings with dignity and reason, these trials also reinforce particular political and legal values that will, it is hoped, be adopted by the state emerging from war and violence. All of this is lost without the "declarative finality" of punishment.[21] It is punishment that gives a trial the capacity to serve the ends of history, memory, and justice.

In the years after the Nuremberg trials, punishment ceased to be a reflection of crimes and victims. It became instead a complicated and unremitting political liability. Although the United States never consented to amnesty of war criminals, the collective impact of their actions had an analogous effect. Beginning with the Peck Panel's reconsideration of the sentences, and continuing through subsequent reevaluations of the cases for purposes of clemency and parole, the truth of the crimes receded ever further from consideration and discussion. The Americans' ultimate abandonment of punishment, the temporal and material articulation of justice, and the standing reproach for Nazi crime and its ideological foundations thereby

CONCLUSION

undermined the message Nuremberg was designed to enforce and sustain. Consequently, Nuremberg's potential as a tool for social rehabilitation and reconciliation was left untested.

There is an unsettling irony in this. Although the trial program failed in its objectives of justice and education, it does not, on the surface, appear to have mattered very much. In time, West Germany stabilized, democratized, and eventually even apologized and made (and Germany continues to make) restitution to victims. Many credit this development to the decision by West Germany's political leadership, guided by Adenauer, to pursue a policy of amnesty and incorporation of former Nazis into German society. Of course, one can accept the cold reality that lower-level perpetrators and collaborators had to be reintegrated, and that a judicial response was simply impossible for these many thousands of helpers and supporters. Nonetheless, the logic of the Nuremberg indictment posed a challenge to the German national conscience. Beginning with support for the Nazi Party and aggressive war, and the alliance between the military and other institutions and agents of the Nazi state, which in combination allowed for the pursuit of racial and ideological goals on an international scale, the crimes the Americans prosecuted at court implicated the German nation as a whole. By contrast, U.S. posttrial policy failed to press home the necessity of this national self-examination.[22]

A new national identity emerged from the ashes in what would become West Germany. Its premise was that the Germans were victims of a criminal regime, of a disastrous defeat, of national division, and of arbitrary Allied policies. It claimed that Germans had been ignorant of Nazi crimes, and that there had been "another" Germany—of resistance against Nazism.[23] The battle over the Wehrmacht record was (and continued to be) integral to this national self-image.[24] This new nationalism supplanted the memory of genocide, it obviated a sense of guilt, and it shifted discussion from the German people's actions to the Allies' actions. The Germans' rejection of collective responsibility and attempts to distance themselves from the crimes of the alleged "minority" became more deeply entrenched with the principle of the "zero hour" and the general effort to "draw a line under the past." Two press reactions to the 1951 Landsberg decisions are telling in this regard: "We Germans want to search for peace with the great communities of the world on the basis of confidence. . . . We have asked that the fateful chain of guilt and death be cut"; and "everything left to us after the collapse of the Nazi Regime is a bitter heritage which must be liquidated."[25] One can sympathize with the rationale, and certainly Germany was not unique in its approach to the past. One finds the pattern repeated in other countries with similarly tortured and traumatic histories. To many minds, a distancing from the former regime would augment the legitimacy of the successor government, and a break with the past was necessary for civil peace and to protect the nascent democracy from being overwhelmed by a preoccupation with crime and torn apart by vengeance. It was commonly felt that only time and silence would allow the wounds to heal.[26]

But in truth West Germany's relationship with the past was much more ambiguous and contained elements of connection and continuity as well. Adenauer's concurrent policies of making reparations payments to Israel and restoring pensions to veterans and Nazi civil servants are particularly revealing of West Germany's Janus-faced approach to its immediate history. In the same year (1952) that President Theodor Heuss dramatically declared at Bergen-Belsen, "No one will lift this shame from us!," Adenauer, a majority of political parties, the German churches, and other institutions were hammering away at occupation officials to grant amnesty or early release to convicted war criminals.[27] As Jeffrey Herf reminds us, the few early (and notable for their rarity) expressions of contrition never connected with justice.[28] These measures were substitutes, not symptoms, of national self-reflection.[29] Adenauer's policy of amnesty and integration, while perhaps making for a smoother transition to democracy, exacted a debt to truth and justice.

Scholarship has long shown that it took a generation for West Germans to undertake a far-reaching confrontation with the past. There are many identifiable moments when this occurred, beginning in the 1960s: the Eichmann trial in Jerusalem (1961), the Auschwitz trial in Frankfurt (1963–1965), Willy Brandt's kneeling at the Warsaw Ghetto Memorial (1970), the Maidanek trials (1975–1981), the television broadcast of the miniseries *Holocaust* in West Germany (1979), the Bitburg affair and Chancellor Richard von Weizsäcker's Bundestag Speech on the fortieth anniversary of the war's end (1985), the Historikerstreit (1986–1989), the Wehrmacht exhibition (1995), the translation into German of Daniel Goldhagen's controversial book *Hitler's Willing Executioners: Ordinary Germans and the Holocaust* (1996), and most recently the opening of the Berlin Holocaust Memorial (2005). Several institutions and movements have also focused on the Nazi past. The Ludwigsburg Central Office of the State Justice Administration for the Investigation of National Socialist Crimes, established in 1958, assumed a mandate to investigate and prosecute German nationals suspected of war crimes. Although laudable in its ambition, of the tens of thousands of investigations, only a fraction reached the courts, an even smaller number concerned capital cases, and fewer still ended in convictions.[30]

There were as well the student movements of 1968. Impressed by the

Frankfurt Auschwitz trial, this generation of activists had grown up in rela-
tive ignorance of the enormity of Nazi crimes and their parents' involvement
in them.[31] They believed that their parents' generation possessed a moral
and political duty to examine its attitudes and actions during the Nazi era.[32]
At the extreme end of this movement, members turned to terrorist tactics
to force their message on the public.[33] In the main, however, these students
promoted discussion around the issues of complicity, responsibility, and
memory. When they became teachers, open and thorough study of the Third
Reich became more common in German schools and universities.[34]

Over time, the memory of the war has become part of Germany's political culture in positive, if also imperfect, ways. The German government's
willingness to grant restitution and reparations and to offer apologies
remains unequalled. On the other hand, German memory of the Nazi
period has focused primarily on the Holocaust. One understands this tendency. The Holocaust epitomized the depth of Nazi depravity; Auschwitz
had no parallel. However, this emphasis on the crimes against the Jews has
left many other crimes, as well as victim and perpetrator groups, in the shad-
ows. Recognizing the breadth of Nazi depravity—the crimes of the military—took much longer to filter into public consciousness. Moreover,
despite these many moments and movements aiming at reconciling with the
past, most perpetrators never faced justice.

Were the Americans unrealistic, even arrogant, in assigning extralegal
goals to the Nuremberg trial program? Looking at the records, it is difficult
to be critical of the Americans' ambition, optimism, and idealism when proceedings were being planned. One cannot help note the sincerity and hope
that infused their work. Any evaluation of the project must also be sensitive
to the context. The mixed results of the trials speak to the innovation of the
entire Nuremberg enterprise. The planners were dealing with unparalleled
crime and using novel tools and idioms to give them meaning and bring
them within a court's jurisdiction. Aside from undertaking the custody of
convicted war criminals, occupation officials were overseeing the social,
political, and economic reconstruction of West Germany at a time of worldwide political realignment. While regretting the various decisions the American administration made that deliberately subordinated punishment to
politics, one can still appreciate the complexity of the tasks they faced and
their position as progenitors of transitional justice. The potential of their
vision for Nuremberg merits reflection and admiration. It would be short-
sighted to collapse the significance of the whole project under the weight
of its first disappointing results. The failure of Nuremberg's educative mission is not necessarily an argument against didactic trials.

Whether didactic trials possess social value remains a topic of lively debate. Some scholars have expressed doubt that trials held immediately after war in a climate of exhaustion, deprivation, and inflamed passions can benefit society. They suggest that time alone, counted in decades, will "bind up wounds."[35] However, this advice does not account for the urgent and undeniable need societies have for reconstruction and reconciliation after mass violence. It does not provide any direction for what is to be done with the perpetrators and victims in their midst. To leave known atrocity perpetrators in peace, in Justice Jackson's words, would "mock the dead and make cynics of the living."[36] Justice delayed is similarly unsatisfactory. Over time, evidence disappears. Memories fade. Witnesses scatter. All this diminishes the impact and success of atrocity trials. Just as the postwar, postatrocity time period is critical to the pursuit of justice, so too is the court as a venue. No other public institution possesses both the capacity and authority for the investigation and punishment of mass atrocity crimes and the public confidence and prestige elicited by courts of law.

We have moved beyond the question of whether atrocity trials should serve extralegal ends. They do. Both in their meaning and practice, trials show that justice and memory are inextricably linked, each completing and reinforcing the other. Successful prosecution reinforces the rule of law and reintroduces a sense of justice. Justice is completed by the imposition of punishment. Adherence to punishment signals the depth of society's collective memory of the crime. And memory honors the value of the victim, sustaining rejection of the perpetrators' acts. Memory is not dependent on trials; it will surface whether summoned or not. The trajectory of Germany's confrontation with the past confirms that, whether in violent public spasms in the 1960s and 1970s or in quiet, painful discussions with one's father in the 1990s, the encounter inevitably came. What is most regrettable about the German case is that justice rarely accompanied memory's return. Whereas trials focus principally on justice, as much as they concentrate public attention and stimulate discussion about the past, they have the added potential to shape memory soon after the events, in socially, politically, legally, and morally positive ways. Trials, unlike any other social ritual, thus present moments of "transformative opportunity."[37]

The generations since Nuremberg have witnessed the patterns of mass violence and genocide repeated. In response, a varied and imaginative range of transitional justice processes has emerged that seeks to harness and direct trials' transformative potential for the societies affected by these crimes. Political circumstances have at times forestalled the initiation of these processes. Nonetheless, the core goals of Nuremberg—justice and education—echo through their proceedings. The National Commission on Disappeared Persons of Argentina, South Africa's Truth and Reconciliation

Commission, and Rwanda's Gacaca tribunals are only three examples of transitional justice models that put the experience of the victim at the center of their work. By honing and strengthening the link between memory and justice, they consciously seek to pay homage to the victims and promote social reconciliation among perpetrators, survivors, and bystanders. Certainly there is still much work to do if these goals are to be achieved. Martha Minow has written that in the ongoing pursuit of postatrocity justice, one must balance humility about the potential of trials to face and transcend complex criminal pasts with a willingness to be inspired.[38] In having created the very vocabulary of international criminal law and the precedents for punishing perpetrators of mass atrocity, Nuremberg remains the source of that inspiration.[39] Subsequent experiences of genocide and mass violence have not diminished our longing for justice. For providing hope that justice is possible in the wake of catastrophe, we have Nuremberg to thank.

Appendix 1

The High Command Case

Official name: *United States v. Wilhelm von Leeb et al.*

Tribunal: John Young (Presiding): former chief justice, Colorado
                  Supreme Court
                  Winfield Hale: judge of the Tennessee Court of Appeals
                  Justin Harding: district judge of the First Division,
                  Alaska

Defendants: Johannes Blaskowitz, Karl Hollidt, Hermann Hoth,
                  Georg von Kuechler, Wilhelm von Leeb,
                  Rudolf Lehmann, Hermann Reinecke, Hans Reinhardt,
                  Karl von Roques, Hans von Salmuth, Otto Schniewind,
                  Hugo Sperrle, Walter Warlimont, Otto Woehler

Indictment filed: 28 November 1947
Arraignment: 30 December 1947
Prosecution opening statement: 5 February 1948
Prosecution closing statement: 10 August 1948
Prosecution trial days: 26
Prosecution evidence exhibits: 1,778
Prosecution witnesses: 23
Defense opening statements: 12 April 1948
Defense closing pleas: 11–13 August 1948
Defense trial days: 85
Defense evidence exhibits: 2,122
Defense witnesses: 66
Judgment and sentencing: 27–28 October 1948
Court adjourned: 29 October 1948

Chief of counsel: Telford Taylor

Prosecution counsel: Morton Barbour, Eugene Dobbs,
George Fulkerson, James Higgins,
Paul Horecky, Arnost Horlick-Hochwald,
James McHaney (deputy chief of counsel),
Paul Niederman (chief prosecutor and director,
Military and S.S. Division, Office of the Chief
of Counsel, War Crimes), Walter Rapp (director
of the Evidence Division)

Defense counsel: Kurt Behling, Stefan Fritsch,
Friedrich Frohwein, Kurt Gollnick,
Rupprecht von Keller, Hans Laternser,
Paul Leverkuehn, Hans Meckel,
Heinz Mueller-Torgow, Gerhard Rauschenbach,
Hans Surholt, Edmund Tipp

Appendix 2

German Army Field Formations and Basic Command Structure

Formation:	Army Group
Commanded by:	a Feldmarschall (American equivalent: five-star general) or a Generaloberst (four-star general)
Function:	exercised tactical command over its armies

Formation:	Army
Commanded by:	a Feldmarschall, a Generaloberst, or a General (five, four- and three-star generals, respectively)
Function:	directed its subordinate units and acted as field headquarters for matters of administration and supply, etc.

By the end of the war, there were eleven army groups and twenty-two armies in the German army. An army generally controlled two to seven corps. A corps, in turn, controlled two to seven divisions. The division was the basic self-contained unit of the army and contained varying numbers of specialized regiments or battalions. Therefore, in descending order of size (with the approximated manpower strength in brackets), the army formations were as follows:

Army Group (96,000 to 1,700,000)
Army (48,000 to 425,000)
Corps (24,000 to 85,000)
Division (12,000 to 17,000)
Regiment (1,000 to 1,200)
Battalion (500)[1]

Army group, army, and corps headquarters varied in size according to the total force it commanded, but each included a commanding officer aided by a staff that was in turn headed by a chief of staff. Divisions could be moved from one army to another. The standard German division contained infantry and artillery regiments and various other specialized battalions. Other divisions included the Panzer (or armored) division. The corps controlled a group of divisions typically predominated by infantry divisions. In cases where Panzer divisions constituted the majority, the corps was called a Panzer Corps. During 1942, the armored groups deployed against the Soviet Union were given the status of armies and designated Panzer Armies. By mid-1945, six of the Reich's twenty-two armies were Panzer Armies.[2]

Appendix 3

Wartime Positions of the High Command Case Field Commanders

GENERAL JOHANNES BLASKOWITZ[1]

Commander in chief 1st, 2nd, 8th, 9th, and 25th Armies (intermittently, September 1939–April 1945)
Commander in chief East (October 1939–May 1940)
Military commander, Northern France (June 1940)
Acting commander in chief Army Group G (May–September 1944)
Commander in chief Army Group G (December 1944–January 1945)
Commander in chief Army Group H (January–April 1945)
Commander in chief Netherlands (April 1945)

GENERAL KARL HOLLIDT

Chief of staff 5th Army (September–October 1939)
Chief of staff to the commander in chief East (October 1939–May 1940)
Chief of staff 9th Army (May–October 1940)
Commander 50th Infantry Division (October 1940–January 1942)
Commanding general XVII Corps (January–December 1942)
Commander of army (Armeeabteilung) (December 1942–March 1943)
Commander in chief 6th Army (March 1943–April 1944)

GENERAL HERMANN HOTH

Commanding general XV Corps (November 1938–November 1940)
Commander Panzer Group 3 (November 1940–October 1941)
Commander in chief 17th Army (October 1941–April 1942)
Commander in chief 4th Panzer Army (May 1942–December 1943)

214

APPENDIX THREE

FIELD MARSHAL GEORG KARL-FRIEDRICH-WILHELM VON KUECHLER

Commander in chief 3rd Army (September 1939)
Commander East Prussian Defense Zone (October–November 1939)
Commander in chief 18th Army (November 1939–January 1942)
Commander in chief Army Group North (January 1942–January 1944)

FIELD MARSHAL WILHELM VON LEEB

Commander in chief 12th Army (September 1939–May 1941)
Commander in chief Army Group North (June 1941–January 1942)

GENERAL HANS REINHARDT

Commander 4th Panzer Division (October 1938–February 1940)
Commanding general XLI Corps (February 1940–October 1941)
Commander Panzer Group 3 (later 3rd Panzer Army) (October 1941–
    August 1944)
Acting commander in chief Army Group Center (August 1944–August
    1945)

LIEUTENANT GENERAL KARL VON ROQUES

Commander of rear area Army Group South (March 1941–June 1942)
Commander of Group (Armeegruppe) (September–October 1941)
Commander of rear area Army Group A (July–December 1942)

GENERAL HANS VON SALMUTH

Chief of staff Army Group Command 1 (1937–August 1939)
Chief of staff Army Group North (September–October 1939)
Chief of staff Army Group B (October 1939–May 1941)
Commanding general XXX Corps (May 1941–February 1942)
Acting commander in chief 17th Army (April–May 1942)
Acting commander in chief 4th Army (June–July 1942)
Commander in chief 2nd Army (July 1942–February 1943)
Commander in chief 15th Army (August 1943–August 1944)

LIEUTENANT GENERAL OTTO WOEHLER

Operations officer (Ia) Army Group 5 (later AOK 14) (April 1938)
Chief of staff XVII Corps (October 1939–October 1940)
Chief of staff 11th Army (October 1940–May 1942)
Chief of staff Army Group Center (May 1942–July 1943)
Commanding general I Corps (February–July 1943)
Acting commander XXVI Corps (July–August 1943)
Commander in chief 8th Army (August 1943–December 1944)
Commander in chief Army Group South (December 1944–April 1945)

Appendix 4

The High Command Case Defendants' Sentence Expiration and Parole and Clemency Release Dates

High Command case convicts considered in the January 1951 Landsberg revisions: Hoth, von Kuechler, Reinecke, Reinhardt, Warlimont, von Salmuth, and Woehler. Although the Peck Panel interviewed Woehler, he was already scheduled for good conduct time release in 1951 and was not included in the Landsberg report on McCloy's decisions.

High Command case convicts still in Landsberg at the time the Interim Mixed Clemency and Parole Board began its work in November 1953: Hoth, Reinecke, and Warlimont.

IMPORTANT DATES

31 August 1953: Interim Mixed Parole and Clemency Board established
11 August 1955: Mixed Clemency and Parole Board established
9 May 1958: last inmate released from Landsberg
4 June 1958: Mixed Clemency and Parole Board reduced all remaining parolees' sentences to time served

HERMANN HOTH

Original length of sentence: 15 years
Original date for expiration of sentence: 28 October 1963, later 3 December 1960[1]
10 March 1949 review: sentence confirmed
Good time credit release date: 19 November 1957, later 3 June 1955
31 January 1951 review: no change

New sentence expiration date: NA
Paroled: 7 April 1954
Release from parole/sentence reduced to time served: 11 June 1957

GEORG VON KUECHLER

Original length of sentence: 20 years
Original date for expiration of sentence: 28 October 1968
10 March 1949 review: sentence confirmed
Good time credit release date: 27 September 1962
31 January 1951 review: 12 years
New sentence expiration date: 28 October 1960
Paroled: 18 February 1953 (medical grounds)
Release from parole/sentence reduced to time served: 30 January 1954

RUDOLF LEHMANN

Original length of sentence: 7 years
Original date for expiration of sentence: 28 October 1955
10 March 1949 review: sentence confirmed
Good time credit release date: 16 August 1950
31 January 1951 review: NA
New sentence expiration date: NA
Paroled: NA
Release from parole/sentence reduced to time served: NA

HERMANN REINECKE

Original length of sentence: life
Original date for expiration of sentence: (life)
10 March 1949 review: sentence confirmed
Good time credit release date: NA
31 January 1951 review: no change
New sentence expiration date: NA
Interim Mixed Parole and Clemency Board recommendation: reduction of
    sentence to 27 years—sentence backdated to 4 June 1945
New sentence expiration date: 7 May 1972
Good conduct release date: 25 June 1963
Paroled: 27 September 1954

Release from parole/sentence reduced to time served: 15 August 1957
Note: Reinecke served the longest in Landsberg of any High Command
case defendant

HANS REINHARDT

Original length of sentence: 15 years
Original date for expiration of sentence: 28 October 1963
10 March 1949 review: sentence confirmed
Good time credit release date: 19 November 1957
31 January 1951 review: no change
New sentence expiration date: NA
Paroled: 14 June 1952 (compassionate grounds)
Release from parole/sentence reduced to time served: NA

HANS VON SALMUTH

Original length of sentence: 20 years
Original date for expiration of sentence: 28 October 1968
10 March 1949 review: sentence confirmed
Good time credit release date: 21 March 1962
31 January 1951 review: 12 years and sentence backdated to 3 June 1945
New sentence expiration date: 28 October 1960, later 2 July 1957
Good time credit release date: summer 1953
Release from parole/sentence reduced to time served: NA

WALTER WARLIMONT

Original length of sentence: life
Original date for expiration of sentence: (life)
10 March 1949 review: sentence confirmed
Good time credit release date: NA
31 January 1951 review: 18 years—sentence backdated to 9 May 1945
New sentence expiration date: 8 May 1963
Paroled: 9 June 1954
Release from parole/sentence reduced to time served: clemency denied 30
    August 1954; parole lifted in fall 1955 in interests of United States
    Army, Europe, Historical Division project; sentence reduced to time
    served mid-July 1957

OTTO WOEHLER

Original length of sentence: 8 years
Original date for expiration of sentence: 28 October 1956, later 23 June
    1953
10 March 1949 review: sentence confirmed
Good time credit release date: 29 February 1952
31 January 1951 review: NA
New sentence expiration date: NA
Good time credit release date: 1 February 1951—based on sentence being
    backdated to 1945
Release from parole/sentence reduced to time served: NA

OTHER DEFENDANTS

Johannes Blaskowitz: committed suicide 5 February 1948
Otto Schniewind: not guilty
Hugo Sperrle: not guilty
Wilhelm von Leeb: sentenced to time served and released upon announce-
    ment of the verdict and sentences
Karl Hollidt: sentenced to 5 years; released on good time credit 22 Decem-
    ber 1949
Karl von Roques: sentenced to 20 years; released on medical parole 17
    December 1949; died 25 December 1949

Notes

ABBREVIATIONS USED IN NOTES

BAK   Bundesarchiv Koblenz
BMA   Bundesmilitärarchiv Freiburg
CULS-ADLL   Columbia University Law School, Arthur Diamond Law
                Library, New York
IfZ   Institut für Zeitgeschichte, Munich
LCMD   Library of Congress—Manuscripts Division
NAMP   National Archives Microfilm Publication
NAMP 898   Records of the United States Nuernberg War Crimes Trials—
                United States of America v. Wilhelm von Leeb et al. (Case XII):
                November 28, 1947—October 28, 1949
NAMP 1019   Records of the United States Nuernberg War Crimes Trials
                Interrogations, 1946–1949
NARG   National Archives and Records Administration, College Park,
                Maryland, Record Group
NARG 153   Records of the Office of the Judge Advocate General
NARG 238   National Archives Collection of World War II War Crimes
                Records
NARG 260   Records of U.S. Occupation Headquarters, World War II
                (OMGUS)
NARG 466   Records of the U.S. High Commissioner for Germany
                (HICOG)
NARG 549   Records of U.S. Army Europe
TLI   Truman Library Institute, Independence, Missouri

CHAPTER ONE: FROM WAR CRIMES TO WAR CRIMES TRIALS

Epigraph from Interim Report for President Harry S. Truman from Justice Robert H. Jackson, 7 June 1945, TLI, Office Files, Box 1007, Folder: 325 (1945–1949).

1. Gerhard Weinberg, *A World at Arms: A Global History of World War II* (Cambridge: Cambridge University Press, 1994), 894.

2. Arieh Kochavi, *Prelude to Nuremberg: Allied War Crimes Policy and the Question of Punishment* (Chapel Hill: University of North Carolina Press, 1998), 11–16;

Bradley Smith, *Reaching Judgment at Nuremberg* (New York: Basic Books, 1977), 20–21.

3. Kochavi, *Prelude to Nuremberg*, 15.

4. St. James Palace Declaration, 13 January 1942, signed by Belgium, Czechoslovakia, Greece, Luxembourg, the Netherlands, Norway, Poland, Yugoslavia, and the Free French National Committee, in Telford Taylor, "The Nuremberg War Crimes Trials," *International Conciliation* 450 (April 1949), annotated manuscript, CULS-ADLL, Telford Taylor Papers, Entry 8, Subentry 1, Box 1, Folder: 14, 3. Emphasis added.

5. Although the number of victims may have been grossly underestimated, the events that later came to be called the Holocaust were well-known to Allied officials on both sides of the Atlantic during the war. On 17 December 1942, the State Department issued a press release entitled "German Policy of Extermination of the Jewish Race." (British Secretary of the Foreign Office Anthony Eden also read it aloud in the House of Commons.) It declared, "The German authorities are now carrying into effect Hitler's oft-repeated intention to exterminate the Jewish people from Europe. From all the occupied centers of Europe Jews are being transported in conditions of appalling horror and brutality to Eastern Europe. In Poland, which has been made the principal Nazi slaughterhouse, the ghettos established by the Nazi invaders are being systematically emptied of all Jews except a few highly skilled workers required for war industries. None of those taken away are ever heard from again. The able-bodied are slowly worked to death in labor camps. The infirm are left to die of exposure and starvation, or are deliberately massacred in mass executions. The number of victims of these bloody cruelties is reckoned in many hundreds of thousands of entirely innocent men, women and children." Robert H. Jackson, *Report of Robert H. Jackson, United States Representative to the International Conference on Military Trials, London, 1945* (Washington, D.C.: Department of State, 1949), 9–10.

6. The term "United Nations" was used after the 1 January 1942 Declaration of the United Nations, which announced a common war effort of twenty-six nations against Germany and Japan. Michael Marrus, ed., *The Nuremberg War Crimes Trial, 1945–46: A Documentary History* (Boston: Bedford Books, 1997), 9, n. 3. As a condition of their participation, the Soviet Union demanded recognition of its annexations of the Baltic states and several other republics, as well as extra voting rights. When the Allies refused, the Soviet Union declined cooperation. For a detailed account of the formation of the United Nations War Crimes Commission (as it was eventually named), see Kochavi, *Prelude to Nuremberg*, 27–28, 36–49.

7. On 8 September 1942, Churchill announced to the House of Commons, "Those who are guilty of the Nazi crimes will have to stand up before tribunals in every land where their atrocities have been committed in order that an indelible warning may be given to future ages." Marrus, *Nuremberg War Crimes Trial*, 19. On

7 October 1942, Roosevelt declared, "It is our intention that just and sure punishment shall be meted out to the ringleaders responsible for the organized murder of thousands of innocent persons in the commission of atrocities which have violated every tenet of the Christian faith." Jackson, *Report of Robert H. Jackson*, 9.

8. Kochavi, *Prelude to Nuremberg*, 235. In a memorandum from Samuel Rosenman to President Harry Truman on 2 May 1945 on the status and recommendations of the UNWCC, Rosenman stated plainly, "The commission has not been a success," adding that the information it had gathered did not really pertain to the major criminals. He declared that the commission's recommendation that the Allies establish a "treaty civilian court" had already been rejected (although not publicly) as "too cumbersome and too dilatory." Samuel Rosenman, "Memorandum for the President," 2 May 1945, TLI, President's Secretary's Files 1945–1953, Box 121, Folder: War Crimes Commission.

9. Smith, *Reaching Judgment*, 21; Marrus, *Nuremberg War Crimes Trial*, 20.

10. These trials were named for the towns in which they were held: Krasnodar and Kharkov. Encouraged by the turn in the tide of the war, and drawing broadly on the Geneva Convention, on 19 April 1943, the presidium of the USSR Supreme Soviet decreed the death penalty or hard labor for "German fascist criminals" guilty of crimes against Soviet citizens. From 14 to 16 July 1943, in Krasnodar, eleven Soviet citizens were tried for treason for collaborating with Nazi forces. Referencing the April edict, the judgment passed eight death sentences and three terms of twenty years' hard labor. Significantly, during questioning, prosecution counsel sought to elicit evidence that the crimes charged were committed under German supervision, that these cruelties were part of a regular system, and that true responsibility rested at the very highest echelons of the Nazi state—all principles that would eventually find expression at the joint Allied postwar trial. The second Soviet trial was held shortly after—and, the Soviets claimed, in direct accordance with the publication of the November 1943 Joint Allied Declaration on War Crimes, also known as the Moscow Declaration. This time, three Germans and one Russian were included in the indictment. The same principles asserted at Krasnodar were confirmed at Kharkov, with the qualification that the existence of superior orders constituted no valid defense—also a principle of the eventual Nuremberg trial. On the Krasnodar and Kharkov trials, see George Ginsburgs and V. N. Kudriavtsev, eds., *The Nuremberg Trial and International Law* (Dordrecht: Martinus Nijhoff, 1990), 18–21 and 25–27.

11. Moscow Declaration on German Atrocities in Occupied Europe, 30 October 1943, in Taylor, "Nuremberg War Crimes Trials," 4–5.

12. Kochavi, *Prelude to Nuremberg*, 239–240.

13. Ibid., 231–232. These trials became known as the Leipzig trials. Article 227 of the Versailles Treaty publicly arraigned Kaiser Wilhelm I "for a supreme offense against international morality and the sanctity of treaties" and committed the United

States, Britain, France, Italy, and Japan to constitute a tribunal in order to try him and other persons accused of war crimes. The treaty further obligated the Germans to hand over the accused as well as the documents that constituted evidence of their crimes. In November 1918, Kaiser Wilhelm fled to Holland, which in turn refused to extradite him. With the prime defendant beyond reach, the victor nations called on the German government to hand over 854 men the Allies accused of war crimes. Significantly, the list included such prominent military officers as Erich Ludendorff, Alfred von Tirpitz, and Paul von Hindenburg. The German government flatly refused, declaring that it was "morally impossible" to extradite them. Instead, the German authorities agreed to try a limited number of men (ultimately forty-five) before the Supreme Court in Leipzig. The British, who of all the Allied powers were the most committed to seeing the trials through to conclusion, submitted three cases of flagrant crimes by submarine crews. The most important of these was the case involving a U-boat torpedoing of the British hospital ship *Llandovery Castle* in June 1918. Not only had the German crew ignored the protection legally afforded to hospital ships, but they had also fired on the few survivors who had found their way into lifeboats. In this case, the two accused were sentenced to four years' imprisonment but were "accompanied to prison by a cheering crowd." Their sentences were reduced shortly thereafter by nonjudicial process. The two convicts "escaped" with help from their German captors. British reaction to the Leipzig trials ranged from angry protestations over the "scandalous failure of justice" (*Times*) to a resigned acceptance that the "principle" of punishment had been upheld (albeit by light sentences). With cold political calculation, the British government concluded that the time had come to allow war crimes punishment "to pass into oblivion" in order to restore peaceful relations with Germany. Major works on these trials include Gerd Hankel, *Die Leipziger Prozesse: Deutsche Kriegsverbrechen und ihre strafrechtliche Verfolgung nach dem Ersten Weltkrieg* (Hamburg: Hamburger Edition, 2003); Claud Mullins, *The Leipzig Trials: An Account of the War Criminals' Trials and a Study of the German Mentality* (London: H. F. & G. Witherby, 1921); and James Willis, *Prologue to Nuremberg: The Politics and Diplomacy of Punishing War Criminals of the First World War* (Westport, Conn.: Greenwood Press, 1982). See also Peter Maguire, *Law and War: An American Story* (New York: Columbia University Press, 2001); Robert Woetzel, *The Nuremberg Trials in International Law* (London: Stevens & Sons, 1962).

14. Kochavi, *Prelude to Nuremberg*, 232.

15. When Samuel Rosenman traveled to London in April 1945 to win over the British to the trial plan, he also met with Charles de Gaulle, the head of France's provisional government. De Gaulle stated clearly that he favored trial over summary execution, and thereafter, France was included as one of the major powers that organized and prosecuted the trial. See Telford Taylor, *The Anatomy of the Nuremberg Trials: A Personal Memoir* (Boston: Little, Brown, 1992), 32. In the negotiations at

London in summer 1945, the French team was led by Robert Falco of the Cour de Cassation (later also the French alternate judge at the tribunal). Described as "over-legalistic" in his approach, he spoke very little during the conference. Indeed, "his very occasional comments in the transcripts of the sessions come as a startling reminder that he was there at all." Ann Tusa and John Tusa, *The Nuremberg Trial* (London: Macmillan London, 1983), 74.

16. Ibid., 231. For the British view, see British Lord Chancellor Sir John Simon, memorandum, "Major War Criminals," 4 September 1944, in *The American Road to Nuremberg: The Documentary Record, 1944–1945*, ed. Bradley Smith (Stanford: Hoover Institution Press, 1982), 32. This volume contains a collection of the original documents relevant to the planning and preparation of the Nuremberg trial.

17. Smith, *American Road*, 5; Smith, *Reaching Judgment*, 20–21; Robert Conot, *Justice at Nuremberg* (New York: Harper & Row, 1983), 10.

18. Smith, *American Road*, 6; War Department, War Department Handbook of Military Government for Nazi Germany, Table "D"—Nazi Police, Party, Para-Military and Governmental Officers to be Interned, 1 September 1944, in Smith, *American Road*, 15–16. Henry Stimson's memoirs have been published as Henry Stimson and McGeorge Bundy, *On Active Service in Peace and War* (New York: Harper & Brothers, 1948).

19. Smith, *American Road*, 7.

20. American Jewish Conference, statement on war crimes submitted by the American Jewish Conference to the secretary of state, 25 August 1944, in Smith, *American Road*, 17–20.

21. Maguire, *Law and War*, 87.

22. Ibid.

23. Ibid., 88.

24. Henry Morgenthau Jr., "Memorandum for President Roosevelt" (the Morgenthau Plan), 5 September 1944, in Marrus, *Nuremberg War Crimes Trial*, 24–25.

25. Franklin Roosevelt, presidential memorandum for the secretary of war, 26 August 1944, in *From the Morgenthau Diaries*, vol. 3, *Years of War, 1941–1945*, ed. John Morton Blum (Boston: Houghton Mifflin, 1967), 348–349.

26. Smith, *Reaching Judgment*, 24; Henry L. Stimson, note to Henry Morgenthau Jr., 5 September 1944, in Smith, *American Road*, 30. Stimson's opposition to the Morgenthau Plan was informed by Germany's response to the Versailles Treaty. He feared a vengeful peace could give rise to a second "stab in the back" myth. Maguire, *Law and War*, 90–91.

27. Henry L. Stimson to Franklin Roosevelt, 9 September 1944, in Smith, *American Road*, 30–31.

28. Lord Simon, memorandum, "Major War Criminals," 4 September 1944, in Smith, *American Road*, 32. Emphasis in original.

29. Maguire, *Law and War*, 89; Smith, *American Road*, 10.

30. Maguire, *Law and War,* 92. Described by Telford Taylor as a slender, sallow-complexioned man with white hair and cavernous eyes, Murray Bernays was of Lithuanian–Jewish descent and was trained in law at Harvard, Columbia, and Fordham universities. Taylor, *Anatomy,* 48; Conot, *Justice at Nuremberg,* 10.

31. Murray C. Bernays, memorandum, "Trial of European War Criminals," 15 September 1944, in Smith, *American Road,* 35. Lidice was a small Czech village whose population the Nazis brutally murdered and deported in June 1942 in retaliation for the assassination of RSHA leader Reinhard Heydrich in Prague.

32. Ibid., 36.

33. Ibid. Emphasis added.

34. Ibid., 36–37. Bernays's proposal to try organizations under criminal charges may have been inspired by an advance copy of Rafael Lemkin's book, *Axis Rule in Occupied Europe: Laws of Occupation, Analysis of Government, Proposals for Redress* (Washington, D.C.: Carnegie Endowment for International Peace, Division of International Law, 1944), which he obtained from Colonel Marcus in the Army Civil Affairs Division. In it, Lemkin (also the originator of the terms "genocide" and "crimes against humanity") argued that the S.S., Gestapo, and other Nazi groups were essentially "criminal organizations of volunteer gangsters." Bernays expanded on this view that organizations could be called criminal conspiracies. It should also be noted that it was Herbert Pell, the American representative to the UNWCC, who helped formulate the principle of trying war criminals for offenses against their own nationals before the war and who lobbied doggedly to see it incorporated into the eventual trial procedure. See Kochavi, *Prelude to Nuremberg,* 235–236.

35. Maguire, *Law and War,* 94.

36. Colonel Ammi Cutter, memorandum for Mr. McCloy, 1 October 1944, in Smith, *American Road,* 38.

37. Henry L. Stimson, letter to Secretary of State Cordell Hull, 27 October 1944, in Smith, *American Road,* 39–41.

38. "Three Secretaries' Memorandum," 11 November 1944, in Smith, *American Road,* 43.

39. William Chanler, memorandum, 30 November 1944, in Smith, *American Road,* 74.

40. Smith, *American Road,* 75–78.

41. Ibid., 78 and 83; Smith, *Reaching Justice,* 33.

42. Herbert Wechsler, memorandum for the attorney general (Francis Biddle) from the assistant attorney general (Herbert Wechsler), 29 December 1944, in Smith, *American Road,* 84–90.

43. Smith, *American Road,* 52.

44. Ibid., 137–138. Operating under the assumption that proceedings would include Hitler, Himmler, Mussolini, Göring, Ribbentrop, and Goebbels, Simon sought to devise a method of punishment that would avoid both summary execu-

tion without trial and a "long drawn-out process with endless witnesses as to details who would have to be cross-examined with all the paraphernalia of an immense state trial." He suggested that the Allies draw up a "document of arraignment" that would set out the defendants' offenses. The defendants would have an opportunity to dispute the document's accuracy before an inter-Allied judicial tribunal, which would rule on its truthfulness. By avoiding charges derived from or building on international law, Simon explained, challenges of ex post facto prosecution could be avoided, and persecutions perpetrated against Axis nationals before the war could be included without jurisdictional challenge. Lord Simon, "Memorandum to Judge Rosenman from Lord Simon," 6 April 1945, in Smith, *American Road,* 149–152.

45. Smith, *Reaching Judgment,* 37; Smith, *American Road,* 138.

46. Colonel Ammi Cutter, draft of argument in support of trial of war criminals, 20 April 1945, in letter and memorandum from McCloy to Rosenman, 23 April 1945, TLI, Samuel Rosenman Papers, Box 9, Folder: War Crimes (7).

47. Ibid.

48. Robert H. Jackson, speech before the American Society of International Law, 12 April 1945, in Eugene Gerhardt, *America's Advocate: Robert H. Jackson* (Indianapolis: Bobbs-Merrill, 1958), 317.

49. Executive Order 9547: "Providing for the Representation of the United States in Preparing and Prosecuting Charges of Atrocities and War Crimes against the Leaders of the European Axis Powers and their Principal Agents and Accessories," 2 May 1945, NARG 238: Office of the Chief of Counsel for War Crimes 1933–1949, Chief of Counsel, Entry 159: General Records, Correspondence, Reports and Other Records 1945–1949, Box 1, Folder: Executive Orders 9547 and 9679.

50. Gerhardt, *America's Advocate,* 34–35.

51. Joseph Persico, *Nuremberg: Infamy on Trial* (New York: Viking Penguin, 1994), 9.

52. Gerhardt, *America's Advocate,* 136, 193, 231.

53. Tusa and Tusa, *Nuremberg Trial,* 68.

54. Ibid., 70.

55. Gerhardt, *America's Advocate,* 318. For more on the proceedings at San Francisco, see Smith, *Reaching Judgment.*

56. The State Department published a record of the London talks (26 June to 8 August 1945) including minutes, summary records of informal meetings, and relevant supporting documents in 1949, as Jackson, *Report of Robert H. Jackson.*

57. Tusa and Tusa, *Nuremberg Trial,* 85; Taylor, *Anatomy,* 64. The charter was signed on 8 August 1945. Nineteen other nations also endorsed the charter: Greece, Denmark, Yugoslavia, the Netherlands, Czechoslovakia, Poland, Belgium, Ethiopia, Australia, Honduras, Norway, Panama, Luxembourg, Haiti, New Zealand, India, Venezuela, Uruguay, and Paraguay.

58. Taylor, *Anatomy,* 63–64.

59. Tusa and Tusa, *Nuremberg Trial*, 85.

60. Ibid., 83.

61. Charter of the International Military Tribunal, International Military Tribunal, *Trial of Major War Criminals before the International Military Tribunal*, 42 vols. (Nuremberg, Germany, 1947–1949), 1:12.

62. Robert Jackson, "Report for the President," 7 June 1945, LCMD, Robert H. Jackson Papers, Box 108, Folder: Nuremberg War Crimes Trial—Office Files— U.S. Chief of Counsel—Reports, Final Report to the President October 7, 1946, 6.

63. Tusa and Tusa, *Nuremberg Trial*, 87.

64. International Military Tribunal, *Trial of Major War Criminals*, 1:11.

65. Ibid., 11. The crimes charged as defined by the charter were as follows: "(a) CRIMES AGAINST PEACE: namely, planning, preparation, initiation or waging of a war of aggression, or a war in violation of international treaties, agreements or assurances, or participation in a common plan or conspiracy for the accomplishment of any of the foregoing; (b) WAR CRIMES: namely, violations of the laws or customs of war. Such violations shall include, but not be limited to, murder, ill-treatment or deportation to slave labor or for any other purpose of civilian population of or in occupied territory, murder and ill-treatment of prisoners of war or persons on the seas, killing of hostages, plunder of public or private property, wanton destruction of cities, towns or villages, or devastation not justified by military necessity; (c) CRIMES AGAINST HUMANITY: namely, murder, extermination, enslavement, deportation, and other inhumane acts committed against any civilian population, before or during the war, or persecutions on political, racial or religious grounds in execution of or in connection with any crime within the jurisdiction of the tribunal, whether or not in violation of the domestic law of the country where perpetrated. Leaders, organizers, instigators and accomplices participating in the formulation or execution of a common plan or conspiracy to commit any of the foregoing crimes are responsible for all acts performed by any persons in execution of such a plan." In the draft of the charter that was signed on 8 August 1945, under the description of the charge "crimes against humanity," there was a semicolon between the words "war" and "or persecutions." This formulation expanded the interpretation of the charge in that murder, extermination, enslavement, deportation, and so on need not be connected with the crime of aggressive war. Because this went against what the London Conference had actually agreed on, the semicolon was replaced with a comma in a protocol signed on 6 October. Predictably, the tribunal read the charge according to this narrower construction. Unfortunately, this effectively cut off all persecution of German Jews before the war from the court's jurisdiction. See Roger S. Clark, "Crimes against Humanity at Nuremberg," in Ginsburgs and Kudriavtsev, *Nuremberg Trial and International Law*, 190–193. In a letter home to her parents, Katherine Fite Lincoln, an assistant to the American prosecution team, remarked on this grammatical "error" in the signed charter and attributed it to "rushed [and]

sloppy work." See Katherine ("Titter") Fite Lincoln, letter to parents, 8 October 1945, TLI, Katherine Fite Lincoln Papers, Box 1, Folder: Nuremberg Letters.

66. Tusa and Tusa, *Nuremberg Trial*, 88.

67. Smith, *American Road*, 257.

68. Robert Jackson, opening statement, International Military Tribunal, *Trial of Major War Criminals*, 2:104; Robert H. Jackson, report for President Truman, 7 June 1945, TLI, Office Files, Box 1007, Folder: 325 (1945–1949), 8.

69. Some of the most important works on the Nuremberg trial (by participants and observers of the proceedings) are: Francis Biddle, *In Brief Authority* (Westport, Conn.: Greenwood Press, 1976); Hans Fritzsche, *The Sword in the Scales* (London: Allan Wingate, 1953); Kilmuir (Sir David Maxwell-Fyfe), *Political Adventure: The Memoirs of Lord Kilmuir* (London: Weidenfeld and Nicolson, 1964); Airey Neave, *Nuremberg: A Personal Record* (London: Hodder and Stoughton, 1978); Boris Polevoi, *The Final Reckoning: Nuremberg Diaries* (Moscow: Progress Publishers, 1978); Hjalmar Schacht, *Account Settled* (London: Weidenfeld and Nicolson, 1949); Lord Hartley Shawcross, *Life Sentence; The Memoirs of Lord Shawcross* (London: Constable, 1995); Taylor, *Anatomy;* Herbert Wechsler, *Principles, Politics and Fundamental Law: Selected Essays* (Cambridge: Harvard University Press, 1961); Franz von Papen, *Memoirs* (London: André Deutsch, 1952); Rebecca West, *A Train of Powder* (New York: Viking Press, 1955). Edited collections of key documents include Marrus, *Nuremberg War Crimes Trial;* Smith, *American Road.* Monographs include Conot, *Justice at Nuremberg;* Ginsburgs and Kudriavtsev, *Nuremberg Trial and International Law;* Whitney Harris, *Tyranny on Trial: The Evidence at Nuremberg* (Dallas: Southern Methodist University Press, 1954); Werner Maser, *Nuremberg: A Nation on Trial* (London: Allen Lane, 1979); Persico, *Nuremberg: Infamy on Trial;* Smith, *Reaching Judgment;* Tusa and Tusa, *Nuremberg Trial;* Woetzel, *Nuremberg Trials in International Law.*

70. Tusa and Tusa, *Nuremberg Trial*, 83.

71. Gerhardt, *America's Advocate*, 21.

72. West, *Train of Powder*, 8; Taylor, *Anatomy*, 61.

73. Tusa and Tusa, *Nuremberg Trials*, 84.

74. Shawcross, *Life Sentence*, 101.

75. Tusa and Tusa, *Nuremberg Trial*, 148. In fact, only twenty-one defendants stood trial. Martin Bormann was tried in absentia, Robert Ley committed suicide before the trial's first session, and Gustav Krupp was declared unfit to stand trial after he was named to the indictment.

76. Tusa and Tusa, *Nuremberg Trials*, 146.

77. Robert H. Jackson, opening statement, International Military Tribunal, *Trial of Major War Criminals*, 2:98–99.

78. Lawrence Douglas, "The Shrunken Head of Buchenwald: Icons of Atrocity at Nuremberg," *Representations* 63 (Summer 1998): 39.

79. West, *Train of Powder*, 3. The charges were divided up among the four participants. The Americans, wanting to keep "the bulk of the case in American hands," went first, presenting the conspiracy charge, which included evidence on the other three counts. The British followed with the case of crimes against peace. The French presented on war crimes and crimes against humanity in the West. The Russians concluded the prosecution's presentations with the case on war crimes and crimes against humanity in the East. See Tusa and Tusa, *Nuremberg Trial*, 103.

80. West, *Train of Powder*, 7–8.

81. Shawcross, *Life Sentence*, 115.

82. West, *Train of Powder*, 8; International Military Tribunal, *Trial of Major War Criminals*, 4:319 and 11:415.

83. International Military Tribunal, *Trial of Major War Criminals*, 9:417–421, 9:507–508.

84. Tusa and Tusa, *Nuremberg Trial*, 190.

85. Ibid., 198.

86. West, *Train of Powder*, 60.

87. Robert H. Jackson, opening statement, International Military Tribunal, *Trial of Major War Criminals*, 2:99. Emphasis added.

88. Joint Chiefs of Staff Directive 1023/3, 25 September 1944, in Telford Taylor, *Final Report to the Secretary of the Army on Nuernberg War Crimes Trials under Control Council Law No. 10* (Washington, D.C.: U.S. Government Printing Office, 15 August 1949), 1–2. In fact, in anticipation of imminent collapse, Dwight D. Eisenhower's staff at SHAEF had prepared a "Handbook for Military Government in Germany" several months earlier in June 1944. The handbook called for the automatic arrest and detention of all high-ranking Nazis, as well as all members of the Gestapo; S.S., S.D., S.A., party, police, and Hitler Youth officials; and army officers—a total approximated at a quarter of a million men. See Frank Buscher, *The U.S. War Crimes Trial Program in Germany, 1946–1955* (New York: Greenwood Press, 1989), 13; Smith, *American Road*, 15–16. Although the handbook never received presidential approval, it was distributed widely at the outset of the occupation and served as temporary guidelines for military government officers as they entered a German city. See Daniel Nelson, *A History of U.S. Military Forces in Germany* (Boulder, Colo.: Westview Press, 1987), 13. The handbook infuriated Secretary of the Treasury Morgenthau, who thought it too soft, and in response, he composed his now infamous plan. Roosevelt also criticized the handbook in a letter to Secretary of War Stimson. To fill the policy void, the War Department formulated a new occupation directive, which came to be called by its cable reference: Joint Chiefs of Staff 1067. McCloy was its chief architect. It was adopted as official U.S. occupation policy on 11 May, under President Truman, and remained U.S. occupation policy until 27 July 1947. This directive called for the arrests and detention of those suspected of planning or perpetrating war crimes or atrocities. See Buscher, *U.S. War Crimes Trial*, 13, 18–19.

89. Taylor, *Final Report*, 2–3.

90. Robert H. Jackson, Report for President Truman, 7 June 1945, TLI, Office Files, Box 1007, Folder: 325 (1945–1949).

91. Taylor, *Final Report*, 3.

92. Holger Lessing, *Der Erste Dachauer Prozess (1945/46)* (Baden-Baden: Nomos Verlagsgesellschaft, 1993), 349.

93. For all mass atrocity cases tried before American military commissions, the novel concept of a "common design" to commit war crimes was the central charge. Similar in concept to the IMT charge of conspiracy, it differed in that the prosecution did not have to prove the existence of a previously conceived plan to commit the crime in question. See Lt. Col. C. E. Straight, *Report of the Deputy Judge Advocate for War Crimes, European Command, June 1944 to July 1948*, NARG 549, Box 13: 3–4.

94. Joshua Greene, *Justice at Dachau: The Trials of an American Prosecutor* (New York: Broadway Books, 2003), 40–54.

95. War Crimes Branch, Judge Advocate General, "Memorandum on War Crimes Activities," 17 August 1949, NARG 549: Judge Advocate Division, War Crimes Branch, Entry 2236: General Administrative Records 1942–1957, organization file—cables, Box 9, Folder: Policy Files, Prior 1952. Works on the Dachau Trials include Greene, *Justice at Dachua*; Lessing, *Der Erste Dachauer Prozesse;* and Robert Sigel, *Im Interesse der Gerechtigkeit: Die Dachauer Kriegsverbrecherprozesse, 1945–1948* (Frankfurt am Main: Campus Verlag, 1992). Harold Marcuse includes a short description of the trial at Dachau of the former Dachau personnel in *Legacies of Dachau: The Uses and Abuses of a Concentration Camp, 1933–2001* (Cambridge: Cambridge University Press, 2001). See also Lisa Yavnai, "Military Justice: The U.S. Army Trials of War Criminals in Germany, 1944–1947" (Ph.D. diss., London School of Economics and Political Science, 2007).

96. "Directive on the Identification and Apprehension of Persons suspected of War Crimes and other Offenses and Trial of Certain Offenders" (JCS 1023/10), 8 July 1945, in Taylor, *Final Report*, 4–6.

97. "Directive on the Identification and Apprehension of Persons suspected of War Crimes and other Offenses and Trial of Certain Offenders" (JCS 1023/10), 8 July 1945, in Taylor, *Final Report*, 244–245.

98. Edward C. Betts, theater judge advocate, letter to Robert Jackson, 19 October 1945, LCMD, Robert H. Jackson Papers, Box 110, Folder: Robert H. Jackson Legal File, Nuremberg War Crimes Trial Office Files—U.S. Chief of Counsel Subsequent Files—1.

99. Robert H. Jackson, draft of letter to Edward Betts, 24 October 1945, LCMD, Robert H. Jackson Papers, Box 110, Folder: Robert H. Jackson Legal File, Nuremberg War Crimes Trial Office Files—Chief of Counsel Subsequent Trials—1.

100. Telford Taylor's Biographical Data, May 1946, LCMD, Robert H. Jackson

Papers, Box 110, Folder: Robert H. Jackson Legal File, Nuremberg War Crimes Office Files, U.S. Chief of Counsel Subsequent Trials—2.

101. "Status Report on Military Government of Germany," 15 March 1946, NARG 466: U.S. High Commissioner for Germany, Historical Division, Entry 17: Publications relating to the U.S.'s occupation of Germany, 1945–1953, Status Report on OMGUS through certain International and U.S. Policy, Box 1, Folder: Status Report on Military Government of Germany, 15 March 1946.

102. Taylor, *Final Report*, 6.

103. Military Government Ordinance 7 (MGO 7): "Organization and Powers of Certain Military Tribunals," 18 October 1946, NARG 238: Textual Records of the U.S. Military Tribunals, Nuremberg, Records of Military Tribunals, Entry 145: Correspondence, Memoranda, Reports and other Records 1947–1949, Archives History A-D, Box 1, Folder: Authority for War Crimes Trials.

104. Ibid., and Donald Bloxham, *Genocide on Trial: War Crimes Trials and the Formation of Holocaust History and Memory* (Oxford: Oxford University Press, 2001), 5. For the excerpts from the Roechling trial documents, see Germany (Territory under Allied Occupation, 1945–1955: U.S. Zone), Military Tribunals, *Trials of War Criminals before the Nuernberg Military Tribunals under Control Council Law No. 10; Nuernberg, October 1946–April 1949* (Buffalo: William S. Hein, 1997), 14:1061–1143. For a summary of the trials held in the French Zone under Control Council Law No. 10 and certain other ordinances of the French Supreme Commander in Germany, see Yveline Pendaries, *Les Procès de Rastatt (1946–1954): Le Jugement des crimes de guerre en zone française d'occupation en Allemagne* (Bern: Peter Lang, 1995).

105. Taylor, "Nuremberg War Crimes Trials," 11.

106. On the results of Soviet trials of German war criminals, see Annette Weinke, *Die Verfolgung von NS-Tätern im geteilten Deutschland* (Paderborn: Schöningh, 2002), and Hermann Wentker, *Justiz in der Sowjetischen Besatzungszone/ Deutsche Demokratische Republik, 1945–1953* (Munich: Oldenbourg, 2001).

107. Telford Taylor, letter to Charles Horsky, 7 August 1947, LCMD, Robert H. Jackson Papers, Box 110, Folder: Robert H. Jackson Legal File, Nuremberg War Crimes Trial Office Files—U.S. Chief of Counsel Subsequent Trials—2. The British did not set up their own tribunals under Control Council Law No. 10 as the Americans had hoped, but did proceed with a few cases under the "Royal Warrant." Passed on 14 June 1945 (before the London Charter), it established special jurisdiction and procedure to try to punish individuals for violations of "law and usages of war" committed anytime after 2 September 1939. Because the offenses charged were committed while the defendants were on active service, the trials were modeled on courts-martial, and the accused were subject to military law. The trials were conducted in military courts with military officers presiding. The courts could impose punishments ranging from fines to the death penalty. For the Royal Warrant, see

Taylor, *Final Report*, 254–257. One of the best-known Royal Warrant trials was the prosecution of Field Marshal Albert Kesselring in Venice for his part in the Ardeantine Caves Massacre, in which German occupation forces shot 335 Italian civilians in reprisal for a partisan attack that claimed thirty-three German lives. See Bloxham, *Genocide on Trial*, 77. The defense attorney for the OKW at the IMT and the chief defense attorney at the High Command case, Hans Laternser, served as Kesselring's counsel. In the preparation of the High Command case, the Americans had uncovered damning evidence against Field Marshals Walther von Brauchitsch, Gerd von Rundstedt, Erich von Manstein, and General Adolf Strauss, all of whom were in British custody. The British elected to try these men themselves under the Royal Warrant, although von Brauchitsch died before proceedings began, and von Rundstedt and Strauss were found unfit to stand trial. Von Manstein was eventually tried in August 1949, and the records of the High Command case constituted the majority of the evidence against him. (His attorney, Paul Leverkuehn, served at the High Command case as well.) He was sentenced to eighteen years, which was progressively whittled down on the basis of pretrial time served and "good time" remissions. He was released in August 1952. Kesselring, who had originally been sentenced to death but whose sentence was commuted to life imprisonment, was released on medical parole one month before. See Donald Bloxham, "Punishing German Soldiers during the Cold War: The Case of Erich von Manstein," *Patterns of Prejudice* 33, no. 4 (1999): 25–45. No British convicts of war crimes remained in prison after 1957. On the British prosecution of German military officers, see also J. H. Hoffmann, "German Field Marshals as War Criminals: A British Embarrassment," *Journal of Contemporary History* 23 (1988): 17–35.

108. Telford Taylor, letter to Charles Horsky, 7 August 1947, LCMD, Robert H. Jackson Papers, Box 110, Folder: Robert H. Jackson Legal File, Nuremberg War Crimes Trial Office Files—U.S. Chief of Counsel Subsequent Trials—2.

109. Joseph T. McNarney, memorandum for the chief of staff, War Department, "Organization for Further Proceedings against Axis War Criminals and Certain other Offenders," 5 December 1945, NARG 260: Records of the Executive Office, Records of the Adjutant General, Entry: 4(A1)/5: Military Government Ordinances and Related Records 1945–1949, Box 64, Folder: Military Government Ordinance No. 7. Emphasis added.

110. Ibid.; Telford Taylor, "Memorandum on Further Trials for Robert Jackson," 20 January 1946, NARG 260: Records of Functional Offices and Divisions, Records of the OCCWC, Entry 8(A1)/1: Administrative Division Records re. Defendants and Internal Administration, Box 2, Folder: Subsequent Proceedings Division 013.1.

111. Taylor, *Anatomy*, 152.

112. Telford Taylor, memorandum for Benjamin Cohen on American participation in further international trials of Nazi war criminals, 13 May 1946, TLI, Harry S. Truman Papers, President's Secretary's Files, Box 179: Subject File, Foreign Affairs

File (Germany—German Reparations), Folder: Subject File, Foreign Affairs—Germany, Nuremberg War Crimes.

113. Taylor, *Final Report*, 23.

114. Robert H. Jackson, report for President Truman on the form of the Subsequent Proceedings, 13 May 1946, TLI, Harry S. Truman Papers, President's Secretary's Files, Box 179: Subject File, Foreign Affairs File (Germany–German Reparation), Folder: Subject File, Foreign Affairs—Germany, Nuremberg War Crimes.

115. Samuel Rosenman, letter to Harry Truman, 27 May 1946, TLI, Harry S. Truman Papers, President's Secretary's Files, Box 179: Subject File, Foreign Affairs File (Germany—German Reparation), Folder: Subject File, Foreign Affairs—Germany, Nuremberg War Crimes.

116. Charles Fahy, "Memorandum for the Secretary on Further International Trials of Axis War Criminals," 24 July 1946, NARG 153: (Army) War Crimes Branch, Entry 1018: Nuremberg Administrative Files 1944–1949, Box 1, Folder: 2 International Trial folder II 84-1.

117. Telford Taylor, "Memorandum for the Secretary of War," 29 July 1946, TLI, Harry S. Truman Papers, President's Secretary's Files, Box 179: Subject File, Foreign Affairs File (Germany—German Reparation), Folder: Subject File, Foreign Affairs—Germany, Nuremberg War Crimes. Indeed, two of the six subsections of the Subsequent Proceedings Division had been dedicated exclusively to the preparation of cases against the Krupp and IG Farben companies. These and one more case against the steel magnate Friedrich Flick and five of his associates were prosecuted with success. The Americans presented evidence concerning the rearmament of Germany in preparation for war and support of the German war machine, the expropriation of Jewish industrial and mining properties in the late 1930s and spoliation of industrial resources in the occupied territories, the exploitation of slave labor, and extensive dealings with the S.S. Twenty-four of the forty-two indicted defendants received prison sentences. See Taylor, *Final Report*, 39, and Taylor, "Nuremberg War Crimes Trials," 3.

118. Taylor, *Final Report*, 27.

119. Taylor, "Nuremberg War Crimes Trials," 17–21. In a report for the deputy military governor, Taylor explained that of the eighteen originally planned trials, the case concerning the destruction of Warsaw had been abandoned because of the "primarily Polish interest" in it, and that the Government Administration case and the Propaganda and Education cases had been combined. See Telford Taylor, memorandum for Deputy Military Governor, OMGUS, 20 May 1947, NARG 549: Judge Advocate Division, War Crimes Branch, Entry 2236: General Administrative Records 1942–1957, Box 1, Folder: Organization—1947. In a subsequent memorandum, Taylor remarked that budgetary and time limitations and the difficulty in obtaining judges to staff the military tribunals had forced the further reduction of

projected trials from sixteen to from twelve to fourteen. However, this would be accomplished by consolidating trials, instead of abandoning particular cases altogether. Although Taylor concluded that the single most limiting factor in the prosecution of the remaining war crimes proceedings was the difficulty in obtaining judges, he noted that because the defendants had occupied high positions and had not for the most part committed murder or other crimes with their own hands, developing and presenting conclusive proof of the defendants' guilt was extremely time-consuming. The accusations in turn opened the door to lengthy defenses. "In these respects, the OCC trials are every bit as difficult, and frequently more difficult than the IMT," Taylor declared. See Telford Taylor, "Memorandum for Deputy Military Governor, OMGUS," 4 September 1947, TLI, Alvin Rockwell Papers, Box 38: OMGUS File: Subject File 1944–(1948), 1952—Selected Opinions—Legal Division, January 1, 1952–June 30, 1952, to War Crimes, Correspondence—Folder: War Crimes—Press Releases—Summary of Memo 4 September 1947.

120. Although condemned by the IMT judgment as a "ruthless military caste," the tribunal could not declare the OKW a criminal organization, because as a group, its bonds of membership were too loose to constitute a coherent organization within the meaning of the charter. See Robert Jackson, "Final Report of Robert H. Jackson," 7 October 1946, LCMD, Robert H. Jackson Papers, Box 108, Folder: Nuremberg War Crimes Trial—Office Files—U.S. Chief of Counsel—Reports, Final Report to the President 7 October 1946, and Telford Taylor, "The Meaning of the Nuremberg Trials," CULS-ADLL, Telford Taylor Papers, Speeches, Box 53, "The Meaning of the Nuremberg Trials," address delivered in French to the International Association of Democratic Lawyers at the Palais de Justice, Paris, 25 April 1947.

121. Taylor, speech, "Meaning of the Nuremberg Trials."

122. The IMTFE consisted of eleven judges from Australia, Canada, China, England, France, India, the Netherlands, New Zealand, the Philippines, the United States, and the USSR. An American, Joseph Keenan, served as the chief prosecutor. Twenty-eight defendants stood trial, all former Japanese officers. Proceedings lasted two and a half years, from 29 April 1946 to 12 November 1948. Charges reflected the principles of the Nuremberg Charter and included the crimes of conspiracy, aggressive war, war crimes, and crimes against humanity, but the Tokyo Charter's wording differed on some points. Ultimately the tribunal handed down seven death sentences and sixteen terms of life imprisonment. See B. V. A. Röling and C. F. Rüter, eds., *The Tokyo Judgment: The International Military Tribunal for the Far East (IMTFE), 29 April 1946–12 November 1948* (Amsterdam: APA—University Press, Amsterdam, 1977), 1:xi–xiii and 1:465–466.

CHAPTER TWO: THE RESPONSE TO THE TRIALS

Epigraph from Theophil Wurm, letter to General Gross, American Military Governor of Baden-Württemberg, 3 May 1949, Theophil Wurm, Martin Niemöller, and Karl Hartenstein, *Memorandum by the Evangelical Church in Germany on the Question of War Crimes Trials before American Military Courts* (Waiblingen-Stuttgart: Gust. Stürner, 1949), NARG 238: Advisory Board on Clemency for War Criminals, Office of the U.S. High Command for Germany, 1947–1950, Entry 213: Correspondence and other Records, 1950, Box 4, Folder: Memorandum by the Evangelical Church.

1. Anna Merritt and Richard Merritt, eds., *Public Opinion in Occupied Germany: The OMGUS Surveys, 1945–1949* (Urbana: University of Chicago Press, 1970), 3.

2. Ibid., 34–35.

3. Ibid., 34.

4. OMGUS Opinion Survey Report, "Majority of Germans Believe Nurnberg Trials Fair: Guilt of Defendants and Organizations Conclusive, Reactions of Population to Trials Favorable," 7 August 1946, NARG 260: Records of Information Control Division, Records of the Opinion Surveys Branch, Entry 16(A1)/9: Records Relating to Public Opinion 1945–1949, Box 153, Folder: Opinion Survey Reports—Index and Nos. 1–20. See also Merritt and Merritt, *OMGUS Surveys*, 34.

5. OMGUS Opinion Survey Report 68, "The Trend in Attitudes toward National Socialism," 10 October 1947, NARG 260: Records of Information Control Division, Records of the Opinion Surveys Branch, Entry 16(A1)/9: Records Relating to Public Opinion 1945–1949, Box 153, Folder: Opinion Survey Reports 61–80. See also Merritt and Merritt, *The OMGUS Surveys*, 32.

6. OMGUS Opinion Survey Report 68, "Trend in Attitudes."

7. Benjamin Ferencz, letter to Sheldon Glueck, quoted in letter from Sheldon Glueck to Robert H. Jackson, 31 October 1947, LCMD, Robert H. Jackson Papers, Box 110, Folder: Robert H. Jackson Legal File, Nuremberg War Crimes Trial Office File, U.S. Chief of Counsel Subsequent Trials—2.

8. "Germans Show Lack of Interest in War Trials: AMG Strives to Remedy Situation Ascribed to One-Sided News Reports," *New York Herald Tribune*, 5 March 1948, NARG 238: Office of the Chief of Counsel for War Crimes 1933–1949, Executive Office, Publications Division, Entry 196: Correspondence, Reports and other Records 1948–1949, War Crimes Data, Newspaper Clippings, Box 2, Folder: Newspaper Clippings, War Crimes Trials at Nuremberg.

9. Merritt and Merritt, *The OMGUS Surveys*, 18.

10. "Report of the Special Commission appointed by the Secretary of the Army Royall to study Nutrition in Bizonal Germany," May 1948, TLI, Harry S. Truman Papers, Student Research File (B file), U.S. Policy in Occupied Germany, Folder:

U.S. Policy in occupied Germany—Denazification, Decartelization, Demilitarization—Introductory.

11. In Bavaria from 25 December 1948 to 25 January 1949, a total of 273,761 people attended Amerika Haus programs, and these centers recorded a book circulation of 184,955 volumes. See Office of the Military Government for Bavaria, "Monthly Report of Exhibitions and Information Centers Branch, ISD, OMBG (25 December 1948–25 January 1949)," for the Director, Information Service Division, OMBG APO 407-A, U.S. Army, 25 January 1949, NARG 260: Records of Information Control Division, Records of Information Centers and Exhibits Branch, Entry 16 (A1)/25: Land Level Reports 1949, Box 351, Folder: ICE Bavaria—1949. The ultimate impact of the Amerika Haus program was a complex force to measure. Although overall relatively few Germans regularly attended program events, those who did tended to occupy prominent roles in their communities. According to the November 1948 OMGUS survey, only 4 percent of respondents had been to an Amerika Haus, but the majority of those who did were from the better-educated classes, particularly community and opinion leaders. See Merritt and Merritt, *OMGUS Surveys*, 15.

12. Tom Bower, *Blind Eye to Murder: Britain, America and the Purging of Nazi Germany—A Pledge Betrayed* (London: Granada, 1981), 186. On the denazification program, see Lutz Niethammer, *Entnazifizierung in Bayern: Säuberung und Rehabilitierung unter amerikanischer Besatzung* (Frankfurt am Main: Fischer, 1972); Steven Remy, *The Heidelberg Myth: The Nazification and Denazification of a German University* (Cambridge: Harvard University Press, 2002); Clemens Vollnhals and Thomas Schlemmer, *Entnazifizierung: Politische Säuberung und Rehabilitierung in den vier Besatzungszonen, 1945–1949* (Munich: Deutscher Taschenbuch Verlag, 1991).

13. Bower, *Blind Eye to Murder*, 191.

14. Merritt and Merritt, *OMGUS Surveys*, 37; Michael Kater, "Problems of Political Reeducation in West Germany, 1945–1960," *Simon Wiesenthal Center Annual* 4 (1987): 99–105.

15. Constantine FitzGibbon, *Denazification* (London: Michael Joseph, 1969), 167.

16. Bower, *Blind Eye to Murder*, 188–189; Merritt and Merritt, eds., *OMGUS Surveys*, 37.

17. Bower, *Blind Eye to Murder*, 204; Kai Bird, *The Chairman: John J. McCloy—The Making of the American Establishment* (New York: Simon & Schuster, 1992), 329–330.

18. Timothy Vogt, *Denazification in Soviet-Occupied Germany: Brandenburg, 1945–1948* (Cambridge: Harvard University Press, 2000), 8.

19. FitzGibbon, *Denazification*, 165.

20. Bower, *Blind Eye to Murder*, 195 and 204.

21. Ibid., 195. The certificates were colloquially referred to as "Persilscheine," from *Persil,* the brand name of a popular laundry detergent, and *-scheine,* "certificates."

22. Bower, *Blind Eye to Murder,* 207; David Buxton, "To What Extent Was the Failure of Denazification in Germany 1945–48 a Result of Apathy of the Allies?" *Historian* 78 (Summer 2003): 18–21.

23. Bishop Theophil Wurm, Bishop Hans Meiser, Bishop Bender (first name not indicated), Bishop Wuestemann (first name not indicated), Church President Martin Niemöller, letter to General Lucius D. Clay, 20 May 1948, NARG 549: Judge Advocate Division, War Crimes Branch, Entry 2237: Records Relating to Post Trial Activities 1945–1947, Box 9, Folder: Bishop of Wurms [*sic*].

24. "Prosecutor Scores War-Crimes Judge: General Taylor Sees Dangers to U.S. in Wennershum's [*sic*] Nuremberg Remarks," *New York Times,* 23 February 1948, NARG 238: Office of the Chief of Counsel for War Crimes 1933–1949, Executive Office, Publications Division, Entry 196: Correspondence, Reports and other Records 1948–1949, War Crimes Data, Newspaper Clippings, Box 2, Folder: Newspaper Clippings—War Crimes Trials at Nuremberg. The trial was officially called *U.S. v. Wilhelm List et al.* There were only oblique references to this attitude in the tribunal's judgment. Near its conclusion it read: "It has been suggested that an element of unfairness exists from the inherent nature of the organizational character of the tribunal. It is true, of course, that the defendants are required to submit their case to a panel of judges from a victor nation. It is unfortunate that the nations of the world have taken no steps to remove the basis of this criticism. The lethargy of the world's statesmen in dealing with this matter . . . is well known. . . . A tribunal of this character should through its deliberations and judgment disclose that it represents all mankind in an effort to make contribution to a system of international law and procedure, devoid of nationalistic prejudices. This we have endeavored to do. To some this may not appear to be sufficient protection against bias and prejudice. Any improvement however, is dependent upon the affirmative action by the nations of the world. It does not rest within the scope of the functions of the tribunal." See Germany (Territory under Allied Occupation, 1945–1955: U.S. Zone), Military Tribunals, *Trials of War Criminals before the Nuernberg Military Tribunals under Control Council Law No. 10 Nuernberg, October 1946–April 1949* (Buffalo: William S. Hein, 1997), 11:1316–1317. In his interview with the *Chicago Tribune,* Wennerstrum also claimed that the only thing the trials were teaching the Germans was that they had lost to a "tough conqueror." See Telford Taylor, letter to Judge Wennerstrum, 21 February 1948; "War Crimes Judge Assails Trials; Taylor Accuses Him of 'Smear,'" 23 February 1948, Provenance not indicated, TLI, Alvin Rockwell Papers, Box 38, Folder: War Crimes—Correspondence. Wennerstrum's remarks were picked up by the major news service Reuters and published in all major papers, including the *New York Times* and the *Washington Post.* See above and "Editorial,"

Washington Post, 24 February 1948, TLI, John Young Papers, Box 57, Folder: 7: Extra Exhibits. Apparently Wennerstrum was the only one of the three-member tribunal who harbored these views, because the other two judges, Edward Carter (of the Nebraska Supreme Court) and George Burke (general counsel for the University of Michigan), stated only that they felt the trial had been "well thought out" and "tried fairly" and avoided all comment on Wennerstrum's outburst. See "Wennerstrum Backs Charges," 24 February 1948, provenance not indicated, TLI, Alvin Rockwell Papers, Box 38, Folder: War Crimes—Correspondence. The bristling over Wennerstrum's remarks was soon overtaken by speculation over how Taylor had come to know about the interview, because his reply appeared before the contents of the interview had even been published. Journalist Hal Foust blamed army wiretapping and followed up his piece on Wennerstrum with an article about that. Ultimately a staff member of the army's Public Information Office admitted having received the piece from a German operator for Press Wireless. See Office of Military Government (U.S.) Incoming Message from Department of the Army, 25 February 1948, TLI, Alvin Rockwell Papers, Box 38, Folder: War Crimes—Correspondence.

25. Telford Taylor, letter to Charles S. Wennerstrum, 21 February 1948, TLI, Alvin Rockwell Papers, Box 38, Folder: War Crimes—Correspondence.

26. "Wennerstrum Backs Charges," 24 February 1948, article provenance not indicated, TLI, Alvin Rockwell Papers, Box 38, Folder: War Crimes—Correspondence.

27. Otto Kranzbuehler, Conrad Boettcher, Hans Laternser, telegram to President Truman, 27 February 1948, NARG 238: Textual Records of the U.S. Military Tribunals, Nuremberg, Records of Military Tribunals, Entry 145: Correspondence, Memoranda, Reports and Other Records 1947–1949, Box 1, Folder: Defendants' Clemency Petitions—General. The telegram read: "Recent statement by high American judge confirms misgivings prevailing among defense counsel as to administration of justice before U.S. Military Tribunals at Nuernberg. All endeavors to secure fair trial so far frustrated on account of rules originating from American military authorities. Spokesmen of defense counsel in industrial and military cases now pending before Military Tribunals most fervently appeal to you for help and relief." The telegram was reported in the *Stars and Stripes.* See "Defense Asks Truman Aid in Crimes Cases," *Stars and Stripes,* 29 February 1948, TLI, John Young Papers, Box 72, Folder: Records Books and Binders; "Attorneys Appeal to Truman," *New York Times,* 23 February 1948, 5. This latter article, which had the German attorneys claiming that "intimidation and other illegal methods had been used to obtain evidence," is quoted in Frank Buscher, *The U.S. War Crimes Trial Program in Germany, 1946–1955* (New York: Greenwood Press, 1989), 36.

28. Ernst Klee, *Persilscheine und falsche Pässe: Wie die Kirchen den Nazis halfen* (Frankfurt am Main: Fischer Taschenbuch Verlag, 1992), 7. On the clergy's inter-

vention on behalf of war criminals, see also Jörg Friedrich, *Die kalte Amnestie: NS-Täter in der Bundesrepublik* (Frankfurt: Fischer Taschenbuch Verlag, 1984).

29. Suzanne Brown-Fleming, *The Holocaust and Catholic Conscience: Cardinal Aloisius Muench and the Guilt Question in Germany* (Notre Dame: University of Notre Dame Press, 2006), 13–14. See also Michael Phayer, *The Catholic Church and the Holocaust, 1930–1965* (Bloomington: Indiana University Press, 2000), 134; Norbert Frei, *Adenauer's Germany and the Nazi Past: The Politics of Amnesty and Integration* (New York: Columbia University Press, 2002), 306.

30. Phayer, *The Catholic Church and the Holocaust*, 134.

31. Ibid., 133–138. By describing the first and last drafts of the August 1945 Fulda statement, Phayer highlights the particular issues about which the bishops were most sensitive—and most equivocal. For the full text of the Stuttgart Declaration of Guilt and a lengthy analysis of the Protestant Church's response to the Nazi past, see Matthew Hockenos, *A Church Divided: German Protestants Confront the Nazi Past* (Bloomington: Indiana University Press, 2004). On the distinction among criminal guilt, political responsibility, and moral guilt, see Kurt Tauber, *Beyond Eagle and Swastika: German Nationalism since 1945* (Middletown: Wesleyan University Press, 1967), 1:37–43.

32. Evangelical Church of Germany Council, "Stuttgart Declaration of Guilt," October 1945, in Hockenos, *Church Divided*, 187.

33. Daily Intelligence Digest 124, "An Interview with Pastor Niemoeller," 4 March 1946, NARG 260: Records of Information Control Division, Records of the Opinion Surveys Branch, Entry 16(A1)/9: Records Relating to Public Opinion 1945–1949, Box 145, Folder: D.I.D.

34. Evangelical Church of Germany Council, "Stuttgart Declaration of Guilt," October 1945, in Hockenos, *Church Divided*, 187.

35. Phayer, *The Catholic Church and the Holocaust*, 139; Brown-Fleming, *Holocaust and Catholic Conscience*, 162.

36. Daily Intelligence Digest 133, "Clergy continues to favor Cause of Interned Nazis," 15 March 1946, NARG 260: Records of Information Control Division, Records of the Opinion Surveys Branch, Entry 16(A1)/9: Records Relating to Public Opinion 1945–1949, Box 145, Folder: D.I.D.

37. "Forgive Germany, Pope Urges World," *New York Times*, 16 April 1948, NARG 238: Office of the Chief of Counsel for War Crimes 1933–1949, Executive Office, Publications Division, Entry 196: Correspondence, Reports and Other Records 1948–1949, War Crimes Data, Newspaper Clippings, Box 2, Folder: Newspaper Clippings, War Crimes Trials at Nuremberg.

38. Brown-Fleming, *Holocaust and Catholic Conscience*, 17–18. For a more detailed discussion of the pope's view of Catholic Germans, see Phayer, *The Catholic Church and the Holocaust*, chap. 9, "The Holocaust and the Priorities of Pius XII during the Cold War," 159–183.

39. Brown-Fleming, *Holocaust and Catholic Conscience*, chap. 2, "Excusing the Holocaust," 44–65.

40. Ibid., 22 and 45. It does not appear as though Muench composed "One World in Charity" for the benefit of a German audience, although he expressed some satisfaction when unofficial translations appeared in Germany in late December 1946 to early January 1947. Catholic clergy (notably including Bishop von Galen) and laity alike distributed several excerpted versions at the local parish level. All versions retained three points: (1) the exoneration of the majority of Germans' guilt or responsibility, (2) emphasis on German suffering, and (3) the equation of Allied and Nazi "crimes." Remarkably, the letter was still in circulation in Germany in 1951. See Brown-Fleming, *Holocaust and Catholic Conscience*, 44–65. OMGUS surveyors attempted to determine German attitudes toward collective guilt. In the last two weeks of December 1946, they polled American zone citizens on seven interrelated questions designed to reveal these opinions, such as whether they shared responsibility for Hitler's regime because they supported it, whether they shared responsibility for the war because they gave power to a war-minded government, whether the war was justified as a response to the harsh Versailles Treaty, and whether Germans tortured and murdered millions of helpless Europeans. They tabulated conclusions by consolidating answers that rejected guilt or rationalized behavior on each of the questions. They arranged answers on a scale of 1 to 7, where 1 signified a rejection of collective guilt on any single question and 7 signified rejection of collective responsibility for all seven questions. The average score for the total population was just under 4, meaning the population surveyed rejected collective guilt for almost four (i.e., over half) of seven questions. For a detailed breakdown of responses, see "Attitudes toward Collective Guilt in the American Zone of Germany," Report Number 51, ODIC Opinion Surveys HQ, 2 April 1947, NARG 260: Records of Information Control Division, Records of the Opinion Surveys Branch, Entry 16(A1)/9: Records Relating to Public Opinion 1945–1949, Box 153, Folder: Opinion Survey Reports—Index and Nos. 1–20.

41. Archbishop Josef Frings of Cologne (also chairman of the Fulda Bishops Conference) and Bishop Otto Dibelius (Berlin-Brandenburg) were also particularly active on behalf of war criminals.

42. Theophil Wurm, letters to Robert Kempner, 19 February 1948 and 30 March 1948, in Wurm et al., *Memorandum by the Evangelical Church in Germany*, NARG 238: Advisory Board on Clemency for War Criminals, Office of the U.S. High Command for Germany 1947–1950, Entry 213: Correspondence and other Records, 1950, Box 4, Folder: Memorandum by the Evangelical Church. There were moments of unhappy resignation to the verdicts as well. After the trials, Cardinal Frings declared, "As Christians we refuse to recognize the Nuremberg verdicts as justice, but we have to accept them, as a defeated people, as acts of reprisal imposed by the victor." See "German Bishops on War Crimes Trials," *Christian Century* 66 (1949): 725–726, as quoted in Buscher, *U.S. War Crimes Trial*, 100.

43. Lisa Yavnai, "Military Justice: The U.S. Army Trials of War Criminals in Germany, 1944–1947" (Ph.D. diss., London School of Economics and Political Science, 2007). Although the first trial took place in June 1945, the rest of the cases occurred over roughly eighteen months before December 1947. There were a total of 462 cases. These included so-called flyer cases, which prosecuted 640 Axis nationals (mostly Germans) for the killing or assaulting of 1,244 downed Americans who had parachuted into enemy territory. Eight cases were classified as "mass atrocity" cases, concerned with the staffs of the Dachau, Buchenwald, Mauthausen, Flossenburg, Nordhausen, and Muehldorf concentration camps, as well as the Hadamar euthanasia installation. This category also included the Malmedy massacre case, which is discussed at length in this chapter. A total of 286 defendants were involved in these eight cases. Because the concentration camps themselves were so large and so complex, a second entry (called "subsequent" cases) of camp-related trials was held involving 746 defendants. See Summary Report, "War Crimes Activities," 17 August 1949, NARG 549: Judge Advocate Division, War Crimes Branch, Entry 2236: General Administrative Records 1942–1957, Box 9, Folder: Policy Files Prior 1952.

44. Tomaz Jardim, "The Mauthausen War Crimes Trial and American Justice in Germany" (PhD diss., University of Toronto, 2009), 25.

45. Summary Report, "War Crimes Activities."

46. Jardim, "Mauthausen War Crimes Trial," 26.

47. The commander in chief's jurisdiction was described as follows: "Regulations for the trials of war criminals provide that the record of the trial be reviewed by staff officers of the appointing officer and that the written review and recommendations be submitted to the appointing officer for his approval or disapproval. The appointing officer, in his capacity as the reviewing authority, may confirm or set aside any finding; affirm, suspend, reduce, commute, or modify any sentence." See "Conduct of Ilse Koch War Crimes Trial, Interim Report of the Investigations Subcommittee of the Committee on Expenditures in the Executive Departments Pursuant to S. Res. 189 (80th Congress)," submitted, under the authority of the order of the Senate on 27 December 1948, by Mr. Ferguson, TLI, Alvin Rockwell Papers, Box 38, Folder: War Crimes (press releases, telegrams, letters, and reports, 2 of 2).

48. As of March 1947, General Lucius Clay, already military governor, became theater commander. It should be noted that his jurisdiction over the Dachau sentences extended from his position as head of U.S. military forces, not as military governor. All in all, the Dachau courts sentenced 1,416 defendants, of which 426 men were sentenced to death. Clay eventually commuted 127 of these sentences to life imprisonment and reduced many more prison terms. Therefore, Clay was responsible for 299 executions. See Lucius Clay, *Decision in Germany* (Garden City: Doubleday & Company, 1950), 253. Clay insisted that he took great care in the revision of all sentences before him. However, given the sheer volume of material and

the breadth of his responsibilities for all facets of occupation government, it is doubt-ful that he was able to conduct exhaustive reviews of all cases. He was greatly assisted by the five review boards, whose recommendations he largely followed.

49. Colonel J. L. Harbaugh, Headquarters, European Command, Office of the Judge Advocate, office memorandum No. 4, "Establishment of Board of Review for War Crimes Cases," 29 August 1947, NARG 549: Judge Advocate Division, War Crimes Branch, Entry 2236: General Administrative Records 1942–1957, Box 1, Folder: Organization—1947.

50. Internal Route Slip, Headquarters, U.S. Forces, European Theater, "War Crimes Clemency Program," 30 September 1947, NARG 549: Judge Advocate Division, War Crimes Branch, Entry 2237: Records Relating to Post Trial Activi-ties 1945–1947, Box 2, Folder: Clemency Files 1947—General Admin.

51. Summary Report, "War Crimes Activities." The trial (officially called *U.S. v. Valentin Bersin et al.*) actually involved charges for killing between 538 and 749 Allied POWs and over 90 Belgian citizens. However, it was the Malmedy massacre by Joachim (Jochen) Peiper's First S.S. Panzer Division that received the most atten-tion. For a fascinating account of the trial and American lead defense attorney Willis Everett's lifelong pursuit to nullify the judgment, see James Weingartner, *A Peculiar Crusade: Willis M. Everett and the Malmedy Massacre* (New York: New York Uni-versity Press, 2000). Also on the Malmedy massacre and trial, see James Weingart-ner, *Crossroads of Death: The Story of the Malmedy Massacre and Trial* (Berkeley: University of California Press, 1979). On the leader of the S.S. group that perpe-trated the massacre and the chief defendant in the Malmedy trial, see Charles Whit-ing, *Jochen Peiper: Battle Commander S.S. Liebstandarte Adolf Hitler* (Barnsley: Leo Cooper, 1999).

52. Johann Neuhäusler, letter to Honorable Francis Case, John Vorys, W. Versell, Overton Brooks, Ed Cox (members of U.S. Congress), 23 March 1948, NARG 549: Judge Advocate Division, War Crimes Branch, Entry 2237: Records Relating to Post Trial Activities 1945–1947, Box 11, Bishop Neuhäusler—Admin Files.

53. Weingartner, *Peculiar Crusade,* 120–121. Also helpful on the debacle over the Malmedy trial is Buscher, *U.S. War Crimes Trial,* especially chap. 2, "Doubts about the U.S. War Crimes Program," 29–48.

54. Weingartner, *Peculiar Crusade,* 123–124.

55. Ibid., 130–131.

56. Ibid., 138–141.

57. Ibid., 147–162. See also Buscher, *U.S. War Crimes Trial,* 38–39.

58. Johann Neuhäusler, letter to Honorable Francis Case, John Vorys, W. Versell, Overton Brooks, Ed Cox (members of U.S. Congress), 23 March 1948, NARG 549: Judge Advocate Division, War Crimes Branch, Entry 2237: Records Relating to Post Trial Activities 1945–1947, Box 11, Bishop Neuhäusler—Admin Files.

59. Robert Kempner, letter to Theophil Wurm, 12 May 1948; Theophil Wurm, letter to Robert Kempner, 5 May 1948, in Wurm et al., *Memorandum by the Evangelical Church in Germany*, NARG 238: Advisory Board on Clemency for War Criminals, Office of the U.S. High Command for Germany 1947–1950, Entry 213: Correspondence and other Records, 1950, Box 4, Folder: Memorandum by the Evangelical Church.

60. Annexes IV to VI, IX to XI: sworn statements by Werner Sternebeck, Hans Siptrott, Paul Zwigart, Valentin Bersin, Max Rieder, and Tomczak [no first name], respectively, "Report on Documentary Statements Submitted by Bishop of Wurms [*sic*] to the Secretary of the Army," sent to Theater Judge Advocate, EUCOM, undated but after 29 May 1948, NARG 549: Judge Advocate Division, War Crimes Branch, Entry 2237: Records Relating to Post Trial Activities, Box 9, Folder: Bishop Wurms [*sic*].

61. Annex VII: "Malmedy Trial before the General Court in Dachau" in "Report on Documentary Statements Submitted by Bishop of Wurms [*sic*] to the Secretary of the Army," sent to Theater Judge Advocate, EUCOM, undated but after 29 May 1948, NARG 549: Judge Advocate Division, War Crimes Branch, Entry 2237: Records Relating to Post Trial Activities, Box 9, Folder: Bishop Wurms [*sic*] and Theophil Wurm; letter to Robert Kempner, 5 June 1948, in Wurm et al., *Memorandum by the Evangelical Church in Germany*.

62. Weingartner, *Peculiar Crusade*, 145.

63. Department of the Army memorandum for the press, 6 January 1949; memorandum for the Secretary of the Army, "Survey of the Trials of War Crimes held at Dachau, Germany" (the Simpson Commission Report), 6 January 1949; and Appendix 3, "List of cases in which clemency has been recommended," undated, TLI, Alvin Rockwell Papers, Box 38, Folder: War Crimes—press releases, telegrams, letters, and reports (2 of 2). The order for the creation of the Simpson Commission came from the Department of the Army; however, there is evidence that the impetus for the board originated with General Clay, who wanted an independently conducted review. See Jean Edward Smith, ed., *The Papers of General Lucius D. Clay: Germany, 1945–49* (Bloomington: Indiana University Press, 1974), 2:742–743; Clay, *Decision in Germany*, 253.

64. Weingartner, *Peculiar Crusade*, 163, 166–167. Van Roden later published one of these speeches, which appeared under the title "American Atrocities in Germany" in the February 1949 issue of *The Progressive*. See Buscher, *U.S. War Crimes Trial*, 41.

65. The Dachau courts implemented a similar strategy as the designers and prosecutors of the Nuremberg trials. However, instead of indicting defendants on the charge of participation in the "common plan or conspiracy," they charged them with having "encouraged, aided, abetted and participated in the common criminal design." Individuals were not charged with specific crimes such as murder or assault,

nor did they have to be proven guilty of having personally committed "any specific act or acts of violence." The reasoning behind this charge was that "one who joins in a common design to commit unlawful acts is responsible for all acts committed in furtherance of the common design. Any act committed by one participant in furtherance of a common design is, in law, the act of all, and all are equally guilty." In practice, however, the extent of a person's participation could be a mitigating factor when determining the sentence. See "Conduct of Ilse Koch War Crimes Trial."

66. "Conduct of Ilse Koch War Crimes Trial." For Clay's explanation of his decision, see Smith, *Papers of General Lucius D. Clay*, 2:888–889.

67. "Conduct of Ilse Koch War Crimes Trial."

68. Ibid.

69. Harry Truman, letter to Kenneth Royall, 17 October 1948; "Trial of Ilse Koch Report," 1948, TLI, Harry S. Truman Papers, White House Confidential Files, Box 3, Folder: Army, Department of the, May 1945–September 1949; Memorandum, Subject: Ilse Koch Case, 16 November 1948, Folder: Army, Department of the, September 1948–August 1948. A handwritten note at the bottom of the memorandum reads: "there was a pretty clear abuse of discretion."

70. John O'Donnell, "Capitol Stuff," *New York News*, 4 October 1948, TLI, Vertical File, World War, 1939–1945—War Criminal.

71. "Conduct of Ilse Koch War Crimes Trial." Also on the Ferguson Subcommittee review, particularly the Buchenwald case lead prosecutor William Denson's involvement, see Joshua Greene, *Justice at Dachau: The Trials of an American Prosecutor* (New York: Broadway Books, 2003), 321–342.

72. "Conduct of Ilse Koch War Crimes Trial"; "Ilse Koch Hangs Herself in Cell: Nazi 'Beast of Buchenwald' Was Serving Life Term," *New York Times*, 3 September 1967, TLI, Vertical File, World War, 1939–1945—War Criminal. Konrad Morgen is well-known for his investigations into corruption and criminality at Auschwitz, and his findings were critical for the adjudication of the 1963 Auschwitz trial of camp personnel. See Rebecca Wittmann, *Beyond Justice: The Auschwitz Trial* (Cambridge: Harvard University Press, 2005).

73. At the same time, the committee noted, "the distinction between changing the sentence after it becomes final and the exercise of clemency should be noted. Under our democratic system clemency may be exercised at any time by the proper authorities. This is an added protection against possible injustice to the accused and is not a violation of the rule of finality." "Conduct of Ilse Koch War Crimes Trial."

74. Ibid. General Clay would later write that perhaps he had erred in reducing Koch's sentence, but he added that he had not had all the records (meaning some of the most damaging) available to him at the time of his review. He smarted at the accusations that he had been too lenient—as in the course of his duties as commander in chief, he had confirmed nearly 300 death sentences. See Clay, *Decision in Germany*, 254. As for Ilse Koch, while the original indictment was sweeping in its

inclusion of offenses against non-German nationals, it had not accounted for crimes against Germans. In January 1949, General Clay referred her file to the Bavarian Ministry of Justice. With the assistance of the provost marshal general of the army, the judge advocate, and the OMGUS Legal Division, a German special prosecutor prepared a case. See Summary Report, "War Crimes Activities." Koch was rearrested upon her release in October 1949 and tried at Augsburg for crimes against German nationals. The court found her guilty of murder, attempted murder, and physical mistreatment and sentenced her to life imprisonment. In 1967, she hanged herself in her cell. See "Ilse Koch Hangs Herself in Cell."

75. Resolution taken at the Bishops' Conference in Fulda on 26 August 1948 to the American Military Government, "The German Bishops' Attitude to the Nuremberg and Dachau Trials," in Wurm et al., *Memorandum by the Evangelical Church in Germany.*

76. Report of War Crimes Board of Review No. 2, Crawford, Haefele, and McClintock, 5 January 1949, NARG 549: Judge Advocate Division, War Crimes Branch, Entry 2237: Records Relating to Post Trial Activities 1945–1947, Box 11, Folder: Bishop Meiser—Admin Files.

77. Ibid.

78. Memorandum for the Secretary of the Army, "Survey of the Trials of War Crimes held at Dachau, Germany" (the Simpson Commission Report), 6 January 1949, TLI, Alvin Rockwell Papers, Box 38, Folder: War Crimes—press releases, telegrams, letters, and reports (2 of 2).

79. Ibid.

80. Clay, *Decision in Germany,* 253; Smith, *Papers of General Lucius D. Clay,* 2:962, 2:1013, 2:1043, 2:1045.

81. On Clay's confirmation of death sentences, see Smith, *Papers of General Lucius D. Clay,* 2:1054–1056, 2:059–1061. A recurring issue in Clay's official correspondence in early spring 1949 was the desire simply to proceed with the executions before the establishment of the High Commission for Germany. For example, he wrote, "I would not like to have a mass execution and yet I do want to free my successor from this thankless task and give him a clearer and more constructive task. It is one of my inheritances I do not want to pass on." Ibid., 2:1062. See also 2:1038 and 2:1041.

82. Weingartner, *Peculiar Crusade,* 176. On domestic American criticism of the war crimes trial program, see William Bosch, *Judgment on Nuremberg: American Attitudes toward the Major German War-Crime Trials* (Chapel Hill: University of North Carolina Press, 1970); John Mendelsohn, "War Crimes Trials and Clemency in Germany and Japan," in *Americans as Proconsuls: United States Military Government in Germany and Japan, 1944–1952,* ed. Robert Wolfe (Carbondale: Southern Illinois University Press, 1984).

83. Weingartner, *Peculiar Crusade,* 189.

84. Weingartner, *Peculiar Crusade,* 196; Buscher, *U.S. War Crimes Trial,* 41–42.
85. Buscher, *U.S. War Crimes Trial,* 42.
86. Weingartner, *Peculiar Crusade,* 197.
87. Drexel Sprecher, letter to Telford Taylor, October 1948, NARG 238: Textual Records of the U.S. Military Tribunals, Nuremberg, Records of Military Tribunals, Entry 159: General Records, Box 2, Folder: Weekly Reports—Brigadier General Telford Taylor.
88. Judge Powers also based his dissent on the interpretation of the crimes against peace count, as well as the war crimes and crimes against humanity counts vis-à-vis plunder and spoliation and the destruction of the Jews. Regarding the latter, Powers contested that the Foreign Office was aware of the exterminations of Jews. Rather, he argued that the entire program "was handled with the greatest of secrecy" and that "not over 100 people in all were informed about the matter." See Dissenting Opinion in *United States v. Ernst von Weizsäcker et al.,* in Wurm et al., *Memorandum by the Evangelical Church in Germany.*
89. Germany (Territory under Allied Occupation, 1945–1955: U.S. Zone), *Trials of War Criminals before the Nuernberg Military Tribunals,* 14:871; Theophil Wurm, letter to General Gross, American Military Governor of Württemberg-Baden, 3 May 1949, Hans Meiser, letter to Lucius Clay, 25 April 1949, and Hans Meiser, letter to General Hübner, 15 June 1949, in Wurm et al., *Memorandum by the Evangelical Church in Germany.*
90. Internal Route Slip, Headquarters, European Command, "Aschenauer, Rudolf," 10 October 1950, NARG 549: Judge Advocate Division, War Crimes Branch, Entry 2236: General Administrative Records 1942–1957, Box 5, Folder: Aschenauer. Aschenauer acted as defense counsel in the Justice and IG Farben cases as well.
91. Klee, *Persilscheine und falsche Pässe,* 81.
92. Internal Route Slip, Headquarters, European Command, "Aschenauer, Rudolf," 10 October 1950, NARG 549: Judge Advocate Division, War Crimes Branch, Entry 2236: General Administrative Records 1942–1957, Box 5, Folder: Aschenauer.
93. Ibid., and Klee, *Persilscheine und falsche Pässe,* 139.

CHAPTER THREE: PROSECUTING HITLER'S HIGH COMMAND

Epigraph from Telford Taylor, letter to Charles Horsky, 7 August 1947, LCMD, Papers of Robert H. Jackson, Box 110, Folder: Robert H. Jackson Legal File— Nuremberg War Crimes Trial Office Files—U.S. Chief of Counsel Subsequent Trials—2.
1. Telford Taylor, *Final Report to the Secretary of the Army on the Nuernberg War Crimes Trials under Control Council Law No. 10* (Washington, D.C.: United States

Government Printing Office, 15 August 1949), 84. Emphasis in original. Taylor was also undoubtedly referring to the criticism by some American officers to the trial of German military personnel. For more on this see Telford Taylor, *The Anatomy of the Nuremberg Trials: A Personal Memoir* (Boston: Little, Brown, 1992), 147–149, 180–186, 238–240. Ronald Smelser has also written on the American military's opposition to the trial of German officers at Nuremberg during the postwar years. See Ronald Smelser and Edward Davies II, *The Myth of the Eastern Front: The Nazi–Soviet War in American Popular Culture* (Cambridge: Cambridge University Press, 2007), esp. chap. 2, "The Cold War and the Emergence of a Lost Cause Mythology."

2. Prosecution Opening Statement, NAMP 898, Roll 1, 21–22.

3. The prosecution evidence consisted of orders, reports, photographs, diaries, witness affidavits, and courtroom testimony. The documentary evidence ranged from a single page to several hundred pages in length each.

4. The charges were divided as follows: count 1: crimes against Peace: invasions of or declarations of war upon Austria (March 1938), Czechoslovakia (October 1938 and March 1939), Poland (September 1939), France and Great Britain (September 1939), Norway and Denmark (April 1940), Belgium, the Netherlands and Luxembourg (May 1940), Greece and Yugoslavia (April 1940), the USSR (June 1941), and the United States (December 1941); count 2: War Crimes and Crimes against Humanity related to Enemy Belligerents and Prisoners of War, including the Commissar Order, the Commando Order, prohibited labor of POWs, murder and ill-treatment of POWs, the Terror Flier Order; count 3: War Crimes and Crimes against Humanity related to Crimes against Civilians, including the deportation and enslavement of civilians, plunder of public and private property, wanton destruction and devastation not justified by military necessity, murder, ill-treatment, and persecution of civilian populations, the Barbarossa Jurisdiction Order, the Night and Fog Decree, the Terror and Sabotage Decrees, and antipartisan measures; and last, count 4: the Common Plan or Conspiracy. This last charge did not receive significant attention during the course of the trial because the evidence related to count 1 suggested its existence. The prosecution produced evidence connecting each defendant to each of the crimes just listed wherever possible. This led to a great deal of repetition in the trial and in the briefs. Given the constraints of time and space, this chapter will highlight those military campaigns and military orders and policies that produced the most devastating consequences and most directly implicated the greatest number of defendants.

5. In January 1938, Hitler demanded Blomberg's resignation after it was made public that his new wife had an allegedly sordid past. At the same time, Himmler presented Hitler with a file alleging that von Fritsch had engaged in homosexual activity. The charge was a lie, as a court of honor confirmed a couple of months later. Nonetheless, von Fritsch was forced from his post in February. In order to disguise

the departure of two of the most senior army leaders, Hitler removed twelve additional generals. The Blomberg–von Fritsch affair ushered in a new relationship between Hitler and the Wehrmacht. Just as apprehensions from within the military leadership over Hitler's foreign policy ambitions began to surface, Hitler asserted his dominance over this institution. See Ian Kershaw, *Hitler: 1936–1945: Nemesis* (London: Penguin Books, 2000), 51–60; Geoffrey Megargee, *Inside Hitler's High Command* (Lawrence: University Press of Kansas, 2000), 39–41, 45.

6. On the labyrinthine organization and at times highly inefficient functioning of the OKW, see Megargee, *Inside Hitler's High Command,* a much-needed accessible synthesis of the literature. Walter Warlimont, one of the defendants, also wrote a book on the OKW entitled *Inside Hitler's Headquarters, 1939–1945* (Novato, Calif.: Presidio Press, 1964). It appeared two years earlier in German under the title *Im Hauptquartier der deutschen Wehrmacht, 1939–1945.* Although interesting for its firsthand viewpoint, it is tainted by the author's self-serving depiction of events.

7. Chief of Counsel for War Crimes, "Military Tribunal Case No. 12 *U.S. vs. Leeb et al.* Basic Information," January 1948, TLI, John C. Young Papers, Box 12, Folder: Case 12 (High Command) Background Data.

8. United States Office of Chief of Counsel for Prosecution of Axis Criminality, *Nazi Conspiracy and Aggression: Opinion and Judgment* (Washington, D.C.: U.S. Government Printing Office, 1946–1947), 105.

9. Ibid., 107.

10. Ibid., 107.

11. The List case indicted two field marshals and ten generals, none of whom were staff officers. Their crimes concerned the murders of hundreds of thousands of mainly Greek, Yugoslavian, and Albanian civilians. Doctors, lawyers, clergymen, artists, farmers, and laborers, regardless of age or sex, were taken from the street, their homes, and their workplaces and held in camps and shot or hanged when attacks against German forces or installations took place. The indictment also included charges related to plunder and looting and wanton destruction in Norway, Greece, Yugoslavia, and Albania; ill-treatment and murder of POWs; and murder, torture, systematic terrorization, imprisonment in concentration camps, arbitrary forced labor, deportation to slave labor, and imprisonment and murder of Jews, Romani, democrats, and nationalists. Neither the Milch nor List case raised the charge of crimes against peace. See Germany (Territory under Allied Occupation, 1945–1955: U.S. Zone), Military Tribunals, *Trials of War Criminals before the Nuernberg Military Tribunals under Control Council Law No. 10: Nuernberg, October 1946–April 1949* (Buffalo: William S. Hein, 1997), 11:764–775. In the List case, the tribunal acquitted two defendants, sentenced eight to prison terms, and released two for time already served. See Telford Taylor, "Information Bulletin No. 162: Nuremberg Trials—Synthesis and Projection," 31 May 1949, TLI, John C. Young Papers, Nuremberg War Crimes Trials, Publications File, Box 78, Folder: Publica-

tions and Telephone Directories, Folder: 1. Excerpts of the Milch trial records can be found in Germany (Territory under Allied Occupation, 1945–1955: U.S. Zone), *Trials of War Criminals*, vol. 2. Milch was sentenced to life imprisonment.

12. Telford Taylor, letter to Charles Horsky, 7 August 1947, LCMD, Robert H. Jackson Papers, Box 110, Folder: Robert H. Jackson Legal File—Nuremberg War Crimes Trial Office Files—U.S. Chief of Counsel Subsequent Trials—2. Telford Taylor, who spearheaded the preparation of the trial, was deeply concerned that about half of the principal defendants identified by their investigations (including Field Marshals von Manstein, von Brauchitsch, and von Rundstedt) were in British custody and that the British showed no desire to try them. Taylor hoped either that these men would be extradited to the U.S. zone or that the Americans and British could hold a joint trial. Ultimately, to Taylor's profound disappointment, neither option materialized. Taylor, *Final Report to the Secretary of the Army*, 82–83. In 1948, the British decided to try the three field marshals; however, von Brauchitsch died before preparations were finalized, and von Rundstedt was declared medically unfit to stand trial. Von Manstein was put on trial in August 1949. He was found guilty of war crimes and sentenced to eighteen years in prison. However, pretrial incarceration and good conduct time credits led to repeated reductions in his sentence, and he was released in August 1952. See chap. 1, n. 107. The British prosecuted several other prominent military figures, however, including Student, Falkenhorst, Blumentritt, Kesselring, Mackensen, Maelzer, and a few others.

13. Significantly, this office transferred to S.S. supervision in October 1944.

14. Chief of Counsel for War Crimes, "Military Tribunal Case No. 12 *U.S. vs. Leeb et al.* Basic Information."

15. In December 1941, von Brauchitsch resigned, and Hitler, already commander in chief of the armed forces, took the title of commander in chief of the army for himself, resulting in some overlap in the functions of the OKW and the OKH. He relieved Halder of duty in September 1942. Over the course of the next three years, three generals served as army chief of staff, the best known being Colonel General Heinz Guderian. Generally, army field commanders answered directly to the OKH. However, depending on the campaign or the time concerned, armies sometimes came under the direct supervision of the OKW. Consequently, the responsibilities of both these offices were periodically difficult to differentiate. See Chief of Counsel for War Crimes, "Military Tribunal Case No. 12 *U.S. vs. Leeb et al.* Basic Information."

16. Chief of Counsel for War Crimes, "Military Tribunal Case No. 12 *U.S. v. Leeb et al.* Basic Information." See Appendix 2 in this book for an overview of the command structure and approximate manpower strength of the army field formations.

17. On the Wehrmacht's prohibition against voting, see Georg von Kuechler, Testimony, Transcript, NAMP 898, Roll 4, 2791–2792. Under the Weimar Repub-

lic, members of the military swore an oath to defend the constitution. Upon the death of President Hindenburg in August 1934, von Blomberg and von Reichenau arranged for soldiers to swear an oath of personal allegiance to Hitler. It declared, "I swear by God this holy oath, that I will render to Adolf Hitler, leader of the German nation and people, supreme commander of the armed forces, unconditional obedience, and I am ready as a brave soldier to risk my life at any time for this oath." Certain top-level officers went even further, proudly wearing the Nazi Party badge on their uniforms. On the mixed loyalties of OKW officers to Nazism (from the most dedicated to the most doubtful), see Megargee, *Inside Hitler's High Command,* 17–36.

18. Report of the HICOG Advisory Board on Clemency for War Criminals, "Case Number 12, Tribunal V," 1 September 1950, NARG 466: Office of the U.S. High Commissioner for Germany, Bonn, Entry 48: Security-Segregated Records of the Prisons Division, Box 6, Folder: Report of the HICOG Advisory Board on Clemency for War Criminals, 1 September 1950, Part II.

19. Karl von Roques had retired from active service in 1933 but was called back in April 1940 as preparations for Operation Barbarossa got under way. He was appointed commander in chief of the rear area of Army Group South. Wilhelm von Leeb retired on 28 February 1938 (upon the Blomberg–Fritsch affair) but was called back into service in July 1938 and participated in the planning for the invasion of Czechoslovakia.

20. Report of the HICOG Advisory Board on Clemency for War Criminals, "Case Number 12, Tribunal V," 1 September 1950.

21. Prosecution Opening Statement, NAMP 898, Roll 1, 88.

22. Taylor elaborated upon his argument that the generals and Nazis allied because of their mutual need of each other for the attainment of shared goals such as rearmament, the restoration of Germany's status, and military conquest. Seeing the generals as having been irrevocably shaped during the Kaiserreich by a "narrow, caste-conscious authoritarianism," Taylor concluded that their behavior under Hitler was entirely in keeping with their training and worldview. He wrote, "To 'blame' such men, as individuals, for failing to risk their careers to preserve democracy in Germany is too much like blaming the crow for not singing sweetly. To expect German generals to 'renounce war as an instrument of national policy' is to blind one's eyes to the hard facts of life." Telford Taylor, *Sword and Swastika: Generals and Nazis in the Third Reich* (New York: Simon and Schuster, 1952), 368. More recent works on the generals' early and continuing allegiance to Hitler argue similarly that the dominant military culture in Germany "was ripe for cooperation [with Hitler] before the Nazis ever became a factor in . . . politics." Megargee, *Inside Hitler's High Command,* 231. For a study of the deep roots of racism, hierarchy, and control and the ideology of total destruction in German military culture, see Isabel Hull, *Absolute Destruction: Military Culture and the Practices of War in Imperial Germany* (Ithaca: Cornell University Press, 2004).

23. Prosecution Opening Statement, NAMP 898, Roll 1, 43 and 52.

24. Prosecution Opening Statement, NAMP 898, Roll 1, 52. Ernst Roehm was a World War I veteran, one of the *alte Kämpfer* ("old fighter," that is, original) Nazis and leader of the S.A., the brown-shirted army of the party whose job it was to disrupt meetings of political opponents and act as Hitler's personal bodyguard. Roehm had aspirations of the S.A. becoming the "people's army," swallowing up the Reichswehr in the process. Impatient with the pace of the National Socialist revolution and dissatisfied with Hitler's leadership, the S.A. began to stockpile arms in anticipation of open conflict. When, after Hitler's advances, Roehm refused to stand down, he and other S.A. leaders were killed during the night of 30 June 1934. The Roehm purge (also called "the night of the long knives"), along with the Reichstag Fire and the Blomberg–Fritsch affair, are considered the primary events in Hitler's assertion of dominance over the state, and in particular over the military.

25. Prosecution Opening Statement, NAMP 898, Roll 1, 22 and 24.

26. Ibid., 23.

27. "Memorandum Brief of the Prosecution, Crimes against Peace: Counts One and Four: Planning, Preparing, Initiating and Waging of Wars of Aggression and Invasions, the Common Plan or Conspiracy," 26 August 1948, NAMP 898, Roll 58, 2.

28. Prosecution Opening Statement, NAMP 898, Roll 1, 124.

29. Prosecution Memorandum of Law and Facts, "Responsibility of Wilhelm von Leeb under Counts Two and Three of the Indictment," July 1948, NAMP 898, Roll 57, 130.

30. Prosecution Memorandum of Law and Facts, "Responsibility of Georg Karl Friedrich-Wilhelm von Kuechler under Counts Two and Three of the Indictment," 12 August 1948, NAMP 898, Roll 57, 26.

31. Ibid., 3.

32. Taylor, *Final Report to the Secretary of the Army*, 85.

33. Given that at the time the Philippines was under U.S. control, and proceeding from the Moscow Declaration's and the London Charter's stipulations that "lesser" criminals could be prosecuted in the nations where their crimes took place and judged according to the laws of those locations, an American military commission organized and administered the trial. It is important to note that this trial preceded the trials of the International Military Tribunal for the Far East against Japanese leaders in Tokyo. Richard Lael, *The Yamashita Precedent: War Crimes and Command Responsibility* (Wilmington, Del.: Scholarly Resources, 1982), 79–80. On the Yamashita trial, see also Lawrence Taylor, *A Trial of Generals: Homma, Yamashita, MacArthur* (South Bend, Ind.: Icarus Press, 1981).

34. Lael, *Yamashita Precedent*, 97.

35. Ibid., 80, 83.

36. Ibid., 95.

37. Germany (Territory under Allied Occupation, 1945–1955: U.S. Zone), *Trials of War Criminals*, 11:1230.

38. Prosecution Memorandum of Law and Facts, "Responsibility of Wilhelm von Leeb under Counts Two and Three of the Indictment," July 1948, NAMP 898, Roll 57, 8.

39. Prosecution Memorandum of Law and Facts, "Responsibility of Karl von Roques under Counts Two and Three of the Indictment," 20 August 1948, NAMP 898, Roll 58, 6.

40. Prosecution Memorandum of Law and Facts, "Responsibility of Wilhelm von Leeb under Counts Two and Three of the Indictment," July 1948, NAMP 898, Roll 57, 73.

41. Ibid., 7.

42. Judgment, *U.S. v. Wilhelm von Leeb et al.*, Germany (Territory under Allied Occupation, 1945–1955: U.S. Zone), *Trials of War Criminals*, 11:563.

43. Prosecution Memorandum of Law and Facts, "Responsibility of Wilhelm von Leeb under Counts Two and Three of the Indictment," July 1948, NAMP 898, Roll 57, 46.

44. Prosecution Memorandum of Law and Facts, "Responsibility of Georg Karl Friedrich-Wilhelm von Kuechler under Counts Two and Three of the Indictment," 12 August 1948, NAMP 898, Roll 57, 5.

45. Ibid., 7.

46. Ibid., 11.

47. Prosecution Memorandum of Law and Facts, "Responsibility of Wilhelm von Leeb under Counts Two and Three of the Indictment," July 1948, NAMP 898, Roll 57, 6–7.

48. Closing Statement for the United States of America, 10 August 1948, NAMP 898, Roll 57, 94–95.

49. Prosecution General Legal Brief, 26 August 1948, NAMP 898, Roll 58, 27.

50. Ibid., 26.

51. Closing Statement for the United States of America, 10 August 1948, NAMP 898, Roll 57, 90.

52. Prosecution General Legal Brief, 26 August 1948, NAMP 898, Roll 58, 27; Closing Statement for the United States of America, 10 August 1948, NAMP 898, Roll 57, 88.

53. Prosecution General Legal Brief, 26 August 1948, NAMP 898, Roll 58, 28. Article 2, Paragraph 4(b) of Control Council Law No. 10 declared, "The fact that any person acted pursuant to the order of his government or of a superior does not free him from responsibility for a crime but may be considered in mitigation." See Prosecution Memorandum of Law and Facts, "Responsibility of Karl von Roques under Counts Two and Three of the Indictment," 20 August 1948, NAMP 898, Roll 58, 104. One of the prerequisites of the superior orders plea was duress. That is, unless

there was fear of severe reprisal for disobedience, obedience was to be considered voluntary. Prosecutors in the case against Otto Ohlendorf and twenty-three other Einsatzgruppen leaders had dealt with the issue at length. In the judgment of that case, jurists held that the threat of reprisal had to be "imminent, real and inevitable," which no German defense attorney in this case, or in any other, had been able to prove. Judgment, *U.S. v. Otto Ohlendorf et al.*, in Germany (Territory under Allied Occupation, 1945–1955: U.S. Zone), *Trials of War Criminals*, 4:470–488, quoted at 4:480.

54. Yoram Dinstein, *The Defense of "Obedience to Superior Orders" in International Law* (Leyden: A. W. Sijthoff, 1965), 7–9, 11–15, and 87–90. On the evolution of the interpretation of the superior orders defense, see also Mark Osiel, *Obeying Orders: Atrocity, Military Discipline and the Law of War* (New Brunswick, N.J.: Transaction Publishers, 1999); Albin Eser, "Defenses in War Crimes Trials," in Yoram Dinstein and Mala Tabory, eds., *War Crimes in International Law* (The Hague: Martinus Nijhoff, 1996), 256–260. During the late 1950s and 1960s, the Ludwigsburg-based Central Agency for the State Administration of Justice, West Germany's office for the investigation of Nazi crimes, reviewed every instance where a defendant claimed superior orders to ascertain whether disobedience would have been punished by death or deportation to a camp. They were unable to authenticate a single case. Indeed, in the vast majority of instances, German courts rejected the superior orders defense for lack of evidence. One expert in postwar trials of Nazis called the superior orders defense "one facet of the collective German strategy of exoneration," wherein perpetrators depicted themselves as victims. See Ruth Bettina Birn, "War Crimes Prosecution: An Exercise in Justice? A Lesson in History?," in *Lessons and Legacies*, vol. 4, *Reflections on Religion, Justice, Sexuality, and Genocide*, ed. Larry Thompson (Evanston, Ill.: Northwestern University Press, 2003), 101–127, quoted at 110.

55. Closing Statement for the United States of America, 10 August 1948, NAMP 898, Roll 57, 14.

56. Ibid., 91.

57. Prosecution Memorandum of Law and Facts, "Responsibility of Wilhelm von Leeb under Counts Two and Three of the Indictment," July 1948, NAMP 898, Roll 57, 129.

58. Prosecution General Legal Brief, 26 August 1948, NAMP 898, Roll 58, 1.

59. The seizures of Austria and Czechoslovakia were not charged as crimes in the IMT indictment; however, the IMT judgment did find them to be "invasions" and "acts of aggression." Consequently, Control Council Law No. 10 included the concept of "invasions of other countries." See Memorandum Brief of the Prosecution, "Crimes against Peace: Counts One and Four: Planning, Preparing, Initiating and Waging of Wars of Aggression and Invasions, the Common Plan or Conspiracy," 26 August 1948, NAMP 898, Roll 58, 15–16.

60. Ibid., 3.

61. Ibid., 8.

62. Ibid., 11. Article IX of Military Government Ordinance No. 7 had stipulated that IMT findings were binding on the SNP. It declared: "The determinations of the International Military Tribunal in the judgments in case No. 1 that invasions, aggressive acts, aggressive wars, crimes, atrocities or inhuman acts were planned or occurred, shall be binding on the tribunals established hereunder and shall not be questioned except insofar as the participation therein or knowledge thereof by any particular person may be concerned. Statements of the International Military Tribunal in the judgment in case No. 1 constitute proof of the facts stated, in the absence of substantial new evidence to the contrary." Memorandum Brief of the Prosecution, "Crimes against Peace: Counts One and Four: Planning, Preparing, Initiating and Waging of Wars of Aggression and Invasions, the Common Plan or Conspiracy," 26 August 1948, NAMP 898, Roll 58, 16.

63. Ibid., 17–19.

64. Ibid., 19.

65. In a November 1948 report entitled "An Outline of the Research and Publication Possibilities of the War Crimes Trials," Taylor recommended that because the Halder diaries were "of such major historical proportions," they should be published in their entirety. In shorthand, Halder made impressively detailed notes of conferences and conversations connected to his position as army chief of staff. Closely linked to officials in the Foreign Office, Halder addressed both political and military issues and events in his diary. See Taylor, "An Outline of the Research and Publication Possibilities of the War Crimes Trials," TLI, John C. Young Papers, Box 14, Folder: An Outline of the Research and Publication Possibilities of the War Crimes Trials, Telford Taylor, November 1948. The Halder diaries were first published in German in the early 1960s by the Arbeitskreis für Wehrforschung as *Kriegstagebuch: Tägliche Aufzeichnungen des Chefs des Heeres, 1939–1942*, 3 vols. (Stuttgart: W. Kohlhammer, 1962–1964). They are available in English as Charles Burdick and Hans-Adolf Jacobsen, eds., *The Halder War Diary, 1939–1942* (Novato, Calif.: Presidio Press, 1988). Halder, a career staff officer who replaced the outspoken and critical Ludwig Beck, was religious and conservative, believed strongly in the "moral element of command," and possessed a profound sense of duty. He participated in the plans for a coup in 1938 in anticipation of the outbreak of war over the Czech question, which was undermined when Britain and France conceded to Hitler's demands at Munich. See Megargee, *Inside Hitler's High Command*, 53–55. Halder was arrested after the July 1944 assassination attempt against Hitler and imprisoned at Dachau. Released in spring 1945, he surrendered to American troops and spent the next two years in a POW camp. He testified at the High Command case in 1948. In the 1950s, he worked as an advisor to the American army's historical division. He died in 1972. On the Halder biography, see Christian Hartmann, *Halder: Generalstabschef Hitlers, 1938–1942* (Paderborn: Schöningh, 1991).

66. Memorandum Brief of the Prosecution, "Crimes against Peace: Counts One and Four: Planning, Preparing, Initiating and Waging of Wars of Aggression and Invasions, the Common Plan or Conspiracy," 26 August 1948, NAMP 898, Roll 58, 22. Ludwig Beck was chief of the army General Staff from 1933 to 1938. On 29 May 1938, he wrote, "Regular, informed advice to the supreme commander of the armed forces in questions of warfare and above all of military operations must be called for in the same measure as a clear delimitation of and respect for responsibilities. If measures are not taken soon to change current relationships, which have become unbearable, and if the present anarchy remains the dominant condition over the long term, the further fate of the armed forces in peace and war, as well as the fate of Germany in a future war, can be seen only in the blackest terms." Memoranda and meetings with fellow generals continued throughout the summer of 1938, culminating with Beck's recommendation that they should resign en masse if Hitler refused to heed their warnings about provoking war. His comrades did not support him. Beck resigned his position in August 1938, leaving a written prophecy in the internal records of the General Staff declaring that "a final German victory is impossible." See Megargee, *Inside Hitler's High Command*, 49–52. Upon the failure of the 1944 coup attempt (in which he was involved), Beck shot himself. On Beck's position and activities as chief of the army General Staff, see Klaus-Jürgen Müller, *General Ludwig Beck: Studien und Dokumente zur politisch-militärischen Vorstellungswelt und Tätigkeit des Generalstabschef des deutschen Heeres, 1933–1938* (Boppard am Rhein: H. Boldt, 1980).

67. Memorandum Brief of the Prosecution, "Crimes against Peace: Counts One and Four: Planning, Preparing, Initiating and Waging of Wars of Aggression and Invasions, the Common Plan or Conspiracy," 26 August 1948, NAMP 898, Roll 58, 25–27.

68. Memorandum Brief of the Prosecution, "Crimes against Peace: Counts One and Four: Planning, Preparing, Initiating and Waging of Wars of Aggression and Invasions, the Common Plan or Conspiracy," 26 August 1948, NAMP 898, Roll 58, 30.

69. Ibid., 34.

70. Prosecution Opening Statement, NAMP 898, Roll 1, 65.

71. Memorandum Brief of the Prosecution, "Crimes against Peace: Counts One and Four: Planning, Preparing, Initiating and Waging of Wars of Aggression and Invasions, the Common Plan or Conspiracy," 26 August 1948, NAMP 898, Roll 58, 46–47.

72. Ibid., 49. A particularly valuable account of the Polish invasion, and in particular the relationship between Nazi ideology and German military practice, is Alexander Rossino's *Hitler Strikes Poland: Blitzkrieg, Ideology, and Atrocity* (Lawrence: University Press of Kansas, 2003). This book details the scope of racial and political crimes of this early campaign and draws parallels with what was still

to come with Operation Barbarossa. See also his article, "Destructive Impulses: German Soldiers and the Conquest of Poland," *Holocaust and Genocide Studies* 7 (1997): 351–365.

73. Memorandum Brief of the Prosecution, "Crimes against Peace: Counts One and Four: Planning, Preparing, Initiating and Waging of Wars of Aggression and Invasions, the Common Plan or Conspiracy," 26 August 1948, NAMP 898, Roll 58, 63–64. Emphasis added.

74. Ibid., 64.

75. Closing Statement for the United States of America, 10 August 1948, NAMP 898, Roll 57, 45.

76. Ibid.

77. Memorandum Brief of the Prosecution, "Crimes against Peace: Counts One and Four: Planning, Preparing, Initiating and Waging of Wars of Aggression and Invasions, the Common Plan or Conspiracy," 26 August 1948, NAMP 898, Roll 58, 73–76.

78. Ibid., 76.

79. Ibid., 83.

80. An indispensable guide to the vast German and English historiography of the eastern campaign is Rolf-Dieter Müller and Gerd Ueberschär, eds., *Hitler's War in the East: A Critical Assessment* (New York: Berghahn Books, 2002), particularly Gerd Ueberschär's essay, "The Ideologically Motivated War of Annihilation in the East." Other articles surveying the literature of the Wehrmacht and its complicity in racial and political crimes are: Omer Bartov, "Professional Soldiers," in *The German Army and Genocide: Crimes against War Prisoners, Jews and Other Civilians in the East, 1939–1944*, ed. Hamburg Institute for Social Research (New York: New Press, 1999); Omer Bartov, "German Soldiers and the Holocaust: Historiography, Research and Implications," *History and Memory* 9, no. 1/2 (Fall 1997): 162–188; Jörg Echternkamp, "At War, Abroad and at Home: The Essential Features of German Society in the Second World War," in *Germany and the Second World War*, vol. 9:1, *German Wartime Society, 1939–1945: Politicization, Disintegration and the Struggle for Survival*, ed. Jörg Echternkamp (Oxford: Clarendon Press, 2008); Norman Naimark, "War and Genocide on the Eastern Front, 1941–1945," *Contemporary European History* 16, no. 2 (2007): 259–274; and Bill Niven, "The Crimes of the Wehrmacht," in *Facing the Nazi Past: United Germany and the Crimes of the Third Reich* (London: Routledge, 2001), 143–174.

81. Memorandum Brief of the Prosecution, "Crimes against Peace: Counts One and Four: Planning, Preparing, Initiating and Waging of Wars of Aggression and Invasions, the Common Plan or Conspiracy," 26 August 1948, NAMP 898, Roll 58, 106.

82. Closing Statement for the United States of America, 10 August 1948, NAMP 898, Roll 57, 37–38.

83. Ibid., 106 and Prosecution Exhibit 1359, NOKW-3140, NAMP 898, Roll 24.

84. Prosecution Memorandum of Law and Facts, "Responsibility of Hans Reinhardt under Counts Two and Three of the Indictment," 26 August 1948, NAMP 898, Roll 57, 7.

85. Memorandum Brief of the Prosecution, "Crimes against Peace: Counts One and Four: Planning, Preparing, Initiating and Waging of Wars of Aggression and Invasions, the Common Plan or Conspiracy," 26 August 1948, NAMP 898, Roll 58, 115.

86. Prosecution Opening Statement, NAMP 898, Roll 1, 88.

87. Interestingly, one of the first German pieces of historical writing on the Wehrmacht and Nazi crimes was Institut für Zeitgeschichte historian Hans-Adolf Jacobsen's lengthy report on the Commissar Order for the 1964 Auschwitz trial, "Kommissarbefehl und Massenexecutionen sowjetische Kriegsgefangener," published in Hans Buchheim, Martin Broszat, Hans-Adolf Jacobsen, and Helmut Krausnick, eds., *Anatomie des S.S.-Staates: Gutachten des Instituts für Zeitgeschichte*, vol. 2 (Munich: Deutscher Taschenbuch Verlag, 1965). This and other works by Volker Berghahn, "NSDAP und 'Geistige Führung' der Wehrmacht," *Vierteljahrshefte für Zeitgeschichte* 17 (1969): 17–21; Jürgen Förster, "The Wehrmacht and the War of Extermination against the Soviet Union," *Yad Vashem Studies* 14 (1981): 7–34; Manfred Messerschmidt, *Die Wehrmacht im NS-Staat: Zeit der Indoktrination* (Hamburg: R.v. Decker's Verlag, 1969); Klaus-Jürgen Müller, *Das Heer und Hitler: Armee und nationalsozialistisches Regime, 1933–1940* (Stuttgart: Deutsche Verlags-Anstalt, 1969); Benjamin Segalowitz, "The Wehrmacht's Guilt," *Yad Vashem Bulletin* 21 (1967): 10–18; Alfred Streim, *Die Behandlung sowjetischer Kriegsgefangener im "Fall Barbarossa": Eine Dokumentation* (Heidelberg: Müller, Juristischer Verlag, 1981); and Christian Streit, *Keine Kameraden: Die Wehrmacht und die sowjetischen Kriegsgefangenen* (Stuttgart: Deutsche Verlags-Anstalt, 1978), laid the foundation for showing that the Wehrmacht leadership had willingly and approvingly subjected their troops to extensive ideological indoctrination, had participated in the planning and execution of conquest and occupation as a whole, and had played a central role in doing away with the conventional rules and regulations of warfare. It should be noted, however, that the connection between the war in the East and the program for the destruction of the Jews was not firmly established until somewhat later, in the early 1980s. Publication on the link between the Wehrmacht and other racially based crimes has accelerated in recent years, but surprisingly with little or no mention of the first major and systematic confrontation with the question of the Wehrmacht's criminal liability for racially based crimes and without benefit of the material produced by this endeavor. Helmut Krausnick and Hans-Heinrich Wilhelm, in *Die Truppe des Weltanschauungskrieges: Die Einsatzgruppen der Sicherheitspolizei und des SD, 1938–1942*, 2 vols. (Stuttgart: Deutsche Verlags-Anstalt, 1981), were among the first to make the connection between the

activities of the Einsatzgruppen and the Wehrmacht. Also, since 1979, the Militärgeschichtliches Forschungsamt (Military History Office; formerly of Freiburg, now based in Potsdam) has been publishing a massive ten-volume series on the Third Reich and World War II entitled *Das Deutsche Reich und der Zweite Weltkrieg* (Stuttgart: Deutsche Verlagsanstalt (1979–present). The series is available in English translation up to volume 9:1 as Militärgeschichtliches Forschungsamt, *Germany and the Second World War* (Oxford: Clarendon Press, 1990–2008). Most of the articles in this series are written by experienced historians and are of very high quality. See especially vol. 4, *The Attack on the Soviet Union* (1998), for the background and course of Germany's war against the Soviet Union, and the army's role in this unprecedented campaign of annihilation.

    88. Prosecution Opening Statement, NAMP 898, Roll 1, 88, 108. Hitler first raised the issue of executing commissars at a 28 March 1941 conference with his generals. Warlimont initialed an early draft of the order in mid-May and continued working on it with Lehmann until early June. See High Command case indictment, in Germany (Territory under Allied Occupation, 1945–1955: U.S. Zone), *Trials of War Criminals*, 10:30.

    89. Ibid., and Prosecution Memorandum of Law and Facts, "Responsibility of Georg Karl Friedrich-Wilhelm von Kuechler under Counts Two and Three of the Indictment," 12 August 1948, NAMP 898, Roll 5, 12.

    90. Prosecution Exhibit 57, NOKW-1076, NAMP 898, Roll 12.

    91. Ibid. See also Prosecution Opening Statement, NAMP 898, Roll 1, 112. Von Brauchitsch further stipulated that nonhostile commissars were to be left alone. However, given the overall tone of the war in the East and a host of other orders and directives calling for the wholesale murder of entire groups, in addition to the countless reports showing that the Commissar Order was implemented regularly and extensively, it is clear that these amendments did not act as a significant brake on the order's application.

    92. Prosecution Exhibit 57, NOKW-1076, NAMP 898, Roll 12.

    93. For examples of these reports, see Prosecution Memorandum of Law and Facts, "Responsibility of Georg Karl Friedrich-Wilhelm von Kuechler under Counts Two and Three of the Indictment," 12 August 1948, NAMP 898, Roll 57, 12–21. Ultimately Hoth, Reinhardt, and von Roques were also found guilty of enforcing the Commissar Order; see their briefs for more examples of ground-level reports detailing its implementation.

    94. Indictment, in Germany (Territory under Allied Occupation, 1945–1955: U.S. Zone), *Trials of War Criminals*, 10:31, and Prosecution Opening Statement, NAMP 898, Roll 1, 93–98.

    95. Closing Statement for the United States of America, 10 August 1948, NAMP 898, Roll 57, 62, and Indictment, Germany (Territory under Allied Occupation, 1945–1955: U.S. Zone), *Trials of War Criminals*, 10:31–32.

96. Prosecution Memorandum of Law and Facts, "Responsibility of Wilhelm von Leeb under Counts Two and Three of the Indictment," July 1948, NAMP 898, Roll 57, 47. The most important early work done on Soviet POWs was Heidelberg historian Christian Streit's 1978 *Keine Kameraden* (reissued in 1997). Emphasizing POW planning at the OKW and OKH levels, including the formulation of criminal orders, Streit details the Wehrmacht's cooperation with the Einsatzgruppen in murdering POWs and the subsequent policies for the use of POWs for slave labor. The later edition contains an overview of more recent research into the treatment of POWs. Shortly after Streit's book appeared, Alfred Streim, a German state prosecutor who had worked on bringing Nazi criminals to justice, confirmed Streit's findings. His book, *Die Behandlung sowjetischer Kriegsgefangener im "Fall Barbarossa,"* uses primary sources that he had gathered for trials of former Nazis.

97. Doris Bergen, *War and Genocide: A Concise History of the Holocaust* (Lanham, Md.: Rowman & Littlefield, 2003), 157.

98. Prosecution Memorandum of Law and Facts, "Responsibility of Hermann Reinecke under Counts Two and Three of the Indictment," 26 August 1948, NAMP 898, Roll 57, 3 and 7.

99. Ibid., 5.

100. Ibid., 16.

101. Ibid., 18–20.

102. Ibid., 20, and Prosecution Exhibit 362, NO-3414, NAMP 898, Roll 15.

103. Prosecution Memorandum of Law and Facts, "Responsibility of Hermann Reinecke under Counts Two and Three of the Indictment," 26 August 1948, NAMP 898, Roll 57, 20.

104. Prosecution Memorandum of Law and Facts, "Responsibility of Georg Karl Friedrich-Wilhelm von Kuechler under Counts Two and Three of the Indictment," 12 August 1948, NAMP 898, Roll 57, 47–48, and Prosecution Exhibit 244, NOKW-2423, NAMP 898, Roll 14.

105. Closing Statement for the United States of America, 10 August 1948, NAMP 898, Roll 57, 64.

106. Prosecution Memorandum of Law and Facts, "Responsibility of Karl von Roques under Counts Two and Three of the Indictment," 20 August 1948, NAMP 898, Roll 58.

107. Prosecution Memorandum of Law and Facts, "Responsibility of Hermann Reinecke under Counts Two and Three of the Indictment," 26 August 1948, NAMP 898, Roll 57, 7.

108. Ibid., 26–27.

109. Prosecution Memorandum of Law and Facts, "Responsibility of Hermann Reinecke under Counts Two and Three of the Indictment," 26 August 1948, NAMP 898, Roll 57, 28–29.

110. Ibid., 28.

111. Ibid., 30. Indeed, the USSR had not signed the Geneva Convention, but the prosecution, like Canaris, held that Germany's adherence to it indicated its awareness of the convention's contents as representative of contemporary customary law regarding POWs. Significantly, Canaris's memorandum did not contain any moral arguments; rather, it addressed only the practical implications of the policy for the German military. For example, he reasoned that treating POWs harshly would provoke insubordination, making guarding them more difficult. Further, he believed that these decrees would be used for anti-German propaganda. He also argued that mistreating these POWs would irrevocably alienate them from German forces, and that they would refuse to work for the reconstruction of the occupied areas upon release. Interestingly, Canaris, chief of the Abwehr, the German military intelligence agency, was later executed for his involvement in the 20 July 1944 assassination plot. See Richard Bassett, *Hitler's Spy Chief: The Wilhelm Canaris Mystery* (London: Weidenfeld & Nicolson, 2005), and Heinz Höhne, *Canaris* (London: Secker & Warburg, 1979).

112. Prosecution Memorandum of Law and Facts, "Responsibility of Hermann Reinecke under Counts Two and Three of the Indictment," 26 August 1948, NAMP 898, Roll 57, 106. By the end of 1941, over 3.3 million Soviet POWs had been captured. Most were dead by spring 1942. Overall estimates for the war vary, but it is generally accepted that around 5.5 million Soviet POWs were captured and over 3 million died. This figure does not include Soviet commissars and Jews from the POW population who were shot outright upon capture. In early 1942, the food and shelter the Germans provided to Soviet POWs began to improve in order that they might be exploited for slave labor. Although mortality rates decreased, they still perished in numbers far exceeding prisoners of other nationalities. Notably, Soviet military doctrine dictated that soldiers were to fight to the death and were prohibited from surrendering. Stalin considered Soviet POWs as having "given themselves up to imprisonment" and accordingly made little attempt to protect those who were captured. The Red Cross attempted to broker a convention on Soviet POWs, but Hitler rejected their offer. See Rüdiger Overmann, "Die Kriegsgefangenenpolitik des Deutschen Reiches 1939–1945," in Militärgeschichtliches Forschungsamt, *Das Deutsche Reich und der Zweite Weltkrieg*, vol. 9:2, *Die deutsche Kriegsgesellschaft 1939 bis 1945: Ausbeutung, Deutungen, Ausgrenzung* (Stuttgart: Deutsche Verlags-Anstalt, 2005), 729–877; Ueberschär, "Ideologically Motivated War," 214–217. On the fate of POWs in German custody, see also Gerd Ueberschär and Wolfram Wette, eds., *"Unternehmen Barbarossa," der deutsche Überfall auf die Sowjetunion 1941: Berichte, Analysen, Dokumente* (Paderborn: Ferdinand Schöningh, 1984). For a comparison of the treatment of Western and Eastern POWs by the Germans, see David Rolf, *Prisoners of the Reich: Germany's Captives, 1939–1945* (London: Cooper, 1988). The general consensus regarding the fate of German prisoners of war under Soviet control is that of 3.15 million taken, 1.2 million died, mainly after January 1943. By

1947, approximately 2 million still remained in Soviet custody. See Ueberschär, "Ideologically Motivated War," 248–252. For more on the fate of German POWs, see Frank Biess, *Homecomings: Returning POWs and the Legacy of Defeat in Postwar Germany* (Princeton: Princeton University Press, 2006), and Robert Moeller, *War Stories: the Search for a Usable Past in the Federal Republic of Germany* (Berkeley: University of California Press, 2001).

113. Prosecution Memorandum of Law and Facts, "Responsibility of Hermann Reinecke under Counts Two and Three of the Indictment," 26 August 1948, NAMP 898, Roll 57, 46.

114. Prosecution Memorandum of Law and Facts, "Responsibility of Hermann Hoth under Counts Two and Three of the Indictment," 16 August 1948, NAMP 898, Roll 58, 15.

115. Closing Statement for the United States of America, 10 August 1948, NAMP 898, Roll 57, 63–64.

116. Prosecution Memorandum of Law and Facts, "Responsibility of Karl von Roques under Counts Two and Three of the Indictment," 20 August 1948, NAMP 898, Roll 58, 40–41. Supply for POWs was the responsibility of the Oberquartiermeister, a staff officer in every army, subordinate to the chief of staff, who was in turn subordinate to the commander of the army group. In the rear areas, responsibility rested with an inspector for prisoners of war, who also answered to the military commander of the area.

117. Prosecution Memorandum of Law and Facts, "Responsibility of Wilhelm von Leeb under Counts Two and Three of the Indictment," July 1948, NAMP 898, Roll 57, 43.

118. Prosecution Memorandum of Law and Facts, "Responsibility of Hermann Reinecke under Counts Two and Three of the Indictment," 26 August 1948, NAMP 898, Roll 57, 52–56. Rudolf Hess, the former commandant at Auschwitz, describes the Zyklon B experiments involving Soviet POWs in his memoir, *Death Dealer: The Memoirs of the S.S. Kommandant at Auschwitz* (New York: Da Capo Press, 1996), 155–157.

119. Prosecution Memorandum of Law and Facts, "Responsibility of Wilhelm von Leeb under Counts Two and Three of the Indictment," July 1948, NAMP 898, Roll 57, 45; Prosecution Exhibit 283, 081-PS, NAMP 898, Roll 14.

120. Prosecution Exhibit 283, 081-PS, NAMP 898, Roll 14.

121. Prosecution Memorandum of Law and Facts, "Responsibility of Hermann Reinecke under Counts Two and Three of the Indictment," 26 August 1948, NAMP 898, Roll 57, 68.

122. Ibid., 101–105.

123. Ibid., 75–76.

124. Prosecution Opening Statement, NAMP 898, Roll 1, 108.

125. Prosecution Memorandum of Law and Facts, "Responsibility of Wilhelm

von Leeb under Counts Two and Three of the Indictment," July 1948, NAMP 898, Roll 57, 102–103, and Prosecution Exhibit 594, C-50, NAMP 898, Roll 16.

126. Prosecution Memorandum of Law and Facts, "Responsibility of Wilhelm von Leeb under Counts Two and Three of the Indictment," July 1948, NAMP 898, Roll 57, 104–107.

127. Prosecution Opening Statement, NAMP 898, Roll 1, 126–127. On the army's campaign against partisans, see Hannes Heer's essay, "The Logic of the War of Extermination: The Wehrmacht and the Anti-Partisan War," in *War of Extermination: The German Military in World War II, 1941–1944*, ed. Hannes Heer and Klaus Naumann (New York: Berghahn Books, 2000), and Ben Shepherd, *War in the Wild East: The German Army and Soviet Partisans* (Cambridge: Harvard University Press, 2004).

128. Prosecution Memorandum of Law and Facts, "Responsibility of Georg Karl Friedrich-Wilhelm von Kuechler under Counts Two and Three of the Indictment," 12 August 1948, NAMP 898, Roll 57, 110.

129. Prosecution Memorandum of Law and Facts, "Responsibility of Wilhelm von Leeb under Counts Two and Three of the Indictment," July 1948, NAMP 898, Roll 57, 109–110. Emphasis added.

130. Prosecution Memorandum of Law and Facts, "Responsibility of Georg Karl Friedrich-Wilhelm von Kuechler under Counts Two and Three of the Indictment," 12 August 1948, NAMP 898, Roll 57, 110 and Prosecution Exhibit 611, C-148, NAMP 898, Roll 16. Emphasis in original.

131. Prosecution Opening Statement, NAMP 898, Roll 1, 104–106.

132. Prosecution Memorandum of Law and Facts, "Responsibility of Wilhelm von Leeb under Counts Two and Three of the Indictment," July 1948, NAMP 898, Roll 57, 110–119; Prosecution Memorandum of Law and Facts, "Responsibility of Georg Karl Friedrich-Wilhelm von Kuechler under Counts Two and Three of the Indictment," 12 August 1948, NAMP 898, Roll 57, 83–89.

133. Prosecution Memorandum of Law and Facts, "Responsibility of Hans Reinhardt under Counts Two and Three of the Indictment," 26 August 1948, NAMP 898, Roll 57, 79; Prosecution Exhibit 652, NOKW-2345, NAMP 898, Roll 17.

134. Prosecution Opening Statement, NAMP 898, Roll 1, 126.

135. Prosecution Memorandum of Law and Facts, "Responsibility of Hans Reinhardt under Counts Two and Three of the Indictment," 26 August 1948, NAMP 898, Roll 57, 80.

136. Ibid., 113–115.

137. Ibid., 115.

138. Prosecution Opening Statement, NAMP 898, Roll 1, 100–102.

139. On the Wehrmacht's complicity in crimes against Jews, see especially Andrej Angrick, *Besatzungspolitik und Massenmord: Die Einsatzgruppe D in der südlichen Sowjetunion, 1941–1943* (Hamburg: Hamburger Edition, 2003); Hannes Heer,

"Killing Fields: The Wehrmacht and the Holocaust in Belorussia, 1941–1942," *Holocaust and Genocide Studies* 7 (1997): 79–101; Hannes Heer, *Tote Zonen: Die deutsche Wehrmacht an der Ostfront* (Hamburg: Hamburger Edition, 1999); Walter Manoschek, *"Serbien ist Judenfrei": Militärische Besatzungspolitik und Judenvernichtung in Serbien, 1941/42* (Munich: R. Oldenbourg, 1993); Walter Manoschek, ed., *Die Wehrmacht im Rassenkrieg: Der Vernichtungskrieg hinter der Front* (Vienna: Picus Verlag, 1996); Jürgen Förster, "Wehrmacht, Krieg und Holocaust," in *Die Wehrmacht: Mythos und Realität,* ed. Rolf-Dieter Müller and Hans-Erich Volkmann (Munich: R. Oldenbourg, 1999); Edward Westermann, "Partners in Genocide: The German Police and the 'Wehrmacht' in the Soviet Union," *Journal of Strategic Studies* 31, no. 5 (2008): 771–796; Wolfram Wette, *The Wehrmacht: History, Myth, Reality* (Cambridge: Harvard University Press, 2006); and Hans-Heinrich Wilhelm, *Rassenpolitik und Kriegführung: Sicherheitspolizei und Wehrmacht in Polen und der Sowjetunion* (Passau: Wissenschaftsverlag Richard Rothe, 1991).

140. Prosecution Memorandum of Law and Facts, "Responsibility of Georg Karl Friedrich-Wilhelm von Kuechler under Counts Two and Three of the Indictment," 12 August 1948, NAMP 898, Roll 57, 116, and Prosecution Exhibit 587, NOKW-1531, NAMP 898, Roll 16.

141. Prosecution Exhibit 847, NOKW-2080, NAMP 898, Roll 18.

142. Ibid., and Prosecution Memorandum of Law and Facts, "Responsibility of Wilhelm von Leeb under Counts Two and Three of the Indictment," July 1948, NAMP 898, Roll 57, 72–73.

143. Closing Statement for the United States of America, 10 August 1948, NAMP 898, Roll 57, 80.

144. Ohlendorf testimony, *U.S. vs. Wilhelm von Leeb et al.* Trial Transcript, NAMP 898, Roll 10, 9268–9491. See also Hilary Earl, *The Nuremberg Einsatzgruppen Trial, 1945–1958: Atrocity, Law, History* (New York: Cambridge University Press, 2009). See also her article, "Scales of Justice: History, Testimony, and the Einsatzgruppen Trial at Nuremberg," in *Lessons and Legacies,* vol. 6, *New Currents in Holocaust Research,* ed. Jeffry Diefendorf (Evanston, Ill.: Northwestern University Press, 2004), 325–351.

145. *U.S. vs. Wilhelm von Leeb et al.* Trial Transcript, NAMP 898, Roll 21, 9115–9117.

146. Prosecution Memorandum of Law and Facts, "Responsibility of Georg Karl Friedrich-Wilhelm von Kuechler under Counts Two and Three of the Indictment," 12 August 1948, NAMP 898, Roll 57, 138.

147. Prosecution Memorandum of Law and Facts, "Responsibility of Wilhelm von Leeb under Counts Two and Three of the Indictment," July 1948, NAMP 898, Roll 57, 71.

148. Ibid., 79–80; Prosecution Exhibit 956, L-180, NAMP 898, Roll 20.

149. Prosecution Exhibit 956, L-180, NAMP 898, Roll 20, and Prosecution

Memorandum of Law and Facts, "Responsibility of Wilhelm von Leeb under Counts Two and Three of the Indictment," July 1948, NAMP 898, Roll 57, 79–81.

150. Prosecution Exhibit 956, L-180, NAMP 898, Roll 20; Prosecution Memorandum of Law and Facts, "Responsibility of Wilhelm von Leeb under Counts Two and Three of the Indictment," July 1948, NAMP 898, Roll 57, 82.

151. Prosecution Memorandum of Law and Facts, "Responsibility of Karl von Roques under Counts Two and Three of the Indictment," 20 August 1948, NAMP 898, Roll 58, 67. Although the prosecution could not determine the total number of Jews killed in von Roques's rear area of Army Group South, it cited Einsatzgruppe C's own calculations that between June and November 1941, they shot 80,000 civilians, of whom 75,000 were Jews. In only three days in August, units of Higher Police S.S. and Police Leader Friedrich Jeckeln murdered 23,000 Jews at Kamieniec-Podolsk. The next month, in only two days, they shot 33,000 Jews at Babi Yar near Kiev. Apart from the Einsatzgruppe having submitted reports to von Roques attesting to this, von Roques was in the habit of eating with Jeckeln every night. The prosecution could scarcely believe that the foregoing actions had never come up in conversation, as the defendant claimed. Prosecution Memorandum of Law and Facts, "Responsibility of Karl von Roques under Counts Two and Three of the Indictment," 20 August 1948, NAMP 898, Roll 58, 72–73 and 78.

152. Prosecution Memorandum of Law and Facts, "Responsibility of Karl von Roques under Counts Two and Three of the Indictment," 20 August 1948, NAMP 898, Roll 58, 55–56.

153. Ibid., 67.

154. Prosecution Memorandum of Law and Facts, "Responsibility of Wilhelm von Leeb under Counts Two and Three of the Indictment," July 1948, NAMP 898, Roll 57, 92. The defendants von Salmuth and Woehler were also heavily implicated in crimes against Jews. Woehler went so far as to request that all wristwatches belonging to Jews shot by Einsatzgruppe D under Otto Ohlendorf be turned over to the army. See Closing Statement for the United States of America, 10 August 1948, NAMP 898, Roll 57, 83.

155. Prosecution Memorandum of Law and Facts, "Responsibility of Wilhelm von Leeb under Counts Two and Three of the Indictment," July 1948, NAMP 898, Roll 57, 93–94.

156. Prosecution Opening Statement, NAMP 898, Roll 1, 137. Similarly, an order from within Reinhardt's Third Panzer Army dated 31 October 1943 declared, "It appears a propitious moment to again recall to our troops the crimes which the Jews at one time committed in Germany against the German people with the help of their devilish and insidiously treacherous intellectuals who now again appear with their propaganda material and the same aims. It is [an] eternal tribe of parasites which has been gnawing at the strength of the Western peoples for over 1000 years and which now, through Bolshevist evil, is probably committing its last work of

decomposition. The brave German Western individual still is not energetic enough with their hellish monsters. He still treats the Jewish monster too much in accordance with decent concepts, instead of releasing his entire hatred and will of destruction against the breed of a 1000 year old infernal world. The misfortune which the Jewish poison has brought up to now upon the Western people is inconceivable and now it again threatens the tortured peoples with the help of the Bolshevistic mask. I expect all company and battery commanders indefatigably to use the appearance of the Jewish–Bolshevist propaganda in order to open the eyes of our brave German soldiers at every possible opportunity to fill their hearts with deep hatred and will of destruction. With such an attitude of the German soldier we would not worry about the future of our National Socialist Reich. The Reich will then remain ours." Prosecution Memorandum of Law and Facts, "Responsibility of Hans Reinhardt under Counts Two and Three of the Indictment," 26 August 1948, NAMP 898, Roll 57, 99–100, and Prosecution Exhibit 661, NOKW-2436, NAMP 898, Roll 17.

157. Prosecution Memorandum of Law and Facts, "Responsibility of Georg Karl Friedrich-Wilhelm von Kuechler under Counts Two and Three of the Indictment," 12 August 1948, NAMP 898, Roll 57, 102–103.

158. Ibid., 104, and Prosecution Exhibit 1359, NOKW-3140, NAMP 898, Roll 24.

159. Prosecution Memorandum of Law and Facts, "Responsibility of Georg Karl Friedrich-Wilhelm von Kuechler under Counts Two and Three of the Indictment," 12 August 1948, NAMP 898, Roll 57, 104–106.

160. Prosecution Memorandum of Law and Facts, "Responsibility of Hans Reinhardt under Counts Two and Three of the Indictment," 26 August 1948, NAMP 898, Roll 57, 86–87.

161. Prosecution Opening Statement, NAMP 898, Roll 1, 138–143. On the use of civilians from all over occupied Europe for slave labor in the Reich, see Ulrich Herbert, ed., *Europa und der "Reicheinsatz": Ausländische Zivilarbeiter, Kriegsgefangene und KZ-Häftlinge in Deutschland, 1938–1945* (Essen: Klartext Verlag, 1991). According to Rolf-Dieter Müller's calculations, about 20 million Soviets were pressed into service, of whom 3 million were deported to the Reich. See "The Occupation," in Müller and Ueberschär, *Hitler's War in the East*, 309.

162. Indictment, in Germany (Territory under Allied Occupation, 1945–1955: U.S. Zone), *Trials of War Criminals*, 10:37–38.

163. Prosecution Memorandum of Law and Facts, "Responsibility of Georg Karl Friedrich-Wilhelm von Kuechler under Counts Two and Three of the Indictment," 12 August 1948, NAMP 898, Roll 57, 67–68, and Prosecution Rebuttal Exhibit 24, NOKW-3379, NAMP 898, Roll 27.

164. Report dated 6 March 1944 submitted to the Third Panzer Army under Reinhardt, Prosecution Memorandum of Law and Facts, "Responsibility of Hans

Reinhardt under Counts Two and Three of the Indictment," 26 August 1948, NAMP 898, Roll 57, 42.

165. For example, in dealing with the issue of the army's relationship to the Einsatzgruppen, the prosecution commented: "That those security tasks [i.e., of the Einsatzgruppen] embraced the extermination of those races and classes which might endanger or only inconvenience the future of Hitler's thousand year Reich, escaped their attention somehow." Closing Statement for the United States of America, 10 August 1948, NAMP 898, Roll 57, 72.

166. General Legal Brief, 26 August 1948, NAMP 898, Roll 58, 28.

167. Closing Statement for the United States of America, 10 August 1948, NAMP 898, Roll 57, 1.

168. Prosecution Opening Statement, NAMP 898, Roll 1, 146.

169. Closing Statement for the United States of America, 10 August 1948, NAMP 898, Roll 57, 93.

170. General Johannes Blaskowitz committed suicide the day the indictment was read, leaving thirteen defendants to stand trial. On Blaskowitz's biography, see Richard Giziowski, *The Enigma of General Blaskowitz* (New York: Hippocrene Books, 1997).

CHAPTER FOUR: THE SOLDIERS' DEFENSE

Epigraph from Paul Leverkuehn, Opening Statement for Walter Warlimont, NAMP 898, Roll 61, 15.

1. Manfred Messerschmidt, "Forward Defense: The 'Memorandum of the Generals' for the Nuremberg Court," in *War of Extermination: The German Military in World War II, 1941–1944*, ed. Hannes Heer and Klaus Naumann (New York: Berghahn Books, 2000), 381. The original of this memorandum can be found in Siegfried Westphal, *Der deutsche Generalstab auf der Anklagebank: Nürnberg, 1945– 1948. Mit einer Denkschrift von Walter von Brauchitsch, Erich von Manstein, Franz Halder, Walter Warlimont, Siegfried Westphal* (Mainz: v. Hase & Koehler, 1978). On the role the memorandum played in the formation of German public memory about the Wehrmacht's role in the war, see Hannes Heer, "The Difficulty of Ending a War: Reactions to the Exhibition: Crimes of the Wehrmacht 1941 to 1944," *History Workshop Journal* 46 (1998): 187–203. Interestingly, the memorandum was written at the behest of Major General Bill Donovan, the wartime chief of the American Office of Strategic Services and Robert Jackson's first deputy during the preparation stage of the IMT. Donovan was opposed to indicting field commanders of the German army, believing they had "only been doing their duty." He was not as generous in his view of staff officers, and he hoped the memorandum could be used to incriminate Keitel and Jodl at trial. It turned out to be useless for this purpose, as

the generals placed all the blame for the war on Hitler. See Telford Taylor, *The Anatomy of the Nuremberg Trials: A Personal Memoir* (Boston: Little, Brown, 1992), 148 and 180.

2. Messerschmidt, "Forward Defense," 381–382.

3. Ibid.

4. Ibid., 383–385.

5. Ibid., 383, 393.

6. Ibid., 394.

7. Ibid., 388.

8. Ibid., 396.

9. See Rolf-Dieter Müller, "Die Wehrmacht—Historische Last und Verantwortung: Die Historiographie im Slannungsfeld von Wissenschaft und Vergangenheitsbewältigung," in *Die Wehrmacht: Mythos und Realität*, ed. Rolf-Dieter Müller and Hans-Erich Volkmann (Munich: R. Oldenbourg, 1999), 3–38; Geoffrey Megargee, "Selective Realities, Selective Memories: The German Generals and National Socialism" (unpublished paper, 2000).

10. In the scholarly literature, a consensus emerges that World War II actualized a culmination of thought among a critical mass of the officer corps on race, politics, and military strategy that rationalized war and ideological policies toward civilians as militarily necessary and legitimate. In her study of the imperial army, Isabel Hull finds a long and entrenched tradition of racism and antisemitism and an institutional approach to and conduct in war that aimed at total destruction and that targeted civilians and combatants alike. Although she does not refer to the Holocaust, her work is nonetheless extremely valuable to understand the link between the Wehrmacht and the eastern campaign and genocide. See Isabel Hull, *Absolute Destruction: Military Culture and the Practices of War in Imperial Germany* (Ithaca, N.Y.: Cornell University Press, 2004). Wolfram Wette argues that the experience of the Russian revolution, Germany's defeat in World War I, and the political upheaval of the interwar period attracted many of the senior officer corps toward a radical nationalism that conflated anti-Communism with antisemitism. Hitler did not have to invent the image of a menacing Jewish Bolshevism; he merely adopted and intensified it. In planning war against the Soviet Union, the distinctions among military, political, racial, and ideological enemies disappeared. Wolfram Wette, *The Wehrmacht: History, Myth, Reality* (Cambridge: Harvard University Press, 2006). On the interplay between the war and ideological policies toward civilians and belligerents, see especially the works of Omer Bartov: *The Eastern Front, 1941–45: German Troops and the Barbarisation of Warfare* (Oxford: Macmillan, 1985), *Hitler's Army: Soldiers, Nazis, and War in the Third Reich* (Oxford: Oxford University Press, 1992), and "Operation Barbarossa and the Origins of the Final Solution," in *The Final Solution: Origins and Implementation*, ed. David Cesarani (New York: Routledge, 1994), 119–136; Jürgen Förster, "Complicity or Entanglement? Wehrmacht,

War and Holocaust," in *The Holocaust and History: The Known, the Unknown, the Disputed and the Reexamined,* ed. Michael Berenbaum and Abraham Peck (Bloomington: Indiana University Press, 1998); Heer and Naumann, *War of Extermination;* Geoffrey Megargee, "A Blind Eye and Dirty Hands: The Sources of Wehrmacht Criminality in the Campaign against the Soviet Union," in *The Germans and the East,* ed. Charles Ingrao and Franz Szabo (West Lafayette, Ind.: Purdue University Press, 2008), 310–327; Manfred Messerschmidt, "The Wehrmacht and the Volksgemeinschaft," *Journal of Contemporary History* 18 (1983): 719–744; Manfred Messerschmidt, *Die Wehrmacht im NS-Staat: Zeit der Indoktrination* (Hamburg: R. v. Decker's Verlag, 1969). See also Rolf-Dieter Müller, "Die Wehrmacht," 3–38; Geoffrey Megargee, "Selective Realities."

11. Rebecca Wittmann, *Beyond Justice: The Auschwitz Trial* (Cambridge: Harvard University Press, 2005), 207. Hans Laternser wrote three books about defending military men in Allied courts and his defense work in the Auschwitz trials. See *Die andere Seite im Auschwitz-Prozess, 1963/65* (Stuttgart: Seewald, 1966), and *Verteidigung deutscher Soldaten: Plädoyers vor alliierten Gerichten* (Bonn: R. Bohnemeier, 1950). His defense for the OKW before the IMT was published as *Plaedoyer vor dem Internationalen Militärgerichtshof zu Nürnberg* (Nuremberg: Deutsche Lager-Kommandantur, 1946).

12. Spruchkammer Wiesbaden, Spruch mit Begründing gegen Dr. Hans Laternser, 9 July 1948, BMA N431/978: Hans Laternser, Spruchkammerverfahren und Fragebogen gegen Hans Laternser (1948).

13. Johann-Georg Schätzler (former defense attorney at the International Military Tribunal at Nuremberg), interview with the author, at Wachtberg, Germany, 23 July 2002.

14. Hans Laternser, opening statement for Wilhelm von Leeb, NAMP 898, Roll 61, 2.

15. Ibid., 3–4.

16. Ibid., 8.

17. Ibid., 6–8. The book, based on his past military experience in defensive warfare, was called simply *Defense.*

18. Ibid., 10, 20.

19. Ibid., 21.

20. Ibid., 20.

21. Ibid., 12, 51.

22. Ibid., 21–22.

23. Ibid. 30.

24. Ibid., 35, 38.

25. Ibid., 39.

26. Ibid., 40.

27. Ibid., 46–51.

28. Ibid., 61.

29. Ibid., 64–67.

30. Hans Laternser, "Looking Back at the Nuremberg Trials with Special Consideration of the Processes against Military Leaders," *Whittier Law Review* 8 (1986): 574. This article is Laternser's summation of and reflection on the difficulties he encountered in his defense of military men during the various postwar war crimes trials in which he served. Published posthumously, it contains the objections and protests raised during the proceedings.

31. Ibid., 572; Paul Leverkuehn, opening statement for Walter Warlimont, NAMP 898, Roll 61, 9.

32. Laternser, "Looking Back," 561–562; Heinz Müller-Torgow, opening statement for Hermann Hoth, NAMP 898, Roll 61, 1–2; Hans Surholt, opening statement for Hermann Reinecke, NAMP 898, Roll 61, 2; Edmund Tipp, opening statement for Karl von Roques, NAMP 898, Roll 61, 1.

33. Public Information Office, List of Defense Counsel, 27 January 1949, NARG 238: Office of the Chief of Counsel for War Crimes, 1933–1949, Chief of Counsel, Entry 164: Public Information Office, Box 1, Folder: List of Defense Counsel. Notably, Paul Leverkuehn, Walter Warlimont's counsel in the High Command case, went on to defend Field Marshal Erich von Manstein before a British military court. His account of his work there was published as Paul Leverkuehn, *Verteidigung Manstein* (Hamburg: H. H. Nölke, 1980).

34. Edmund Tipp, opening statement for Karl von Roques, NAMP 898, Roll 61, 2.

35. Major Robert Schaeffer, Chief, Defense Center, report for the Secretary General, Military Tribunals, "Activities of the Defense Center, Secretariat for Military Tribunals," 31 March 1948, TLI, John C. Young Papers, Box 18, Folder: Record File.

36. Ibid.

37. Despite persistent claims and impressions otherwise, contemporary research into German opinions on the trials found that most thought that they had been conducted fairly and impartially. See August von Knierim, *Nürnberg: Rechtliche und Menschliche Probleme* (Stuttgart: E. Klett, 1952), and Wilbourn Benton and Georg Grimm, ed., *Nuremberg: German Views of the War Crimes Trials* (Dallas: Southern Methodist University Press, 1955). On the rights of the defense at Nuremberg, see Benjamin Ferencz, "Nuremberg Trial Procedure and the Rights of the Accused," *Journal of Criminal Law and Criminology of Northwestern University* 39, no. 2 (August 1948): 145–151. Although in the American Nuremberg military cases defense attorneys were permitted access to Washington, D.C., archives to draw their evidence, the same was not true of the attorneys representing S.S. defendants. See John Mendelsohn, "Trial by Document: The Problem of Due Process for War Criminals at Nuremberg," *Prologue* 8 (1975): 228–234.

38. Paul Leverkuehn, opening statement for Walter Warlimont, NAMP 898, Roll 61, 14.

39. Heinz Müller-Torgow, closing brief for Hermann Hoth, NAMP 898, Roll 61, 29.

40. Ibid.; Heinz Müller-Torgow, opening statement for Hermann Hoth, NAMP 898, Roll 61, 16–17.

41. Heinz Müller-Torgow, closing brief for Hermann Hoth, NAMP 898, Roll 61, 30–31.

42. Heinz Müller-Torgow, opening statement for Hermann Hoth, NAMP 898, Roll 61, 16–17.

43. Ibid., 32. *Sonderbehandlung* ("special treatment"), like *Endlösung* ("final solution") and *Aussiedlung nach Ost* ("resettlement to the East"), was a seemingly innocuous term, typical of the bureaucratic language used by the Nazi regime to veil the murderous policies to which they referred. For a discussion of the origins and usage of this kind of vocabulary to conceal genocidal policies, see "Endlösung der Judenfrage" and "Sonderbehandlung" in Cornelia Schmitz-Bering, *Vokabular des National-Sozialismus* (Berlin: de Gruyter, 1998), 174–176, 584–587; and Berel Lang, *Act and Idea in the Nazi Genocide* (Chicago: University of Chicago Press, 1990), 88, as cited in Jeffrey Herf, "The 'Jewish War': Goebbels and the Antisemitic Campaigns of the Nazi Propaganda Ministry," *Holocaust and Genocide Studies* 19, no. 1 (2005): 51–80.

44. Friedrich Frohwein, closing brief for Hans Reinhardt, NAMP 898, Roll 62, 98.

45. Heinz Müller-Torgow, closing brief for Hermann Hoth, NAMP 898, Roll 61, 98.

46. Ibid., 99.

47. Hans Surholt, opening statement for Hermann Reinecke, NAMP 898, Roll 61, 4.

48. Paul Leverkuehn, opening statement for Walter Warlimont, NAMP 898, Roll 61, 3–6.

49. NAMP 1019, interrogation summary No. 380, interrogation of Hermann Reinecke, 30 October 1946.

50. Heinz Müller-Torgow, opening statement for Hermann Hoth, NAMP 898, Roll 61, 7.

51. Kurt Behling, opening statement for Georg von Kuechler, NAMP 898, Roll 61, 7–11.

52. Ibid.; Heinz Müller-Torgow, opening statement for Hermann Hoth, NAMP 898, Roll 61, 4–7.

53. Hans Surholt, opening statement for Hermann Reinecke, NAMP 898, Roll 61, 8.

54. Heinz Müller-Torgow, closing brief for Hermann Hoth, NAMP 898, Roll 61, 21.

55. Hans Surholt, opening statement for Hermann Reinecke, NAMP 898, Roll 61, 5; Friedrich Frohwein, closing brief for Hans Reinhardt, NAMP 898, Roll 62, 21.

56. Hans Surholt, opening statement for Hermann Reinecke, NAMP 898, Roll 61, 5; Paul Leverkuehn, opening statement for Walter Warlimont, NAMP 898, Roll 61, 12.

57. Paul Leverkuehn, opening statement for Walter Warlimont, NAMP 898, Roll 61, 12; Friedrich Frohwein, closing brief for Hans Reinhardt, NAMP 898, Roll 62, 21.

58. Georg von Kuechler, testimony, Transcript, NAMP 898, Roll 4, 2911. Other defendants offered similar explanations for their decision to remain and fight. Hoth's counsel quoted Halder's testimony: "If there is a war there is no question for a soldier for what reason the war has broken out. Then his soldierly duty transcends everything, and his duty consists in fighting for his troops and his country. A resignation at that moment would be desertion." Heinz Müller-Torgow, closing brief for Hermann Hoth, NAMP 898, Roll 61, 12. Reinhardt's attorney declared, "Never will a soldier come to the conclusion that at the outbreak of war he could be dutifully required to desert his fatherland at that moment just because his fatherland is waging a war of aggression." Friedrich Frohwein, closing brief for Hans Reinhardt, NAMP 898, Roll 62, 2.

59. Georg von Kuechler, testimony, Transcript, NAMP 898, Roll 4, 2982.

60. A great deal of research has been done on the Wehrmacht's internalization and promotion of the ideological aspects of the war. Some of the best-known works on this subject are: Bartov's *The Eastern Front, 1941–45, Hitler's Army,* and "Operation Barbarossa and the Origins of the Final Solution." Bartov concludes that German soldiers were "brutalized" by their experience of war in the East, with its huge losses, impenetrable geography, and harsh climate, as well as the scale of fighting, the prevalence of disease, and inadequate supplies. Combined with the troops' view of the enemy as alien and primitive, the war in the East quickly devolved into what felt like a primeval battle for survival, an "apocalyptic event" in which traditional legal and moral values no longer mattered. However, using letters soldiers sent home from the front, Bartov shows that their views were not solely created by their combat experience. Rather, they had internalized the racist and ideological ideas of the Nazi state and found these ideas confirmed once they were in the East. Soldiers had been and continued to be instructed to view the war as a racial war and a war of competing ideologies. Believing that "Jewish Bolshevism" sought world domination, the ideological dimension of the war assumed monumental importance. Bartov and others, for example, Stephen Fritz, in *Frontsoldaten: The German Soldier in World War II* (Lexington: University Press of Kentucky, 1997), and "'We are trying . . . to change the face of the world': Ideology and Motivation in the Wehrmacht on the Eastern Front: The View from Below," *Journal of Military History* 60 (1996): 683–710, have justifi-

ably focused on Operation Barbarossa, when undoubtedly the ideological aspect of the war reached its zenith. However, Alexander Rossino, in his study of the invasion of Poland, reminds us that "the evolution of German military practice to include the eradication of political and ideological enemies, as defined in racial-biological terms by National Socialism, . . . began in 1939." *Hitler Strikes Poland: Blitzkrieg, Ideology, and Atrocity* (Lawrence: University Press of Kansas, 2003), xv. Significantly, also by using soldiers' personal correspondence, he demonstrates their genuine belief in the political goals of the war, even before the deterioration of the battlefront that Bartov cites in the brutalization of German forces in the Soviet theater. Other recent publications similarly emphasize the massive anti-Jewish indoctrination program applied in the military and its acceptance by officers and the rank and file alike. See Jürgen Förster, "Ideological Warfare in Germany, 1919–1945," in Militärgeschichtliches Forschungsamt, *Germany and the Second World War*, vol. 9:1, *German Wartime Society, 1939–1945: Politicization, Disintegration and the Struggle for Survival*, ed. Jörg Echternkamp (Oxford: Clarendon Press, 2008); Manfred Oldenburg, *Ideologie und militärisches Kalkül: Die Besatzungspolitik der Wehrmacht in der Sowjetunion 1942* (Cologne: Boehlau, 2004); Christoph Rass, *"Menschenmaterial": Deutsche Soldaten an der Ostfront: Innenansichten einer Infanteriedivision, 1939–1945* (Paderborn: Ferdinand Schöningh Verlag, 2003). Notably, Oldenburg's study draws attention to Hermann Hoth's 17th Army as having taken part systematically in the pursuit and murder of Jews and quotes from Hoth's instructions to his troops. Ernst Klee and Willi Dreßen have published two collections of firsthand accounts revealing ordinary soldiers' support for the war of annihilation and active complicity in the murder of Jewish (and non-Jewish) civilians in occupied USSR. They are: *"Gott mit uns": Der deutschen Vernichtungskrieg im Osten, 1939–1945* (Frankfurt am Main: S. Fischer, 1989), and *"The Good Old Days": The Holocaust as Seen by Its Perpetrators and Bystanders* (New York: Free Press, 1991). The latter was originally published in German under the title *"Schöne Zeiten": Judenmord aus der Sicht der Täter und Gaffer* (Frankfurt am Main: S. Fischer, 1988). In a similar way that the idea of the *Volksgemeinschaft* (people's community) has been used to help explain the German population's support for and loyalty to Hitler, even into war and destruction, Thomas Kühne argues that soldierly comradeship (a more profound bond than "camaraderie") helps explain the cohesion within the military and its complicity in nonmilitary murder policies. See *Kameradschaft: Die Soldaten des nationalsozialistischen Krieges und das 20. Jahrhundert* (Göttingen: Vandenhoeck & Ruprecht, 2006). Scholars are also increasingly turning their attention to regional studies to uncover new insights and details regarding the local interpretation, application, and at times initiative of anti-Jewish (and anti-Soviet and anti-Communist) policies and actions. See, for example, Karel Berkhoff, *Harvest of Despair: Life and Death in Ukraine under Nazi Rule* (Cambridge: Harvard University Press, 2004), and Wendy Lower, *Nazi Empire-Building and the Holocaust in Ukraine* (Chapel Hill: University of North Carolina Press, 2005).

61. Kurt Behling, opening statement for Georg von Kuechler, NAMP 898, Roll 61, 16.

62. Heinz Müller-Torgow, opening statement for Hermann Hoth, NAMP 898, Roll 61, 10; Friedrich Frohwein, opening statement for Hans Reinhardt, NAMP 898, Roll 61, 8.

63. Kurt Behling, opening statement for Georg von Kuechler, NAMP 898, Roll 61, 17.

64. Heinz Müller-Torgow, opening statement for Hermann Hoth, NAMP 898, Roll 61, 10.

65. Edmund Tipp, opening statement for Karl von Roques, NAMP 898, Roll 61, 14–15. The effort to depict the war against Russia as a preventive strike, although first enunciated at the war crimes trials at Nuremberg and elsewhere, persisted long into the postwar period. See Hartmut Schustereit, *Vabanque: Hitlers Angriff auf die Sowjetunion 1941 als Versuch durch den Sieg im Osten den Westen zu bezwingen* (Bonn: Mittler, 1988); Bernd Stegemann, "Der Entschluss zum Unternehmen Barbarossa: Strategie oder Ideologie?," *Geschichte in Wissenschaft und Unterricht* 33 (1982): 205–213; Bernd Stegemann, "Geschichte und Politik: Zur Diskussion über den deutschen Angriff auf die Sowjetunion 1941," *Blätter zur Konfliktforschung* 17, no. 1 (1987): 1287–1300. These works were soundly refuted by such writings as Andreas Hillgruber, "Noch einmal: Hitlers Wendung gegen die Sowjetunion 1940," *Geschichte in Wissenschaft und Unterricht* 33 (1982): 214–226; Gerd Ueberschär, "Hitler's Decision to Attack the Soviet Union in Recent German Historiography," in *Operation Barbarossa: The German Attack on the Soviet Union, June 22, 1941*, special issue of *Soviet Union* 18, no. 1–3 (1991): 297–315. However, the thesis did not disappear and enjoyed renewed currency within a larger effort to rationalize the military's crimes against Soviet civilians as having been inspired and provoked by Soviet methods of totalitarian control and warfare. During the mid-1980s, a *Historikerstreit*, or "historians' dispute," erupted around the place of the German–Soviet war in the broader European historical context. Some argued that the Soviet dictatorship and interwar policies were comparable to the policies of the Nazis. See Gerd Ueberschär, "'Historikerstreit' und 'Präventivkriegsthese.' Zu den Rechtfertigungsversuchen des deutschen Überfalls auf die Sowjetunion 1941," *Tribüne: Zeitschrift zum Verständnis des Judentums* 26, no. 103 (1987): 108–116. The German historian Ernst Nolte, in *Das Vergehen der Vergangenheit: Antworten an meine Kritiker im sogenannten Historikerstreit* (Berlin: Ullstein, 1993), went so far as to suggest that German crimes against Jews, Romani, and Slavs were simply a reaction to "Asiatic barbarities." The general argument drew parallels between Auschwitz and the gulag, relativized the crimes of the Nazi state, and attempted to cast doubt on their unique and unprecedented status. It drew passionate opposition. See Dan Diner, ed., *Ist der Nationalsozialismus Geschichte? Zur Historisierung und Historikerstreit* (Frankfurt am Main: Fischer Taschenbuch Verlag, 1987); Jürgen Habermas, *Eine Art Schadensabwicklung*

(Frankfurt am Main: Suhrkamp, 1987); Rudolf Augstein, *"Historikerstreit": Die Dokumentation der Kontroverse um die Einzigartigkeit der nationalsozialistischen Judenvernichtung* (Munich: R. Piper, 1987). The revisionist side of the *Historikerstreit,* although vociferously advocated, emerged late enough in the development of the historiography of the Third Reich that its theses never really threatened to offset the consensus on the origins and aims of Hitler's war in the East, let alone provided any significant insights. As one historian referred to it, the debate created "more heat than light." However, its emergence bears witness to the compelling version of events as presented at Nuremberg by the defense, and to the failure of the prosecution and judgments to have soundly impressed the truth of this history on German public consciousness. On the history of the *Historikerstreit,* see Augstein, *"Historikerstreit";* Peter Baldwin, ed., *Reworking the Past: Hitler, the Holocaust and the Historians' Debate* (Boston: Beacon Press, 1990); Martin Broszat and Saul Friedländer, "A Controversy about the Historicization of National Socialism," *Yad Vashem Studies* 19 (1988): 310–324; Richard Evans, *In Hitler's Shadow: West German Historians and the Attempt to Escape from the Nazi Past* (New York: Pantheon Books, 1989); Gerd Ueberschär, "Avoiding and Coming to Terms with the Past," in *Hitler's War in the East: A Critical Assessment,* ed. Rolf-Dieter Müller and Gerd Ueberschär (New York: Berghahn Books, 2002), 367–374.

66. Kurt Behling, opening statement for Georg von Kuechler, NAMP 898, Roll 61, 5–6; Paul Leverkuehn, opening statement for Walter Warlimont, NAMP 898, Roll 61, 14.

67. Paul Leverkuehn, opening statement for Walter Warlimont, NAMP 898, Roll 61, 14.

68. Heinz Müller-Torgow, closing brief for Hermann Hoth, NAMP 898, Roll 61, 17–18.

69. Defense Exhibit Index, NAMP 898, Roll 1.

70. Trial Transcript, NAMP 898, Roll 4, 3330.

71. Defense Exhibit Index, NAMP, Roll 1; Heinz Müller-Torgow, closing brief for Hermann Hoth, NAMP 898, Roll 61, 14, 27, 47, 74–77, 124.

72. See chap. 3, n. 91.

73. Paul Leverkuehn, closing brief for Walter Warlimont, NAMP 898, Roll 62, 65.

74. Ibid., 67.

75. Ibid., 68–69, 73.

76. Georg von Kuechler, testimony, Transcript, NAMP 898, Roll 4, 2921.

77. Ibid., 2922.

78. Ibid., 2833.

79. Heinz Müller-Torgow, closing brief for Hermann Hoth, NAMP 898, Roll 61, 20; Hermann Hoth, testimony, Transcript, NAMP 898, Roll 4, 3082.

80. Hermann Hoth, testimony, Transcript, NAMP 898, Roll 4, 3084.

81. Ibid., 3085–3086.

82. Ibid., 3085, 3087.

83. Ibid., 3144.

84. Ibid., 3143–3144.

85. Ibid., 3133.

86. Heinz Müller-Torgow, closing brief for Hermann Hoth, NAMP 898, Roll 61, 83.

87. Ibid., 77, 81.

88. Hermann Hoth, testimony, Transcript, NAMP 898, Roll 4, 3147.

89. Friedrich Frohwein, closing brief for Hans Reinhardt, NAMP 898, Roll 62, 130.

90. Hans Reinhardt, testimony, Transcript, NAMP 898, Roll 4, 3491–3492.

91. Friedrich Frohwein, closing brief for Hans Reinhardt, NAMP 898, Roll 62, 135.

92. Ibid., 155.

93. Ibid., 167; Hans Reinhardt, testimony, Transcript, NAMP 898, Roll 4, 3494.

94. Georg von Kuechler, testimony, Transcript, NAMP 898, Roll 4, 2868–2869.

95. Ibid., 2869.

96. Ibid.

97. Ibid., 2876–2877.

98. Ibid., 2877.

99. Interrogation Summary No. 14, interrogation of Otto Woehler and Otto Ohlendorf, no date, NAMP 1019.

100. Otto Ohlendorf, testimony, Transcript, NAMP 898, Roll 10, 9115–9117.

101. Heinz Müller-Torgow, closing brief for Hermann Hoth, NAMP 898, Roll 61, 109; Friedrich Frohwein, closing brief for Hans Reinhardt, NAMP 898, Roll 62, 119.

102. Paul Leverkuehn, closing brief for Walter Warlimont, NAMP 898, Roll 62, 186.

103. Georg von Kuechler, testimony, Transcript, NAMP 898, Roll 4, 2962.

104. Ibid., 2892–2893.

105. Ibid., 2900, 2972.

106. Ibid., 2977.

107. Ibid., 2862–2863.

108. Ibid., 2892–2893, 2962.

109. Ibid., 2878, 2954, 2955.

110. Hoth's instructions to his troops in furtherance of the von Reichenau order are discussed in chapter 3.

111. Order, 17 November 1941, cited in prosecution opening statement, NAMP 898, Roll 1, 137.

112. Hermann Hoth, testimony, Transcript, NAMP 898, Roll 4, 3164–3165.

113. Ibid., 3164.

114. Ibid., 3166.

115. Ibid., 3167.

116. Ibid., 3169.

117. Ibid., 3170.

118. Ibid., 3171.

119. Ibid., 3173.

120. Ibid., 3174. General Friedrich Sixt, the chief of the General Staff of Corps subordinate to Hoth's army, appeared in court on Hoth's behalf. He corroborated Hoth's depiction of events, claiming that the order was only intended to "wake the German soldiers from their 'dangerous indifference' and to tell them of the dangers which were threatening them." Transcript, NAMP 898, Roll 4, 3291–3923.

121. Hermann Hoth, testimony, Transcript, NAMP 898, Roll 4, 3183. The Führer Order was a reference to Hitler's alleged order to exterminate all Soviet Jewish men, women, and children. It was discussed at great length in the Nuremberg Einsatzgruppen trial. On this, see Hilary Earl, *The Nuremberg Einsatzgruppen Trial,* chap. 5, "Trial." Although it is clear that a decision for the wholesale destruction of European Jews was made sometime in the latter half of 1941, no order has been found that can be traced back to Hitler directly. For a detailed overview of the timing of the decision, see Christopher Browning, with contributions by Jürgen Matthäus, *The Origins of the Final Solution* (Lincoln: University of Nebraska Press, 2004), 277–374.

122. Heinz Müller-Torgow, closing brief for Hermann Hoth, NAMP 898, Roll 61, 98.

123. Hermann Reinecke, testimony, Transcript, NAMP 898, Roll 8, 7330; Hans Surholt, closing brief for Hermann Reinecke, NAMP 898, Roll 62, 76.

124. Hans Surholt, closing brief for Hermann Reinecke, NAMP 898, Roll 62, 9, 199–202a.

125. Ibid., 70.

126. Ibid., 71; Hans Surholt, closing brief for Hermann Reinecke, NAMP 898, Roll 62, 7359. German soldiers constituted the largest single group of prisoners of war captured during World War II (11 million in over twenty countries). It is estimated that the Red Army captured one third of these, or 3.2 million, of whom one third died. They received far worse treatment from the Soviets than from Western captors; however, their death rates still pale in comparison to the fate of Soviet POWs in German custody during the war. Although in the early 1950s the estimated number of German prisoners still held in Russian custody was greatly exaggerated, it is true that the last captives did not return from the USSR until 1956. Rolf-Dieter Müller, "The Results of the War," in Müller and Ueberschär, *Hitler's War in the East,* 345–366.

127. Hans Surholt, closing brief for Hermann Reinecke, NAMP 898, Roll 62, 77.

128. Hermann Hoth, testimony, Transcript, NAMP 898, Roll 4, 3101. *Boche* comes from the French word *caboche*, a colloquial term for "head," and is used in phrases denoting pigheadedness, for example, "avoir la caboche dur." During the late nineteenth century, the shortened *boche* became a slang nickname for all Germans as a result of their reputation in France for obstinacy. The term gained currency during World War I. From http://www.billcasselman.com/wording_room/boche.htm (accessed July 2009).

129. Georg von Kuechler, testimony, Transcript, NAMP 898, Roll 4, 2844.

130. Ibid., 2842–2843.

131. Ibid., 2851.

132. Maximilian Himmel, testimony, Transcript, NAMP 898, Roll 5, 3745.

133. Ibid., 3745–3746. Several defendants, with obvious pride, made a point of stating that they had never accepted any gifts or money from Hitler in return for their loyalty. The historian Norm Goda has shown that Hitler generously bribed his military officers throughout the war. See "Black Marks: Hitler's Bribery of His Senior Officers during World War II," *Journal of Modern History* 72, no. 2 (2000): 413–452.

134. Otto Heidkämper, testimony, Transcript, NAMP 898, Roll 5, 3852.

135. Ibid., 3851–3852.

136. Friedrich Frohwein, closing brief for Hans Reinhardt, NAMP 898, Roll 62, 177.

137. Ibid., 178.

138. Georg von Kuechler, testimony, Transcript, NAMP 898, Roll 4, 2806–2809.

139. Wette, *Wehrmacht,* 101–102.

140. Kurt Behling, opening statement for Georg von Kuechler, NAMP 898, Roll 61, 18.

141. Wilhelm von Leeb, closing statement on behalf of all the generals, NAMP 898, Roll 65, 9997–10,000.

142. Gerd Ueberschär, "Avoiding and Coming to Terms with the Past," in Müller and Ueberschär, *Hitler's War in the East,* 367. On the politics of West Germany's *Vergangenheitsbewältigung,* see especially Norbert Frei, *Adenauer's Germany and the Nazi Past: The Politics of Amnesty and Integration* (New York: Columbia University Press, 2002); Jeffrey Herf, *Divided Memory: The Nazi Past in the Two Germanys* (Cambridge: Harvard University Press, 1997); Robert Moeller, *War Stories: The Search for a Usable Past in the Federal Republic of Germany* (Berkeley: University of California Press, 2001); Hans Mommsen, "The Legacy of the Holocaust in German National Identity," Leo Baeck Memorial Lecture (New York: The Leo Baeck Institute, 1999); and Bill Niven, *Facing the Nazi Past: United Germany and the Legacy of the Third Reich* (London: Routledge, 2002). Although the volume and tenor of the rhetoric of victimization have not been constant, but rather have ebbed and flowed with such public debates as those around the 1980s *Historikerstreit* (discussed elsewhere in these notes) and the 1990s Wehrmacht exhibit (discussed in the conclusion), the overall

development of the historiography has tended toward a more nuanced, accurate, and contextualized view of German victimization and German victimizing. See, for example, Frank Biess, *Homecomings: Returning POWs and the Legacy of Defeat in Postwar Germany* (Princeton: Princeton University Press, 2006); Hannes Heer, *The Discursive Construction of History: Remembering the Wehrmacht's War of Annihilation* (New York: Palgrave Macmillan, 2008); Hannes Heer, *Vom Verschwinden der Täter: der Vernichtungskrieg fand statt, aber keiner war dabei* (Berlin: Aufbau-Verlag, 2004); Katharina von Kellenbach, "Vanishing Acts: Perpetrators in Postwar Germany," *Holocaust and Genocide Studies* 17, no. 2 (2003): 305–329; Robert Moeller, "On the History of Man-Made Destruction," *History Workshop Journal* 61 (2006): 103–134; W. G. Sebald, *On the Natural History of Destruction* (Toronto: Alfred A. Knopf, 2003).

CHAPTER FIVE: PRESIDING JUDGE JOHN CARLTON YOUNG AND
THE HIGH COMMAND CASE JUDGMENT

Epigraph from John Young, letter to "Sons and Families," 14 March 1948, TLI, John C. Young Papers, Box 12, Folder 1: (Correspondence 1947–1948).

1. Telford Taylor, *Final Report to the Secretary of the Army on the Nuernberg War Crimes Trials under Control Council Law No. 10* (Washington, D.C.: U.S. Government Printing Office, 15 August 1949), 19–36.

2. G. Scott Briggs, "John Carlton Young, Sr.," in "Six of the Greatest: A Tribute to Outstanding Lawyers in Colorado History," *Colorado Lawyer* 23, no. 7 (July 1994): 1497–1498.

3. John Young, letter to Lee Pace, Colorado Springs News, 30 January 1948, TLI, John C. Young Papers, Box 12, Folder: Chronological Correspondence File 1948.

4. Briggs, "John Carlton Young, Sr.," 1498.

5. John Young, letter to John C. Young Jr., 27 January 1948, TLI, John C. Young Papers, Box 12, Folder: Chronological Correspondence File 1948.

6. Ibid.; John Young, letter to John and Rush, 22 January 1948, TLI, John C. Young Papers, Box 12, Folder 1: (Correspondence 1947–1948).

7. John Young, letter to John and Rush, 26 June 1948, TLI, John C. Young Papers, Box 12, Folder 1: (Correspondence 1947–1948).

8. John Young, letter to John, Rush, Mary, Evelyn, and grandchildren, 28 December 1947, TLI, John C. Young Papers, Box 12, Folder 1: (Correspondence 1947–1948).

9. John Young, letter to Rush, 9 January 1948, TLI, John C. Young Papers, Box 12, Folder 1: (Correspondence 1947–1948).

10. Ibid.

11. John Young, letter to John C. Young Jr., 27 January 1948, TLI, John C. Young Papers, Box 12, Folder: Chronological Correspondence File 1948.

12. Ibid. and John Young, purchase request to Wehmann Brothers, for *Easy Method for Learning German Quickly* and *German, Self-Taught*, TLI, John C. Young Papers, Box 12, Folder: Chronological Correspondence File 1948.

13. John Young, letter to Rush, 28 January 1947 [*sic*—should be 1948], TLI, John C. Young Papers, Box 12, Folder 1: (Correspondence 1947–1948).

14. John Young, letter to John C. Young, Jr., 27 January 1948, TLI, John C. Young Papers, Box 12, Folder: Chronological Correspondence File 1948, and John Young, letter to Walter D. Baker, 30 January 1948, TLI, John C. Young Papers, Box 12, Folder: Chronological Correspondence File 1948.

15. Ibid., and John Young, letter to Rush, 28 January 1947 [*sic*—should be 1948], TLI, John C. Young Papers, Box 12, Folder 1: (Correspondence 1947–1948).

16. John Young, letter to John T. Haney, 3 February 1948, TLI, John C. Young Papers, Box 12, Folder: Chronological Correspondence File 1948.

17. John Young, letter to John Jr., 22 January 1948, TLI, John C. Young Papers, Box 12, Folder 1: (Correspondence 1947–1948).

18. John Young, letter to Honorable Benjamin C. Hilliard, 4 March 1948, TLI, John C. Young Papers, Box 12, Folder: Chronological Correspondence File 1948.

19. Ibid.

20. John Young, letter to "Firm," 28 February 1948, TLI, John C. Young Papers, Box 12, Folder 1: (Correspondence 1947–1948).

21. John Young, letter to "Sons and Families," 14 March 1948, TLI, John C. Young Papers, Box 12, Folder 1: (Correspondence 1947–1948).

22. John Young, letter to "Sons," 30 June 1948, TLI, John C. Young Papers, Box 12, Folder 1: (Correspondence 1947–1948).

23. Winfield Hale, "Nuremberg War Crimes Tribunals," *Tennessee Law Review* 21 (1949): 18.

24. John Young, letter to Boys, 12 February 1948, TLI, John C. Young Papers, Box 12, Folder 1: (Correspondence 1947–1948). He may not have liked the defendants much, but his sense of professionalism dictated that he should at least pronounce their names correctly while in court. Among his papers is a list of the defendants' names accompanied by their phonetic spelling. Warlimont became "Varlemont"; von Kuechler, "fon Kuechler"; von Salmuth, "fon Sarlmoot"; etc. No author, list of phonetic pronunciation of defendants' names, no date, TLI, John C. Young Papers, Box 73, Folder: John Carlton Young Book 1.

25. John Young, letter to "Dear Ones," 7 July 1949, TLI, John C. Young Papers, Box 12, Folder 1: (Correspondence 1947–1948). Young handwrote the majority of his letters, but he typed this one himself. Clearly out of practice with the machine, he apologized at the beginning of his letter for the uncharacteristically awkward syntax and spelling.

26. John Young, letter to "Firm," 20 April 1948, TLI, John C. Young Papers, Box 12, Folder 1: (Correspondence 1947–1948).

27. John Young, letter to "Sons," 23 August 1948, TLI, John C. Young Papers, Box 13, Folder 2: (Correspondence 1947–1948).

28. John Young, letter to "Sons and Families," 14 March 1948, TLI, John C. Young Papers, Box 12, Folder 1: (Correspondence 1947–1948); John Young, letter to "Boys," 20 March 1948, TLI, John C. Young Papers, Box 12, Folder 1: (Correspondence 1947–1948); John Young, letter to "Sons," 15 July 1948, TLI, John C. Young Papers, Box 12, Folder 1: (Correspondence 1947–1948).

29. John Young, letter to Rush and John, 1 April 1948, TLI, John C. Young Papers, Box 12, Folder 1: (Correspondence 1947–1948).

30. John Young, letter to "Sons," 20 July 1948, TLI, John C. Young Papers, Box 12, Folder 1: (Correspondence 1947–1948).

31. John Young, letter to John and Rush, 26 June 1948, TLI, John C. Young Papers, Box 12, Folder 1: (Correspondence 1947–1948).

32. John Young, letter to "Folks," 31 August 1948, TLI, John C. Young Papers, Box 13, Folder 2: (Correspondence 1947–1948).

33. John Young, letter to "Sons and Families," 1 May 1948, TLI, John C. Young Papers, Box 12, Folder 1: (Correspondence 1947–1948).

34. John Young, letter to "Kids," 26 July 1948, TLI, John C. Young Papers, Box 13, Folder 2: (Correspondence 1947–1948).

35. Ibid.

36. John Young, letter to "Sons," 23 August 1948, TLI, John C. Young Papers, Box 13, Folder 2: (Correspondence 1947–1948); John Young, letter to Winfield Hale, 24 September 1948, TLI, John C. Young Papers, Box 13, Folder 2: (Correspondence 1947–1948).

37. John Young, letter to "Sons," 20 July 1948, TLI, John C. Young Papers, Box 12, Folder 1: (Correspondence 1947–1948).

38. John Young, "Some Suggestions and Bright Ideas in Here," notes for judgment, no date, TLI, John C. Young Papers, Box 14, Folder: Draft and Notes of Trial.

39. John Young, letter to Judge Wilbur Walter, 8 August 1948, TLI, John C. Young Papers, Box 12, Folder: Chronological Correspondence File 1948; John Young, letter to Winfield Hale, 24 September 1948, TLI, John C. Young Papers, Box 13, Folder 2: (Correspondence 1947–1948).

40. John Young, letter to Winfield Hale, 24 September 1948, TLI, John C. Young Papers, Box 13, Folder 2: (Correspondence 1947–1948).

41. John Young, letter to "Folks," 9 September 1948, TLI, John C. Young Papers, Box 13, Folder 2: (Correspondence 1947–1948).

42. John Young, letter to Winfield Hale, 24 September 1948, TLI, John C. Young Papers, Box 13, Folder 2: (Correspondence 1947–1948).

43. Irene Young, letter to "Dear Ones All," 5 October 1948, TLI, John C. Young Papers, Box 13, Folder 2: (Correspondence 1947–1948).

44. John Young, letter to Judge H. P. Burke, 5 August 1948, TLI, John C. Young Papers, Box 12, Folder: Chronological Correspondence File 1948.

45. John Young, letter to "Sons," 20 July 1948, TLI, John C. Young Papers, Box 12, Folder 1: (Correspondence 1947–1948).

46. Eugene Phillips, Public Information Office, interoffice memo for Judge Young, 22 October 1948, TLI, John C. Young Papers, Box 13, Folder 2: (Correspondence 1947–1948).

47. Public Information Office, list of correspondents in Nuremberg to cover the High Command Case judgment, 26 October 1948, TLI, John C. Young Papers, Box 13, Folder: Correspondence (1947–48), folder 2—Young Papers.

48. John Young, letter to Winfield Hale, 6 October 1948, TLI, John C. Young Papers, Box 17, Folder 3: Official Memoranda.

49. "Nullum crimen, nulla poena sine praevia lege poenali," Latin for "No crime, no punishment without a previous penal law," prohibits law to be applied retroactively. That is, an act is not considered a crime until it has first been proscribed by law.

50. Transcript, NAMP 898, Roll 24, 10001–10025.

51. Ibid., 10026.

52. Ibid., 10027–10028.

53. Ibid., 10035.

54. Ibid., 10028–10038.

55. Ibid., 10038–10047.

56. Ibid., 10043.

57. Ibid., 10048.

58. Ibid., 10059–10060.

59. Ibid., 10060–10061.

60. Ibid., 10063–10064.

61. Ibid., 10062–10064.

62. Ibid., 10077.

63. Ibid., 10078.

64. Ibid., 10080.

65. Ibid., 10083.

66. Ibid., 10087.

67. Ibid.

68. Ibid., 10088–10089.

69. Ibid., 10090.

70. Ibid., 10091.

71. Ibid., 10092–10101.

72. Ibid., 10109.

73. Ibid., 10111.

74. Ibid., 10113.

75. Ibid., 10114.
76. Ibid., 10108.
77. Ibid., 10114–10116.
78. Ibid., 10121.
79. Ibid.
80. Ibid.
81. Ibid.
82. Germany (Territory under Allied Occupation, 1945–1955: U.S. Zone), Military Tribunals, *Trials of War Criminals before the Nuernberg Military Tribunals under Control Council Law No. 10; Nuernberg, October 1946–April 1949* (Buffalo: William S. Hein, 1997), 11:563.
83. Ibid., 566 and 588.
84. Ibid., 604–610.
85. Ibid., 648.
86. Ibid., 683.
87. Ibid., 661.
88. Antrag auf Erlass eines Writ of Habeas Corpus to the U.S. District Court for the District of Columbia, 29 November 1948; Antrag auf Erlass eines Writ of Habeas Corpus to the U.S. Supreme Court, IfZ, ED 418/3: Lehmann, Rudolf: general.
89. Transcript, NAMP 898, Roll 24, 10108.
90. Telford Taylor, letter to Kenneth Royall, 12 May 1948, Alvin Rockwell Papers, TLI, Box 38, Folder: War Crimes, Press Releases, Letters, Telegrams and Reports (1 of 2).
91. Telford Taylor, statement for the International News Service, 9 May 1949, CULS-ADLL, Telford Taylor Papers, [5-1-1 9TMs] (9 May 1949).
92. Germany (Territory under Allied Occupation, 1945–1955: U.S. Zone), *Trials of War Criminals*, 11:553–563.
93. Ibid., 564–565.
94. Ibid., 565–580.
95. Ibid., 580–596.
96. Ibid., 596–614.
97. Ibid., 614–625.
98. Ibid., 625–629.
99. Ibid., 629–630.
100. Ibid., 630–648.
101. Ibid., 648–661.
102. Ibid., 661–683.
103. Ibid., 683–690.
104. Ibid., 690–695.

CHAPTER SIX: THE DEBATE OVER IMPRISONED SOLDIERS AND
THE POLITICS OF PUNISHMENT, 1949 TO 1952

Epigraphs from John J. McCloy, letter to David Peck, Presiding Justice, Supreme Court Appellate Division, 5 February 1951, NARG 466 U.S. High Commander, John J. McCloy, Entry 1: Classified General Records, 1949–1952, 1951, no. 1–134, Box 24, Folder: January 1951—D(51)1–D(51)126 War Crimes, and Office of the U.S. High Commissioner for Germany Public Affairs Division, "Review of German and Foreign Press Reaction to the Clemency Decisions on Landsberg War Crimes Cases," 10 February 1951, NARG 466: U.S. High Commander, John J. McCloy, Entry 1: Classified General Records, 1949–1952, 1951, no. 1–134, Box 24, Folder: January 1951—D(51)1–D(51)126 War Crimes.

1. Kai Bird, *The Chairman: John J. McCloy—The Making of the American Establishment* (New York: Simon & Schuster, 1992), 309–311.

2. Ibid., 328.

3. Konrad Adenauer, *Memoirs, 1945–1953* (Chicago: Henry Regnery, 1966), 409.

4. HICOG Office of Political Affairs memorandum: "The War Criminals Question," 22 December 1942, NARG 466: Entry 10A: Security-Segregated Records, 1949–1952 (later: 1953–1955), Box 28, Folder: 321.6 German War Criminals—General.

5. German Federal Government, letter to the High Commissioners, undated, BAK, B305/141: Auswärtiges Amt, Deutsche Kriegsverurteilte in Landsberg 1949–1952.

6. Ibid.

7. Dr. Gebhard Müller, Staatspräsident, Land Württemberg-Hohenzollern, letter to Chancellor Adenauer re. Decree of an Amnesty for Germans who were sentenced by Allied military courts, 21 October 1949, BAK, B305/141: Auswärtiges Amt, Deutsche Kriegsverurteilte in Landsberg, 1949–1952, and Rudolf Aschenauer, letter to Bundesjustizminister Dr. Thomas Dehler, 10 November 1949, BAK, B305/132: Deutsche Kriegsverurteilte in Landsberg: Allgemeines und Einzelfälle: 1949–1952.

8. HICOG Administration of Justice and Prisons Division, memorandum for C. A. McLain: "Clemency for Nuremberg War Crimes Prisoners," 28 December 1949, NARG 466: Office of the High Commissioner for Germany Prisons Division, Entry 48: Security Segregated Records of the Prisons Division, Box 10, Folder: War Crimes Trials—War Crimes Clemency Program and Mortimer Kollender; Mortimer Kollender, memorandum for Robert Bowie: "Power of the High Commissioner to Alter, after Confirmation, the Sentences Imposed by the Military Tribunals at Nuremberg," 11 October 1949, NARG 466: U.S. High Commander, John J. McCloy, Entry 1: Classified General Records, 1949–1952, Box 3, Folder: D(49)271–292.

9. HICOG Administration of Justice and Prisons Division, memorandum for C. A. McLain: "Clemency for Nuremberg War Crimes Prisoners," 28 December 1949, NARG 466: Prisons Division, Entry 48: Security Segregated Records of the Prisons Division, Box 10, Folder: War Crimes Trials—War Crimes Clemency Program.

10. Ibid.

11. Ibid.

12. In December 1949, the good conduct credit amounted to five days' remission per month of good behavior; John J. McCloy, letter to General Thomas Handy, 19 December 1949, NARG 238: Advisory Board on Clemency for War Criminals Office of the High Command for Germany 1947–1950, Miscellaneous Correspondence, Entry 213: Correspondence and Other Records, 1950, Box 1, Folder: Box 1. In order to match domestic U.S. penal practice, and on the request of the Advisory Board on Clemency for War Criminals (also called the Peck Panel), which was established in spring 1950 to advise McCloy on clemency matters, the good conduct credit was doubled to ten days' remission per month of good behavior. HICOG, letter to Colonel Damon Gunn, JAG, 22 May 1950, and Robert Bowie, HICOG General Counsel, memorandum for John J. McCloy, 3 August 1950, NARG 238: Advisory Board on Clemency for War Criminals Office of the High Command for Germany 1947–1950, Miscellaneous Correspondence, Entry 213: Correspondence and Other Records, 1950, Box 2, Folder: Clemency Committee, General File.

13. John McCloy, letter to Mr. C. M. Bolds, Office of the Land Commissioner for Bavaria, March 1950, NARG 238: Advisory Board on Clemency for War Criminals Office of the High Command for Germany 1947–1950, Miscellaneous Correspondence, Entry 213: Correspondence and Other Records, 1950, Box 2, Folder: Clemency Committee, General File.

14. John Bross, Assistant General Counsel, HICOG, HICOG Office memorandum for Gerald Fowlie: "Clemency Committee Program," 18 May 1950, NARG 238: Advisory Board on Clemency for War Criminals, Office of the High Command for Germany 1947–1950, Miscellaneous Correspondence, Entry 213: Correspondence and Other Records, 1950, Box 2, Folder: Clemency Committee, General File.

15. Office of the High Commissioner for Germany, staff announcement No. 117: "Establishment of Advisory Board on Clemency for War Criminals," 18 July 1950, NARG 238: Advisory Board on Clemency for War Criminals, Office of the High Command for Germany 1947–1950, Miscellaneous Correspondence, Entry 213: Correspondence and Other Records, 1950, Box 2, Folder: Clemency Committee, General File.

16. Ibid.

17. Major Joseph Haefele, Chief, War Crimes Section, Judge Advocate, Euro-

pean Command, memorandum for Colonel Stanley Jones, Judge Advocate, EUCOM: "Conference, re. War Crimes, with HICOG," 3 August 1950, NARG 549: Judge Advocate Division, War Crimes Branch, Entry 2237: Records Relating to Post Trial Activities 1945–1947, Box 2: Clemency Files 1947-Clemency Files 1950, Folder: Clemency Files 1949–1950 General Administration.

18. Office of the U.S. High Commissioner for Germany, "Landsberg: A Documentary Report," 31 January 1951, NARG 466: Office of the U.S. High Commissioner for Germany Historical Division, Entry 17: Publications Relating to the U.S.'s Occupation of Germany, 1945–1953, Displaced Populations through the Special Projects Program, Box 3, Folder: Landsberg, A Documentary Report 31 January 1951.

19. Gerald Fowlie, letter to Peck, Moran, and Snow, 24 July 1950, NARG 466: Office of the U.S. High Commissioner for Germany, Prisons Division, Entry 49: General Records, Box 36, Folder: W.C. Clemency Board—Operational History. By contrast, lawyers working on the review of a single case for Military Governor Clay had taken seven months to complete their investigation. Given the time allotted to the Peck Panel, its members simply could not read through the 330,000 pages of Subsequent Nuremberg Proceedings material, so they didn't. See Bird, *Chairman*, 335–336.

20. Gerald Fowlie, letter re. Board Hearings to Peck, Snow, and Moran, 20 July 1950, NARG 238: Advisory Board on Clemency for War Criminals, Office of the High Command for Germany 1947–1950, Miscellaneous Correspondence, Entry 213: Correspondence and Other Records, 1950, Box 1, Folder: Research for the Board and Office of the U.S. High Commission for Germany, "Rules of Procedure in Clemency Board Hearings," 22 July 1950, NARG 466: Office of the U.S. High Commissioner for Germany, Prisons Division, Entry 49: General Records, Box 36, Folder: War Crimes Clemency Board—Operational History.

21. Robert Bowie, General Counsel, memorandum for John J. McCloy, U.S. High Commissioner: "War Crimes Clemency Program," 3 August 1950, NARG 238: Advisory Board on Clemency for War Criminals, Office of the High Command for Germany 1947–1950, Miscellaneous Correspondence, Entry 213: Correspondence and Other Records, 1950, Box 2, Folder: Clemency Committee, General File.

22. Benjamin Ferencz, chief prosecutor at the Einsatzgruppen trial, offered to consult with the panel but received no reply. See Bird, *Chairman*, 336.

23. Gerald Fowlie, Clemency Committee Administrative Secretary, Office of the HICOG Advisory Board on Clemency for War Criminals, rules of procedure in clemency board hearings, 22 July 1950, NARG 466: Office of the U.S. High Commissioner for Germany, Prisons Division, Entry 49: General Records, Box 36, Folder: War Crimes Clemency Board—Operational History. Although the hearings and deliberations were not transcribed, the defendants' and their counsels' petitions with supporting documentation survive in the archives.

24. Friedrich Frohwein, petition to the U.S. High Commissioner John J. McCloy in behalf of Hans Reinhardt, 19 June 1950, and Hans Reinhardt, statement for John J. McCloy, 26 June 1950, NARG 466: Office of the U.S. High Commissioner for Germany, Prisons Division, Entry 53: Petitions for Clemency or Parole and Related Records of Persons Convicted by the U.S. Military Tribunals at Nuremberg 1947–1957, Box 28, Folders: Reinhardt, Hans Case No. 12, Folder 2, Petitions and Reinhardt, Hans Case No. 12, Folder 3, Petitions.

25. Rudolf Lehmann, statement for the clemency board, 24 June 1950, NARG 466: Office of the U.S. High Commissioner for Germany, Prisons Division, Entry 53: Petitions for Clemency or Parole and Related Records of Persons Convicted by the U.S. Military Tribunals at Nuremberg 1947–1957, Box 18, Folder: Lehmann, Rudolf Case No. 12, Folder 3, Petitions.

26. Heinz Müller-Torgow, statement for the members of the clemency board, no date, NARG 466: Office of the U.S. High Commissioner for Germany, Prisons Division, Entry 53: Petitions for Clemency or Parole and Related Records of Persons Convicted by the U.S. Military Tribunals at Nuremberg 1947–1957, Box 11, Folder: Hoth, Hermann Case No. 12, Folder 2, Petitions.

27. Bundesminister der Justiz, "Investigations in the cases of Germans sentenced to confinement in the prison of Landsberg by American Tribunals in Nürnberg," for the clemency board, 28 July 1950, NARG 238: Advisory Board on Clemency for War Criminals Office of the High Command for Germany 1947–1950, Miscellaneous Correspondence, Entry 213: Correspondence and Other Records, 1950, Box 2, Folder: General File Concerning all Cases.

28. "Einleitung," no date, BAK, Findbuch B305: Zentrale Rechtsschutzstelle.

29. Gerhard Rauschenbach, letter to the Zentrale Rechtsschutzstelle, 4 August 1950, BAK, B305/4775: Zentrale Rechtsschutzstelle, Otto Woehler.

30. Gustav Harteneck, "Ein Aufruf an alle, die helfen wollen, ein Unrecht wieder gut zu machen!," October 1949, BAK, B305/142: Zentrale Rechtsschutzstelle, Deutsche Kriegsverurteilte in Landsberg—Allgemeines und Einzelfälle 1949–1952.

31. Georg von Kuechler, letter to the U.S. High Commissioner for Germany, 26 June 1950, NARG 466: Office of the U.S. High Commissioner for Germany, Prisons Division, Entry 53: Petitions for Clemency or Parole and Related Records of Persons Convicted by the U.S. Military Tribunals at Nuremberg 1947–1957, Box 37, Folder: von Kuechler, Georg, Case No. 12, Folder 3, Petitions; Niedersächsisches Landvolk, Kreisverband Burgdorf, petition for an earlier release of former general Otto Woehler, 30 May 1950, NARG 466: Office of the U.S. High Commissioner for Germany, Prisons Division, Entry 53: Petitions for Clemency or Parole and Related Records of Persons Convicted by the U.S. Military Tribunals at Nuremberg 1947–1957, Box 39, Folder: Woehler, Otto Case No. 12, Folder 3, Petitions; Otto Bitthorn, statement for the clemency board on behalf of Hermann Reinecke,

12 June 1950, NARG 466: Office of the U.S. High Commissioner for Germany, Prisons Division, Entry 53: Petitions for Clemency or Parole and Related Records of Persons Convicted by the U.S. Military Tribunals at Nuremberg 1947–1957, Box 27, Folder: Reinecke, Hermann, Case No. 12, Folder 2, Petitions.

32. Office of the U.S. High Commissioner for Germany, "Landsberg: A Documentary Report."

33. Ibid.

34. Robert Bowie, General Counsel, HICOG, memorandum for John J. McCloy, U.S. High Commissioner: "War Crimes Clemency Program," 3 August 1950, NARG 238: Advisory Board on Clemency for War Criminals Office of the High Command for Germany 1947–1950, Miscellaneous Correspondence, Entry 213: Correspondence and Other Records, 1950, Box 2, Folder: Clemency Committee, General File.

35. Office of the U.S. High Commissioner for Germany, "Landsberg: A Documentary Report."

36. Ibid.

37. Bird, *Chairman*, 361.

38. Robert Bowie, secret office memorandum, Office of the U.S. High Commissioner for Germany, for John J. McCloy: Report of Advisory Board on Clemency for War Criminals, 31 October 1950, NARG 466: Office of the U.S. High Commissioner for Germany, Bonn, Entry 10A: Security-Segregated Records, 1949–1952 (later: 1953–1955), Box 28, Folder: 321.6 German War Criminals—General. This memorandum was prepared in consultation with several members of the HICOG legal staff: John Bross, assistant general counsel; Jonathan Rintels, chief of the Administration of Justice Division; Mr. Weigert, chief of the German Justice Branch under Rintels; Gerald Fowlie, who acted as administrative assistant to the clemency board; and Colonel Raymond, who was the former legal advisor to General Clay.

39. Ibid.

40. Dennis Bark and David Gress, *A History of West Germany*, vol. 1, *From Shadow to Substance, 1945–1963* (New York: Basil Blackwell, 1989), 280.

41. Thomaz Alan Schwartz, *America's Germany: John J. McCloy and the Federal Republic of Germany* (Cambridge: Harvard University Press, 1991), 231. On the European Defense Community, see Edward Fursdon, *The European Defence Community: A History* (New York: St. Martin's Press, 1980).

42. For example, Heinz-Joachim Schmidt, a former colonel of the Luftwaffe General Staff, wrote to McCloy, "At every possibility the public opinion of Germany had been incited against the German soldiers by both the newspapers and the broad-cast [*sic*] from abroad. In a lot of cases the historical facts not only had been neglected but had been falsified, even in speeches made by official people.... Now, it seems to be a political necessity to return arms to the Germans, to the same soldiers the caricature of whom went during the last years all over the world. Should

it not be conceivable, that a German soldier must have certain doubts that he shall be wellcome [*sic*] as an esteemed member of the united forces of the western world . . . ? It is my personal opinion that especially those German soldiers who had to fight in Russia, against Bolshevism and its Red Army are well aware of the deadly danger coming from the East and I think that the Germans will do their bounden duty in the same manner as the Americans, British, French and others in case of an aggression against the Western Free World but only in the true honorable comradeship and forgetting all and every ressentments [*sic*] once caused by a mislead [*sic*] 'public opinion.'" Heinz-Joachim Schmidt, letter to John J. McCloy, 23 January 1951. See also General (ret.) Gustav Harteneck, letter to John J. McCloy, 15 December 1950: "For several years these men have been serving sentences imposed upon them for crimes which neither they nor I acknowledge as such despite the most careful searching of our consciences." Both letters: NARG 466: U.S. High Commander, John J. McCloy, Entry 1: Classified General Records, 1949–1952, 1951, no. 1–134, Box 24, Folder: January 1951—D(51)126 War Crimes.

43. Admiral (Ret.) Gottfried Hansen, letter to John J. McCloy, 31 December 1950, NARG 466: U.S. High Commander, John J. McCloy, Entry 1: Classified General Records, 1949–1952, 1951, no. 1–134, Box 24, Folder: January 1951—D(51)126 War Crimes.

44. Ibid.

45. General Heinz Guderian, letter to John J. McCloy, 1 January 1951, NARG 466: U.S. High Commander, John J. McCloy, Entry 1: Classified General Records, 1949–1952, 1951, no. 1–134, Box 24, Folder: January 1951—D(51)1–D(51)30.

46. Draft memorandum: "Meeting between Mr. McCloy and Delegation from Bundestag, 9 January 1951," NARG 466: U.S. High Commander, John J. McCloy, Entry 1: Classified General Records, 1949–1952, 1951, no. 1–134, Box 24, Folder: January 1951—D(51)1–D(51)30.

47. John J. McCloy, letter to Gottfried Hansen, 22 January 1951, NARG 466: U.S. High Commander, John J. McCloy, Entry 1: Classified General Records, 1949–1952, 1951, no. 1–134, Box 24, Folder: January 1951—D(51)126 War Crimes.

48. Draft memorandum: "Meeting between Mr. McCloy and Delegation from Bundestag, 9 January 1951," NARG 466.

49. Ibid.

50. Bird, *Chairman*, 363.

51. Dwight Eisenhower, quoted in Charles Thayer, *The Unquiet Germans* (London: Michael Joseph, 1957), 240–241. See also David Clay Large, *Germans to the Front: West German Rearmament in the Adenauer Era* (Chapel Hill: University of North Carolina Press, 1996), 114.

52. G. Whitman, Office of the U.S. High Commissioner for Germany, memorandum for Col. Gerhardt, 24 January 1951, NARG 466: U.S. High Commander, John J. McCloy, Entry 1: Classified General Records, 1949–1952, 1951, no. 1–134,

Box 24, Folder: January 1951 D(51)55–D(51)93B. Lieutenant General Hans Speidel—brother of Luftwaffe General Wilhelm Speidel—was a participant in the 20 July 1944 plot to assassinate Hitler and later became a member of the Allied–German defense committee, representing West Germany at NATO. Lieutenant General Adolf Heusinger was chief of operations of the High Command during the war, and was slightly wounded in the July 1944 assassination attempt. He had no use for antisemitic ideology, and he was tried by the People's Court for his connection to the July plot. He was later released. After the war, he was involved in military affairs and served from 1957 to 1961 as general inspector of the Bundeswehr, and from 1961 to 1964 as chairman of NATO Armed Forces in Washington.

53. Large, *Germans to the Front;* Public Relations Division, Office of Public Affairs, Office of the High Commissioner for Germany press release No. 568: "Statement by General Eisenhower upon his Departure," 23 January 1951, NARG 466: U.S. High Commander, John J. McCloy, Entry 1: Classified General Records, 1949–1952, 1951, no. 1–134, Box 24, Folder: January 1951 D(51)55–D(51)93B.

54. Ibid.

55. Thayer, *Unquiet Germans,* 242. See also Bird, *Chairman,* 363.

56. Thayer, *Unquiet Germans,* 242.

57. Ibid., 243.

58. Office of the U.S. High Commissioner for Germany, "Landsberg: A Documentary Report." See also Thomas Alan Schwartz, "John J. McCloy and the Landsberg Cases," in *American Policy and the Reconstruction of West Germany, 1945–1955,* ed. Jeffry Diefendorf, Axel Frohn, and Hermann-Josef Rupieper (New York: Cambridge University Press, 1993), 433–454.

59. John J. McCloy, secret telegram to Kellermann: McCloy's final decisions on Landsberg war criminals, 30 January 1951, NARG 466: U.S. High Commander, John J. McCloy, Entry 1: Classified General Records, 1949–1952, 1951, no. 1–134, Box 24, Folder: January 1951 D(51)94–D(51)134. The Landsberg report contained a statement by McCloy explaining the basis for the clemency review, the decisions on the sentences for each defendant (which also briefly summarized each of the trials), the Peck Panel's report, a short description of the crimes committed by those convicts whose death sentences were confirmed, and a statement from General Handy as well as his final decisions regarding the Dachau trial convicts. Copies of the London Agreement of 8 August 1945, Control Council Law No. 10, and Military Government Ordinance No. 7 were also included. Altogether, the report comprised twenty-five pages. The English version had one extra page of photographs taken at concentration camps.

60. Office of the U.S. High Commissioner for Germany, "Landsberg: A Documentary Report."

61. John J. McCloy, letter to David Peck, Presiding Justice, Supreme Court Appellate Division, 5 February 1951.

62. Office of the U.S. High Commissioner for Germany Public Affairs Division, "Review of German and Foreign Press Reaction to the Clemency Decisions on Landsberg War Crimes Cases," 10 February 1951, NARG 466: U.S. High Commander, John J. McCloy, Entry 1: Classified General Records, 1949–1952, 1951, no. 1–134, Box 24, Folder: January 1951—D(51)1–D(51)126 War Crimes. This review surveyed press coverage of the Landsberg decisions in twenty-nine German newspapers and cited statements by leading German Bundestag members. It also examined the responses in several major American, British, and European newspapers.

63. Ibid.

64. Ibid.; Anderson, confidential incoming message, Office of the U.S. High Commissioner for Germany, 15 February 1951, NARG 466: U.S. High Commander, John J. McCloy, Entry 1: Classified General Records, 1949–1952, 1951, no. 1–134, Box 24, Folder: January 1951—D(51)1–D(51)126 War Crimes.

65. Office of the U.S. High Commissioner for Germany Public Affairs Division, "Review of German and Foreign Press Reaction to the Clemency Decisions on Landsberg War Crimes Cases," 10 February 1951.

66. Ibid.

67. Ibid.

68. B. R. Shute, Director, Office of Intelligence, HICOG, office memorandum for John J. McCloy: "Analysis of Letters on Landsberg Decisions," 9 March 1951, NARG 466: U.S. High Commander, John J. McCloy, Entry 1: Classified General Records, 1949–1952, Box 24, Folder: January 1951—D(51)126 War Crimes.

69. B. R. Shute, Director, Office of Intelligence, HICOG, confidential memorandum: "Analysis of letters on the Landsberg decisions," 19 March 1951, NARG 466: Bonn, Entry 10A: Security-Segregated Records, 1949–1952 (later: 1953–1955), Box 28, Folder: 321.6 German War Criminals—General.

70. Ibid.

71. Ibid.

72. Ibid.

73. Ibid.; B. R. Shute, Director, Office of Intelligence, HICOG, confidential office memorandum, Office of the U.S. High Commissioner for Germany for John J. McCloy: "Analysis of Letters on Landsberg Decisions," 9 March 1951.

74. Heinz-Joachim Schmidt, letter to John J. McCloy, 4 February 1951, NARG 466: U.S. High Commander, John J. McCloy, Entry 1: Classified General Records, 1949–1952, 1951, no. 1–134, Box 24, Folder: January 1951—D(51)1–D(51)126 War Crimes.

75. Ibid.

76. Lieutenant Colonel Gerhard Matzky, German Liaison Director, Headquarters European Command, Labor Services Division, Labor Service Liaison Detachment (German), letter to commander in chief, European Command, 2 Feb-

ruary 1951, forwarded by Colonel Edward J. O'Neill, deputy chief of staff for administration, headquarters, European Command, Office of the Commander in Chief, to John J. McCloy, 3 March 1951, NARG 466: Office of the U.S. High Commissioner for Germany, Bonn, Entry 10A: Security-Segregated Records, 1949–1952 (later: 1953–1955), Box 28, Folder: 321.6 German War Criminals—General.

77. Ibid.

78. Ibid.

79. B. R. Shute, Confidential Office Memorandum, Office of the U.S. High Commissioner for Germany for John J. McCloy, Subject: "Analysis of Letters on Landsberg Decisions," 9 March 1951. See also General (ret.) Gustav Harteneck, letter to John J. McCloy, 15 December 1950, NARG 466: U.S. High Commander, John J. McCloy, Entry 1: Classified General Records, 1949–1952, 1951, no. 1–134, Box 24, Folder: January 1951—D(51)126 War Crimes, and B. R. Shute, Director, Office of Intelligence, HICOG, confidential memorandum: "Analysis of Letters on the Landsberg Decisions," 19 March 1951.

80. Bishop Theophil Wurm, letter to John J. McCloy, 2 February 1951, NARG 466: U.S. High Commander, John J. McCloy, Entry 1: Classified General Records, 1949–1952, Box 24, Folder: January 1951—D(51)126 War Crimes.

81. John J. McCloy, letter to Theophil Wurm, 10 February 1951, NARG 466: U.S. High Commander, John J. McCloy, Entry 1: Classified General Records, 1949–1952, Box 24, Folder: January 1951—D(51)126 War Crimes.

82. Adelbert Weinstein, "A Mortgage of a Special Kind," editorial in *Frankfurter Allgemeine Zeitung,* 18 August 1952, NARG 466: Office of the U.S. High Commissioner for Germany, Bonn, Office of the Executive Director General, Entry 10A: Security Segregated Records 1949–1952 (later 1953–1955), 321.4–321.6, Box 28, Folder: 321.6 German War Criminals—General. This editorial referred to related charges in five other newspapers and journals.

83. John J. McCloy, letter to Baron von Falkenhausen, 28 February 1951, NARG 466: U.S. High Commander, John J. McCloy, Entry 1: Classified General Records, 1949–1952, 1951, no. 1–134, Box 24, Folder: January 1951—D(51)1–D(51)126 War Crimes.

84. Ibid.

85. John J. McCloy, letter to Mrs. Eleanor Roosevelt, 12 March 1951, NARG 466: U.S. High Commander, John J. McCloy, Entry 1: Classified General Records, 1949–1952, 1951, no. 1–134, Box 24, Folder: January 1951—D(51)1–D(51)126 War Crimes.

86. B. R. Shute, Director, Office of Intelligence, HICOG, confidential memorandum: "Analysis of Letters on the Landsberg Decisions," 19 March 1951.

87. Ibid.; Dean Acheson, classified telegram for U.S. Foreign Service Offices in Bonn, London, and Paris, 7 October 1952, NARG 466: Office of the U.S. High Commissioner for Germany, Bonn, Entry 10A: Security-Segregated Records,

1949–1952 (later: 1953–1955), Box 28, Folder: 321.6 German War Criminals—General.

88. Richard C. Hagan, confidential office memorandum, Office of the High Commissioner for Germany, for Eli Whitney Debevoise: "Comments on Concessions to War Criminals," 24 September 1951, NARG 466: Office of the U.S. High Commissioner for Germany, Bonn, Entry 10A: Security-Segregated Records, 1949–1952 (later: 1953–1955), Box 28, Folder: 321.6 German War Criminals—General.

89. Ibid.

90. Ibid.

91. Charles Thayer, chief, Reports Division, Office of Political Affairs, HICOG, report: "Some German Comments on the continued Allied Imprisonment of German Generals," 12 March 1952, NARG 466: Office of the U.S. High Commissioner for Germany, Bonn, Entry 10A: Security-Segregated Records, 1949–1952 (later: 1953–1955), Box 28, Folder: 321.6 German War Criminals—General.

92. Erich Mende, Free Democratic Party, letter to John J. McCloy, 27 November 1951, BAK, B305/131: Deutsche Kriegsverurteilte in Landsberg, Allgemeines und Einzelfälle 1949–1952. Emphasis added.

93. Norbert Frei, *Adenauer's Germany and the Nazi Past: The Politics of Amnesty and Integration* (New York: Columbia University Press, 2002), 190.

94. Ibid., 195. *Endlösung* is the term the Nazis used to refer to the mass extermination of the Jews.

95. At this time, 318 men sentenced by the Dachau trials were also imprisoned at Landsberg. Eli Whitney Debevoise, HICOG General Counsel, report: "Summary Background War Criminal Information," 6 September 1952, NARG 466: Office of the U.S. High Commissioner for Germany, Bonn, Entry 10A: Security-Segregated Records, 1949–1952 (later: 1953–1955), Box 28, Folder: 321.6 German War Criminals—General.

96. Ibid.; Donnely, Foreign Service of the United States of America classified telegram summarizing Bundestag debate, 7 September 1952, NARG 466: Office of the U.S. High Commissioner for Germany Prisons Division, Entry 10A: Security-Segregated Records, 1949–1952 (later: 1953–1955), 321.4–321.6, Box 28, Folder: 321.6 German War Criminals—General; and Dr. Erich Mende, letter to Konrad Adenauer, 19 July 1952, NARG 466: Office of the U.S. High Commissioner for Germany Prisons Division, Entry 10A: Security-Segregated Records, 1949–1952 (later: 1953–1955), 321.4–321.6, Box 28, Folder: 321.6 German War Criminals—General. On 8 September 1952, the *Frankfurter Allgemeine Zeitung* ran the following article: "Mende Threatens with a 'No.'" It read in part: "Bundestag member Dr. Mende (Free Democratic Party) declared at a meeting of the Association of German Soldiers (Verband deutscher Soldaten) in Bielefeld: 'If the Allies are not ready now after seven years to end the so-called war criminals question, I

shall, despite all my approval of Western Defense, vote against the European Defense Treaty." NARG 466: Office of the U.S. High Commissioner for Germany, Prisons Division, Entry 56: War Criminal Case Files and Related Records, Box 1, Folder: War Crimes/Material from Mr. Hulse.

97. Eli Whitney Debevoise, HICOG General Counsel, report: "Summary Background War Criminal Information," 6 September 1952.

98. Admiral (ret.) Gottfried Hansen, letter to General Ridgway, commander in chief, Atlantic Pact Forces, Paris, 10 August 1952, and Verband Deutscher Soldaten and Bund der Berufssoldaten, "Resolution," 6 September 1952, NARG 466: Office of the U.S. High Commissioner for Germany Prisons Division, Entry 10A: Security-Segregated Records, 1949–1952 (later: 1953–1955), 321.4–321.6, Box 28, Folder: 321.6 German War Criminals—General. Copies of both the letter and the resolution were sent to HICOG as well. As a group, veterans' associations were never a decisive political force in 1950s West Germany. Immediately after the war, Wehrmacht and veterans' groups were disbanded, and all active and retired or discharged officers and troops were stripped of state benefits and prohibited from forming associations. In the earliest postwar years, then, soldiers had to integrate themselves into other social and economic milieus. Only gradually were they permitted to form associations. The first of these were founded for the purpose of achieving the restoration of benefits to those men (and their families) who had been disabled by the war. Later, other veterans groups formed to lobby for the reinstatement of professional soldiers' pensions. These associations quickly learned how much more effectively and successfully they could pursue their claims when they operated within the processes established by the occupation governments, and later by the West German Republic. In contrast to the interwar years, former soldiers did not form an isolated, alienated pocket of resentment. There was no post-1945 incarnation of the Freikorps. On the issue of rearmament, veterans' groups were divided. A significant proportion of former soldiers sided with the "Ohne Mich" ("Without Me"/"Count me out") campaign, which condemned proposals for the re-creation of a German military. Their opposition was based on the view that West German rearmament decisively closed the door on reunification, and that rearmament under Allied terms (that is, as part of the EDC, while former soldiers still remained in prison) implied a critique of the Wehrmacht. They vowed to withhold their support and did so vocally. As will be explained below, even after rearmament was ensured, the Americans remained concerned that persistent resentment over the imprisonment of soldiers convicted of war crimes would prevent the new army from attracting experienced officers, or the right kind of young men to fill its ranks. For more on the involvement of former Wehrmacht generals and veterans' associations in the debate surrounding rearmament and West Germany's contribution to the military security of the West, including the Ohne Mich campaign, see especially: James Diehl, *The Thanks of the Fatherland: German Veterans after the Second World War*

(Chapel Hill: University of North Carolina Press, 1993); Frei, *Adenauer's Germany;* Large, *Germans to the Front;* Jay Lockenour, *Soldiers as Citizens: Former Wehrmacht Officers in the Federal Republic of Germany, 1945–1955* (Lincoln: University of Nebraska Press, 2001); Robert Moeller, *War Stories: The Search for a Usable Past in the Federal Republic of Germany* (Berkeley: University of California Press, 2001); and Alaric Searle, *Wehrmacht Generals, West German Society, and the Debate on Rearmament, 1949–1959* (Westport, Conn.: Praeger, 2003).

99. Frank Buscher, *The U.S. War Crimes Trial Program in Germany, 1946–1955* (New York: Greenwood Press, 1989), 107.

100. HICOG translation of an editorial by Adelbert Weinstein, "A Mortgage of a Special Kind," *Frankfurter Allgemeine Zeitung,* 18 August 1952.

101. Eli Whitney Debevoise, report: "Summary Background War Criminal Information," 6 September 1952.

102. Confidential-Security Political Brief No. 5: "Political Aspects of the War Criminals Question," undated but likely January 1953, NARG 466: Office of the U.S. High Commissioner for Germany Prisons Division, Entry 48: Security Segregated Records of the Prisons Division, Box 10, Folder: War Crimes Trial—War Crimes—118; Buscher, *U.S. War Crimes Program Trial,* 91.

103. Samuel Reber, telegram for Secretary of State Kellermann: "Public Affairs Guidance No. 181," 28 July 1952, NARG 466: Office of the U.S. High Commissioner for Germany, Bonn, Office of the Executive Director General, Entry 10A: Security-Segregated Records, 1949–1952 (later: 1953–1955), 321.4–321.6, Box 28, Folder: 321.6 German War Criminals—General.

104. *Die Neue Zeitung,* 9–10 August 1952, quoted in Frei, *Adenauer's Germany,* 211.

105. Eli Whitney Debevoise, report: "Summary Background War Criminal Information," 6 September 1952; Confidential-Security Political Brief No. 5: "Political Aspects of the War Criminals Question."

106. F. G. Hulse, HICOG office memorandum for Eli Whitney Debevoise: "Publication of the Records and Justments [*sic*] made and given in the Trials conducted at Nuremberg under Control Council Law 10," 22 July 1952, NARG 466: Office of the U.S. High Commissioner for Germany Prisons Division, Entry 48: Security-Segregated Records of the Prisons Division, Box 6, Folder: Control Council Law No. 10 (Exchange of information re. persons transferred pursuant to Control Council Law No. 10, 1952).

107. Eli Whitney Debevoise, Report: "Summary Background War Criminal Information," 6 September 1952; Eli Whitney Debevoise, HICOG office memorandum for Assistant High Commissioner Reber: "Publication of the Records and Judgments made and given in the Trials conducted at Nuremberg under Control Council Law 10," undated but after 22 July 1952, NARG 466: Office of the U.S. High Commissioner for Germany Prisons Division, Entry 48: Security Segregated

Records of the Prisons Division, Box 6, Folder: Control Council Law No. 10 (Exchange of information re. persons transferred pursuant to Control Council Law No. 10, 1952).

108. Telford Taylor, *Final Report to the Secretary of the Army on Nuernberg War Crimes Trials under Control Council Law No. 10* (Washington, D.C.: United States Government Printing Office, 15 August 1949), 100.

109. Ibid., 101.

110. Ibid., 102.

111. Drexel Sprecher and Paul Gantt, memorandum for Telford Taylor: "Official Publication of Records in the Nurnberg Proceedings, English and German Editions," 25 August 1948, NARG 238: Office of the Chief of Counsel for War Crimes 1933–1949, Executive Office, Publications Division, Entry 196: Correspondence, Reports and Other Records, 1948–1949, Correspondence, Memos, Bulletins, Box 1, Folder: Volume IX Publication Paul H. Gantt; Drexel Sprecher, memorandum for the OMGUS Control Division, OMGUS Legal Division and OCCWC Executive Office: "Publication of Condensed Records (English and German) of the Twelve Cases held in Nurnberg since the Trial before the International Military Tribunal," 1 October 1948, NARG 238: Office of the Chief of Counsel for War Crimes 1933–1949, Executive Office, Publications Division, Entry 196: Correspondence, Reports and Other Records, 1948–1949, Correspondence, Memos, Bulletins, Box 1, Folder: Volume IX Publication Paul H. Gantt.

112. Drexel Sprecher and Paul Gantt, memorandum for Telford Taylor: "Official Publication of Records in the Nurnberg Proceedings, English and German Editions," 25 August 1948.

113. Drexel Sprecher, memorandum for the OMGUS Control Division, OMGUS Legal Division, and OCCWC Executive Office: "Publication of Condensed Records (English and German) of the Twelve Cases held in Nurnberg since the Trial before the International Military Tribunal," 1 October 1948.

114. Ibid. Eventually the German manuscripts were prepared to be the same in content as the English ones, because Paul Gantt, director of the publications division for the German edition, did not have adequate staff to make appropriate selections of the material. Gantt argued in any case that equivalent volumes would save money in editorial costs and would "avoid considerable criticism." He recommended that if U.S. authorities insisted on shortened German versions, then only the indictments and decisions should be published. See Drexel Sprecher, memorandum for Telford Taylor: "Publication problems requiring your immediate consideration and action," 8 February 1949, NARG 238: Office of the Chief of Counsel for War Crimes 1933–1949, Executive Office, Publications Division, Entry 196: Correspondence, Reports and Other Records, 1948–1949, Correspondence, Memos, Bulletins, Box 1, Folder: Volume IX Publication Paul H. Gantt.

115. Telford Taylor, memorandum for U.S. military governor for Germany: "Pub-

lication of the Nurnberg Trial Proceedings under Law No. 10 in the German Language," 15 April 1949, NARG 238: Office of the Chief of Counsel for War Crimes 1933–1949, Executive Office, Publications Division, Entry 196: Correspondence, Reports and Other Records, 1948–1949, Correspondence, Memos, Bulletins, Box 1, Folder: Volume XV Publications (A) English (B) German Paul H. Gantt; Paul Gantt, memorandum: "Telephone Conversation with Mr. Thomas Carson on 18 May 1949," 18 May 1949, NARG 238: Office of the Chief of Counsel for War Crimes 1933–1949, Executive Office, Publications Division, Entry 196: Correspondence, Reports and Other Records, 1948–1949, Correspondence, Memos, Bulletins, Box 1, Folder: Volume XV Publications (A) English (B) German Paul H. Gantt.

116. Drexel Sprecher, memorandum for Telford Taylor: "Weekly Report," 29 December 1948, NARG 238: Office of the Chief of Counsel for War Crimes 1933–1949, Executive Office, Publications Division, Entry 196: Correspondence, Reports and Other Records, 1948–1949, Correspondence, Memos, Bulletins, Box 1, Folder: Volume IX Publication Paul H. Gantt.

117. Drexel Sprecher, memorandum for Colonel Edward H. Young: "Requests by Germans for copies of German and English edition of the official publication on the Subsequent Proceedings," 18 March 1949, NARG 238: Office of the Chief of Counsel for War Crimes 1933–1949, Executive Office, Publications Division, Entry 196: Correspondence, Reports and Other Records, 1948–1949, Correspondence, Memos, Bulletins, Box 1, Folder: Volume XV Publications (A) English (B) German Paul H. Gantt; Drexel Sprecher, letter to Dr. P. Barandon, 16 December 1948, NARG 238: Office of the Chief of Counsel for War Crimes 1933–1949, Executive Office, Publications Division, Entry 196: Correspondence, Reports and Other Records, 1948–1949, Correspondence, Memos, Bulletins, Box 1, Folder: Volume IX Publication Paul H. Gantt.

118. Drexel Sprecher, memorandum for the OMGUS Control Division, OMGUS Legal Division and OCCWC Executive Office: "Publication of Condensed Records (English and German) of the Twelve Cases held in Nurnberg since the Trial before the International Military Tribunal," 1 October 1948. Paul Gantt, letter to Thomas Carson, 21 June 1949, NARG 238: Office of the Chief of Counsel for War Crimes 1933–1949, Executive Office, Publications Division, Entry 196: Correspondence, Reports and Other Records, 1948–1949, Correspondence, Memos, Bulletins, Box 1, Folder: Volume XV Publications (A) English (B) German Paul H. Gantt.

119. Drexel Sprecher, memorandum for Telford Taylor: "Publication problems requiring your immediate consideration and action," 8 February 1949, NARG 238: Office of the Chief of Counsel for War Crimes 1933–1949, Executive Office, Publications Division, Entry 196: Correspondence, Reports and Other Records, 1948–1949, Correspondence, Memos, Bulletins, Box 1, Folder: Volume IX Publication Paul H. Gantt.

120. Telford Taylor, memorandum for U.S. military governor for Germany: "Publication of the Nurnberg Trial Proceedings under Law No. 10 in the German Language," 15 April 1949.

121. Ibid.

122. Paul Gantt, memorandum: "Telephone Conversation with Mr. Thomas Carson on 18 May 1949," 18 May 1949, NARG 238: Office of the Chief of Counsel for War Crimes 1933–1949, Executive Office, Publications Division, Entry 196: Correspondence, Reports and Other Records, 1948–1949, Correspondence, Memos, Bulletins, Box 1, Folder: Volume XV Publications (A) English (B) German Paul H. Gantt.

123. Fred Niebergall, memorandum for Paul Gantt: "Telephone conversation with Mr. T. Carson in Berlin," 9 June 1949, NARG 238: Office of the Chief of Counsel for War Crimes 1933–1949, Executive Office, Publications Division, Entry 196: Correspondence, Reports and Other Records, 1948–1949, Correspondence, Memos, Bulletins, Box 1, Folder: Volume XV Publications (A) English (B) German Paul H. Gantt; Hays (OMGUS), cable to Department of the Army and Office of Chief of Counsel for War Crimes, 17 June 1949, NARG 238: Office of the Chief of Counsel for War Crimes 1933–1949, Executive Office, Publications Division, Entry 196: Correspondence, Reports and Other Records, 1948–1949, Correspondence, Memos, Bulletins, Box 1, Folder: Volume IX Publication Paul H. Gantt.

124. Taylor, *Final Report*, 106.

125. Gordon Gray, letter to Honorable Emanuel Celler, 31 October 1949, and Major Abraham S. Hyman, acting advisor on Jewish affairs, headquarters, European Command, letter to John J. McCloy: "Publication in German of records of major Nurnberg War Crimes trials," 19 December 1949, NARG 466: Office of the U.S. High Commissioner for Germany Prisons Division, Entry 56: War Criminal Case Files and Related Records, Box 1, Folder: Publication—German Text—Major Nurnberg Trials. The English fifteen-volume edition, called *Trials of War Criminals before the Nuernberg Military Tribunals under Control Council Law No. 10, Nuernberg 1946–April 1949* was published in installments by the Washington, D.C., U.S. Government Printing Office between 1949 and 1953. (It does not appear that it was made available to the occupation staff in Germany, however.) It is commonly referred to as the Green Series because of the books' green covers. A private Buffalo, New York, publisher reissued the series in 1997. No equivalent in German exists.

126. Major Abraham S. Hyman, acting advisor on Jewish affairs, headquarters, European Command, letter to John J. McCloy: "Publication in German of records of major Nurnberg War Crimes trials," 19 December 1949.

127. Frederick G. Hulse, HICOG office memorandum for Eli Whitney Debevoise: "Publication of the Records and Justments [*sic*] made and given in the Trials conducted at Nurenberg under Control Council Law 10," undated but after

22 July 1952. It should be noted that none of the Dachau trial records were pub-lished in German or English. In any case, there was less material to release. Under the army's procedure, a transcript of the testimony was made and the trial ended in a verdict of guilty or not guilty. The verdicts were not supported with any written opinions. See Eli Whitney Debevoise, report: "Summary Background War Crimi-nal Information," 6 September 1952.

128. Jonathan Rintels, letter to Sheperd Stone, 27 February 1951, NARG 466: Office of the U.S. High Commissioner for Germany, Prisons Division, Entry 56: War Criminal Case Files and Related Records, Box 1, Folder: War Crimes (materials from Mr. Hulse).

129. Ibid.

130. Eli Whitney Debevoise, office memorandum for Assistant High Commis-sioner Reber: "Publication of the Records and Judgments made and given in the Trials conducted at Nuremberg under Control Council Law 10," undated but after 22 July 1952. On 6 September 1952, Debevoise wrote: "The end result is that the German press is in a position to work on the ignorance of the population without let or hindrance and without specific reference to any fact, theory or principle, legal, ethical or otherwise." NARG 466: Office of the U.S. High Commissioner for Ger-many, Bonn, Entry 10A: Security-Segregated Records, 1949–1952 (later: 1953–1955), Box 28, Folder: 321.6 German War Criminals—General.

131. Frederick G. Hulse, HICOG office memorandum for Eli Whitney Debevoise: "Publication of the Records and Justments [*sic*] made and given in the Trials conducted at Nurenberg under Control Council Law 10," undated but after 22 July 1952. Emphasis in original.

132. Eli Whitney Debevoise, office memorandum for Assistant High Commis-sioner Reber: "Publication of the Records and Judgments made and given in the Trials conducted at Nuremberg under Control Council Law 10," undated but after 22 July 1952.

133. Samuel Reber, telegram for Secretary of State Kellermann: "Public Affairs Guidance No. 181," 28 July 1952.

134. Francis C. Lindaman, Public Affairs officer, letter to Hans B. Meyer, act-ing chief, Policy Staff, Office of Public Affairs, HICOG, 6 September 1952, NARG 466: Office of the U.S. High Commissioner for Germany, Bonn, Entry 10A: Secu-rity-Segregated Records, 1949–1952 (later: 1953–1955), Box 28, Folder: 321.6 Ger-man War Criminals—General.

135. Ibid.

136. Frederick Hulse, memorandum for Mr. Davies: "Judgment of the United States Military Tribunal V—*U.S. vs. von Leeb et al.* (Case No. 12)," 20 August 1952, NARG 466: Office of the U.S. High Commissioner for Germany, Prisons Division, Entry 56: War Criminal Case Files and Related Records, Box 1, Folder: War Crimes Materials from Mr. Hulse.

137. Frederick G. Hulse, HICOG office memorandum for Eli Whitney Debevoise: "Publication of the Records and Justments [*sic*] made and given in the Trials conducted at Nurenberg under Control Council Law 10," undated but after 22 July 1952.

138. Frederick Hulse, memorandum for Mr. Davies: "Judgment of the United States Military Tribunal V—*U.S. vs. von Leeb et al.* (Case No. 12)," 20 August 1952.

139. Eli Whitney Debevoise, report: "Summary Background War Criminal Information," 6 September 1952.

140. Ibid.

141. Ibid.

142. Acheson added, "We are convinced that material should be used moderately rather than as all-out program, so that if it has poor effect it can be modified or discontinued." Dean Acheson, secretary of state, classified telegram, the Foreign Service of the United States of America, 7 October 1952, NARG 466: Office of the U.S. High Commissioner for Germany Prisons Division, Entry 10A: Security-Segregated Records, 1949–1952 (later: 1953–1955), 321.4–321.6, Box 28, Folder: 321.6 German War Criminals—General.

143. Ibid.

144. Classified telegram, the Foreign Service of the United States of America, 20 October 1952, NARG 466: Office of the U.S. High Commissioner for Germany Prisons Division, Entry 10A: Security-Segregated Records, 1949–1952 (later: 1953–1955), 321.4–321.6, Box 28, Folder: 321.6 German War Criminals—General. In supporting their decision not to issue more trial-related publications, they noted: "good effect produced by pamphlet 'Landsberg—A Documentary Report' which HICOG distributed very widely in early 1951 has practically vanished." See also Confidential-Security Political Brief No. 5: "Political Aspects of the War Criminals Question," which states: "Since few Germans think rationally on the subject of war criminals, this problem cannot be eradicated, or perhaps even treated effectively, by rational arguments. For this reason we do not believe that the problem can be solved in any final sense by a propaganda campaign to give the German public fuller, more complete information on the subject."

145. HICOG Office of Political Affairs, memorandum for the State Department: "The War Criminals Question," 22 December 1952.

146. Donnely, Foreign Service classified telegram for the secretary of state, 12 September 1952, NARG 466: Office of the U.S. High Commissioner for Germany Prisons Division, Entry 10A: Security-Segregated Records, 1949–1952 (later: 1953–1955), 321.4–321.6, Box 28, Folder: 321.6 German War Criminals—General.

147. The following letter was representative of the terms and tone of the ongoing campaign to secure the Landsberger prisoners' release. It was written on 10 November 1953 by August Fischer, mayor of the town of Kempten and president of the Association of Returnees, POWs, and Family Members of Missing Germans,

a group encompassing a half million ex-soldiers and the family members of those who remained in foreign custody as POWs or who were still missing in action. It was mailed to all American congressmen and senators. It read in part (emphasis in original): "As you may have read during the last few days, the Kremlin has started an action of releasing certain groups of German POWs. The Red Spider is a master of psychology and it hopes to gain political prestige by having started some whispering campaign in Chancellor Adenauer's Western Germany: 'Say, don't the Soviets begin to outwit the western Powers by granting clemency?' . . . Again and again we had hoped that the U.S. Government would make a quick and overall decision for the solution of this burning 'war criminals issue' by deciding to grant *amnesty* for all so-called 'war criminals'. . . . We ask you to do all in *your* power to have the U.S. members of the Interim Mixed Parole and Clemency Board consent to the clear principle that those Germans sentenced for *supposed* war crimes, who did not act out of *personal motives* should have the benefit of clemency or of remission of parole. . . . We appeal for the release of *all* German prisoners of war who acted by order or out of the cruel necessities of an extra-ordinary situation in modern warfare [. . .] 'How to win friends for the States? OPEN THE LANDSBERG'S PRISON GATES.'" BAK, B305/55: Zentrale Rechtsschutzstelle, Tätigkeit des Gemischten Ausschußes, insb. für die Landsberger Häftlinge.

148. HICOG Office of Political Affairs and Office of Public Affairs, memorandum for the State Department: "The War Criminals Question," 22 December 1952.

149. The Foreign Service of the United States of America, classified telegram to Harben, HICOG, 19 January 1953, NARG 466: Office of the U.S. High Commissioner for Germany, Bonn, Entry 10A: Security-Segregated Records, 1953–1955, 321.4–321.6, Box 164, Folder: 321.6 War Criminals—General 1953–1955.

150. HICOG Office of Political Affairs, memorandum for the State Department: "The War Criminals Question," 22 December 1952.

151. Ibid.

152. Ibid.

153. Ibid.

CHAPTER SEVEN: SETTING THE WAR CRIMINALS FREE

Epigraph from W. S. Nye, Chief, Army Historical Division, letter to Walter Warlimont, 16 June 1954, NARG 466: Prisons Division, Entry 53: Petitions for Clemency or Parole and Related Records of Persons Convicted by the U.S. Military Tribunal at Nuremberg 1947–1957, Box 39, Folder: Warlimont, Walter.

1. Walter Muller, Interim Mixed Parole and Clemency Board Interim Report, 30 November 1954, NARG 466: Prisons Division, Entry 49: General Records, Box 17, Folder: vol. 1.

2. Edwin A. Plitt, American Embassy, Bonn, Foreign Service dispatch to Department of State, Washington, "History of the Interim Mixed Parole and Clemency Board, with Comments for the Guidance of Future Bodies of Similar Assignment," 15 September 1955, NARG 466: Bonn, Entry 10A: Security-Segregated Records 1953–1955, 321.4–321.6, Box 164, Folder: 321.6 War Criminals—Mixed Board 1953–1955. The British and the French also established interim mixed boards to deal with the war criminals in their custody.

3. James Conant and Charles Bolte, Anordnung betreffend Interimistischer Gemischter Parole- und Gnadenausschuss, 31 August 1953, BAK, B305/53: Zentrale Rechtsschutzstelle, Bereinigung der Kriegsgefangenenproblems 1951–1961, Gemischte deutsche-alliierte Ausschüße zur Überprüfung der Urteile.

4. Plitt, Foreign Service dispatch to Department of State, Washington, "History of the Interim Mixed Parole and Clemency Board."

5. Ibid.

6. HICOG Office of Political Affairs, memorandum: "The War Criminals Question," 22 December 1952, NARG 466: Bonn, Office of the Executive Director General, Entry 10A: Security-Segregated Records, 1949–1952, 321.4–321.6, Box 28, Folder: 321.6 German War Criminals—General.

7. James Conant, U.S. High Commissioner for Germany, Order of Parole and Terms and Conditions of Parole, 1 April 1954, NARG 466: Prisons Division, Entry 54: Administrative and Medical Records of Landsberg Prisoners, Box 5, Folder: Hoth, Hermann, Paroled 7 April 1954.

8. Augsburg Military Post, Office of the Surgeon, Report of Physical Examination of Three War Crimes Prisoners, 30 August 1951, NARG 466: Bonn, Entry 10A: Security-Segregated Records 1953–1955, 321.4–321.6, Box 28, Folder: 321.6 German War Criminals—General; Howard Curtis, Prison Director, to Foreign Service of the United States of America, 18 February 1953, NARG 466: Prisons Division, Entry 53: Petitions for Clemency or Parole and Related Records of Persons Convicted by the U.S. Military Tribunal at Nuremberg 1947–1957, Box 37, Folder: Kuechler, Georg v., 1499 Landsberg.

9. Hans Reinhardt, letter to Colonel Graham re. compassionate leave, Landsberg Prison Director, 25 November 1950; Dr. Oron Hale, memorandum for John McCloy, Subject: Family Situation of Colonel-General A. D. Georg-Hans Reinhardt, 28 March 1952; Edgar Gerlach, memorandum: Hans Reinhardt, Landsberg, 23 May 1952, NARG 466: Prisons Division, Entry 53: Petitions for Clemency or Parole and Related Records of Persons Convicted by the U.S. Military Tribunal at Nuremberg 1947–1957, Box 28, Folder: Reinhardt, Hans, 1524 Landsberg.

10. Bowie, memorandum for King: Medical Parole for Hans von Salmuth, 26 March 1951, NARG 466: Prisons Division, Entry 53: Petitions for Clemency or Parole and Related Records of Persons Convicted by the U.S. Military Tribunal at Nuremberg 1947–1957, Box 38, Folder: von Salmuth, Hans Case No. 12, Folder 3,

Petitions; R. Dolinsky, letter to Hans von Salmuth, 7 August 1953, BMA, MSg1/1202: Militärbiographische-Sammlung, Sammel- und Einzelbiographien zu Personen mit Bezug zu militärhistorischen Ereignissen, von Salmuth.

11. Henri Eschbach, Gottfried Kuhnt, Emil Lersch, A. Michelson, Spencer Phenix, and Hellmuth Weber, "To the Signatories of the Convention on the settlement of matters arising out of the war and the occupation signed at Bonn on 26 May 1952": Final Report of the Mixed Board, 21 October 1958, BAK, B305/56: Zentrale Rechtsschutzstelle, Tätigkeit des Gemischten Ausschusses, insb. (Nr. 55 und 56) für die Landsberger Häftlinge.

12. Eberhard Engelhardt, Rechtsschutz für Generaloberst A. D. Hermann Hoth zur Zeit in Landsberg a. Lech, an die Zentrale Rechtsschutzstelle, 26 October 1953, BMA N503/86—Unterlagung zur Verteidigung Hoths.

13. Statements for James Conant, U.S. High Commissioner in support of Hans Reinecke's application for clemency by Hans Gontard, 20 November 1953; Ellen Conrad, 13 November 1953; Bruno Titschenk, 6 November 1953; A. Westhoff, 11 November 1953; Hans Friede, 6 November 1953; Paul Kropf, 23 November 1953; Hans Sommer, 17 November 1953, NARG 466: Prisons Division, Entry 54: Administrative and Medical Records of Landsberg Prisoners, Box 12, Folder: Reinecke, Hermann, Paroled 1 October 1954.

14. Heinz Assmann, Secretary General of the State Church Office for Community Service (Innere Mission), declaration of parole sponsor, 28 June 1954, NARG 466: Prisons Division, Entry 54: Administrative and Medical Records of Landsberg Prisoners, Box 12, Folder: Reinecke, Hermann Paroled 1 October 1954.

15. Annuity Office Hamburg, certificate of pension, 22 June 1954, NARG 466: Prisons Division, Entry 54: Administrative and Medical Records of Landsberg Prisoners, Box 12, Folder: Reinecke, Hermann Paroled 1 October 1954; Landesversorgungsamt Niedersachsen Pensionabteilung, certificate of pension, 11 December 1953, BAK B305/4523: Zentrale Rechtsschutzstelle, Hermann Hoth.

16. Verband der Heimkehrer, Kriegsgefangenen und Vermissten-Angehörigen, Rundschreiben, 30 October 1953, BAK 305/53: Zentrale Rechtsschutzstelle, Bereinigung des Kriegsgefangenenproblems 1951–1961—Gemischte deutsche-alliierte Ausschüße zur Überprüfung der Urteile.

17. E. C. Moore, Landsberg Prison Director, institutional record, Hermann Hoth, 25 November 1953, NARG 466: Prisons Division, Entry 54: Administrative and Medical Records of Landsberg Prisoners, Box 5, Folder: Hoth, Hermann, Paroled 7 April 1954.

18. E. C. Moore, Landsberg Prison Director, institutional record, Hermann Reinecke, 2 February 1954, NARG 466: Prisons Division, Entry 54: Administrative and Medical Records of Landsberg Prisoners, Box 12, Folder: Reinecke, Hermann, Paroled 1 October 1954.

19. E. C. Moore, Landsberg Prison Director, institutional record, Hermann

Reinecke, 1 August 1954, NARG 466: Prisons Division, Entry 54: Administrative and Medical Records of Landsberg Prisoners, Box 12, Folder: Reinecke, Hermann, Paroled 1 October 1954.

20. E. C. Moore, Landsberg Prison Director, institutional record, Walter Warlimont, 31 October 1953, NARG 466: Prisons Division, Entry 54: Administrative and Medical Records of Landsberg Prisoners, Box 17, Folder Warlimont, Walter, Paroled 9 June 1954; A. C. Smith, Chief, Military History, letter confirming Walter Warlimont's work for the Office of the Chief of Military History, 20 October 1953, NARG 466: Prisons Division, Entry 53: Petitions for Clemency or Parole and Related Records of Persons Convicted by the U.S. Military Tribunal at Nuremberg 1947–1957, Box 39, Folder: HRO 12-4 Warlimont, Walter; Bericht über das Wintersemester 1952/53 der Schule des War Criminal Prison No. 1 Landsberg, 31 March 1953, BAK B305/133: Zentrale Rechtsschutzstelle, Deutsche Kriegsverurteilte in Landsberg Allgemeines und Einzelfälle 1949–1952.

21. E. C. Moore, Landsberg Prison Director, institutional record, Walter Warlimont, 31 October 1953.

22. Conant and Bolte, Anordnung betreffend Interimistischer Gemischter Parole- und Gnadenausschuss, 31 August 1953. The relevant paragraph, which outlines some of the prerequisites for parole, reads: "die durch ihr Verhalten bewiesen haben, dass sie die Straftat oder Straftaten, für die sie verurteilt wurden, *bereuen.*" Emphasis added.

23. E. C. Moore, Landsberg Prison Director, institutional record, Walter Warlimont, 31 October 1953.

24. Application for Clemency for Hermann Reinecke, 1 February 1954, RG 466: Prisons Division, Entry 53: Petitions for Clemency or Parole and Related Records of Persons Convicted by the U.S. Military Tribunal at Nuremberg 1947–1957, Box 27, Folder: HRO 12-3 Reinecke, Hermann; E. C. Moore, Landsberg Prison Director, institutional record, Hermann Reinecke, 1 August 1954.

25. E. C. Moore, Landsberg Prison Director, institutional record, Hermann Hoth, 25 November 1953.

26. Hermann Hoth, summary of interview with Landsberg Director Moore, 30 October 1953, BMA N503/86: Unterlagung zur Verteidigung Hoths.

27. Paul Ralf, Investigation of Housing Conditions, 4 August 1954, NARG 466: Prisons Division, Entry 53: Petitions for Clemency or Parole and Related Records of Persons Convicted by the U.S. Military Tribunal at Nuremberg 1947–1957, Box 27, Folder: Amendment to Parole Order—WC Hermann Reinecke; Paul Gernert, memorandum for Richard Hagan, 21 June 1955, NARG 549: Judge Advocate Division, War Crimes Branch, Entry 2237: Records Relating to Post Trial Activities 1945–1947, Box 6, Folder: U.S. Parole Officer—Summarized Activity Reports and Control Visit Reports September 1954–June 1955; Deforest Barton, memorandum for Richard Hagan: "War Criminal Parolee Hermann Rei-

necke," 4 December 1956, NARG 466: Prisons Division, Entry 53: Petitions for Clemency or Parole and Related Records of Persons Convicted by the U.S. Military Tribunal at Nuremberg 1947–1957, Box 27, Folder (untitled).

28. Paul Gernert, Summarized Parole Report for U.S. Embassy, 12 July 1955, NARG 549: Judge Advocate Division, War Crimes Branch, Entry 2237: Records Relating to Post Trial Activities 1945–1947, Box 6, Folder: U.S. Parole Officer—Summarized Activity Reports and Control Visits September 1954–June 1955.

29. Paul Gernert, United States Parole Officer's Observations, Comments, and Recommendation, 30 November 1955, NARG 466: Prisons Division, Entry 53: Petitions for Clemency or Parole and Related Records of Persons Convicted by the U.S. Military Tribunal at Nuremberg 1947–1957, Box 39, Folder: Warlimont, Walter; Toni Schmidhuber, Monthly Report of the Parolee for Paul Gernert, 6 December 1954, NARG 466: Prisons Division, Entry 53: Petitions for Clemency or Parole and Related Records of Persons Convicted by the U.S. Military Tribunal at Nuremberg 1947–1957, Box 39, Folder: HRO 12-4 Warlimont, Walter; Engelseberger, mayor of Rottach-Egern, statement, 7 October 1955, BAK B305/4516: Zentrale Rechtsschutzstelle, Walter Warlimont; Josef Kronast, Catholic priest of Egern, statement, 7 October 1955, BAK B305/819: Zentrale Rechtsschutzstelle, Walter Warlimont.

30. Edward James, chief, Army Historical Division, statement for Paul Gernert, 30 September 1955, BAK B305/4516: Zentrale Rechtsschutzstelle, Walter Warlimont.

31. Deforest Barton, statement for the chairman of the mixed board, 5 June 1957, BAK B305/4516: Zentrale Rechtsschutzstelle, Walter Warlimont.

32. Plitt, Foreign Service dispatch to Department of State, Washington, "History of the Interim Mixed Parole and Clemency Board."

33. Eschbach et al., "To the Signatories."

34. On the protracted debate surrounding Germany's proposed rearmament and later contribution to the EDC and NATO, see David Clay Large, *Germans to the Front: West German Rearmament in the Adenauer Era* (Chapel Hill: University of North Carolina Press, 1996). For more on the history of Germany's rearmament, see Montecue Lowry, *The Forge of West German Rearmament: Theodor Blank and the Amt Blank* (New York: P. Lang, 1990); Alaric Searle, *Wehrmacht Generals, West German Society, and the Debate on Rearmament, 1949–1959* (Westport, Conn.: Praeger, 2003); James Stefan, *The United States and West German Rearmament, 1947–1950* (Chapel Hill: University of North Carolina Press, 1976); Gerhard Wettig, *Entmilitarisierung und Widerbewaffnung in Deutschland, 1943–1955* (Munich: R. Oldenbourg, 1967).

35. American Embassy, Bonn, Foreign Service dispatch to Department of State, Washington: "War Criminals," 3 August 1955, NARG 466: Bonn, Entry 10A: Security Segregated Records 1953–1955, 321.4–321.6, Box 164, Folder: 321.6 War Criminals—Mixed Board 1953–1955.

36. Ibid.

37. Plitt, Foreign Service dispatch to Department of State, Washington, "History of the Interim Mixed Parole and Clemency Board."

38. Eschbach et al., "To the Signatories."

39. Ibid. The literature on German war criminals in British and French custody is sparse. See Norbert Frei, *Adenauer's Germany and the Nazi Past: The Politics of Amnesty and Integration* (New York: Columbia University Press, 2002), for an overall view. The prisons of Werl and Wittlich are still awaiting their historians. It should be noted that while the mixed board voted on applications for clemency or parole, the continued supervision of the releasees, if stipulated, remained the responsibility of the separate Allied powers.

40. Paul Gernert, U.S. Parole Officer, Statistical Report on Parolees as of 1 February 1956, BAK B305/663: Zentrale Rechtsschutzstelle, Auswärtiges Amt Gnadengesüche (1955–1956).

41. Spencer Phenix, Mr. Phenix's Report to the Mixed Board on 10 April 1957, BAK B305/671: Zentrale Rechtsschutzstelle, Handakten Prof. von Weber 1957–1958.

42. Eschbach et al., "To the Signatories."

43. Frei, *Adenauer's Germany*, 225. On the premature release of war criminals convicted in Allied war crimes courts, see also Donald Bloxham, *Genocide on Trial: War Crimes and the Formation of Holocaust History and Memory* (Oxford: Oxford University Press, 2001); Frank Buscher, *The U.S. War Crimes Trial Program in Germany, 1946–1955* (New York: Greenwood Press, 1989); Hilary Earl, *The Nuremberg Einsatzgruppen Trial, 1945–1958: Atrocity, Law, History* (New York: Cambridge University Press, 2009). In his memoirs, Konrad Adenauer contrasted the "magnanimity" and "generosity" of the British and French toward their war criminals when deciding to grant them early release with the Americans' "slow and hesitant" approach. See Konrad Adenauer, *Memoirs, 1945–1953* (Chicago: Henry Regnery, 1966), 445, 447.

CONCLUSION

Epigraph from Martha Minow, *Between Vengeance and Forgiveness: Facing History after Genocide and Mass Violence* (Boston: Beacon Press, 1998), x.

1. Hannes Heer, "The Difficulty of Ending a War: Reactions to the Exhibition: War of Extermination: Crimes of the Wehrmacht 1941 to 1944," *History Workshop Journal* 46 (1998): 189; Omer Bartov, Atina Grossmann, and Mary Nolan, Introduction to *Crimes of War: Guilt and Denial in the Twentieth Century*, ed. Omer Bartov, Atina Grossman, and Mary Nolan (New York: New Press, 2002), xiv.

2. Omer Bartov, "Professional Soldiers," in *The German Army and Genocide:*

Crimes against War Prisoners, Jews, and Other Civilians, 1939–1944, ed. Hamburg Institute for Social Research (New York: New Press, 1999), 11.

3. On the early literature connecting the Wehrmacht to racial and ideological crimes, see chap. 3, n. 87.

4. Heer, "The Difficulty of Ending a War," 188. Shortly before the exhibition was scheduled to open in New York City in 1999, three academic articles appeared accusing the exhibit organizers of misrepresentation. An independent panel of scholars was appointed to review the documents and photos. They concluded that in some images, the perpetrators belonged to other agencies such as the S.S. and S.D., and that some victims were justifiable targets (e.g., actual partisans). In a very few cases (from eight to eleven), the photographs depicted victims of the Soviet Secret Police who had been killed before the German army's arrival. The exhibition organizers decided to suspend it, and they launched a revised version in 2001. Although opponents attempted to use the controversy to discredit the exhibit entirely, these (albeit regrettable) errors in no way negated the exhibit's main conclusion. The Wehrmacht had been a willing and indispensable partner in planning and executing a war of unprecedented destruction. See Samson Madievski, "The War of Extermination: The Crimes of the Wehrmacht in 1941 to 1944," *Rethinking History* 7, no. 2 (2003): 243–254, and Omer Bartov, "Germany's Unforgettable War: The Twisted Road from Berlin to Moscow and Back," *Diplomatic History* 25, no. 3 (2001): 405–423.

5. Bartov et al., Introduction to *Crimes of War*, x–xiv. Other works on the Wehrmacht exhibition and its reception in Germany and Austria are: Bartov, "Germany's Unforgettable War"; Hannes Heer, ed., *The Discursive Construction of History: Remembering the Wehrmacht's War of Annihilation* (New York: Palgrave Macmillan, 2008); Anke Immenroth, *Die Wehrmacht im Blick der Öffentlichkeit: Analyse zweiter Ausstellungen unter konzeptionellen Gesichtspunkten* (Marburg: Tectum-Verlag, 2004); Walter Manoschek, "Austrian Reaction to the Exhibition 'War of Extermination: Crimes of the Wehrmacht 1941–1944,'" *Contemporary Austrian Studies* 7 (1999): 193–200; Klaus Naumann, "Wenn ein Tabu bricht: Die Wehrmachts-Ausstellung in der Bundesrepublik," *Mittelweg* 36 (1996): 11–24; Bill Niven, *Facing the Nazi Past: United Germany and the Legacy of the Third Reich* (London: Routledge, 2002); Hans-Günther Thiele, ed., *Die Wehrmachtsausstellung: Dokumentation einer Kontroverse: Dokumentation der Fachtagung in Bremen am 26. Februar 1997 und der Bundestagsdebatten am 13. März und 24. April 1997* (Bremen: Edition Temmen, 1997); and Wolfram Wette, *The Wehrmacht: History, Myth, Reality* (Cambridge: Harvard University Press, 2006).

6. Telford Taylor, *Final Report to the Secretary of the Army on the Nuernberg War Crimes Trials under Control Council Law No. 10* (Washington, D.C.: U.S. Government Printing Office, 15 August 1949), 100.

7. Roger Dow, Chief, Reports and Analysis Division, HICOG, report: "West German Reactions to the Landsberg Decisions," 19 March 1951, NARG 466: Bonn, Entry 10A: Security Segregated Records 1953–1955, 321.4–321.6, Box 164, Folder: 321.6 War Criminals—Mixed Board 1953–1955. Emphasis added.

8. Lucius Clay, *Decision in Germany* (Garden City, N.Y.: Doubleday, 1950), 254–255.

9. Mark Osiel, *Mass Atrocity, Collective Memory, and the Law* (New Brunswick, N.J.: Transaction Publishers, 1997), 30.

10. Lawrence Douglas, *The Memory of Judgment: Making Law and History in the Trials of the Holocaust* (New Haven: Yale University Press, 2001), 3.

11. Telford Taylor, "Nuremberg Trials: Synthesis and Projection," *Information Bulletin* 162 (31 May 1949), TLI, John C. Young Papers, Box 78, Folder 1: Publications and Telephone Directories.

12. Lotte Kohler and Hans Saner, eds., *Hannah Arendt–Karl Jaspers Correspondence, 1926–1969* (New York: Harcourt Brace Jovanovich, 1992), 54.

13. Arendt was particularly critical of Israel's exclusive claim to jurisdiction over Eichmann's crimes. She argued that an international tribunal raising the crimes against humanity charge—instead of an Israeli court raising the crimes against the Jewish people charge—would have more accurately reflected Eichmann's offenses. Nonetheless, Eichmann's crimes—acts that "grievously hurt and endangered . . . the international order and mankind in its entirety," served as ultimate justification for the death sentence. Hannah Arendt, *Eichmann in Jerusalem: A Report on the Banality of Evil* (New York: Penguin Books, 1992), 274–279.

14. Yosal Rogat, "The Measures Taken: The Eichmann Trial and the Rule of Law," *Second Coming Magazine* (March 1962): 11.

15. Prosecution Opening Statement, NAMP 898, Roll 1, 88.

16. Lawrence Douglas, "Toward a Jurisprudence of Atrocity" (unpublished paper, 2008), 16.

17. Jean Améry, *At the Mind's Limits: Contemplations by a Survivor of Auschwitz and Its Realities* (Bloomington: Indiana University Press, 1980), 70.

18. Moshe Landau, Benjamin Halevi, Yitzchak Raveh, Judgment, District Court of Jerusalem, Criminal Case No. 40/61, the Accused: Adolf, son of Karl Adolf, Eichmann, http://www.nizkor.org/ftp.py?people/e/eichmann.adolf/transcripts/Judgment/Judgment-006, point 32 (accessed July 2009).

19. Minow, *Between Vengeance and Forgiveness,* 12.

20. Osiel, *Mass Atrocity,* 31.

21. Douglas, "Toward a Jurisprudence of Atrocity," 17.

22. Donald Bloxham, *Genocide on Trial: War Crimes and the Formation of Holocaust History and Memory* (Oxford: Oxford University Press, 2001), 179.

23. Frank Buscher, *The U.S. War Crimes Trial Program in Germany, 1946–1955* (New York: Greenwood Press), 161, and Robert Moeller, "What Has 'Coming to

Terms with the Past' Meant in Post–World War II Germany? From History to Memory to the 'History of Memory,'" *Central European History* 35, no. 2 (2002): 231–232.

24. Bloxham, *Genocide on Trial,* 129–130, and Michael Geyer, "Cold War Angst: The Case of West German Opposition to Rearmament and Nuclear Weapons," in *The Miracle Years: A Cultural History of West Germany, 1949–1968,* ed. Hanna Schissler (Princeton: Princeton University Press, 2001), 384.

25. Office of the U.S. High Commission for Germany, Public Relations Division, "Review of German and Foreign Press Reaction to the Clemency Decisions on Landsberg War Crimes Cases," 10 February 1951, NARG 466: U.S. High Commander, John J. McCloy, Entry 1: Classified General Records, 1949–1952, 1951, no. 1–134, Box 24, Folder: January 1951—D(51)1–D(51)126 War Crimes.

26. W. James Booth, "The Unforgotten: Memories of Justice," *American Political Science Review* 95, no. 4 (December 2001): 778–783.

27. Jeffrey Herf, "The Emergence and Legacies of Divided Memory: Germany and the Holocaust since 1945," in *Memory and Power in Postwar Europe: Studies in the Presence of the Past,* ed. Jan-Werner Müller (Cambridge: Cambridge University Press, 2002), 190–191.

28. Ibid., 203.

29. Richard Evans, *In Hitler's Shadow: West German Historians and the Attempt to Escape from the Nazi Past* (New York: Pantheon Books, 1989), 12.

30. On Germany's domestic investigation and prosecution of Nazi crime, see Dick de Mildt, *In the Name of the People: Perpetrators of Genocide in the Reflection of Their Post-War Prosecution in West Germany—The "Euthanasia" and "Aktion Reinhard" Trial Cases* (The Hague: Martinus Nijhoff Publishers, 1996). De Mildt found that between 1945 and 1992, West German judicial authorities investigated 103,823 citizens for their involvement in Nazi offenses. About 6 percent (6,487 cases) resulted in convictions. Of these, only 1,793 cases (about 15 percent) related to capital crimes committed during the war. Regarding trials related to the Holocaust, the numbers are less impressive still. For the same time period, 755 people were charged for the persecution and killing of Jews. In 283 cases, these trials resulted in acquittals, the dismissal of charges, or no punishment. See de Mildt, *In the Name of the People,* 20–21. Edith Raim makes the argument that despite the limited results, some German prosecutors have pursued the investigation and prosecution of Nazi crime with "stubbornness which demands respect." "Coping with the Nazi Past: Germany and the Legacy of the Third Reich," *Contemporary European History* 12, no. 4 (2003): 559.

31. Susanne Karstedt, "The Nuremberg Tribunal and German Society: International Justice and Local Judgment in Post-Conflict Reconstruction," in *The Legacy of Nuremberg: Civilizing Influence or Institutionalized Vengeance?,* ed. David A. Blumenthal and Timothy L. H. McCormack (Leiden: Martinus Nijhoff Publishers,

2008), 31; Moeller, "What Has 'Coming to Terms,'" 232; and Ian Buruma, *The Wages of Guilt: Memories of War in Germany and Japan* (New York: Meridian, 1994), 19, 142–148.

32. Alf Lüdtke, "'Coming to Terms with the Past': Illusions of Remembering, Ways of Forgetting Nazism in West Germany," *Journal of Modern History* 65 (September 1993): 557.

33. The best-known terrorist group emerging from the 1968 student movement was the Red Army Faction (Rote Armee Fraktion in German; also in its early days referred to by the press as the Baader-Meinhof Gang, after two of its leading members). This group sought to "punish" Germany for the sins of the Nazi period and for what it interpreted as their repetition through the abuse of police powers, and West German support for American activities in Vietnam (which the RAF termed "genocidal"). The RAF equated West German political and judicial authorities with Nazi perpetrators and viewed their rebellion as a sort of vindication, making up for the absence of German armed resistance during the Third Reich. See Jeremy Varon, *Bringing the War Home: The Weather Underground, the Red Army Faction, and Revolutionary Violence in the Sixties and Seventies* (Berkeley: University of California Press, 2004).

34. Evans, *In Hitler's Shadow*, 14.

35. Gary Jonathan Bass, "War Crimes and the Limits of Legalism," *Michigan Law Review* 9, no. 6 (May 1999): 2116.

36. Interim Report for President Harry S. Truman from Justice Robert H. Jackson, 7 June 1945, TLI, Office Files, Box 1007, Folder 325 (1945–1949).

37. Osiel, *Mass Atrocity*, 2.

38. Minow, *Between Vengeance and Forgiveness*, 51.

39. Erin Daly, "Transformative Justice: Charting a Path to Reconciliation," *International Legal Perspectives* 12 (2001–2002): 75.

APPENDIX TWO: GERMAN ARMY FIELD FORMATIONS AND
BASIC COMMAND STRUCTURE

1. Great Britain, War Office, *General Staff, Handbook of the German Army, December 1940* (London: The Imperial War Museum Department of Printed Books, and Nashville: The Battery Press, 1996), 1–3. Absolute accuracy with regard to manpower strength is difficult to attain because figures varied by type of army and type and place of campaign. The figures cited should be considered a guideline.

2. Chief of Counsel for War Crimes, "Military Tribunal Case No. 12 *U.S. vs. Leeb et al.* Basic Information," January 1948, TLI, John C. Young Papers, Box 12, Folder: Case 12 (High Command) Background Data.

APPENDIX THREE: WARTIME POSITIONS OF THE HIGH COMMAND
CASE FIELD COMMANDERS

1. All of the dates regarding the defendants' posts are contained in the indictment, in *Germany (Territory under Allied Occupation, 1945–1955: U.S. Zone), Military Tribunals, Trials of War Criminals before the Nuernberg Military Tribunals under Control Council Law No. 10; Nuernberg, October 1946–April 1949* (Buffalo: William S. Hein, 1997), 10:11–13.

APPENDIX FOUR: THE HIGH COMMAND CASE DEFENDANTS' SENTENCE
EXPIRATION AND PAROLE AND CLEMENCY RELEASE DATES

1. Some original sentence expiration dates changed when prison terms served were backdated to the date of the prisoner's initial incarceration (usually spring–summer 1945).

Bibliography

ARCHIVAL MATERIAL

National Archives and Records Administration, College Park, Maryland

Record Group (RG) 153: Records of the Office of the Judge Advocate General (Army),
War Crimes Branch
Entry 1018: Nuremberg Administrative Files, 1944–1949
File Numbers for Subsequent Proceedings—Zonal Courts:
84: Subsequent Proceedings (Nuremberg)
84-1: Draft and Memo and Set up of Zonal Courts
85: OCC (Taylor) Nuremberg
86-1: Case Preparation
86-1-D: Military
87: Military Tribunals—Nuremberg
89-1: Info Re. Nuremberg Trials

RG 238: National Archives Collection of World War II War Crimes Records Textual
Records of the U.S. Military Tribunals, Nuremberg
— Records of Military Tribunals
Entry 144: Official Records of Military Tribunals I–VI, 1946–1948
Entry 145: Correspondence, Memoranda, Reports and Other Records, 1947–1949
Entry 146: Correspondence and Other Records Relating to the 12 Cases, 1947–1949
Entry 149: Lists of Contents of Military Tribunal Records and the Tribunal Case
    Records ("Overall Index") 1947–1949

RG 238: National Archives Collection of World War II War Crimes Records
— Office of the Chief of Counsel for War Crimes, 1933–1949, Chief of Counsel
Entry 159: General Records
Entry 164: Public Information Office

RG 238: National Archives Collection of World War II War Crimes Records
— Office of the Chief of Counsel for War Crimes, 1933–1949, Executive
    Council Evidence Division, Interrogation Branch
Entry 184: Reports of High Command Interrogations

Entry 186: Administrative Records, Correspondence and Other Records
Entry 187: Correspondence and Lists

RG 238: National Archives Collection of World War II War Crimes Records
— Office of the Chief of Counsel for War Crimes, 1933–1949, Executive Office,
  Publications Division
Entry 196: Correspondence, Reports and other Records, 1948–1949

RG 238: National Archives Collection of World War II War Crimes Records
— Office of the Chief of Counsel for War Crimes, 1933–1949, Executive Office,
  Nuernberg Military Post
Entry 200: Internee Personnel Records ("201 Files") 1945–1948

RG 238: National Archives Collection of World War II War Crimes Records
— Advisory Board on Clemency for War Criminals, Office of the High
  Command for Germany, 1947–1950
Entry 212: Correspondence, Reports, Petitions for Clemency, and Other Records
  Relating to Defendants in Subsequent Proceedings, 1947–1950
Entry 213: Correspondence and Other Records, 1950

RG 238: National Archives Collection of World War II War Crimes Records
— Office of the Chief of Counsel for War Crimes, Evidence Division, Library
Entry 47: Miscellaneous German Newspapers

RG 260: Records of U.S. Occupation Headquarters, World War II (OMGUS)
— Records of the Executive Office, Records of the Adjutant General
Entry 4(A1)/5: Military Government Ordinances and Related Records, 1945–1949
Entry 4(A1)/6: Records Relating to Allied Control Council Laws, 1946–1948
Entry 4(A1)/21: Records Received from the Office of the Political Advisor to
  OMGUS, 1944–1949

RG 260: Records of U.S. Occupation Headquarters, World War II (OMGUS)
— Records of Functional Offices and Divisions, Records of the OCCWC
Entry 8(A1)/1: Administrative Division Records Re. Defendants and Internal
  Administration, 1946–1949
Entry 8(A1)/5: Publication of Proceedings of U.S. Military Tribunals, 1948–1949

RG 260: Records of U.S. Occupation Headquarters, World War II (OMGUS)
— Records of Information Control Division, Records of the Opinion Surveys
  Branch
Entry 16(A1)/9: Records Relating to Public Opinion, 1945–1949

RG 260: Records of U.S. Occupation Headquarters, World War II (OMGUS)
— Records of Information Control Division, Records of the Press Branch
Entry 16(A1)/13: Scrutiny Reports of German Newspapers, 1945–1949

RG 260: Records of U.S. Occupation Headquarters, World War II (OMGUS)
— Records of Information Control Division, Records of Motion Picture Branch
Entry 16(A1)/19: Records Re. Motion Picture Production and Distribution, 1945–1949

RG 260: Records of U.S. Occupation Headquarters, World War II (OMGUS)
— Records of Information Control Division, Records of the Information
Centers and Exhibits Branch
Entry 16(A1)/25: Land Level Reports, 1949

RG 260: Records of U.S. Occupation Headquarters, World War II (OMGUS)
— Records of Educational and Cultural Relations Division, Records of
Education Branch
Entry 38(A1)/6: Records Relating to Policy and Planning
Entry 38(A1)/12: Records Re. Work of Educational Services Section

RG 466: Records of the U.S. High Commission for Germany (HICOG)
— U.S. High Commissioner, John J. McCloy
Entry 1: Classified General Records, 1949–1952

RG 466: Records of the U.S. High Commission for Germany (HICOG)
— Office of the U.S. High Commissioner for Germany, Bonn
Entry 9: General Records, 1949–1952 (later: 1953–1955)
Entry 10A: Security-Segregated Records, 1949–1952 (later: 1953–1955)

RG 466: Records of the U.S. High Commission for Germany (HICOG)
— Office of the U.S. High Commissioner for Germany, Historical Division
Entry 17: Publications Relating to the U.S. Occupation of Germany, 1945–1953

RG 466: Records of the U.S. High Commission for Germany (HICOG)
— Office of the U.S. High Commissioner for Germany, Prisons Division
Entry 48: Security Segregated Records of the Prisons Division
Entry 49: General Records
Entry 50: Inspection Reports
Entry 53: Petitions for Clemency or Parole and Related Records of Persons Con-
victed by the U.S. Military Tribunals at Nuremberg, 1947–1957
Entry 54: Administrative and Medical Records of Landsberg Prisoners
Entry 56: War Criminal Case Files and Related Records

RG 549: Records of U.S. Army Europe
— Judge Advocate Division, War Crimes Branch
Entry 2236: General Administrative Records, 1942–1957
Entry 2237: Records Relating to Post Trial Activities, 1945–1947
Entry 2240: Records Relating to War Criminal Prison No. 1, Landsberg, 1947–1957

Library of Congress Manuscripts Division, Washington, D.C.

Robert Houghwout Jackson Papers

Diamond Law Library, Columbia University Law School, New York, New York

Telford Taylor Papers

Truman Library Institute, Independence, Missouri

Paul C. Aiken Papers
Eben A. Ayers Papers
Eleanor Bontecou Papers
George M. Elsey Papers
Katherine Fite Lincoln Papers
Alvin J. Rockwell Papers
Samuel I. Rosenman Papers
Charles G. Ross Papers
Harry S. Truman Papers
    Confidential File
        Army, Dept. of—War Crimes
        U.S. Chief of Counsel for Prosecution of Axis
    Official File
        85F: (War Crimes) UN Commission
        158: 9-18-45
        325: War Criminals
        325A: U.S. Chief of Prosecution of Axis Criminals
        325B: International Military Tribunal
    President's Personal File
        2585: 3-21-50
        3200: 4-21-47
    President's Secretary's File
        "Blues"—Robert H. Jackson
        General: War Crimes Commission (UN)

General: War Crimes Trials—1945
Subject: Nuremberg War Crimes
Subject: Supreme Court—Robert H. Jackson
Post-Presidential Name File: Robert H. Jackson
John C. Young Papers
Student Research File: The War Crimes Trials at Nuremberg and Tokyo, 1945–1948
Student Research File: U.S. Policy in Occupied Germany

Bundesarchiv, Koblenz

Nachlass: N/1146: Paul Leverkuehn
14: Vorträge, Pressematerial, u.a. von und über Leverkuehn
19: Papiere Leverkuehns aus der Zeit vor, 1945
24: Verschiedenes aus der Arbeit des Bundestages
36: Kriegsfolgenschlussgesetz
56: Literaturangaben und biographischen Notizen
65: Persönliche Papiere
70: Verschiedenes

Alliierte Prozesse 1: Nürnberger Kriesverbrecherprozesse
Verhandlungsakten, Fall 12
Verhandlungsakten, Fall 7–12

Alliierte Prozesse 3: Behling
61: Angeklagter Georg von Kuechler
62: Angeklagter Georg von Kuechler
63: Angeklagter Georg von Kuechler
64: Angeklagter Georg von Kuechler
65: Angeklagter Georg von Kuechler
66: Angeklagter Georg von Kuechler "Generalien der Verteidigung"
67–74: Untitled

Alliierte Prozesse 3: Gollnick
4: Manuskripte und Notizen des Rechtsanwaltes Kurt Gollnick zu Vorträgen über
   die Nürnberger Prozesses, o. Dat.
7: Presseartikel zu den Nürnberger Prozessen, 1948
12: Handakten zum OKW-Prozess (Fall 12), 1948

Alliierte Prozesse 3: Leverkuehn
1: Material betr. General Warlimont

Alliierte Prozesse 21: Prozesse gegen Deutsche im europäischen Ausland
196–198: Behling

B305: Zentrale Rechtsschutzstelle
1–10: Allgemeines Bände 1–3, 1950–1962
11–12: Rechtsschutz für deutsche Kriegsgefangene, 1948–1962
19–20: Dokumentation der Kriegsverbrechen deutscher Soldaten, 1949–1961
30: Nürnberger Prozesse, 1949–1963
48–49: Kriegsverbrecherprobleme—Allgemeines, 1950–1963
51: Bereinigung der Kriegsverbrecherfrage—Kommission und Ausschüße zur Überprüfung der Urteile, 1952–1953
53–54: Bereinigung der Kriegsgefangenenprobleme, 1951–1961—Gemischte deutsche-alliierte Ausschüße zur Überprüfung der Urteile
55–57: Tätigkeit des Gemischten Ausschußes, insb. für die Landsberger Häftlinge
63: Rechtshilfe für Kriegsverurteilte—Schriftverkehr mit Bundestagsab geordneten, 1960–65
65: Anerkennung entlassener Kreigsverurteilter als Spätheimkehrer Allgemeines, 1955–56
66–71: Begnadigung deutscher Kriegsgefangener betr. Tätigkeit der Gemischten Ausschüße, 1953–1958
78: Presse und Informationsmaterial, 1953–1956
87: Schutz von verurteilten Kriegsgefangenen (re. Genfer Convention)
93–105: Kriegsgefangenenfrage—Allgemeines, 1950–52
131–142: Deutsche Kriegsverurteilte in Landsberg—Allgemeines und Einzelfälle, 1949–1952
143–149: Einzelfälle, 1949–1952
547–549: Betr. Rechtsschutztätigkeit des Deutsche Rote Kreuz—Allgemeines, 1952–1957
652–660: Paroleüberwachung der entlassenen deutschen Kriegsgefangenen, 1953–1957
661: U.S.–Paroleverfahren—Gnadengesuche und Entlassugsanträge des Auswärtigen Amts, 1953–1957
662–665: Allg. und Einzelfälle, 1955–1957
671: Handakten Prof von Weber, 1957–1958
724: Betreuung von Kriegsverurteilten—Einzelfälle: Hermann Hoth
774: Betreuung von Kriegsverurteilten—Einzelfälle: Hermann Reinecke
819: Betreuung von Kriegsverurteilten—Einzelfälle: Walter Warlimont
845–846: Begnadigung von Kriegsverurteilten—Sitzungen des Gemischten Ausschußes: 27 Mai 1957
847: Begnadigung von Kriegsverurteilten—Sitzungen des Gemischten Ausschußes: 27 Juni 1957

848: Begnadigung von Kriegsverurteilten—Sitzungen des Gemischten Ausschußes:
28 Juni 1957
849–851: Begnadigung von Kriegsverurteilten—Sitzungen des Gemischten Ausschußes: 26 Juli 1957
2685: Georg von Kuechler
4516: Walter Warlimont
4523: Hermann Hoth
4548: Hans Reinhardt
4550: Hermann Reinecke
4551: Rudolf Lehmann
4775: Otto Woehler
6771: Hans von Salmuth
14567: Rudolf Lehmann

Bundesmilitärarchiv, Freiburg im Breisgau

Nachlässe
— N 145: Wilhelm von Leeb
6: Dipl. Kfm Hermann Leeb: Materialien zur Lebensgeschichte von Wilhelm Ritter von Leeb (1876–1956)—1960
— N 152: Karl von Roques
5: Amerikanischer Militärgerichtshof V in Nürnberg: Prozeßunterlagen des Gen.d.
Inf. A.D. Karl von Roques: Überwiegend Abschriften (5.8.1936–28.11.1951)
— N 184: Georg von Kuechler
9: Am. M-g. Ng. Fall 12
— N 245: Hans Reinhardt
2: Auszugsweise Abschriften von Briefen des Generals an seine Frau (1939–January
1945)
3: Persönliches Kriegstagebuch (17.6.1941–Ende 1945)
15: OB der H. Gru. Mitte
22: Aufzeichnungen in der Kriegsgefangenschaft
28: Aufstand im Warschauer Ghetto, 1944
29: Persönliche Aufzeichnungen und Korrespondenz zum Nürnberger Prozeß (Fall
12), 1948–49
30: Unterlagen aus der Haftzeit in Landsberg / Lech und zum Spruchkammerverfahren, 1950–53
31: Stellungnahme zu Publikationen und zu militärischen Fragen, Korrespondenz
u.a. mit GM v. Manstein und General Hans Speidel, 1951–1961
38: Erklärung Reinhardt für den amerikanischen Clemency Board (Abschrift) 1950
39: Erinnerungen
41: "Erlebnisbericht über meine Kriegsgefangenschaft, 1945–1952" (1963)

53: Besprechung mit Bundeskanzler Adenauer über die als Kriegsverbrecher verurteilter Soldaten (1952)

55: Generalleutnant a.D. Otto Heidkämper: "An den Freundes- und Bekanntenkreis des Generaloberst Reinhardt" (1949)

62: "Wiedervereinigung und Wiederbewaffnung—kein Gegensatz" (1955)

67: Korrespondenz: Bd. 4: General Hans Speidel (1960)

72: Zehnjährigen Bestehen der GfW—Ansprache aus Jubiläumsfeier des Vorstands, Grußwort des Generalinspektors Foertsch "Grundlinien für die Arbeit der GfW" (1962)

73: Aufzeichnung über eine Besprechung mit dem Verteidigungsminister und den Generalinspektor über Kernfragen der GfW (o. Dat.)

— N 356: Hermann Reinecke

4: "Gutachterliche Äusserung" zur definition des Berufssoldatenbegriffs in der ehemaligen Wehrmacht im Sinne des Wehrgesetzes vom 21. Mai 1935 (21.8.1973)

5: Stellungnahme zu den Buch von Manfred Messerschmidt "Die Wehrmacht im NS-Staat"

6: Desgl. (Zusammengefaßte und gekürzte Klarschrift Reineckes), Sept. 1976

7: Persönliche Erlebnisse vom Ende des Ersten bis zum Ende des Zweites Weltkriegs—1966

— N 431: Hans Laternser

28: "Eidestattliche Erklärung" 17.1.47

29: Zeitungsauschnitte

35: Gedanken zur Frage der West-deutschen Wiederaufrüstung

175: Warlimont-Dossier (vermischte Dokumente) u.a. "Persilscheine" (Entlassungsdokuments der Kirchen) für Warlimont

186: Stellungnahmen Warlimonts zur Judenvernichtung, zur Erklärungen Jodls und Keitels, Dokumentkopien zu Einsatzgruppen

221: Verschiedene Schriftstücke

222: Allgemeine Korrespondenz während des OKW-Prozeßes in Nürnberg 1948

293: Zeitungsausschnitte zum Nürnberger Prozeß IMT und OKW

466: Artikelabschrift aus der "Times" vom 2 und 3.11.1948 "das deutsche Offizierkorps"

490: Fall 12 (OKW-Prozeß): Persönliche Aufzeichnungen FM Ritter von Leeb

492: Die Schuld der Generale von Dr. Velte, Verteidiger von FM Keitel (1947)

619: Intern Schriftwechsel zwischen Rechtsanwälten zu allgemeinen und organisatorischen Fragen (Prozeßführung)

649: Fall 12: Schriftwechsel intern Laternser und von Leeb

926–930: Korrespondenz Laternser für FM von Leeb (Fall 12) (1948)

978: Spruchkammerverfahren und Fragebogen gegen Hans Laternser (1948)

979: Schriftwechsel Laternser zu seinem eigenen Spruchkammerverfahren—mit Dokumenten von 1939 (1947–1948)

1002: Dossier über das Verhalten alliierter Soldaten nach, 1945
1887–1888, 2022, 2024, 2027–2028, 2030–2033, 2036, 2044, 2054, 2080–2083,
   2085–2091, 2094–2095, 2097–2112, 2115, 2119–2120, 2123–2124, 2126, 2143–
   2144, 2151, 2118–2219, 2250: Newspaper articles on various war crimes trials
— N 503: Hermann Hoth
21: Gedenken zur Wiederbewaffnung
66: Schriftwechsel u.a. von Lola Hoth während der Inhaftierung ihres Mannes im
   Landsberg/Lech (1950–54)
72: Stellungnahme zum Nationalsozialismus
82: Die Schuldfrage der Generale und der Begriff des Militarismus
83: Abschriften aus Zeitungsausschnitten zu den Themen "Nürnberger Prozesse,"
   "Atomwaffe," "Deutschlands Situation" (1948–1949)
86: Unterlagung zur Verteidigung Hoths
90: Vorträge auf der Soldatentagung in der Evangelische Akademie—Bad Boll 94:
   Vom 6–9.12.51
94: "Wer nimmt meine Verantwortung ab?" Ein Wort zur Schuldfrage
— N 569: Otto Woehler
1–7: Untitled
— MSG1: Militärbiographische-Sammlung, Sammel- und Einzelbiographien
   zu Personen mit Bezug zu militärhistorischen Ereignissen
53: Kommentar Warlimonts zum Nürnberger Dokument NOKW-65; Bericht des
   ehemaligen Stellvertretenden Chefs des Wehrmachtführungsstabes, General
   der Artillerie Walter Warlimont über den Rußland-Feldzug
202: Gustav Marteneck
220: P. E. Schramm 774: Aufzeichnungen und Unterlagen zum Nürnberger Prozess,
   Fall XII
712: Dr. E. von Wallenberg
775: Zeitungsauschnitte über Blaskowitz
848: Manstein, Erich von, Generalfeldmarschall: Glückwunschschreiben des Gen-
   eralfeldmarschalls von Leeb
1202: Korrespondenz von Salmuth mit R. Dohnisky, v.a. zur Zeit seiner Inhaftierung
1378: Trauerfeier für den Generalobersten Johannes Blaskowitz (+ Febr. 1948)
1584: Prozess gegen Gen.-Oberst Reinhardt, Schriftwechsel mit Rechtsanwalt Dr.
   F. Frohwein
1814: Generaloberst Johannes Blaskowitz—Korrespondenz von Hans Gies mit
   Kameraden und Anna Blaskowitz, Zeitungsausschnitte, Ausarbeitungen
2013: Westhoff, Adolf, Generalmajor
2404: Unterlagen von und über Generalleutnant Paul von Hase
2435: Auszug aus der Anklageschrift von Leeb und andere, hier gegen Generaloberst
   Blaskowitz (Umdruck mit handschriftlichen Randnotizen von Blaskowitz)
2993: Kommentar zu Führerlagebesprechungen

3151: Schriftwechsel, u.a. zur Veröffentlichung "Der Feldzug gegen Sowjetrußland, 1941–1945," von Alfred Philippi und Heim
3331: Johannes Blaskowitz; Hermann Hoth; Georg von Kuechler; Wilhelm von Leeb; Hugo Sperrle

Institut für Zeitgeschichte, Munich

ED 1: Leeb, Wilhelm von, GFM
ED 84: Lehmann, Dr. Rudolf Chef Wehrmachtsrechtswesen i. OKW
ED 106: Behling, Kurt
ED 418/1–6: Lehmann, Rudolf
F 125: Warlimont, Walter, Gen.
Fb 93/7: Warlimont, Walter, Gen.
Fd 48/2 und Fd 48/24: Küchler, Georg v.
Fh 53: Küchler, Georg v., GFM
G 47: Frohwein, Friedr., Dr.
MS 669: Behling, Kurt
ZS 72: Hollidt, Karl, Gen. Obst.
ZS 91: Küchler, Georg v.
ZS 93: Leeb, Wilhelm v., GFM
ZS 312/1–3: Warlimont, Walter, Gen.
ZS 339: Schniewind, Otto, Gen. Adm.
ZS 677/1–2: Lehmann, Rudolf. Gen. Obst. Richter
ZS 1344/1–3: Reinecke, Hermann, Ged. D. Inf.
ZS 1345: Reinhardt, Georg-Hans (GO)
ZS 1532: Sperrle, Hugo, Gen. FM
ZS 1681: Wöhler, Otto, Gen. d. Inf. A.D.
ZS 2029: Blaskowitz, Johann (GO)
ZS 2254: Salmuth, Liselotte v.
ZS 3123: Laternser, [Hans] Dr.
ZS A/31: Salmuth, Liselotte v.

INTERVIEW

Johann-Georg Schätzler: former defense attorney at the International Military Tribunal at Nuremberg, at Wachtberg, Germany, 23 July 2002

PUBLISHED MATERIAL

Adenauer, Konrad. *Memoirs, 1945–1953.* Chicago: Henry Regnery, 1966.

Améry, Jean. *At the Mind's Limits: Contemplations by a Survivor of Auschwitz and Its Realities.* Bloomington: Indiana University Press, 1980.

Angrick, Andrej. *Besatzungspolitik und Massenmord. Die Einsatzgruppe D in der südlichen Sowjetunion, 1941–1943.* Hamburg: Hamburger Edition, 2003.

Appleman, John. *Military Tribunals and International Crime.* Westport, Conn.: Greenwood Press, 1971.

Arad, Yitzhak. "The Holocaust of Soviet Jewry in the Occupied Territories of the Soviet Union." *Yad Vashem Studies* 21 (1991): 1–47.

Arbeitskreis für Wehrforschung, ed. *Kriegstagebuch: Tägliche Aufzeichnungen des Chefs des Generalstabes des Heeres, 1939–1942.* 3 vols. Stuttgart: W. Kohlhammer, 1962–1964.

Arendt, Hannah. *Eichmann in Jerusalem: A Report on the Banality of Evil.* London: Penguin Books, 1994.

Aschenauer, Rudolf. *Landsberg: Ein dokumentarischer Bericht von deutscher Seite.* Munich: Arbeitsgemeinschaft für Recht und Wirtschaft, 1951.

———. *Zur Frage einer Revision der Kriegsverbrecherprozesse.* Nuremberg: R. Aschenauer, 1949.

Augstein, Rudolf. *"Historikerstreit." Die Dokumentation der Kontroverse um die Einzigartigkeit der nationalsozialistischen Judenvernichtung.* Munich: R. Piper, 1987.

Baldwin, Peter, ed. *Reworking the Past: Hitler, the Holocaust and the Historians' Debate.* Boston: Beacon Press, 1990.

Bark, Dennis, and David Gress. *A History of West Germany,* vol. 1, *From Shadow to Substance, 1945–1963.* New York: Basil Blackwell, 1989.

Bartov, Omer. *The Eastern Front, 1941–45: German Troops and the Barbarisation of Warfare.* Oxford: Macmillan, 1985.

———. "German Soldiers and the Holocaust: Historiography, Research and Implications." *History and Memory* 9, no. 1/2 (Fall 1997): 162–188.

———. "Germany's Unforgettable War: The Twisted Road from Berlin to Moscow and Back." *Diplomatic History* 25, no. 3 (2001): 405–423.

———. *Germany's War and the Holocaust: Disputed Histories.* Ithaca, N.Y.: Cornell University Press, 2003.

———. *Hitler's Army: Soldiers, Nazis, and War in the Third Reich.* New York: Oxford University Press, 1992.

———. *Mirrors of Destruction: War, Genocide and Modern Identity.* New York: Oxford University Press, 2000.

———. "The Myths of the Wehrmacht." *History Today* 42 (1992): 30–36.

———. "Operation Barbarossa and the Origins of the Final Solution." In *The Final Solution: Origins and Implementation,* edited by David Cesarani, 119–136. New York: Routledge, 1994.

———. "Professional Soldiers." In *The German Army and Genocide: Crimes against*

War Prisoners, Jews and Other Civilians in the East, 1939–1944, edited by the Hamburg Institute for Social Research, 11–17. New York: New Press, 1999.

Bartov, Omer, Atina Grossman, and Mary Nolan, eds. *Crimes of War: Guilt and Denial in the Twentieth Century.* New York: New Press, 2002.

Bass, Gary Jonathan. *Stay the Hand of Vengeance: The Politics of War Crimes Tribunals.* Princeton: Princeton University Press, 2000.

———. "War Crimes and the Limits of Legalism." *Michigan Law Review* 97, no. 6 (1999): 2103–2116.

Bassett, Richard. *Hitler's Spy Chief: The Wilhelm Canaris Mystery.* London: Weidenfeld & Nicolson, 2005.

Bassiouni, Cherif. "Nuremberg Forty Years After: An Introduction." *Case Western Reserve Journal of International Law* 18 (1986): 261–266.

Battini, Michele. "Sins of Memory: Reflections on the Lack of an Italian Nuremberg and the Administration of International Justice after 1945." *Journal of Modern Italian Studies* 9, no. 3 (2004): 349–362.

Benton, Wilbourn, and Georg Grimm, eds. *Nuremberg: German Views of the War Trials.* Dallas: Southern Methodist University Press, 1955.

Bergen, Doris. *War and Genocide: A Concise History of the Holocaust.* Lanham, Md.: Rowman & Littlefield, 2003.

Berghahn, Volker. "NSDAP und 'Geistige Führung' der Wehrmacht." *Vierteljahrshefte für Zeitgeschichte* 17 (1969): 17–21.

Berkhoff, Karel. *Harvest of Despair: Life and Death in Ukraine under Nazi Rule.* Cambridge: Harvard University Press, 2004.

Biddiss, Michael. "'Victors' Justice'? The Nuremberg Tribunal." *History Today* 49 (October 1993): 40–46.

Biddle, Francis. *In Brief Authority.* Westport, Conn.: Greenwood Press, 1976.

Biess, Frank. *Homecomings: Returning POWs and the Legacy of Defeat in Postwar Germany.* Princeton: Princeton University Press, 2006.

Bird, Kai. *The Chairman: John J. McCloy—The Making of the American Establishment.* New York: Simon & Schuster, 1992.

———. "Die Strafverfolgung nationalsozialistischer Verbrechen." In *Ende des Dritten Reiches—Ende des Zweiten Weltkriegs: Eine perspektivische Rückschau,* edited by Hans-Erich Volkmann. Munich: Piper, 1995.

Birn, Ruth Bettina. "War Crimes Prosecution: An Exercise in Justice? A Lesson in History?" In *Lessons and Legacies,* vol. 4, *Reflections on Religion, Justice, Sexuality, and Genocide,* edited by Larry Thompson, 101–127. Evanston, Ill.: Northwestern University Press, 2003.

Bloxham, Donald. *Genocide on Trial: War Crimes Trials and the Formation of Holocaust History and Memory.* Oxford: Oxford University Press, 2001.

———. "Punishing German Soldiers during the Cold War: The Case of Erich von Manstein." *Patterns of Prejudice* 33, no. 4 (1999): 25–45.

Blum, John Morton, ed. *From the Morgenthau Diaries,* vol. 3, *Years of War, 1941–1945.* Boston: Houghton Mifflin, 1967.

Blumenthal, David A., and Timothy L. H. McCormack, eds. *The Legacy of Nuremberg: Civilising Influence or Institutionalised Vengeance?* Boston: Martinus Nijhoff, 2008.

Boll, Bernd. "Wehrmacht vor Gericht: Kreigsverbrecherprozesse der vier Mächte nach 1945." *Geschichte und Gesellschaft* 24 (1998): 570–594.

Booth, W. James. "The Unforgotten: Memories of Justice." *American Political Science Review* 95, no. 4 (December 2001): 777–791.

Bosch, William. *Judgment on Nuremberg: American Attitudes toward the Major German War-Crimes Trials.* Chapel Hill: University of North Carolina Press, 1970.

Bower, Tom. *Blind Eye to Murder: Britain, America and the Purging of Nazi Germany—A Pledge Betrayed.* London: Granada, 1983.

Breyer, Stephen. "Crimes against Humanity: Nuremberg." *New York University Law Review* 71 (1996): 1161–1164.

Briggs, G. Scott. "John Carlton Young, Sr." In "Six of the Greatest: A Tribute to Outstanding Lawyers in Colorado History," *Colorado Lawyer* 23, no. 7 (July 1994): 1497–1498.

Brochhagen, Ulrich. *Nach Nürnberg: Vergangenheitsbewältigung und Westintegration in der Ära Adenauer.* Hamburg: Junius, 1994.

Broszat, Martin. *Nach Hitler: Der schwierige Umgang mit unserer Geschichte.* Munich: R. Oldenbourg, 1988.

Broszat, Martin, and Saul Friedländer. "A Controversy about the Historicization of National Socialism." *Yad Vashem Studies* 19 (1988): 310–324.

Brown-Fleming, Suzanne. *The Holocaust and Catholic Conscience: Cardinal Aloisius Muench and the Guilt Question in Germany.* Notre Dame: University of Notre Dame Press, 2006.

Browning, Christopher. "Wehrmacht Reprisal Policy and the Mass Murder of Jews in Serbia." *Militärgeschchtliche Mitteilungen* 1 (1983): 31–47.

Browning, Christopher, with contributions by Jürgen Matthäus. *The Origins of the Final Solution.* Lincoln: University of Nebraska Press, 2004.

Buchheim, Hans, Martin Broszat, Hans-Adolf Jacobsen, and Helmut Krausnick, eds. *Anatomie des S.S.-Staates: Gutachten des Instituts für Zeitgeschichte.* 2 vols. Munich: Deutscher Taschenbuch Verlag, 1965.

Burdick, Charles, and Hans-Adolf Jacobsen, eds. *The Halder War Diary, 1939–1942.* Novato, Calif.: Presidio Press, 1988.

Burleigh, Michael, ed. *Confronting the Nazi Past: New Debates on Modern German History.* London: Collins & Brown, 1996.

Buruma, Ian. *The Wages of Guilt: Memories of War in Germany and Japan.* New York: Meridian, 1994.

Buscher, Frank. "The U.S. High Commission and German Nationalism, 1949–1952." *Central European History* 23 (1990): 57–75.

————. *The U.S. War Crimes Trial Program in Germany, 1946–1955.* New York: Greenwood Press, 1989.

Bush, Jonathan. "Telford Taylor Bibliography." *Columbia Journal of Transitional Law* 37 (1999): 1015.

————. "Telford Taylor: The Voice of Conscience." *American Lawyer* (December 1999): 119.

Buxton, David. "To What Extent Was the Failure of Denazification in Germany 1945–48 a Result of Apathy of the Allies?" *Historian* 78 (Summer 2003): 18–21.

Calvocoressi, Peter. *Nuremberg: The Facts, the Law and the Consequences.* London: Chatto and Windus, 1948.

Clay, Lucius. *Decision in Germany.* Garden City, N.Y.: Doubleday, 1950.

Conot, Robert. *Justice at Nuremberg.* New York: Harper & Row, 1983.

Cooper, Belinda, ed. *War Crimes: The Legacy of Nuremberg.* New York: TV Books, 1998.

Dallin, Alexander. *German Rule in Russia, 1941–1945: A Study in Occupation Policies.* London: Macmillan, 1981.

Daly, Erin. "Transformative Justice: Charting a Path to Reconciliation." *International Legal Perspectives* 12 (2001–2002): 73–183.

Deak, Istvan, Jan Gross, and Tony Judt, eds. *The Politics of Retribution in Europe: World War II and Its Aftermath.* Princeton: Princeton University Press, 2000.

de Mildt, Dick. *In the Name of the People: Perpetrators of Genocide in the Reflection of Their Post-War Prosecution in West Germany—The "Euthanasia" and "Aktion Reinhard" Trial Cases.* The Hague: Martinus Nijhoff, 1996.

Diefendorf, Jeffry, ed. *Lessons and Legacies,* vol. 6, *New Currents in Holocaust Research.* Evanston, Ill.: Northwestern University Press, 2004.

Diefendorf, Jeffry, Axel Frohn, and Hermann-Josef Rupiepier, eds. *American Policy and the Reconstruction of West Germany.* New York: Cambridge University Press, 1993.

Diehl, James. *The Thanks of the Fatherland: German Veterans after the Second World War.* Chapel Hill: University of Chapel Hill Press, 1993.

Diner, Dan, ed. *Ist der Nationalsozialismus Geschichte? Zur Historisierung und Historikerstreit.* Frankfurt am Main: Fischer Taschenbuch Verlag, 1987.

Dinstein, Yoram. *The Defense of "Obedience to Superior Orders" in International Law.* Leyden: A. W. Sijthoff, 1965.

————. "The Distinctions between War Crimes and Crimes against Peace." *Israel Yearbook on Human Rights* 24 (1995): 1–17.

Dinstein, Yoram, and Mala Tabory, eds. *War Crimes in International Law.* The Hague: Martinus Nijhoff, 1996.

Douglas, Lawrence. *The Memory of Judgment: Making Law and History in the Trials of the Holocaust.* New Haven: Yale University Press, 2001.

————. "The Shrunken Head of Buchenwald: Icons of Atrocity at Nuremberg." *Representations* 63 (Summer 1998): 39–64.

————. "Toward a Jurisprudence of Atrocity." Unpublished paper, 2008.

Earl, Hilary. *The Nuremberg SS-Einsatzgruppen Trial, 1945–1958: Atrocity, Law, History.* New York: Cambridge University Press, 2009.

————. "Scales of Justice: History, Testimony, and the Einsatzgruppen Trial at Nuremberg." In *Lessons and Legacies,* vol. 6, *New Currents in Holocaust Research,* edited by Jeffry Diefendorf, 325–351. Evanston, Ill.: Northwestern University Press, 2004.

Echternkamp, Jörg. "At War, Abroad and at Home: The Essential Features of German Society in the Second World War." In *Germany and the Second World War,* vol. 9:1, *German Wartime Society, 1939–1945: Politicization, Disintegration and the Struggle for Survival,* edited by Jörg Echternkamp. Oxford: Clarendon Press, 2008.

Eisenhower, Dwight. *Crusade in Europe.* New York: Doubleday, 1948.

Eser, Albin. "Defenses in War Crimes Trials." In *War Crimes in International Law,* edited by Yoram Dinstein and Mala Tabory, 251–273. The Hague: Martinus Nijhoff, 1996.

Evans, Richard. *In Hitler's Shadow: West German Historians and the Attempt to Escape from the Nazi Past.* New York: Pantheon Books, 1989.

Falk, Richard. "Telford Taylor and the Legacy of Nuremberg." *Columbia Journal of Transitional Law* 37, no. 3 (1997): 693–723.

Ferencz, Benjamin. "Nuremberg Trial Procedure and the Rights of the Accused." *Journal of Criminal Law and Criminology of Northwestern University* 39, no. 2 (August 1948): 145–151.

FitzGibbon, Constantine. *Denazification.* London: Michael Joseph, 1969.

Förster, Jürgen. *Der Angriff nach der Sowjetunion.* Frankfurt: Fischer, 1991.

————. "Complicity or Entanglement? Wehrmacht, War and Holocaust." In *The Holocaust and History: The Known, the Unknown, the Disputed and the Reexamined,* edited by Michael Berenbaum and Abraham Peck, 226–283. Bloomington: Indiana University Press, 1998.

————. "The German Army and the Ideological War against the Soviet Union." In *The Policies of Genocide: Jews and Soviet Prisoners of War in Nazi Germany,* edited by Gerhard Hirschfeld, 15–29. Boston: Allen & Unwin, 1986.

————. "Ideological Warfare in Germany, 1919–1945." In Militärgeschichtliches Forschungsamt, *Germany and the Second World War,* vol. 9:1, *German Wartime Society, 1939–1945: Politicization, Disintegration and the Struggle for Survival,* edited by Jörg Echternkamp. Oxford: Clarendon Press, 2008.

————. "The Wehrmacht and the War of Extermination against the Soviet Union." *Yad Vashem Studies* 14 (1981): 7–34.

————. "Wehrmacht, Krieg und Holocaust." In *Die Wehrmacht: Mythos und Realität,* edited by Rolf-Dieter Müller and Hans-Erich Volkmann, 948–963. Munich: R. Oldenbourg, 1999.

Frei, Norbert. *Adenauer's Germany and the Nazi Past: The Politics of Amnesty and Integration.* New York: Columbia University Press, 2002.

————. *1945 und wir: Das Dritte Reich im Bewusstsein der Deutschen.* Munich: C. H. Beck, 2005.

————. "'Vergangenheitsbewältigung' or 'Renazification'? The American Perspective on Germany's Confrontation with the Nazi Past in the Early Years of the Adenauer Era." In *America and the Shaping of German Society, 1945–1955,* edited by Michael Ermarth, 47–59. Providence: Berg Publishers, 1993.

Frei, Norbert, Dirk van Laak, and Michael Stolleis, eds. *Geschichte vor Gericht: Historiker, Richter und die Suche nach Gerechtigkeit.* Munich: C. H. Beck, 2000.

Friedrich, Jörg. *Das Gesetz des Krieges: Das deutsche Heer in Russland, 1941 bis 1945: Der Prozess gegen das Oberkommando der Wehrmacht.* Munich: Piper, 1993.

————. *Die kalte Amnestie: NS-Täter in der Bundesrepublik.* Frankfurt: Fischer Taschenbuch Verlag, 1984.

————. "Nuremberg and the Germans." In *War Crimes: The Legacy of Nuremberg,* edited by Belinda Cooper, 87–106. New York: TV Books, 1998.

Fritz, Stephen. *Frontsoldaten: The German Soldier in World War II.* Lexington: University Press of Kentucky, 1997.

————. "'We are trying . . . to change the face of the world': Ideology and Motivation in the Wehrmacht on the Eastern Front—The View from Below." *Journal of Military History* 60 (1996): 683–710.

Fritzsche, Hans. *The Sword in the Scales.* London: Allan Wingate, 1953.

Fursdon, Edward. *The European Defence Community: A History.* New York: St. Martin's Press, 1980.

Gerhardt, Eugene. *America's Advocate: Robert H. Jackson.* Indianapolis: Bobbs-Merrill, 1958.

Germany (Territory under Allied Occupation, 1945–1955: U.S. Zone), Military Tribunal V. *Fall 12: Das Urteil gegen das Oberkommando der Wehrmacht: Gefällt am 28 Oktober in Nürnberg vom Militärgerichtshof V der Vereinigten Staaten von Amerika.* Berlin: Rütten & Loening, 1960.

Germany (Territory under Allied Occupation, 1945–1955: U.S. Zone), Military Tribunals. *Trials of War Criminals before the Nuernberg Military Tribunals under Control Council Law No. 10: Nuernberg, October 1946–April 1949.* 15 vols. Buffalo: William S. Hein, 1997.

Geyer, Michael. "Cold War Angst: The Case of West German Opposition to Rearmament and Nuclear Weapons." In *The Miracle Years: A Cultural History of West Germany, 1949–1968,* edited by Hanna Schissler, 376–408. Princeton: Princeton University Press, 2001.

Giles, Geoffrey, ed. *Stunde Null: The End and the Beginning Fifty Years Ago.* Washington, D.C.: German Historical Institute, 1997.

Gimbel, John. *The American Occupation of Germany, 1945–1949.* Stanford: Stanford University Press, 1968.

Ginsburgs, George, and V. N. Kudiavtsev, eds. *The Nuremberg Trial and International Law.* Dordrecht: Martinus Nijhoff, 1990.

Giziowski, Richard. *The Enigma of General Blaskowitz.* New York: Hippocrene Books, 1997.

Goda, Norm. "Black Marks: Hitler's Bribery of His Senior Officers during World War II." *Journal of Modern History* 72, no. 2 (2000): 413–452.

Great Britain, War Office, General Staff. *Handbook of the German Army, December 1940.* London: Imperial War Museum, Department of Printed Books, 1996.

Greene, Joshua. *Justice at Dachau: The Trials of an American Prosecutor.* New York: Broadway Books, 2003.

Habermas, Jürgen. *Eine Art Schadensabwicklung.* Frankfurt am Main: Suhrkamp, 1987.

Hale, Winfield. "Nuremberg War Crimes Tribunals." *Tennessee Law Review* 21 (1949): 8–19.

Hamburg Institute for Social Research. *The German Army and Genocide: Crimes against War Prisoners, Jews, and Other Civilians, 1939–1944.* New York: New Press, 1999.

Hankel, Gerd. *Die Leipziger Prozesse: Deutsche Kriegsverbrechen und ihre strafrechtliche Verfolgung nach dem Ersten Weltkrieg.* Hamburg: Hamburger Edition, 2003.

Harris, Whitney. *Tyranny on Trial: The Evidence at Nuremberg.* Dallas: Southern Methodist University Press, 1954.

Hartmann, Christian. *Halder: Generalstabschef Hitlers, 1938–1942.* Paderborn: Schöningh, 1991.

Heer, Hannes. "The Difficulty of Ending a War: Reactions to the Exhibition: Crimes of the Wehrmacht 1941 to 1944." *History Workshop Journal* 46 (1998): 187–203.

———. *The Discursive Construction of History: Remembering the Wehrmacht's War of Annihilation.* New York: Palgrave Macmillan, 2008.

———. "How Amorality Became Normality: The Wehrmacht and the Holocaust." In *Lessons and Legacies*, vol. 5, *The Holocaust and Justice*, edited by Ronald Smelser, 123–139. Evanston, Ill.: Northwestern University Press, 2002.

———. "Killing Fields: The Wehrmacht and the Holocaust in Belorussia, 1941–1943." *Holocaust and Genocide Studies* 7 (1997): 79–101.

———. "The Logic of the War of Extermination: The Wehrmacht and the Anti-Partisan War." In *War of Extermination: The German Military in World War II, 1941–1944*, edited by Hannes Heer and Klaus Naumann, 92–126. New York: Berghahn Books, 2000.

———. *Tote Zonen: Die deutsche Wehrmacht an der Ostfront.* Hamburg: Hamburger Edition, 1999.

————. *Vom Verschwinden der Täter: Der Vernichtungskrieg fand statt, aber keiner war dabei.* Berlin: Aufbau-Verlag, 2004.

Heer, Hannes, and Klaus Naumann, eds. *War of Extermination: The German Military in World War II, 1941–1944.* New York: Berghahn Books, 2000.

Herbert, Ulrich, ed. *Europa und der "Reicheinsatz": Ausländische Zivilarbeiter, Kriegsgefangene und KZ-Häftlinge in Deutschland, 1938–1945.* Essen: Klartext Verlag, 1991.

————. *National Socialist Extermination Policies: Contemporary German Perspectives and Controversies.* New York: Berghahn Books, 2000.

Herf, Jeffrey. *Divided Memory: The Nazi Past in the Two Germanys.* Cambridge: Harvard University Press, 1997.

————. "The Emergence and Legacies of Divided Memory: Germany and the Holocaust since 1945." In *Memory and Power in Post-War Europe,* edited by Jan-Werner Müller, 184–205. Cambridge: Cambridge University Press, 2002.

————. "The 'Jewish War': Goebbels and the Antisemitic Campaigns of the Nazi Propaganda Ministry." *Holocaust and Genocide Studies* 19, no. 1 (2005): 51–80.

Hillgruber, Andreas. "Noch einmal: Hitlers Wendung gegen die Sowjetunion 1940." *Geschichte in Wissenschaft und Unterricht* 33 (1982): 214–226.

Hirschfeld, Gerhard, ed. *The Policies of Genocide: Jews and Soviet Prisoners of War in Nazi Germany.* London: Allen and Unwin, 1986.

Hockenos, Matthew. *A Church Divided: German Protestants Confront the Nazi Past.* Bloomington: Indiana University Press, 2004.

Hoess, Rudolf. *Death Dealer: The Memoirs of the S.S. Kommandant at Auschwitz.* New York: Da Capo Press, 1996.

Hoffmann, Christa. *Stunden Null? Vergangenheitsbewältigung in Deutschland, 1945 und 1989.* Bonn: Bouvier, 1992.

Hoffmann, J. H. "German Field Marshals as War Criminals: A British Embarrassment." *Journal of Contemporary History* 23 (1988): 17–35.

Höhne, Heinz. *Canaris.* London: Secker & Warburg, 1979.

Hoschander, Abraham. "Judgment at Nuremberg: Justice and Morality." *National Jewish Law Review* 5 (1990/1991): 163–174.

Hull, Isabel. *Absolute Destruction: Military Culture and the Practices of War in Imperial Germany.* Ithaca, N.Y.: Cornell University Press, 2004.

Immenroth, Anke. *Die Wehrmacht im Blick der Öffentlichkeit: Analyse zweiter Ausstellungen unter konzeptionellen Gesichtspunkten.* Marburg: Tectum-Verlag, 2004.

Ingrao, Charles, and Franz Szabo, eds. *The Germans and the East.* West Lafayette, Ind.: Purdue University Press, 2008.

International Military Tribunal. *Trial of the Major War Criminals before the International Military Tribunal.* 42 vols. Nuremberg, Germany, 1947–1949.

Jackson, Robert H. *Report of Robert H. Jackson, United States Representative to the*

International Conference on Military Trials, London, 1945. Washington, D.C.: Department of State, 1949.

Jardim, Tomaz. "The Mauthausen War Crimes Trial and American Justice in Germany." Ph.D. diss., University of Toronto, 2009.

Journal of Legal Studies (Special Issue). *50th Anniversary of the Nuremberg Trials.* 6 (1995–1996): 1–304.

Just-Dahlmann, Barbara, and Helmut Just. *Die Gehilfen: NS-Verbrechen und Justiz nach 1945.* Frankfurt am Main: Athenäum, 1988.

Karstedt, Susanne. "The Nuremberg Tribunal and German Society: International Justice and Local Judgment in Post-Conflict Reconstruction." In *The Legacy of Nuremberg: Civilizing Influence or Institutionalized Vengeance?*, edited by David A. Blumenthal and Timothy L. H. McCormack, 13–35. Leiden: Martinus Nijhoff, 2008.

Kater, Michael. "Problems of Political Reeducation in West Germany, 1945–1960." *Simon Wiesenthal Center Annual* 4 (1987): 99–105.

Kempner, Robert. *Anklage einer Epoche: Lebenserinnerungen.* Frankfurt am Main: Ullstein, 1983.

Kershaw, Ian. *Hitler: 1936–1945: Nemesis.* London: Penguin, 2000.

Kesselring, Albert. *The Memoirs of Field Marshal Kesselring.* Translated by Lynton Hudson. London: W. Kimber, 1953.

Kilmuir (Sir David Maxwell-Fyfe). *Nuremberg in Retrospect: A Study in the Dynamic of International Law.* Birmingham: Holdsworth Club of the University of Birmingham, 1956.

———. *Political Adventure: The Memoirs of Lord Kilmuir.* London: Weidenfeld and Nicolson, 1964.

King, Henry. "The Meaning of Nuremberg." *Case Western Reserve Journal of International Law* 3, no. 1 (1998): 143–148.

Kittel, Manfred. *Die Legende von der zweiten Schuld: Vergangenheitsbewältigung in der Ära Adenauer.* Berlin: Ullstein, 1993.

Klee, Ernst. *Persilscheine und falsche Pässe: Wie die Kirchen den Nazis halfen.* Frankfurt am Main: Fischer Taschenbuch Verlag, 1992.

Klee, Ernst, and Willi Dreßen, eds. *"The Good Old Days": The Holocaust as Seen by Its Perpetrators and Bystanders.* New York: Free Press, 1991.

———. *"Gott mit uns": Der deutschen Vernichtungskrieg im Osten, 1939–1945.* Frankfurt am Main: S. Fischer, 1989.

———. *"Schöne Zeiten": Judenmord aus der Sicht der Täter und Gaffer.* Frankfurt am Main: S. Fischer, 1988.

Kochavi, Arieh. *Prelude to Nuremberg: Allied War Crimes Policy and the Question of Punishment.* Chapel Hill: University of North Carolina Press, 1998.

Kohler, Lotte, and Hans Saner, eds. *Hannah Arendt–Karl Jaspers Correspondence, 1926–1969.* New York: Harcourt Brace Jovanovich, 1992.

Krausnick, Helmut, and Hans-Heinrich Wilhelm. *Die Truppe des Weltanschau-ungskrieges: Die Einsatzgruppen der Sicherheitspolizei und des SD, 1938–1942.* 2 vols. Stuttgart: Deutsche Verlags-Anstalt, 1981.

Kühne, Thomas. *Kameradschaft: Die Soldaten des nationalsozialistischen Krieges und das 20. Jahrhundert.* Göttingen: Vandenhoeck & Ruprecht, 2006.

Lael, Richard. *The Yamashita Precedent: War Crimes and Command Responsibility.* Wilmington, Del.: Scholarly Resources, 1982.

Landsman, Stephan. *Crimes of the Holocaust: The Law Confronts Hard Cases.* Philadelphia: University of Pennsylvania Press, 2005.

Lang, Berel. *Act and Idea in the Nazi Genocide.* Chicago: University of Chicago Press, 1990.

Large, David Clay. *Germans to the Front: West German Rearmament in the Adenauer Era.* Chapel Hill: University of North Carolina Press, 1996.

Laternser, Hans. *Die andere Seite im Auschwitz-Prozess, 1963/65.* Stuttgart: Seewald, 1966.

———. "Looking Back at the Nuremberg Trials with Special Consideration of the Processes against Military Leaders." *Whittier Law Review* 8 (1986): 557–580.

———. *Plaedoyer vor dem Internationalen Militärgerichtshof zu Nürnberg.* Nuremberg: Deutsche Lager-Kommandantur, 1946.

———. *Verteidigung deutscher Soldaten: Plädoyers vor alliierten Gerichten.* Bonn: R. Bohnemeier, 1950.

Lemkin, Rafael. *Axis Rule in Occupied Europe: Laws of Occupation, Analysis of Government, Proposals for Redress.* Washington, D.C.: Carnegie Endowment for International Peace, Division of International Law, 1944.

Lessing, Holger. *Der Erste Dachauer Prozess (1945/46).* Baden-Baden: Nomos Verlagsgesellschaft, 1993.

Leverkuehn, Paul. *Verteidigung Manstein.* Hamburg: H. H. Nölke, 1980.

Liddell Hart, Basil. *The German Generals Talk.* New York: Quill, 1979.

Lippmann, Matthew. "The Other Nuremberg: American Prosecutions of Nazi War Criminals in Occupied Germany." *Indiana International and Comparative Law Review* 3, no. 1 (1992): 1–99.

Lockenour, Jay. *Soldiers as Citizens: Former Wehrmacht officers in the Federal Republic of Germany, 1945–1955.* Lincoln: University of Nebraska Press, 2001.

Lower, Wendy. *Nazi Empire Building and the Holocaust in Ukraine.* Chapel Hill: University of North Carolina Press, 2005.

Lowry, Montecue. *The Forge of West German Rearmament: Theodor Blank and the Amt Blank.* New York: P. Lang, 1990.

Lüdtke, Alf, "'Coming to Terms with the Past': Illusions of Remembering, Ways of Forgetting Nazism in West Germany." *Journal of Modern History* 65 (1993): 542–572.

Madievski, Samson. "The War of Extermination: The Crimes of the Wehrmacht in 1941 to 1944." *Rethinking History* 7, no. 2 (2003): 243–254.

Maguire, Peter. *Law and War: An American Story.* New York: Columbia University Press, 2001.

Maier, Charles. *The Unmasterable Past: History, Holocaust and German National Identity.* Cambridge: Harvard University Press, 1988.

Manoschek, Walter. "Austrian Reaction to the Exhibition 'War of Extermination: Crimes of the Wehrmacht, 1941–1944.'" *Contemporary Austrian Studies* 7 (1999): 193–200.

———. *"Serbien ist Judenfrei": Militärische Besatzungspolitik und Judenvernichtung in Serbien, 1941/42.* Munich: R. Oldenbourg, 1993.

Manoschek, Walter, ed. *Die Wehrmacht im Rassenkrieg: Der Vernichtungskrieg hinter der Front.* Vienna: Picus Verlag, 1996.

Marcuse, Harold. *Legacies of Dachau: The Uses and Abuses of a Concentration Camp, 1933–2001.* Cambridge: Cambridge University Press, 2001.

Marrus, Michael. "History and the Holocaust in the Courtroom." In *Lessons and Legacies,* vol. 5, *The Holocaust and Justice,* edited by Ronald Smelser, 215–239. Evanston, Ill.: Northwestern University Press, 2002.

———. "The Holocaust at Nuremberg." *Yad Vashem Studies* 26 (1998): 5–41.

Marrus, Michael, ed. *The Nuremberg War Crimes Trial, 1945–46: A Documentary History.* Boston: Bedford Books, 1997.

Maser, Werner. *Nuremberg: A Nation on Trial.* London: Allen Lane, 1979.

Mayer, Arno. *Der Krieg als Kreuzzug: Das deutsche Reich, Hitler's Wehrmacht und die Endlösung.* Hamburg: Rowohlt, 1989.

Mazower, Mark. "Military Violence and National Socialist Values: The Wehrmacht in Greece, 1941–1944." *Past & Present* 134 (1992): 129–158.

McCloy, John. *The Challenge to American Foreign Policy.* Cambridge: Harvard University Press, 1953.

Megargee, Geoffrey. "A Blind Eye and Dirty Hands: The Sources of Wehrmacht Criminality in the Campaign against the Soviet Union." In *The Germans and the East,* edited by Charles Ingrao and Franz Szabo, 310–327. West Lafayette, Ind.: Purdue University Press, 2007.

———. *Inside Hitler's High Command.* Lawrence: University Press of Kansas, 2000.

———. "Selective Realities, Selective Memories: The German Generals and National Socialism." Unpublished paper, 2000.

Mendelsohn, John. "Trial by Document: The Problem of Due Process for War Criminals at Nuremberg." *Prologue* 8 (1975): 228–234.

Mendelsohn, John, ed. *Punishing the Perpetrators of the Holocaust: The Brandt, Pohl and Ohlendorf Cases.* New York: Garland, 1982.

———. "War Crimes Trials and Clemency in Germany and Japan." In *Americans as Proconsuls: United States Military Government in Germany and Japan, 1944–1952*, edited by Robert Wolfe, 226–259. Carbondale: Southern Illinois University Press, 1984.

Merritt, Anna, and Richard Merritt, eds. *Public Opinion in Occupied Germany: The OMGUS Surveys, 1945–1949*. Urbana: University of Chicago Press, 1970.

———. *Public Opinion in Semisovereign Germany: The HICOG Surveys, 1949–1955*. Chicago: University of Illinois Press, 1980.

Merritt, Richard. *Democracy Imposed: U.S. Occupation Policy and the German Public, 1945–1949*. New Haven: Yale University Press, 1995.

Messerschmidt, Manfred. "Forward Defense: The 'Memorandum of the Generals' for the Nuremberg Court." In *War of Extermination: The German Military in World War II, 1941–1944*, edited by Hannes Heer and Klaus Naumann, 381–399. New York: Berghahn Books, 2000.

———. "The Wehrmacht and the Volksgemeinschaft." *Journal of Contemporary History* 18 (1983): 719–744.

———. *Die Wehrmacht im NS-Staat: Zeit der Indoktrination*. Hamburg: R.v. Decker's Verlag, 1969.

Militärgeschichtliches Forschungsamt. *Das Deutsche Reich und der Zweite Weltkrieg*. 10 vols. Stuttgart: Deutsche Verlags-Anstalt, 1979–present.

———. *Germany and the Second World War*. 9 vols. Oxford: Clarendon Press, 1990–2008.

Minow, Martha. *Between Vengeance and Forgiveness: Facing History after Genocide and Mass Violence*. Boston: Beacon Press, 1998.

Moeller, Robert. "Germans as Victims? Thoughts on a Post–Cold War History of World War II's Legacies." *History and Memory* 17, no. 1–2 (2005): 147–194.

———. "On the History of Man-Made Destruction." *History Workshop Journal* 61 (2006): 103–134.

———. *War Stories: The Search for a Usable Past in the Federal Republic of Germany*. Berkeley: University of California Press, 2001.

———. "What Has 'Coming to Terms with the Past' Meant in Post–World War II Germany? From History to Memory to the 'History of Memory.'" *Central European History* 35, no. 2 (2002): 223–256.

Moeller, Robert, ed. *West Germany under Construction: Politics, Society, and Culture in the Adenauer Era*. Ann Arbor: University of Michigan Press, 1997.

Mommsen, Hans. "The Legacy of the Holocaust in German National Identity." Leo Baeck Memorial Lecture. New York: The Leo Baeck Institute, 1999.

Morrison, Fred. "The Significance of Nuremberg for Modern International Law." *Military Law Review* 149 (1995): 207–215.

Mosse, George. *Fallen Soldiers: Reshaping the Memory of the World Wars*. New York: Oxford University Press, 1990.

Müller, Jan-Werner, ed. *Memory and Power in Post-War Europe: Studies in the Presence of the Past.* Cambridge: Cambridge University Press, 2002.

Müller, Klaus-Jürgen. *General Ludwig Beck: Studien und Dokumente zur politisch-militärischen Vorstellungswelt und Tätigkeit des Generalstabschef des deutschen Heeres, 1933–1938.* Boppard am Rhein: H. Boldt, 1980.

———. *Das Heer und Hitler: Armee und nationalsozialistisches Regime, 1933–1940.* Stuttgart: Deutsche Verlags-Anstalt, 1969.

Müller, Norbert. "Generalstab und Oberkommando der Wehrmacht im Urteil des Nürnberger Tribunals." *Militärgeschichte* 25 (1986): 393–399.

Müller, Rolf-Dieter. "Die Wehrmacht—Historische Last und Verantwortung. Die Historiographie im Spannungsfeld von Wissenschaft und Vergangenheitsbewältigung." In *Die Wehrmacht: Mythos und Realität,* edited by Rolf-Dieter Müller and Hans-Erich Volkmann, 3–35. Munich: R. Oldenbourg, 1999.

Müller, Rolf-Dieter, and Gerd Ueberschär, eds. *Hitler's War in the East: A Critical Assessment.* New York: Berghahn Books, 2002.

Müller, Rolf-Dieter, and Hans-Erich Volkmann, eds. *Die Wehrmacht: Mythos und Realität.* Munich: R. Oldenbourg, 1999.

Mullins, Claud. *The Leipzig Trials: An Account of the War Criminals' Trials and a Study of the German Mentality.* London: H. F. & G. Witherby, 1921.

Naimark, Norman. "War and Genocide on the Eastern Front, 1941–1945." *Contemporary European History* 16, no. 2 (2007): 259–274.

National Archives Microfilm Publications No. 898. Records of the United States Nuernberg War Crimes Trials—*United States of America v. Wilhelm von Leeb et al.* (Case XII): November 28, 1947–October 28, 1948. 69 rolls.

National Archives Microfilm Publications No. 1019. Records of the United States Nuernberg War Crimes Trials Interrogations, 1946–1949. 91 rolls.

Naumann, Klaus. "Wenn ein Tabu bricht: Die Wehrmachts-Ausstellung in der Bundesrepublik." *Mittelweg* 36 (1996): 11–24.

Neave, Airey. *Nuremberg: A Personal Record of the Trial of Major War Criminals.* London: Hodder and Stoughton, 1978.

Nelson, Daniel. *A History of U.S. Military Forces in Germany.* Boulder, Colo.: Westview Press, 1987.

Nelte, Otto. *The Generals: The Nuernberg Judgment and the Guilt of the Generals.* Hannover: Das andere Deutschland Hannover, 1947.

Niethammer, Lutz. *Entnazifizierung in Bayern: Säuberung und Rehabilitierung unter amerikanischer Besatzung.* Frankfurt am Main: Fischer, 1972.

Niven, Bill. *Facing the Nazi Past: United Germany and the Legacy of the Third Reich.* London: Routledge, 2002.

Nobleman, Eli. "American Military Government Courts in Germany." *Annals of the American Academy of Political and Social Science* 267 (1950): 87–97.

Nolte, Ernst. *Das Vergehen der Vergangenheit: Antworten an meine Kritiker im soge-nannten Historikerstreit.* Berlin: Ullstein, 1993.

Office of the High Commissioner for Germany, Information Services Division. *Landsberg: A Documentary Report.* Frankfurt: Office of the U.S. High Commissioner for Germany, 1951.

Oldenburg, Manfred. *Ideologie und militärisches Kalkül: Die Besatzungspolitik der Wehrmacht in der Sowjetunion 1942.* Cologne: Boehlau, 2004.

Osiel, Mark. *Mass Atrocity, Collective Memory, and the Law.* New Brunswick, N.J.: Transaction Publishers, 1997.

———. *Obeying Orders: Atrocity, Military Discipline and the Law of War.* New Brunswick, N.J.: Transaction Publishers, 1999.

Overmann, Rüdiger. "Die Kriegsgefangenenpolitik des Deutschen Reiches 1939–1945." In Militärgeschichtliches Forschungsamt, *Das Deutsche Reich und der Zweite Weltkrieg,* vol. 9, no. 2, *Die deutsche Kriegsgesellschaft 1939 bis 1945: Ausbeutung, Deutungen, Ausgrenzung,* 729–877. Stuttgart: Deutsche Verlags-Anstalt, 2005.

Paget, Reginald. *Manstein, His Campaigns, and His Trial.* London: Collins, 1951.

Pendaries, Yveline. *Les Procès de Rastatt (1946–1954): Le Jugement des crimes de guerre en zone française d'occupation en Allemagne.* Bern: Peter Lang, 1995.

Persico, Joseph. "The Guilt of Alfred Jodl." *Quarterly Journal of Military History* 4, no. 6 (1994): 30–37.

———. *Nuremberg: Infamy on Trial.* New York: Viking Penguin, 1994.

Peterson, Edward. *The Many Faces of Defeat: The German People's Experience in 1945.* New York: Peter Lang, 1990.

Phayer, Michael. *The Catholic Church and the Holocaust, 1930–1965.* Bloomington: Indiana University Press, 2000.

Plischke, Elmer. *The Allied High Commission for Germany.* Bad Godesberg: HICOG Historical Division, 1953.

———. *Allied High Commission Relations with the West German Government.* Bad Godesberg: HICOG Historical Division, 1952.

Polevoi, Boris. *The Final Reckoning: Nuremberg Diaries.* Moscow: Progress Publishers, 1978.

Prittie, Terence. *Konrad Adenauer, 1876–1967.* London: Tom Stacey, 1972.

Przyrembel, Alexandra. "Transfixed by an Image: Ilse Koch, the 'Kommandeuse of Buchenwald.'" *German History* 19, no. 3 (2001): 369–399.

Raim, Edith. "Coping with the Nazi Past: Germany and the Legacy of the Third Reich." *Contemporary European History* 12, no. 4 (2003): 547–559.

Rass, Christoph. *"Menschenmaterial": Deutsche Soldaten an der Ostfront. Innenansichten einer Infanteriedivision, 1939–1945.* Paderborn: Ferdinand Schöningh Verlag, 2003.

Reitlinger, Gerald. *The S.S.: Alibi of a Nation, 1922–1945.* New York: Viking, 1957.

Remy, Steven. *The Heidelberg Myth: The Nazification and Denazification of a German University.* Cambridge: Harvard University Press, 2002.

Rogat, Yosal. "The Measures Taken: The Eichmann Trial and the Rule of Law." *Second Coming Magazine* 1, no. 3 (March 1962): 8–19.

Rolf, David. *Prisoners of the Reich: Germany's Captives, 1939–1945.* London: Cooper, 1988.

Röling, B. V. A., and C. F. Rüter, eds. *The Tokyo Judgment: The International Military Tribunal for the Far East (IMTFE), 29 April 1946–12 November 1948,* vol. 1. Amsterdam: APA–University Press Amsterdam, 1977.

Rossino, Alexander. "Destructive Impulses: German Soldiers and the Conquest of Poland." *Holocaust and Genocide Studies* 7 (1997): 351–365.

———. *Hitler Strikes Poland: Blitzkrieg, Ideology, and Atrocity.* Lawrence: University Press of Kansas, 2003.

Rückerl, Adalbert. *The Investigation of Nazi Crimes, 1945–1978: A Documentation.* Hamdon: Archon Books, 1980.

———. *NS-Verbrechen vor Gericht: Versuch einer Vergangenheitsbewältigung.* Heidelberg: C. F. Mueller Juristischer Verlag, 1982.

Rückerl, Adalbert, ed. *NS-Prozesse: Nach 25 Jahren Strafverfolgung: Möglichkeiten— Grenzen—Ergebnisse.* Karlsruhe: C. F. Mueller, 1971.

Schacht, Hjalmar. *Account Settled.* London: Weidenfeld and Nicolson, 1949.

Schissler, Hanna, ed. *The Miracle Years: A Cultural History of West Germany, 1949–1968.* Princeton: Princeton University Press, 2001.

Schmitz, Helmut. *A Nation of Victims? Representations of German Wartime Suffering from 1945 to the Present.* New York: Rodopi, 2007.

Schmitz-Bering, Cornelia. *Vokabular des National-Sozialismus.* Berlin: de Gruyter, 1998.

Schustereit, Hartmut. *Vabanque: Hitlers Angriff auf die Sowjetunion 1941 als Versuch durch den Sieg im Osten den Westen zu bezwingen.* Bonn: Mittler, 1988.

Schwarz, Hans-Peter. *Die Ära Adenauer, 1949–1957.* Stuttgart: Deutsche Verlags-Anstalt, 1981.

Schwartz, Thomas Alan. *America's Germany: John J. McCloy and the Federal Republic of Germany.* Cambridge: Harvard University Press, 1991.

———. "John J. McCloy and the Landsberg Cases." In *American Policy and the Reconstruction of West Germany, 1945–1955,* edited by Jeffry Diefendorf, Axel Frohn, and Hermann-Josef Rupieper, 433–454. New York: Cambridge University Press, 1993.

Searle, Alaric. *Wehrmacht Generals, West German Society, and the Debate on Rearmament, 1949–1959.* Westport, Conn.: Praeger, 2003.

Sebald, W. G. *On the Natural History of Destruction.* Toronto: Alfred A. Knopf, 2003.

Segalowitz, Benjamin. "The Wehrmacht's Guilt." *Yad Vashem Bulletin* 21 (1967): 10–18.

Segev, Tom. *The Seventh Million: The Israelis and the Holocaust.* New York: Hill and Wang, 1993.

Shawcross, Lord Hartley. *Life Sentence: The Memoirs of Lord Shawcross.* London: Constable, 1995.

Shepherd, Ben. *War in the Wild East: The German Army and Soviet Partisans.* Cambridge: Harvard University Press, 2004.

Shklar, Judith. *Legalism: Law, Morals, and Political Trials.* Cambridge: Harvard University Press, 1964.

Sigel, Robert. *Im Interesse der Gerechtigkeit: Die Dachauer Kriegsverbrecherprozesse, 1945–1948.* Frankfurt am Main: Campus Verlag, 1992.

Smelser, Ronald, and Edward Davies II. *The Myth of the Eastern Front: The Nazi–Soviet War in American Popular Culture.* Cambridge: Cambridge University Press, 2007.

Smith, Bradley. *Reaching Judgment at Nuremberg.* New York: Basic Books, 1977.

———. *The Road to Nuremberg.* New York: Basic Books, 1981.

Smith, Bradley, ed. *The American Road to Nuremberg: The Documentary Record, 1944–1945.* Stanford: Hoover Institution Press, 1982.

Smith, Jean Edward, ed. *The Papers of General Lucius D. Clay: Germany, 1945–1949.* 2 vols. Bloomington: Indiana University Press, 1974.

Stefan, James. *The United States and West German Rearmament, 1947–1950.* Chapel Hill: University of North Carolina Press, 1976.

Stegemann, Bernd. "Der Entschluss zum Unternehmen Barbarossa: Strategie oder Ideologie?" *Geschichte in Wissenschaft und Unterricht* 33 (1982): 205–213.

———. "Geschichte und Politik: Zur Diskussion über den deutschen Angriff auf die Sowjetunion 1941." *Blätter zur Konfliktforschung* 17, no. 1 (1987): 1287–1300.

Steiner, James. *Hitler's Wehrmacht: German Armed Forces in Support of the Führer.* Jefferson, N.C.: McFarland, 2008.

Stimson, Henry, and McGeorge Bundy. *On Active Service in Peace and War.* New York: Harper & Brothers, 1948.

Stolzfus, Nathan, and Henry Friedlander, eds. *Nazi Crimes and the Law.* New York: Cambridge University Press, 2008.

Streim, Alfred. *Die Behandlung sowjetischer Kriegsgefangener im "Fall Barbarossa": Eine Dokumentation.* Heidelberg: Müller, Juristischer Verlag, 1981.

Streit, Christian. *Keine Kameraden: Die Wehrmacht und die sowjetischen Kriegsgefangenen.* Stuttgart: Deutsche Verlags-Anstalt, 1978.

Tauber, Kurt. *Beyond Eagle and Swastika: German Nationalism since 1945.* 2 vols. Middletown: Wesleyan University Press, 1967.

Taylor, Lawrence. *A Trial of Generals: Homma, Yamashita, MacArthur.* South Bend, Ind.: Icarus Press, 1981.

Taylor, Telford. *The Anatomy of the Nuremberg Trials: A Personal Memoir.* Boston: Little, Brown, 1992.

———. *Final Report to the Secretary of the Army on the Nuernberg War Crimes Trials under Control Council Law No. 10.* Washington, D.C.: U.S. Government Printing Office, 15 August 1949.

———. "The Nazis Go Free: Justice and Mercy or Misguided Expediency?" *Nation* (24 February 1951): 170–172.

———. *Nuremberg and Vietnam: An American Tragedy.* Chicago: Quadrangle Books, 1970.

———. *Nuremberg Trials: War Criminals and International Law.* New York: Carnegie Endowment for International Peace, 1949.

———. "The Struggle for the German Mind." *New Republic* 122 (30 January 1950): 15–18.

———. *Sword and Swastika: Generals and Nazis in the Third Reich.* New York: Simon & Schuster, 1952.

Taylor, Telford, Constance Baker Motley, and James K. Feibleman. *Perspectives on Justice: 1973 Rosenthal Lectures, Northwestern University School of Law.* Evanston, Ill.: Northwestern University Press, 1975.

Teitel, Ruti. *Transitional Justice.* New York: Oxford University Press, 2000.

Tent, James. *Mission on the Rhine: Reeducation and Denazification in American-Occupied Germany.* Chicago: University of Chicago Press, 1982.

Teschke, John. *Hitler's Legacy: West Germany Confronts the Aftermath of the Third Reich.* New York: P. Lang, 1999.

Thayer, Charles. *The Unquiet Germans.* New York: Harper, 1957.

Thiele, Hans-Günther, ed. *Die Wehrmachtsausstellung: Dokumentation einer Kontroverse. Dokumentation der Fachtagung in Bremen am 26. Februar 1997 und der Bundestagsdebatten am 13. März und 24. April 1997.* Bremen: Edition Temmen, 1997.

Thompson, Larry, ed. *Lessons and Legacies,* vol. 4, *Reflections on Religion, Justice, Sexuality, and Genocide.* Evanston, Ill.: Northwestern University Press, 2003.

Trippen, Norbert. *Josef Cardinal Frings (1887–1978),* vol. 1, *Sein Wirken für das Erzbistum Köln und für die Kirche in Deutschland.* Paderborn: Ferdinand Schöningh, 2003.

Truman, Harry. *Memoirs: Year of Decisions.* Garden City, N.Y.: Doubleday, 1955.

Tusa, Ann, and John Tusa. *The Nuremberg Trial.* London: Macmillan, 1983.

Ueberschär, Gerd. "Avoiding and Coming to Terms with the Past." In *Hitler's War in the East: A Critical Assessment,* edited by Rolf-Dieter Müller and Gerd Ueberschär, 367–374. New York: Berghahn Books, 2002.

———. "'Historikerstreit' und 'Präventivkriegsthese.' Zu den Rechtfertigungsversuchen des deutschen Überfalls auf die Sowjetunion 1941." *Tribüne: Zeitschrift zum Verständnis des Judentums* 26, no. 103 (1987): 108–116.

———. "Hitler's Decision to Attack the Soviet Union in Recent German Historiography." In *Operation Barbarossa: The German Attack on the Soviet Union, June 22, 1941.* Special issue of *Soviet Union* 18, no. 1–3 (1991): 297–315.

Ueberschär, Gerd, ed. *Die Nationalsozialismus vor Gericht: Die alliierten Prozesse gegen Kriegsverbrecher und Soldaten, 1943–1952.* Frankfurt: Fischer Taschenbuch Verlag, 1999.

Ueberschär, Gerd, and Wolfram Wette, eds. *"Unternehmen Barbarossa," Der deutsche Überfall auf die Sowjetunion, 1941: Berichte, Analysen, Dokumente.* Paderborn: Ferdinand Schöningh, 1984.

United Nations War Crimes Commission. *Law Reports of Trials of War Criminals,* vol. 8, *The German High Command Trial.* New York: H. Fertig, 1949.

United States Office for the Chief of Counsel for the Prosecution of Axis Criminality. *Nazi Conspiracy and Aggression: Opinion and Judgment.* 9 vols. Washington, D.C.: U.S. Government Printing Office, 1946–1947.

Uziel, Daniel. "Wehrmacht Propaganda Troops and the Jews." *Yad Vashem Studies* 29 (2001): 27–63.

Varon, Jeremy. *Bringing the War Home: The Weather Underground, the Red Army Faction, and Revolutionary Violence in the Sixties and Seventies.* Berkeley: University of California Press, 2004.

Vogt, Timothy. *Denazification in Soviet-Occupied Germany: Brandenburg, 1945–1948.* Cambridge: Harvard University Press, 2000.

Vollnhals, Clemens. *Evangelische Kirche und Entnazifizierung, 1945–1949: Die Last der nationalsozialistischen Vergangenheit.* Munich: R. Oldenbourg, 1989.

Vollnhals, Clemens, and Thomas Schlemmer. *Entnazifizierung: Politische Säuberung und Rehabilitierung in den vier Besatzungszonen, 1945–1949.* Munich: Deutscher Taschenbuch Verlag, 1991.

von Kellenbach, Katharina. "Vanishing Acts: Perpetrators in Postwar Germany." *Holocaust and Genocide Studies* 17, no. 2 (2003): 305–329.

von Knierim, August. *Nürnberg: Rechtliche und Menschliche Probleme.* Stuttgart: E. Klett, 1952.

von Papen, Franz. *Memoirs.* London: André Deutsch, 1952.

von Wrochem, Oliver. *Erich von Manstein: Vernichtungskrieg und Geschichtspolitik.* Paderborn: Ferdinand Schöningh, 2006.

Warlimont, Walter. *Inside Hitler's Headquarters, 1939–1945.* Novato, Calif.: Presidio, 1964. First published in German as *Im Hauptquartier der deutschen Wehrmacht: Grundlagen, Formen, Gestalten.* Frankfurt am Main: Bernard & Graefe Verlag, 1962.

Wechsler, Herbert. *Principles, Politics, and Fundamental Law: Selected Essays.* Cambridge: Harvard University Press, 1961.

Weinberg, Gerhard. *A World at Arms: A Global History of World War II.* Cambridge: Cambridge University Press, 1994.

Weindling, Paul. "From International to Zonal Trials: The Origins of the Nuremberg Medical Trial." *Holocaust and Genocide Studies* 14 (2000): 367–389.

Weingartner, James. *Crossroads of Death: The Story of the Malmedy Massacre and Trial.* Berkeley: University of California Press, 1979.

———. *A Peculiar Crusade: Willis M. Everett and the Malmedy Massacre.* New York: New York University Press, 2000.

Weinke, Annette. *Die Verfolgung von NS-Tätern im geteilten Deutschland.* Paderborn: Schöningh, 2002.

Wentker, Hermann. *Justiz in der Sowjetischen Besatzungszone/Deutsche Demokratische Republik, 1945–1953.* Munich: R. Oldenbourg, 2001.

West, Rebecca. *A Train of Powder.* New York: Viking Press, 1955.

Westermann, Edward. "Partners in Genocide: The German Police and the 'Wehrmacht' in the Soviet Union." *Journal of Strategic Studies* 31, no. 5 (2008): 771–796.

Westphal, Siegfried. *Der deutsche Generalstab auf der Anklagebank: Nürnberg, 1945–1948. Mit einer Denkschrift von Walter von Brauchitsch, Erich von Manstein, Franz Halder, Walter Warlimont, Siegfried Westphal.* Mainz: v. Hase & Koehler, 1978.

Wette, Wolfram. *The Wehrmacht: History, Myth, Reality.* Cambridge: Harvard University Press, 2006.

Wettig, Gerhard. *Entmilitarisierung und Widerbewaffnung in Deutschland, 1943–1955.* Munich: R. Oldenbourg, 1967.

Whiting, Charles. *Jochen Peiper: Battle Commander S.S. Liebstandarte Adolf Hitler.* Barnsley: Leo Cooper, 1999.

Wilhelm, Hans Heinrich. *Rassenpolitik und Kriegführung: Sicherheitspolizei und Wehrmacht in Polen und der Sowjetunion.* Passau: Wissenschaftsverlag Richard Rothe, 1991.

Willis, James. *Prologue to Nuremberg: The Politics and Diplomacy of Punishing War Criminals of the First World War.* Westport, Conn.: Greenwood Press, 1982.

Wittmann, Rebecca. *Beyond Justice: The Auschwitz Trial.* Cambridge: Harvard University Press, 2005.

Woetzel, Robert. *The Nuremberg Trials in International Law.* London: Stevens & Sons, 1962.

Wolfe, Robert, ed. *Americans as Proconsuls: United States Military Government in Germany and Japan, 1944–1952.* Carbondale: Southern Illinois University Press, 1984.

Wurm, Theophil, Martin Niemöller, and Karl Haretenstein. *Memorandum by the Evangelical Church in Germany on the Question of War Crimes Trials before American Military Courts.* Waiblingen-Stuttgart: Gust. Stürner, 1949.

Yavnai, Lisa. "Military Justice: The U.S. Army Trials of War Criminals in Germany, 1944–1947." Ph.D. diss., London School of Economics and Political Science, 2007.

Index

Yamashita precedent, 67–68, 137,
    148–149
Yamashita trial, 252n33
Young, John Carlton, 130–139, *131*
    (photo), 140–141, 148–150,
    280n24, 280n25
Young, John Carlton, Jr., 130, 133
Young, Rush, 130, 133

Yugoslavia, 8, 10, 68, 227n57, 248n4,
    249n11

Zentrale Rechtsschutzstelle, 162, 191,
    194
Zhitomir, 94
Zyklon B, 84, 262n118